I0605078

Castrato Phantoms

Castrato Phantoms

Moreschi, Fellini, and the Sacred Vernacular in Rome

Martha Feldman

ZONE BOOKS · NEW YORK

2026

ZONE BOOKS
633 Vanderbilt Street
Brooklyn, NY 11218

Printed in the United States of America
Distributed by Princeton University Press,
Princeton, New Jersey, and Woodstock, United Kingdom

The press gratefully acknowledges a contribution from the Donna Cardamone Jackson Fund and General Fund of the American Musicological Society, supported in part by the National Endowment for the Humanities and the Andrew W. Mellon Foundation, as well as from the Division of the Arts and Humanities at the University of Chicago.

Library of Congress Control Number 2025026623

For the Moreschi and Fellini families,

with special thanks to

Fabio Panconesi

The past is never past. It's not even dead.

—William Faulkner, *Requiem for a Nun* (1951)

Contents

List of Principal Family Members

Alessandro Moreschi (1858–1922), star castrato soloist in the Sistine Chapel and elsewhere in Rome, commonly known in recent decades as "the last castrato."

Guendalina Rinaldi (1873–probably 1957), wife of Alessandro Moreschi, mother of Giulio Moreschi.

Giulio Moreschi (1904–1955), son of Guendalina Rinaldi and son (sometimes "adoptive son") of Alessandro Moreschi, biological father unknown; a tenor and highly regarded voice teacher in Rome.

Vittoria Cevasco (1899–1985), Giulio Moreschi's wife, the financial source of well-being in the Moreschi family from the time of their marriage in 1925, when she was also a soprano and student of Giulio's; also the family memory bank.

Pietro Rinaldi (1844–1924), father of Guendalina Rinaldi, father-in-law of Alessandro Moreschi, grandfather of Giulio Moreschi.

Francesco Saverio Mancini (b. after ca. 1907, d. after 1970), second son of Guendalina Rinaldi and half brother of Giulio Moreschi.

Amerigo Moreschi (1882–1925), nephew of Alessandro Moreschi, possible biological father of Giulio Moreschi.

Domenico Salvatori (1855–1909), castrato in the Sistine Chapel; apparent uncle of Alessandro Moreschi.

Alessandra Moreschi (1926–1994), daughter of Giulio Moreschi and Vittoria Cevasco, sometime singer, wife of Riccardo Fellini and later of Giovanni Antonio ("Chico") Solinas, mother of Maria Rita Fellini.

Riccardo Fellini (1921–1991), first husband of Alessandra Moreschi (married 1944) and the hinge between the Moreschi and Fellini families; singer, actor, sometime director and sometime car salesman, brother of Federico Fellini.

Federico Fellini (1920–1993), iconic auteurist filmmaker and screenwriter, brother of Riccardo Fellini, husband of Giulietta Masina, brother-in-law of Alessandra Moreschi, uncle of Maria Rita Fellini.

Giulietta Masina (1921–1994), widely renowned actress, wife of Federico Fellini, sister-in-law of Riccardo Fellini and Alessandra Moreschi, aunt of Maria Rita Fellini.

Giovanni Antonio ("Chico") Solinas (1914–1970), second husband of Alessandra Moreschi (ca. 1961–1970) and father of Julio Salvador Solinas Moreschi; Italian resident in Mexico City from about 1960.

Maria Rita (Rita) Fellini (1945–2012), daughter of Riccardo Fellini and Alessandra Moreschi, granddaughter of Giulio Moreschi, great-granddaughter of Alessandro Moreschi, niece of Federico Fellini and Giulietta Masina; owner of the *pelletteria* (belt shop) Fellini.

Fabio Panconesi (1951–), husband of Rita Fellini, son-in-law of Alessandra Moreschi and Riccardo Fellini, nephew-in-law of Federico Fellini and Giulietta Masina, co-owner of the *pelletteria* Fellini and the primary interlocutor for this book.

Julio (sometimes Giulio) Salvador Solinas Moreschi (1961–2010), half brother of Rita Fellini through Alessandra Moreschi, a well-known actor, singer, dancer, writer, and director; father of castrato Alessandro Moreschi's great-great-grandson Alessandro Solinas Moreschi.

Emanuela Dessy Saddì (1961–), actress, director, writer, and musician, domestic partner of Julio Salvador Solinas Moreschi; mother of Alessandro Solinas Moreschi.

Alessandro Carlo Leone Solinas Moreschi (2006–), Alessandro Moreschi's great-great-grandson; son of Julio Salvador Solinas Moreschi and Emanuela Dessy Saddì.

PROLOGUE

Castrato Hauntings

The referent haunts the picture like a ghost:
it is a revenant, a return of the lost and dead others.
—Marianne Hirsch, *Family Frames*

1.

The idea for this book emerged from a small, but striking constellation of facts, the first of which fell into my lap in December 2006. That month, I was in Rome, pursuing leads for the six Bloch Lectures I was to give at the University of California, Berkeley, the following autumn. The topic was to be the castrati (*sing.*: castrato), that storied caste of Italian male singers, founders of bel canto, who from the mid-sixteenth century until the later nineteenth century underwent testicular castration before puberty in order to preserve their high, nimble, and (by adulthood) powerful voices, going on to populate chapels, salons, and stages all over Europe.

On one day, my research took me to Fiumicino, on the outskirts of Rome, to the home of the recently deceased Luciano Luciani (1954–2021), a music historian and longtime bass in the Sistine Chapel choir, where I went to peruse his remarkable collection of documents, scores, diaries, pictures, and other items related to the modern history of Roman chapel music.[1] For the most part, my upcoming lectures were to deal with the heyday of castrati, through the 1820s, but one piece of them would turn to the holy grail of castrato vocality, namely, recordings made by the so-called last castrato, Alessandro Moreschi (1858–1922), which count as the only solo disks ever made by a castrato, right at the time when his kind was becoming extinct.

Accompanied by my friend Hilary Poriss, I looked through numerous objects in Luciani's collection and photographed quite a few. Together, we listened to recordings by unaltered disciples of Moreschi's, feasted on soup and roasted chestnuts, and sang through some scores at the keyboard. And then, just as we got up to take our leave, Luciani mentioned that Moreschi had had a son named Giulio, sometimes called "adoptive," with a woman with whom he'd been living for a time. A slender, but tantalizing reference.

Three years later, the Bloch lectures behind me, but publication of them still ahead, I returned to Luciani's.[2] This time he added that at some point "la donna è fuggita" (the woman had fled). And then he dropped a bomb: in subsequent decades, Giulio's daughter had married Federico Fellini's brother.[3]

Having grown up watching Fellini films with my parents and older sister on trips to the old Bandbox art theater in Philadelphia's Germantown neighborhood, I was struck to think that an orthogonal relationship existed between the castrato and that master auteur, whose cinematic obsessions with masculinity, women, *romanità*, boundary creatures, and autobiography are legendary[4] and no less by the fact that knowledge of this familial suture, casually unloosed from unwritten lore, had lain dormant in a corner of the Sistine Chapel for some sixty-five years. It seemed I had stepped on pay dirt. And yet I was too preoccupied with the prime years of the castrato phenomenon to start digging in new terrain. I was caught up in thinking about a set of paradoxes that increasingly appeared fundamental to it, paradoxes of castrati as both old-world figures of sacrifice and new-world figures enmeshed in commercial exchange, deprived of biological reproduction, but reproduced in male systems of kinship and patronage and abjected by castration, yet marshalled in kingly theaters as charismatic substitutes for ever-weakening monarchs—all themes that eventually found their way into the much-reworked publication of the Bloch lectures as *The Castrato: Reflections on Natures and Kinds*, with no real attention to Moreschi except as the exclusive sonic source of solo castrato vocality.[5]

It was that last preoccupation that led me to Moreschi's living descendants just months after my second visit to Luciani. Finding them proved relatively simple. Given the mountains of research on Fellini, it was easy to realize that his only brother, Riccardo Fellini, had married his singing teacher's then-seventeen-year-old daughter, Alessandra Moreschi,[6] and barely more difficult to discover that Riccardo and Alessandra's only offspring, Maria Rita (Rita) Fellini, was running a belt shop (*pelletteria*) in baroque Rome with her husband, Fabio Panconesi—the great-granddaughter and great-grandson-in-law of the castrato, in other words, as well as the niece and nephew-in-law of Federico Fellini. (See the genealogy in figure P.1.) In May 2010, I made a side trip to via del Corso 340 to meet them at their shop, called "Fellini" (figs. P.2 and P.3). I had set myself the task of puzzling out genealogies of vocal pedagogy and praxis that involved castrati and presumed that Rita might be able to tell me something about her father's practicing and singing under the tutelage of the castrato's son.

All this represented a departure from the kinds of research I had done until then, and I had no idea what I would find. As it happened, Rita was out sick that day. Fabio and I walked from the shop to converse around the corner at Taverna Antonina while Rita participated by telephone.[7] Knowing that her father had been taught singing by her grandfather and her grandfather by her castrato great-grandfather, I first used the conversation to search for whatever remnants of a castrato vocal genealogy might have survived, hoping that enough of Rita's memories would have outwitted the fading of time to help me flesh out the vocal lineages that stretch from early modern castrati through various nineteenth- and early twentieth-century singers and on into the era of Callas in ways that

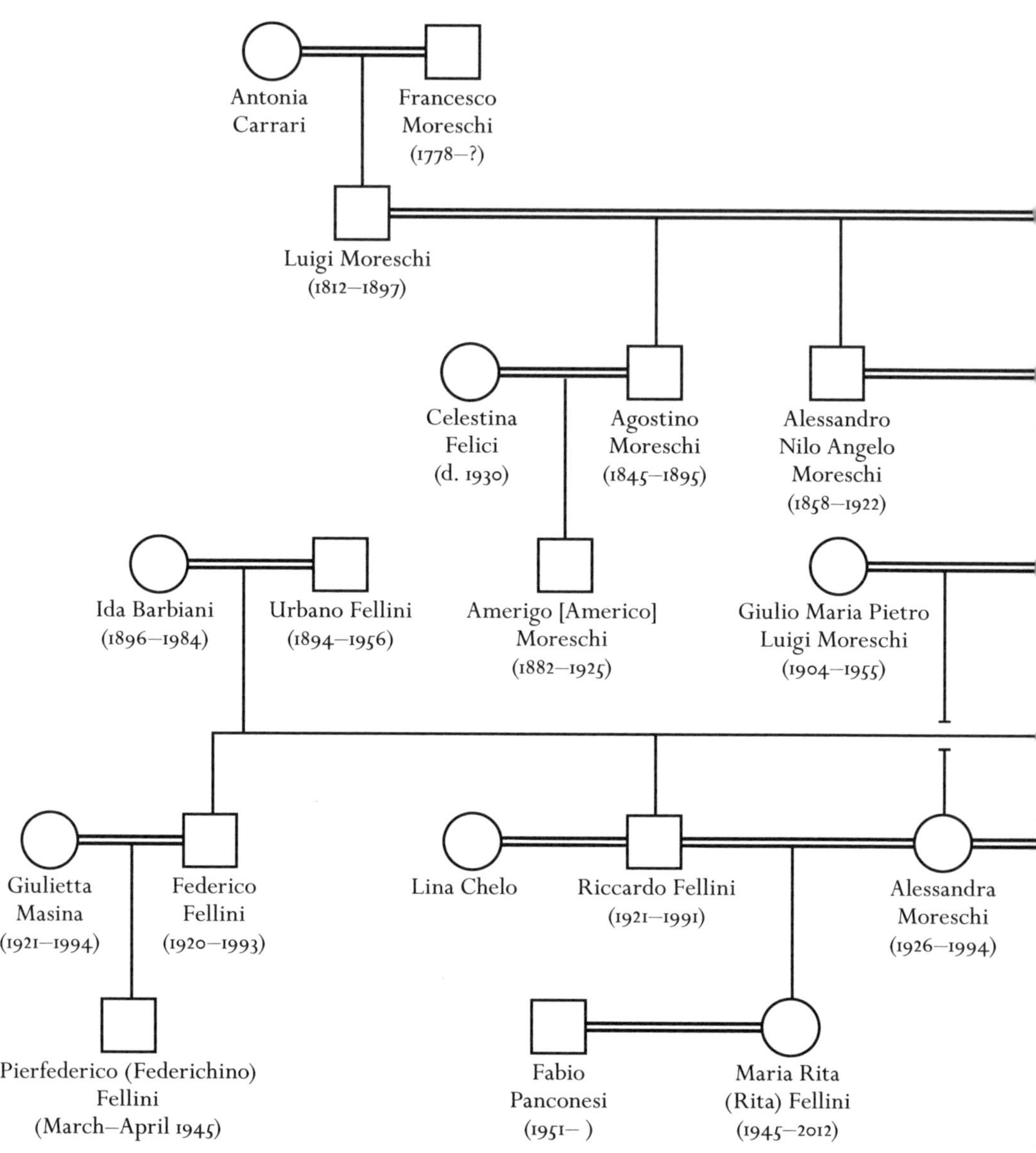

Figure P.1. Selective genealogy of the Moreschi-Fellini family. Compiled by author. Drawing by Shawn Marie Keener.

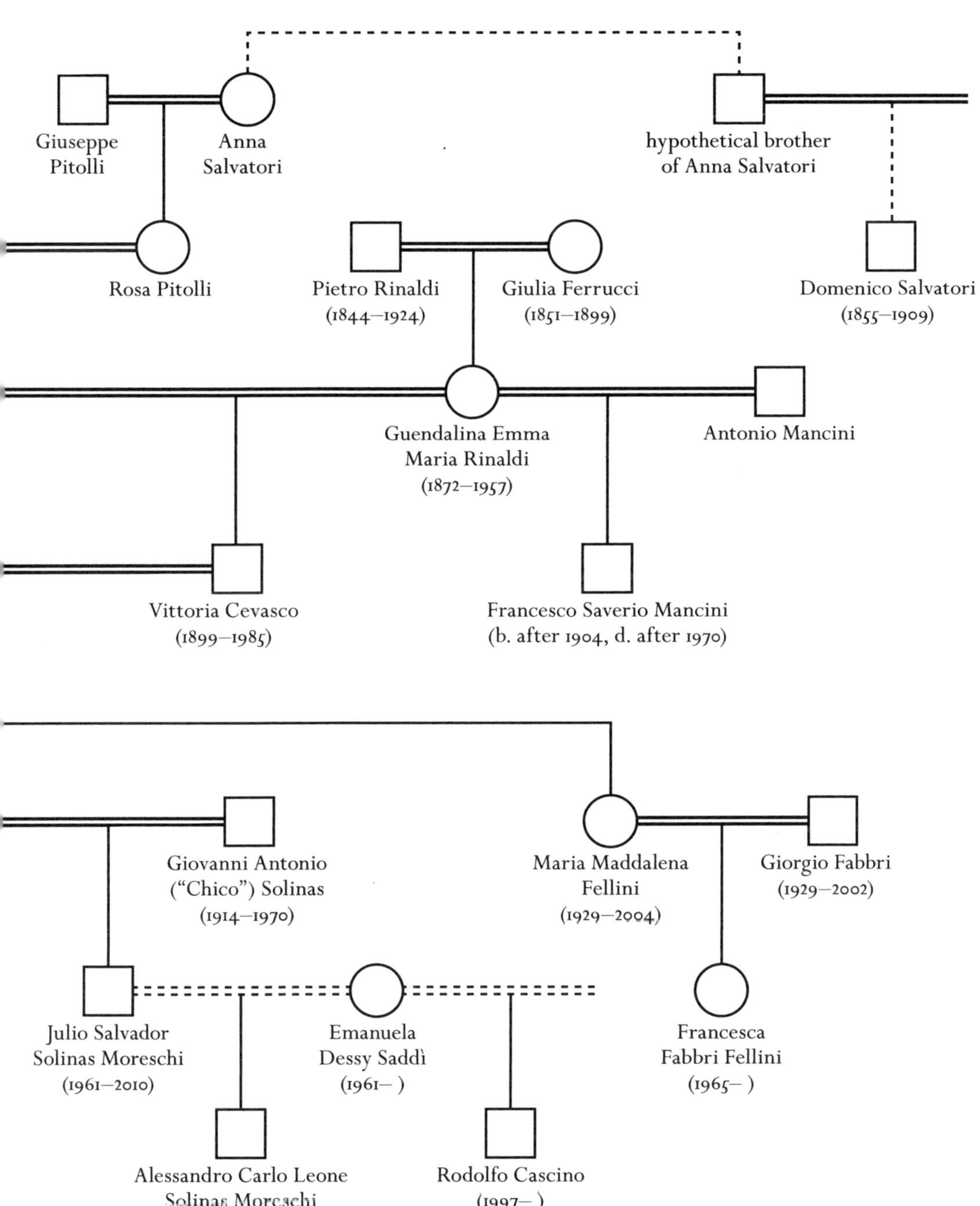
Giuseppe
Pitolli
Anna
Salvatori
hypothetical brother
of Anna Salvatori
Rosa Pitolli
Pietro Rinaldi
(1844–1924)
Giulia Ferrucci
(1851–1899)
Domenico Salvatori
(1855–1909)
Guendalina Emma
Maria Rinaldi
(1872–1957)
Antonio Mancini
Vittoria Cevasco
(1899–1985)
Francesco Saverio Mancini
(b. after 1904, d. after 1970)
Giovanni Antonio
("Chico") Solinas
(1914–1970)
Maria Maddalena
Fellini
(1929–2004)
Giorgio Fabbri
(1929–2002)
Julio Salvador
Solinas Moreschi
(1961–2010)
Emanuela
Dessy Saddì
(1961–)
Francesca
Fabbri Fellini
(1965–)
Alessandro Carlo Leone
Solinas Moreschi
(2006–)
Rodolfo Cascino
(1997–)

Figures P.2 and P.3. The *pelleteria* (belt shop) called Fellini on Rome's via del Corso 340, owned until May 2015 by Federico Fellini's niece, Maria Rita Fellini (died 2012), and her husband, Fabio Panconesi. Photographs by the author.

would go beyond the material detritus of gramophone recordings, scores, anecdotes, and treatises.[8]

Rita listened patiently to my questions, but drew a blank about her family's vocal practices. Her maternal grandfather had died when she was ten, around the same time as her parents' tumultuous marriage ended in separation, after which she and her mother moved to Mexico City via New York City to join her future stepfather.[9] She had had little occasion to hear her father sing, nor, we will see, is it clear he ever practiced much.[10] But there was much else that she and Fabio were eager to tell me. Indeed, their accounts threw me into the midst of an elaborate family history as they began to offer up tales about which they said the family had hitherto been silent, accounts that have become foundational to this book.[11]

2.

To begin approaching them, we might first glance at a family picture with Giulio Moreschi seated at the head of a dinner table next to his wife, Vittoria, who perches herself on the edge of his chair (fig. P.4a). It's a blurry amateur photograph, never before printed, but was valued enough to be made up in the then-popular form of a photo postcard for sending out to friends and relatives with a message handwritten on the back. The couple kept the copy seen here in their collection of family memorabilia with Vittoria's annotation on its verso, "25 anni di Matrimonio Moreschi 1950" (twenty-five years of Moreschi marriage, 1950) (fig. P.4b). The picture condenses a world of allusions, events, and memories. Its focal point is Giulio, a tenor who sang and toured intermittently with the Sistine Chapel choir in between teaching and keeping up a lively social life with various luminaries in Rome—besides the Fellini family, the tenor Giacomo Lauri-Volpi (1892–1979) and J. Paul Getty's last wife, Theodora Getty Gaston (1913–2017) among them. And yet it's Giulio's father, beloved, venerated, and continually nurtured in memory, who looms over the occasion like a benevolent ghost, the trunk of the family tree, despite being unable to procreate.

Alessandro is central among the "castrato phantoms" of my title. He was the last singer known to have been castrated and remains a key figure in the history of the castrati, who have never disappeared, but instead traverse a varied psychic, social, and commercial topography, receding and reemerging in different media over a *longue durée* that extends from the mid-sixteenth century up to the present day.

Explaining how so is one of the projects of this book. From the start, the practice of castrating boys for singing produced a history that occulted and denied castrations, not least in their country of origin. Some Spanish castrati did sing in the papal choir in the earliest years, and many Italian ones soon made their way beyond the peninsula, eventually ranging all over Europe, east and west, north and south, and in careers that varied widely from work in provincial chapels to engagements starring in big churches and cathedrals or performing at courts and in chambers, and above all, on opera stages.[12] Still, Italy was so invariably the place where castrations for singing took place that castrati bore a virtual "Made in Italy" stamp when they traveled abroad.[13]

Paradoxically, although their voices intertwine *avant la lettre* with the birth and apogee of bel canto, the period of the 1820s when the term was codified coincides with their replacement on operatic stages by sopranos, mezzos, contraltos, and tenors.[14] In 1830, the last major castrato star, Giambattista Velluti, exited the operatic stage, already a radical anachronism—a man out of time.[15] By then, the entire phenomenon had come to be concentrated in Italian churches and very soon exclusively in papal Rome, the sole patron of castrati in their sunset years, much as it had been almost three centuries earlier.[16] Below, I argue that the late nineteenth-century Vatican not only chose, cultivated, and supported castrati, but once again functioned as their procurers and virtual manufacturers. Only this time, castrati were islanded. They had turned into cultural carnage because they were anathema to pan-European liberal sensibilities that had been propounding ideals of innocent childhood

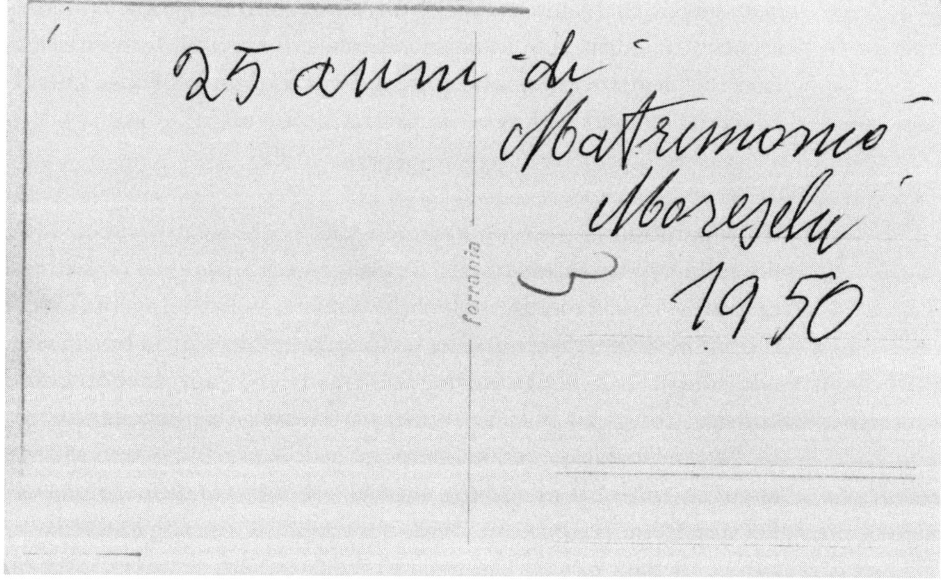

Figure P.4a. Photograph of Giulio Moreschi, tenor and son of the last castrato, at the head of a dinner table celebrating his twenty-fifth anniversary with his wife, Vittoria Cevasco, April 25, 1950. *Seated left to right*: Maria Rita (Rita) Fellini, Alessandra (Sandra) Moreschi, Riccardo Fellini, Vittoria Cevasco, Giulio Moreschi, unknown man (possibly Umberto Giuli), Federico Fellini, Giulietta Masina, and two unknown women. The men standing, also unknown, may be students of Giulio's. Moreschi-Fellini Archive.

Figure P.4b. Verso of the photograph with inscription in the hand of Vittoria Cevasco reading "25 anni di Matrimonio Moreschi 1950" (25 years of Moreschi marriage, 1950). Moreschi-Fellini Archive.

and dimorphic gender with increasing stringency since the mid to late eighteenth century. There are various ironies to reckon with here. For one, castrati were essential to the same institution that denied its own role in bringing them into existence. For another, the church music they sang, both at the Sistine Chapel and in the Cappella Giulia and other papal basilicas and churches in Rome, was far from pristinely sacred, but rather drenched in the worldly sounds of opera.[17] Small wonder that by the turn of the twentieth century, castrati had turned into a fusty vestige of their past, even though they still staffed the Sistine soprano section.[18]

That means, too, that at the time Moreschi made his gramophone recordings, in 1902 and 1904, castrati were already relics whose end was long overdue. In fact, the recording sessions bookended the official termination date of the castrati, November 22, 1903, the feast of St. Cecilia, saint of music, when the pope issued a *motu proprio* that banned them from papal churches. Some nonetheless continued singing in papal churches, sponsored by an institution that had never openly approved of them, much less acknowledged its long-standing role in producing them.[19]

3.

No separation is possible between this peculiar atavism and the unending obfuscations and contradictions that long embedded castrati—in schemes by melophilic patrons and venal agents to ferret out prepubertal choristers for castration; in efforts by princes, nobles, parents, vocal teachers, orphanages, church choirs, and conservatories to hide the means by which they'd been identified and castrated; in euphemistic practices of naming and talking about castrati that muted the very fact of their condition. Precisely because Rome perpetuated these contradictions so late in the day, it can be thought to have carried into the twentieth century a cultural burden that other places could more easily escape—the burden that came with quartering castrati while keeping their origins a secret—and this by a papal regime whose time had itself passed.

Nothing jangled against modernity more than those castrated men, whose treatment by the Roman church, especially as boys, cannot be entirely divorced from the church's notorious treatment of boy acolytes, pupils, and choir boys all too familiar from the twentieth and twenty-first centuries. Like the systems that have protected modern-day priests and bishops from charges of sexual abuse, the systems that allowed the nineteenth-century church minimally to obtain castrated rural village boys — or more realistically, to see to their castrations — was part of a regressive, but inexorable papal machinery that rumbled along well past 1871, the year when Moreschi was castrated, apparently the last to be, but not the last to be formally considered for that fate. Until the bans took hold, the church's powers went largely unimpeded and its desires unchecked.

The papal prehistory up to 1871 is crucial to understanding its anachronistic aftermath. Especially revealing is the most famous verbal expression of papal antiliberalism, the encyclical *Quanta cura* and the appended "Syllabus of Errors." Issued on December 8, 1864 (the Feast of the Immaculate Conception) by Pope Pius IX (reigned 1846 to 1878), the "Syllabus of Errors" rejected calls for Italian unification and lambasted the liberalism of the "modern world," not least the proposition that the pope himself should have to embrace or even acquiesce to various forms of modernization. The proclamation was unmatched in its severity. Reason-based faith, separation of church and state, religious freedom, and every non–Roman Catholic form of Christianity all came under Pius's attack. Not only that, but his dogmatism spilled over from the Risorgimento — generally taken to have lasted from 1848 until the establishment of the Kingdom of Italy in March 1861, when Vittorio Emanuele was recognized as king — continuing up to and beyond the Capture of Rome ("Presa di Roma") on September 20, 1870, when the city was taken by the Italian Army led by Raffaele Cadorna.

The date represents a revealing moment in papal history. While Rome became the capital of Italy, Pius famously imprisoned himself in his palace. He remained intransigent throughout his imprisonment, despite the fact that his properties and revenues had been confiscated—this at a time when the Papal States no longer existed, and papal sovereignty had turned into a thing of the past. Inasmuch as the pope's only remaining territories were those in the region nowadays called Lazio, he had decisively gone from being a monarch with temporal powers to a religious figure with (formally, at least) only spiritual powers.[20] And that difference is all-important. It means that the pope persisted as an archconservative force, even while a liberal revolution was taking place in his own backyard—a revolution that included cries for religious freedom, economic development, and church reform, along with much else that he flat-out rejected.

Because of such overlapping inheritances, to speak of *papal* Rome and the Vatican in this moment is to speak of *Rome itself*. Even after the pope's downfall, papal Rome stood symbolically and practically in a metonymic relationship to Rome as a whole, a city so thoroughly imbricated with the Vatican that it cannot be separated analytically from Roman consciousness, spectacles, customs, and institutions.[21] Castrated male sopranos figured as a naturalized part of this landscape, even as they were deep-seated reminders of something awry in the body politic. One of my claims in this book is that having produced and harbored castrati well beyond their sell-by date carried consequences not just for the Vatican, but for the entire city, and that those consequences were substantial because castrati, while discordant with an emerging modernity, continued to occupy a prominent place in papal symbolism—a symbolism projected visually, but even more dramatically in the Roman soundscape. They were a fixture in the auditory topography of Rome, despite the fact that making them required basic interventions into the sexual functioning, anatomical development, and performance of the human body—not insignificantly the *male* body—with results that could not easily be incorporated into the body social.

Hence even as Rome's post-Risorgimento castrati attracted curiosity seekers and fans, they also drew mixed reactions from visitors and locals from literati like Enrico Panzacchi and socialites such as Lillie de Hegermann-Lindencrone in the 1880s; American recording engineers Fred Gaisberg and William Sinkler Darby in 1902 and 1904; musicians and musicologists such as Franz Haböck in the early twentieth century; and visiting clerics such as the Cecilianists and Solesmes monks who attended the 1904 Gregorian Congress that coincided with the 1904 recording sessions—all of whom I take up in this book. Observers were fascinated by the power and alterity of castrato voices, especially the solo voices of Moreschi and his older colleagues Domenico Mustafà (1829–1912) (never recorded) and Giovanni Cesari (1843–1904) (audible only on 1902 recordings in a choir, if at all).[22] But they were often perturbed by the mismatches of those voices with the bodies that produced them, mismatches engineered by males whose cutting and slicing of other males interfered with both with the smooth, organic materiality of the body and the smoothness of biological time, disrupting the natural course of human development and turning modern ideas of liberality backward and upside down. In the face of such disturbances, castrati could no longer be seamlessly proposed as sacrifices to the church, as they had been in older explanations and justifications for them.[23] Instead, they became outward, embodied instances of savagery toward boys, uncomfortable displays of intolerable practices and impossible thinking, consciousness run amok, and natural time wrenched out of whack.

Meanwhile, their bodies also came to be racialized, not in the sense widely (and problematically) linked to skin tone in today's popular imaginary and political calculus (of census-taking and voting, for example), but in the currency of early modern thinking that worked to separate and categorize bodies and bodily types all told. Michael Omi and Howard Winant refer to fields of signification in which race "symbolizes social conflicts and interests by referring to different types of human bodies."[24] The epistemology that underwrites that notion of race made it easy to align castrati loosely with subjects and social groups negatively typed in the toxic scientific racism promulgated in Cesare Lombroso's criminal anthropology.[25] This is not to say that Lombroso's writings addressed the dying caste of castrati, who would not have fit in with his eugenicist theory of inborn, congenital criminality and the atavistic characteristics he associated with them. Rather it's to observe that at their foundation, Lombroso's writings demanded broad-based racist thinking that promoted uniform, undifferentiated bodies as ideals to hold up against Others demonized as different, whether judged criminal, mentally inferior, physically abnormal, or phenotypically lesser in whatever way.[26]

If castrati themselves were not criminal in Lombroso's terms, the practice of castrating boys for singing was. And it was a Roman crime by association since castrati were understood to be Rome's inheritance and its ongoing liability. I therefore suggest that the shadow they cast — though concealed in the masculinist/nationalist years of Fascism that began formally just after Moreschi's death on April 21, 1922 — persisted long after they had vanished and been all but stripped from historical memory, continuing to stalk the Roman psyche phantasmatically.

4.

Let's curve back to the period of Moreschi's Roman years, after he was taken from the small Lazian town of Montecompatri to Rome by the Vatican musician and agent Nazareno Rosati. Those years, from 1871 to 1922, overlap with what John Pollard calls the years of "Catholic recovery," roughly 1870 to 1914, from the fall of Rome to the start of the Great War.[27] On the front end, Moreschi's arrival in Rome at age twelve or thirteen occurred approximately one year after the pope was effectively dethroned. On the back end, Moreschi's official retirement from the Sistine Chapel in 1913 happened just before the start of the world war, about which Italy was initially neutral and two years before it joined the side of the French and British Entente following a vigorous minority campaign for intervention led by Benito Mussolini.[28]

Historians have asked what was required of Italians, especially Romans, in the momentous years after unification struggles had stripped the pope of temporal power and how they responded. Many have pointed to Catholic retrenchments during the period. Far from Catholicism being lessened, it was buttressed via fortifications of religious feeling and rituals. Liberal secularism became an enemy that institutions were called on to mobilize against. Even though many benefices and properties of lesser Italian churches were removed, clergy impoverished, congregational coffers diminished, and religious orders weakened, reactions against liberalism went almost the opposite way. In Rome and Lazio, religiosity surged, a kind of counterpendulum to the secularism of liberality.[29] Above all, Marian devotions turned out to be key in the Catholic revival of Pius's successor, Leo XIII (reigned 1878 to 1903), who wrote no fewer than eleven encyclicals on the rosary in his twenty-five years as pope — something that surely resonated for Alessandro, only nineteen years old when Leo's pontificate started and himself, as a boy in his small town in rural Lazio, a star vocal product of cults associated with the chapel of the Madonna del Castagno.

5.

To approach these dimensions of Roman experience and consciousness, I move between hierarchically different orders, engaging aesthetic and affective domains at family levels, but also across the broader ones of church and state. In the process, I also shift between the haunted anachrony of the decades surrounding 1900 at one end of the temporal spectrum to the postwar decades of the 1950s to 1970s and on up to the present on the other end. What results is a nonsequential treatment that attends to what Manuel De Landa calls "nonlinear time" and Elizabeth Freeman calls "queer time," time that in my case causes history to fold over on itself, defying sequential schemata and "con-sequential" events in favor of "apparitional" ones.[30] This means thinking about "unconsciousness, haunting, reverie, and the afterlife" in ways that might typically be "invisible to the historicist eye."[31] And it means thinking with specters in terms of what Jacques Derrida called "a *politics* of memory, of inheritance, and of generations."[32] In this book, I am interested therefore not just in Moreschi's time, but in how it's figured in the consciousness of his Roman descendants and cultural heirs, how their pasts produced futures, and how presents are always living with and responding to shades of the past.[33]

Haunted consciousness continually mediates the objective material remnants and facts of existence, especially in the realm of the sonic. Moreschi's son, for instance, painstakingly preserved physical replications of his father's recordings and must have played them repeatedly for students and guests. But like the telephone conversation between Proust's protagonist and his grandmother in *Remembrance of Things Past* elegantly analyzed by Sara Danius, the voice heard through the uncanny medium of the gramophone was a spectral, disembodied materiality.[34] Inevitably, what it produced were shadow memories, reified, yet forever detached from the body responsible for making them and moreover from its lived contexts. Shadow memories are in any case elusive. Like all that is ineffable—not least in music, as famously described by Vladimir Jankélévitch—memories are shaped by experiences that may be touchstones, but are marked by inconsistency, experience to experience, person to person.[35] And in music, those memories are filed away, only to be replayed in ways that may resurrect the revenant without bringing it fully, and most definitely not reliably, back to life.

It's these afterlives that underlie the spectral mode with which I want to think here, a mode that recognizes grounded practices and material forms as inseparable from psychic resonances, individual or collective, which are relatively oblivious to linear time. Temporal folds implicate everything from vocal lineages to family lineages, individual wounds and disavowals to mass cultural ones, personal memories and collective ones. They include psychic fears, anxieties, body dysmorphias, mental disturbances, hidden desires, and troubling fantasies—none easily pinnable to orderly histories, precise chronologies, or specific causes. In this sense, my interests lie in phantom phenomena in the plural sense: those that stand in a peripheral relationship to or outside of consciousness and those that absent conscious collective memory because they are repressed in practice and discourse.

As with Freud's uncanny, what often emerge, too, are Doppelgängers, psychic and functional doubles that interpose themselves between life and death, ghosting the real and the unconscious. Hence, the familiar continually becomes strange and the strange familiar, and this, too, modulates the unpredictable rhythms of time. By exploring the declining and disappearing castrato in late nineteenth-century and twentieth-century Rome, not least as it was submerged in Roman consciousness and finally resurfaced as a return of the repressed, I think about how recent Roman history continually defines yet disrupts the present. That history suggests that through some combination of happenstance and circumstance, manifest as an impossible trace, the psychocultural construct that emerges from the no-longer embodied and manifest castrato—once, but no longer part of an assemblage of Roman landscapes, figures, and soundscapes—continues to resonate as an afterlife.

6.

In my account, then, the castrato is necessarily embedded as a latency or residue, something that shimmers with an afterglow, even in a space that secretes him—indeed, even in one that is ashamed of him. The space that secrets him is a place where time is always hiccupping, as old traditions keep rearranging themselves in new vernaculars. In moving through these folded temporalities and spatial overflows, I work to understand what I call the *sacred vernacular*, a compulsively repeating, reforming, and all-consuming tendency toward vernacularization that constantly (re)familiarizes sacred forms and tropes. Rome, in its sustained modern moment, was an environment that, even more than elsewhere in Italy, was constantly turning religious form and ritual into familiar comforts:

Madonna figurines, angel trinkets, little crucifixes, baptismal ribbons, death cards, and *mattoni* (those wooden, signed remembrance plaques produced for jubilees). It was a place filled with the daily rituals of prayers, blessings, and masses, its landscapes marked by the sartorial forms of arm coverings, veils, cassocks, robes, wedding dresses, and confirmation dresses, its soundscapes ringing with sentimental sacred music: the Latin texts occasionally sung in salons, the religious art songs in the vernacular like Paolo Tosti's "Ideale," the sacred contrafacta of operas once made by Moreschi's teacher Gaetano Capocci, and the oratorios composed by Lorenzo Perosi in the early 1900s. All this to say nothing of the soothing cycles of ritual events that constantly articulated Roman life, from christenings and confirmations to weddings and funerals.

My "sacred vernacular" thus links sacred practices to vernacular tropes, combining what Miriam Hansen, in explaining her term "vernacular modernism," calls "the dimensions of the quotidian, of everyday usage, with connotations of discourse, idiom, and dialect, with circulation, promiscuity, and translatability."[36] Rome's sacred vernacular tropes, like Hansen's modern vernacular ones, are fungible, exchangeable, and infinitely variable, yet always infused somehow with a centripetal force toward the homey and ordinary. Conceived in relation to the volatile sociopolitical environments of late nineteenth-century and early to mid-twentieth-century Italy, both Hansen's category and mine implicate a vast array of forms and instances at the same time as they point up a gravitational pull toward the familiar. But in the Roman case, what counts is the *sacred* as domesticated through radical circulations, always entailing reemergences, dormancies, and overflows from one idiom to another and back in ways that account not only for the general condition of a particular modernity, but for constant passages from the sacred to the secular.

Far from being attenuated by the secularizing impulses of later nineteenth-century liberalism and then of Fascism, vernacular tokens of religiosity were only reinforced, their forms constantly in states of revision. This held true in the period of Catholic recovery, when Romans largely rejected liberalism, and it held true again in the aftermath of World War II, the time of "Catholic triumphalism," when Giulio and Vittoria, their daughter and her husband, and Federico and his wife were all in their prime.[37] Both periods involved moments of severe crisis. The latter-day Catholic triumphalist moment emerged from the cruel, agonizing end to Italian involvement in World War II, starting in 1943, when the Italian state, lacking an effective army, was kneecapped, its monarchy abolished, and when in 1946 it was denied entry to the UN. Starting in those same years, the Christian Democratic Party (aka Democrazia Cristiana, Il Partito della DC, or simply Il DC) made immense gains, allowing the Catholic church to hold vast legal powers concerning the life-and-death matters of marriage, last rites, and funerals and allowing it direct political and social power over workers' associations, political parties, the press, the arts, and on and on, notwithstanding the increased hold of Marxism, represented politically by the chief opposition party, the Italian Communist Party. All this held true until 1958, even though broader secularization became inevitable only after the 1963 launch of the Second Vatican Council under John XXIII (reigned 1958 to 1963). The year 1963 represents the real sea change for Italy, a counterpoint to 1903/1904. John XXIII's policies leaned heavily toward modernization, or better, updating, *aggiornamento*, not on ideological grounds, but on practical ones, and those leanings increased under Paul VI (reigned 1963 to 1978), when *aggiornamento* took root, not least in response to the American and British cultural invasions of pop art, popular music, women's lib, and divorce law.[38]

Through all that, Italy—and markedly, Rome—developed and sustained its own idiomatic vernacularism centered on the sacred. In this book, I'm interested in how a vernacular tropology allows the castrato to exist, sonically and ontologically, in the years surrounding 1900, but also in how the castrato reappears as a psychic remnant at certain historical moments after ostensibly being gone, especially in postwar Rome. How does the temporal dislocatedness of the late-stage castrato come to be translated into different vernacular forms and media? And how do those forms and media work through certain cognitive dilemmas that castrati had long posed in Italy? What's at stake is the pastness or out-of-dateness of the late castrato as hold-over, as well as the paradoxical modernity of the castrato as a haunting remainder — the psychic piece that vexes the modernist puzzle by not fitting in, yet refusing to go away, thus worrying the prevailing cultural logic. Here is how phantoms — materializations of hauntings from the past — intersect with my sacred vernacular. It's also why it's not just the *vernacular* in Hansen's "vernacular modernism" that matters to my story, but the uneasy, troubled, discombobulated, and time-warped *modernism* in it.

The chapters that follow explore the nexus of cultural psychic connections between the Moreschi and Fellini families to think about the castrato as a kind of sacred monster operating along vectors that stretch from divadom to divinity, along which the sacred vernacular operates as a site of constant play, a site of difference with respect to itself. The hybridized style of sacred performances sung by Moreschi and his contemporaries, infusing operatic musical idioms into religious-texted music, is one prominent instance of that. But relevant, too, is that Moreschi recorded some of those performances using the magical new technologies brought to Rome with the phonograph, one of the startling new media to land there just before the turn of the century. For both reasons, Moreschi registered as an inherent problem, representing the sacred, but (like his castrato colleagues) betraying its fissures, fitting into some modern norms and others not at all. Through all this, the sacred adhered to him both through music and by virtue of his stigmata — the wounds that undermined modernist claims of progress by betraying the outdated norms of sacrifice made via bodily mortification that were proper precisely to the old regime they were supposed to suture. Small wonder that his performances met almost as often with puzzlement or even derision as with praise.

Modernity came around slowly, partially, and hesitantly for Moreschi. When new rules for papal singers, including castrati, went into effect in 1891, he was able for the first time to attend the theater "legally" and by some reckoning, at least, to marry, becoming a quasi-legitimate man of the modern Roman world. What he could never overcome was having been cut out of possibilities for procreation, an exclusion that was a timeworn mark of sacredness, but also a permanent humiliation and among the worst of personal and family vicissitudes for a man in Catholic Italy.[39]

7.

As for Giulio's in-law, Federico Fellini, who will figure along with his brother more below: once he started making feature films, codirecting *Luci della varietà / Variety Lights* (with Alberto Lattuada), starring his iconic wife, Giulietta Masina, in the same year of 1950 as Giulio and Vittoria celebrated their twenty-fifth anniversary, his presence in the extended family became increasingly rare. Although Rita and Fabio made fairly frequent trips to the Fellini-Masina residence at Fregene and elsewhere over the years,[40] the photo in figure P.4a remains the only surviving picture of Federico with the Moreschi family, apart from images with Rita. It remains a thin archival trace from the filaments that bound the Moreschi family to the director, who was possessed by his work, distracted by his personal affairs, and resistant to family obligations, however deeply attached he was to his family-oriented wife.[41]

And yet Fellini matters to the story I tell here. During the 1950s, from his first and second solo feature films, *Lo sceicco bianco / The White Sheik* and *I vitelloni* (1953), to the masterpiece, *La dolce vita* (1960), that rocketed him to iconic international stature, Fellini established himself as the master critic of the sacred vernacular as I elaborate it in Chapter 2. All three films created worlds laced throughout with vernacular tokens of sacred tropology: with angels, rosaries, and incense, nuns in habits, priests in robes, lay churchgoers making signs of the cross, stumbling to confession, taking communion. His films not only vernacularized the sacred all told, but offered up a specifically Roman variety of it whose rhythms are shaped by daily encounters: with the majesty of the Vatican palace, squares, colonnades, and museums; with the city's constant parade of robed clerics, its ubiquitous architecture of parish and basilican churches and saintly statuary; and with the endless rituals, from blessings and masses to sacraments and rosaries, that take place in familiar Roman spaces. Indeed, in Fellini, almost everything points Romeward while reminding viewers that Catholicism lies forever close at hand. Even *I vitelloni*, set in a mythical provincial town that recalls the Fellini brothers' hometown of Rimini, ends with one of its protagonists making his way to Rome after embracing a life-size wooden angel.

All of which raises questions about what kind of figure the castrato represented in the late nineteenth and early twentieth centuries. A weirdly anachronistic, but minor fact of Roman life—no more than a small and aberrant blip on the screen of history? Or the expression of something more, something deeply connected to what made Rome what it was? My goal in this book is to contemplate the late castrato in both ways: as an anomalous figure, but also an improbable index of Roman consciousness, both during Moreschi's own life and beyond it.

8.

The phantoms of my title are not identical to sensations and anxieties of haunting. They are more like personifications, though also materializations of them. As such, they point in several directions. They point, first of all, to the secrecy and obfuscations that have always clouded castrato histories and made castrati a cultural millstone for Italy, but especially for Rome, which inherited the burden of them once it became the sole place to perpetuate castrati long after their extinction elsewhere. Second, they point to a family story carried forward over the course of four generations that has repeatedly visited itself on the castrato's descendants, taking shape as a transgenerational secret whose origins date back to a trauma experienced by Alessandro in 1907, aspects of which I contemplate in Chapters 1 and 5. And third, they point to the repression of castrati during the Italian twentieth century (the Novecento), following their disappearance, in the course of which they were muted through a kind of concerted oblivion. That oblivion extends from the aesthetic decadence and warmongering masculinism of Gabriele D'Annunzio (1863–1938) to the masculinist impulses of such futurists as Filippo Tommaso Marinetti (1876–1944) and the Bragaglia brothers Anton Giulio (1890–1960) and Carlo Ludovico (1894–1998). It encompasses the metaphysician Alberto Savinio (1891–1952), whose work I explore in Chapter 4, and was later entangled with the machismo of Fascism and arguably even the postwar neorealist cinema of Roberto Rossellini and Vittorio De Sica, with its rough-hewn, tough-guy focus on the plights of the downtrodden. More ambiguously, the oblivion reaches into the so-called neodecadence of Fellini, who apprenticed with Rossellini and some of his contemporaries, notwithstanding Fellini's preoccupation with the impotence of his male-chauvinistic characters (we can think of *8½*'s Marcello as the quintessential embodiment of the type, but also recall the masculine dilemma at the heart of *Città delle donna /City of Women*). The wager I make here is that these different vectors overlap in meaningful ways and that their overlaps accrete meanings over time that make them more revealing in their sum than their parts.

9.

While this book is an attempt to view the photograph in figure P.4a—to make it sensible and audible along with the wider worlds it inhabits—it is also an acknowledgment that the image cannot be truly seen, much less heard. The occasion depicted lies chronologically at the midpoint between the present story—which is to say, the story I tell from the present that is also *of* the present—and the story of Giulio's much-celebrated father, Alessandro, who in March 1883, just twenty-four years old, entered the private chapel of the pope as an acclaimed soloist and dominated much of Roman church and salon singing over the span of a long career.

And yet the photograph also intersects directly with my own tale. When I first met with Fabio, he encouraged me to write down what he and Rita related, and sketched the beginnings of a genealogical chart that reached back four generations. The sketch was a very rough one, he lamented, because there had been a "break" in family memory prior to their grandparents' generation.[42] He also took me that afternoon to Rome's vast old cemetery, the Cimitero del Verano, to see the family tomb, where Alessandro and various descendants are buried, which Fabio had given one of his regular groomings the week before.

Embedded in the tomb were a number of mysteries. To begin with, it was architecturally impressive, given the castrato's basically middle-class to upper-middle-class means (fig. P.5). Its principal feature consists of a wide, rounded pillar of reddish-brown stone situated beneath a capital assembled from some seven slabs that complete the column, the whole topped by a large crucifix. Second, the pillar is heavily pockmarked along its frontal surface (fig. P.6). Fabio told me that the tomb had been vandalized at some point, though he did not know why or exactly how or when. And last, unlike so many tombs of modern Italian families, whose headstones are overlaid with porcelain-laminated photographs of the dead, this one had only a single photograph, sitting inconspicuously on its marble pedestal, of a man named Pietro Rinaldi (fig. P.7) about whom the family in 2010 knew nothing, presuming that he must have been a family friend.[43] And yet the great marble slab that covers the bodies of the deceased is prominently engraved in large capital letters that read "MORESCHI E RINALDI" (fig. P.8).

That summer, I returned home to a busy administrative schedule chairing my department while a young research assistant in Rome, Martina Piperno—now an outstanding Italianist in her own right—pursued a series of leads that I mapped out for her in daily correspondence and that she pursued with ever greater independence.[44] My conversations with the family continued necessarily mediated by Fabio, though they were disrupted by two untimely deaths. In October 2010, Rita's forty-nine-year-old half brother, the actor, singer, director, writer, and dancer, Julio (sometimes Giulio) Salvador Solinas Moreschi, died of a heart attack on the streets of Rome just months after I went in search of Rita and Fabio.[45] And in February 2012, Rita herself died, aged sixty-six, of heart failure brought on by complications from diabetes, leaving it to Fabio and me to press on.[46] Ultimately, these conversations have become an odyssey in family remembrance, revelation, and reflection, driven by my promise to Rita and Fabio to honor their generosity and candor by uncovering more of their story.

In 2011, in between these deaths, Fabio and Rita asked that I take a donation of some family materials that are among the relatively few to have survived the ravages of time, a donation I accepted as an interim custodian with the understanding that they would be deposited in a public archive after my work was done. Among the materials are many photographs documenting family and professional events, some tourist items collected on trips or received as gifts, Giulio's baptismal ribbon and his spectacles, a guest book from Alessandro's funeral, a couple of stray letters, the mid-nineteenth-century professional scrapbook of Alessandro's teacher Nazareno Rosati, and some framed pictures, along with a manuscript score of Lorenzo Perosi's and a few printed opera scores almost certainly belonging to Giulio. Much else has gone astray.

Making the donation was a hedge against further loss, a way of preserving most of what remained in family hands. The original donation, plus some recent additions (comprising further photographs, documents related to Rita's stepfather, a wedding invitation, and letters, including one from Federico to Rita), combined with historical, musical, and archival research and the fruits of many conversations, have given this book its footings.

In March 2024, I stopped briefly in Rome to discuss the book with Fabio and give him a spiral-bound printout of it. He approved

Figure P.5. Moreschi-Rinaldi tomb, Cimitero del Verano, Rome, May 2010. Photographs by the author.

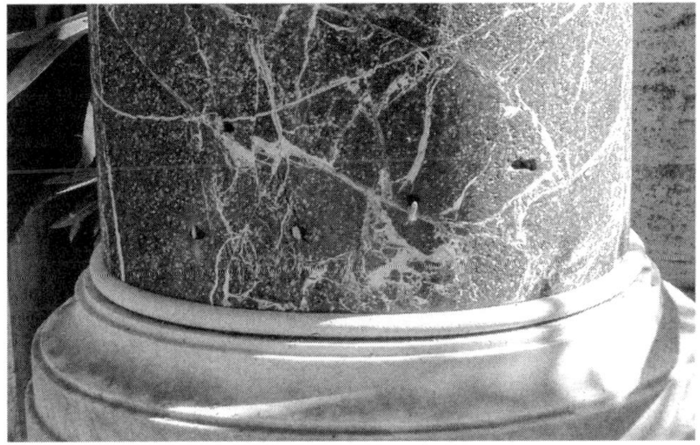

Figure P.6. Close-up showing the central pockmarked column.

Figure P.7. Moreschi-Rinaldi tomb in May 2010, with a single porcelained photograph of the then-unidentified Pietro Rinaldi on the pedestal.

Figure P.8. The great stone slab covering the deceased at the Moreschi-Rinaldi tomb, engraved with large letters "MORESCHI E RINALDI."

the quotations of him and gave his blessing for the book's title, even as the two of us acknowledged that we could not expect to see eye to eye on all nuances of interpretation. My hope is that the book might offer a small compensation for fortunes and things lost in the family's legacy over the decades.

10.

Let's return to figure P.4a, a grainy family photograph that yields its secrets grudgingly. On first inspection, some figures are barely legible. Furthermore, it's hard to know whether the milestone celebrated was only a wedding anniversary or a double celebration that also commemorated the fifth anniversary of Liberation Day, which marked the release from so much that beset the generations depicted there.[47]

When I first began to parse the image, I quickly saw that seated on the viewer's left was Giulio and Vittoria's only child, Alessandra, named for her castrato grandfather. Five-year-old Rita sits on her mother's lap, Alessandra's husband, Riccardo, to her left. But circling clockwise, things for some time were less clear. Across the table, an unidentified man flanks Giulio, and to his left is a couple I first failed to recognize, but only much later realized was lanky Federico Fellini sitting alongside his petite wife, Giulietta.[48] And there they all gather, doubtless not silently, as they seem to us now, but to the sounds of clinking glasses, clattering dishes, chitchat, and bursts of singing, sonic residues of Alessandro, according to Giulio's voice student Teddy (Theodora) Getty, who later reported that at jovial dinners out, Giulio would always break into song.[49] Indeed, singing preoccupied the family, on the job and off. Vittoria had been Giulio's student and was herself an aspiring opera singer. If Federico's accounts can be believed, Riccardo would have been among the first to join in, and the same goes for Alessandra, also a singer and on Rita's jaundiced account an incorrigible show-off.[50] It might also be true for the gentlemen standing in the back, at least some of whom were likely Giulio's singing students.

Still, if the photograph captures a moment before song, it also captures something else. It's the convergence of this upbeat to musical conviviality, a promise of what will or ought to be—hospitality, singing, familial warmth—with the bleaker augur of how things may inevitably turn out and how the image may someday register: precisely not as the warrant of familial bonds, but a record of what failed to happen or went awry. After talking with descendants of this assembled party and studying others, I cannot help associating the picture with experiences of loss and mourning that shadow it, experiences with which the genre of photography has itself been linked. Images, writes Susan Sontag, are "able to usurp reality" because a photograph is not only an image, but "an *interpretation* of the real; it is also a *trace*, something directly stenciled off the real, like a footprint or a death mask."[51] Elegiac and "touched with pathos," this photograph, like countless others, might be taken as what Sontag named a "pseudo-presence and a token of absence," hence, also an "incitement to reverie."[52]

And this is the case not least when encountered in its residue—the form of encounter in which you and I are viewing it now. For in this moment, we see it in parallax, in a condition of obliquity and difference with respect to the object itself. As Roland Barthes noted, whatever the photographic image "grants to vision and whatever its manner, a photograph is always invisible: it is not *it* that we see."[53]

11.

While writing *Castrato Phantoms*, the photograph has kicked up a backwash of questions—about the location, the waiter, the unidentifiable guests, the anonymous photographer . . . were the chairs in the foreground vacated by the three standing gentlemen to let them enter the picture frame, while a fourth clicked the shutter? Someone without skill or a tripod (a blessing, given the fate of a family archive that was later pilfered of things of obvious value, as more legible photos of Fellini would have been)? And how did they get Federico to attend—or was he still pliant enough at age

Figure P.9a. Photograph of Alessandro Moreschi with his circa eight-year-old son, Giulio Moreschi, about 1912 (recto). Moreschi-Fellini Archive.

Figure P.9b. Verso of photograph of figure P.9a, marked in Vittoria's hand, "Giulio e suo padre a Montecompatri" (Giulio and his father at Montecompatri). Moreschi-Fellini Archive.

twenty-nine to acquiesce? Most of all, why the scarcity of smiles? Occasioned by a jubilant milestone, the event also feels freighted by a certain gloom, the picture a study in paradox, with the affable Giulio beaming along with the ever-pleasant, ever-constant Giulietta, Federico raising his champagne flute amiably amid others who look far less genial (the unsmiling Riccardo, Alessandra, and Rita, the sour women to Giulietta's left).

Looking at it, my mind travels back in time, remembering the very different feeling I had seeing a photograph of Giulio with the man Vittoria marked down on its verso as his "father" ("padre") (figs. P.9a and P.9b). Taken around 1912, when the child must have been about eight years old, it is a priceless memento—the only image of the pair to survive and another that has never been published. The two are shod in walking boots, but dressed in the kind of hiking apparel a city dweller might have chosen, young Giulio with his jaunty hat, matching seersucker suit, and knee socks, both nicely knotted at the neck, and both looking as if someone had just handed them walking sticks. The picture, apparently captured on the outskirts of Moreschi's small town of Montecompatri, could easily have felt stiff and antiseptic, posed beforehand by a tourist photographer (as it likely was) but for something in their demeanor, something that hints at a special bond.[54] It comes through in Alessandro's gaze as he lays his hand tenderly on the back of his child, who seems relaxed and cared for, despite all. To be sure, we can see the castrato only in Barthes's condition of obliquity, as what Marianne Hirsch calls a revenant, a figure who looms over Giulio and Vittoria's anniversary party, but is not there. And yet Alessandro, already in his mid-fifties and looking less than fit, has in this moment a softness in his eyes, the kind of supple resignation you see in a person who's done much in life and managed to battle heartache with a certain gratitude.

CHAPTER ONE

Phantoms in the Archive

> Personally I have had the sense that remembering the dead is important for them but also for us. Because not to know anything is as if you had a hole, a black hole—to know that before us there were people in certain places who lived, suffered, got sick, and then suddenly silence, forgetfulness, oblivion descended. And that pushed me to search for others too, other recollections of other persons. . . . I now preserve the names both of persons who lived and I've known, and those that I didn't know. And periodically I name them, let's say I say a prayer. Even if I'm not particularly observant, still I think that to utter the names of the dead helps them, helps the person who has crossed over. At least that's my thought, it's not a certainty, I can't say such a thing as a certainty.
>
> —Fabio Panconesi, March 23, 2015

The Son, the Wife, the Thief, and Her Lover

After Rita's death and through May of 2015, Fabio continued running their belt shop, Fellini, as its sole living proprietor, perhaps the only one of the many business establishments around the world named for Fellini that had actual blood ties to the family.[1] A broad-minded man of innate intelligence, Fabio was first raised in cosmopolitan Cairo by his father, Edoardo, himself descended from a Florentine military man decorated in the African campaign,[2] and did his elementary schooling there in French, one of his family's two languages, along with Italian, even after their return to Italy around the time Fabio began secondary school. Most of what he and Rita knew about Moreschi family history came from Rita's grandmother, Vittoria Cevasco (1899–1985), the strong-willed Genoese woman who married the castrato's son in 1925.[3] In the mid-1920s, Vittoria had been one of Giulio's chief pupils, staged by him in concerts of arias built around the then-fashionable verismo repertory. A program in the Moreschi-Fellini Archive features her in a concert produced by Giulio at the Hotel Plaza on Corso Umberto I six months after their marriage, singing repertory by Tirindelli, Puccini, Ponchielli, and Catalani (his famed "Ebben ne andrò lontano" from *La Wally*) (figs. 1.1a and 1.1b)—this in the same period in which the couple reenacted an operatic scene for the camera (fig. 1.2).

The next year, their daughter, Alessandra, was born, on October 10, 1926, and Vittoria became the family's staunch matriarch. Years later, after eighteen-year-old Alessandra—by then married, but still footloose and fancy-free—had prematurely birthed her own daughter, on March 20, 1945, Vittoria energetically helped rear her fragile granddaughter, Rita. And then once more, from 1973 through 1984, it was Vittoria who housed Rita and Fabio when the two were young newlyweds.[4] Those were the years immediately following their wedding at the Campidoglio on September 14, 1973, which Vittoria attended along with both of Rita's parents, her young half brother, Julio (Alessandra's son, then aged eleven), and the female half of the couple composed of uncle Federico (Fellini) and aunt Giulietta (Masina) (fig. 1.3).[5]

By the time Rita and Fabio married, Vittoria had been widowed for almost two decades and had become the family memory bank and storyteller, despite a poorly executed operation done on her vocal cords that left her with a rough, low-pitched voice.[6] On Vittoria's account, as Rita and Fabio remembered things, Alessandro Moreschi had married a woman named Guendalina, surname unknown to them. That in itself is remarkable. Over the course of

programma del concerto con Vittoria e Giulio Moreschi

HOTEL PLAZA

(CORSO UMBERTO I)

Domenica 20 Settembre 1925

alle ore 21

GRANDE CONCERTO DI GALA

A BENEFICIO DEL

RICREATORIO VITTORIO EMANUELE III

La Direzione si riserva di variare le esecuzioni

È PRESCRITTO L'ABITO NERO

PROGRAMMA

PARTE I

1. — U. GIORDANO
Andrea Chenièr - Monologo
Bar. Sig. Attilio Boschi

2. — BIZET
Carmen - Romanza del fiore
Ten. Sig. Franco Caselli

3. — TIRINDELLI
Romanza - Strana
Sopr. Sig.ra Vittorina Moreschi

4. — PUCCINI
Gianni Schicchi - Preghiera di Lauretta
Sopr. Sig.ra Vittorina Moreschi

PARTE II

1. — PUCCINI
Fanciulla del West - Ch'ella mi creda
Ten. Sig. Franco Caselli

2. — LEONCAVALLO
Zazà - Zazà piccola zingara
Bar. Sig. Attilio Boschi

3. — CATALANI
Wally - Ebben ne andrò lontano
Sopr. Sig.ra Vittorina Moreschi

4. — PONCHIELLI
Gioconda - Duetto I Atto
Sopr. Sig.ra Vittorina Moreschi
Ten. Sig. Franco Caselli

MAESTRO DIRETTORE SIG. GIULIO MORESCHI

Figures 1.1a–b. Program book (outside and inside) for a benefit vocal concert put on by Giulio Moreschi at the Hotel Plaza on Corso Umberto I, featuring his wife, Vittoria Cevasco, Sunday, September 20, 1925, at 9 p.m., to benefit the Recreatory of Vittorio Emanuele III—a kind of black-tie affair ("prescritto l'abito nero"). As director, Giulio reserved the right to change the program, which leaned in a veristic direction. Moreschi-Fellini Archive.

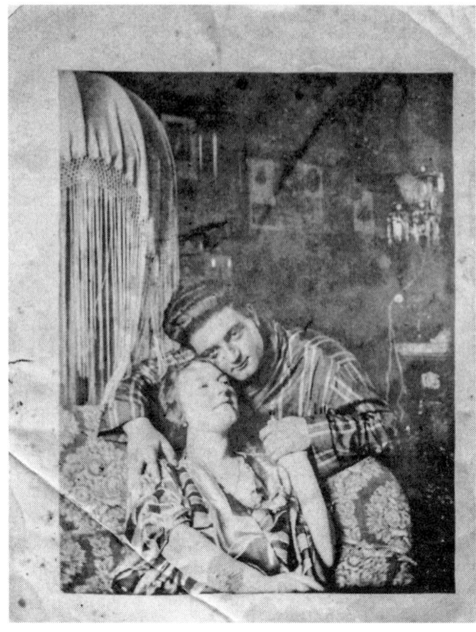

Figure 1.2. Giulio Moreschi and Vittoria Cevasco posing for an unidentified operatic scene, probably 1924. (See Appendix One, 5 and 6.) Moreschi-Fellini Archive.

history, very few castrati ever married, and of those who did, none married Catholic women or did so on Italian soil. (The only possible exception dates from the later sixteenth century, well before the castrato phenomenon had fully taken hold.)[7] The prohibition forbidding castrato marriages traces back to a bull of Sixtus V, "Cum frequenter," dated June 27, 1587, made in answer to a complaint from the bishop of Navarra, albeit without naming the object of the prohibition as singing castrates (see below). Although "Cum frequenter" was evidently bound up at least partly with the advent of castrati, marriage continued to be forbidden to anyone incapable of procreation. And until rules of celibacy were lifted on March 7, 1891, for lay members of the papal chapel, marriage was also forbidden to everyone in the Sistine Chapel.[8]

Even after that, Alessandro's marriage was extraordinary because he was patently incapable of procreating. Yet what the archives reveal about it is even more so. According to parish records (*gli stati delle*

Figure 1.3. Group shot of the wedding party for the marriage of Rita Fellini and Fabio Panconesi. *Left to right*: Julio Salvador Solinas Moreschi, Fabio Panconesi, Riccardo Fellini, Rita Fellini, Alessandra Moreschi, Vittoria Cevasco, and Giulietta Masina. Campidoglio, Rome, September 14, 1973. Moreschi-Fellini Archive.

anime), in 1901 Guendalina (then twenty-eight) and Alessandro (forty-three) were living in an elegant flat steps away from the Pantheon, on the fourth floor of what is now numbered as via della Palombella 38 (fig. 1.4), together with his nineteen-year-old nephew, Amerigo Moreschi (sometimes "Americo") (fig. 1.5), and Pietro Rinaldi (age fifty-seven)—the same man who is buried in the Moreschi-Rinaldi tomb (see fig. P.7).[9] The records list Guendalina as "Guendalina Rinaldi" and Pietro as Guendalina's father, while cemetery documents show that on April 24, 1900, he and Moreschi had become concessionaries of the new joint family tomb (properly, "Moreschi-Rinaldi").[10] Venturing into such a legally and symbolically freighted arrangement suggests a degree of closeness as well as stature and perhaps wealth, plus a goodly amount of initiative on at least one of their parts. But by 1902, the father had absented the flat. Moreover, with the description in that year's parish record of Guendalina as "*fu* Rinaldi," meaning "daughter of the *late* [Pietro] Rinaldi" (figs. 1.6a and 1.6b), the father

Figure 1.4. The apartment building at via della Palombella 38 (= no. 88) near the Pantheon, where Alessandro Moreschi lived on the top floor with Guendalina Rinaldi between at least 1900 and 1905, along with Alessandro's nephew, Amerigo Moreschi, and others. Guendalina birthed Giulio there in 1904. Photograph by the author.

Figure 1.5. Amerigo (Americo) Moreschi (1882–1925). Moreschi-Fellini Archive.

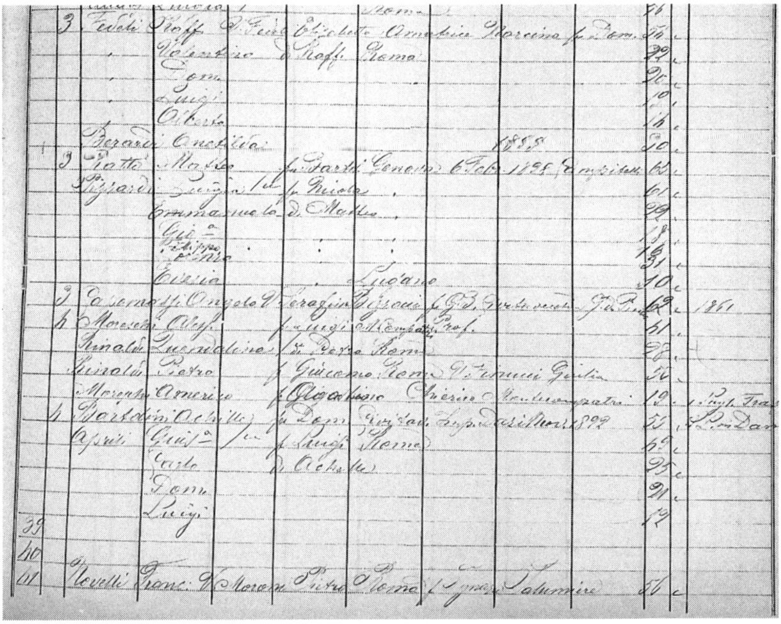

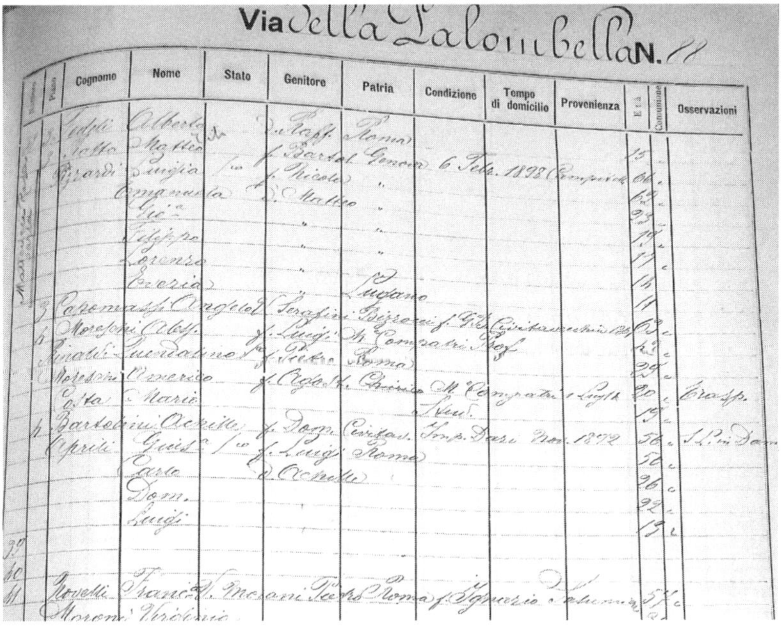
Via della Palombella N. 88

	Piano	Cognome	Nome	Stato	Genitore	Patria	Condizione	Tempo di domicilio	Provenienza	Età	Comunione	Osservazioni

Figures 1.6a–b. 1901 parish record, annotated as being for via della Palombella 88, but coincident with via della Palombella 38, and 1902 parish record for via della Palombella 88 (= via della Palombella 38). In 1901 (figure 1.6a, top), Guendalina's father is listed among those living there, but is represented in 1902 (figure 1.6b, bottom) as deceased through the designation "Rinaldi Guendalina fu Pietro" (i.e., of the late Pietro Rinaldi)—falsely so because he did not die until 1924. Archivio Storico Diocesano del Vicariato di Roma. Reproduced by permission.

was represented as being deceased—falsely so since Rinaldi senior died only in 1924, when, tellingly, he left no heirs, even though Guendalina was alive then and, per family memory, destitute. "*Fu* Rinaldi" therefore sounds more like a claim about their relationship than a life-or-death claim, a way of asserting emancipation or claiming a permanent "estrangement," as if to say, "I used to be his offspring, but no longer am." Whatever the specifics, there has to have been a severe crossing of swords at some point, and a profound falling out between father and daughter.[11]

As for Alessandro and Guendalina, the story continued, although, as choir member and sacred music historian Alessandro Gabrielli (1882–1941) put it years later, Moreschi's "intimate family life was not tranquil."[12] According to government archives, ratified by the private diaries of a chapel singer, Guendalina gave birth to Giulio Maria Pietro Luigi Moreschi on March 15, 1904.[13] Notably, Giulio's surname in official documents was always Moreschi. Vittoria told her grandchildren that Alessandro immediately became Giulio's adoptive father and went on to become his sole parent when Giulio was quite small. She also suggested that the biological father was a young nephew. And though various candidates are possible, and the truth cannot be verified, young Amerigo seems the likeliest candidate.[14]

The rest of the tale has two variants, one even more heartbreaking and scandalous than the other. In both, Guendalina flew the coop not too long after Giulio was born—something the unofficial papal diarist chronicled in June 1907.[15] According to Fabio's recollection of the grandmother's account, she quickly made off with her husband's entire fortune, including precious objects and jewels, which she sold, some on the street, and the proceeds of which her lover, a croupier, promptly lost at the gaming tables such that none of the losses could ever be recouped. According to Rita's recollection, doubtless mined from the same source, Guendalina returned for the jewels (or perhaps it was just the remaining ones) only sometime later. Rita crafted her version of things for her unpublished book *In viaggio con lo zio* (Travels with my uncle), a memoir whose odd-numbered chapters record her explorations of magic with uncle Federico (Fellini) and whose even-numbered chapters mostly record histories and memories of the Moreschi and Fellini families.[16] By contrast with Fabio's account, Rita's elaborates on the deterioration of Alessandro and Guendalina's marriage and its aftermath by painting Guendalina in more forgiving, even quasi-feminist terms.

> The love that my great-grandfather showed his adoptive son was not enough to halt his gradual disaffection for Guendalina. While he resigned himself to accepting her whims, he was unable to prevent her from leaving him. His son remained with him while Guendalina moved away and changed cities, and sometime later, after Alessandro's death, remarried. Little by little, all trace of my great-grandmother, who was reported first in Naples, then in Florence, was lost. It was also found that she had had another son, then nothing more.[17]
>
> After her estrangement from her first husband, Guendalina never learned to adjust to her reduced circumstances, and she was forced to come back to ask for her famous jewels, her effects [*il corredo*, which can also mean dowry or trousseau], her clothes, and all the goods that had belonged to her. It was easy for my great-grandfather to abide by her requests, if only to get her as far away from the child as possible so that she would remain only a faint memory. Years later I did some ancestry research to find out more about her, but despite my efforts I wasn't even able to find the cemetery where she was buried, she had traveled so far and so wide throughout Italy that hardly any trace was left of her movements.[18]

For Rita, as for Alessandro, Giulio, Vittoria, Fabio, and all the others, Guendalina thus endures as an absence, a haunted and haunting figure. Of her jewels and garments, vagaries and caprices, torments and misfortunes, only faded memories survive, fragments of multiple, sometimes conflicting views and recollections, reworked over time in the form of a myth, a tale told again and again, with variants to buttress an ever-shifting set of understandings about family fortunes and misfortunes. In the account of her great-granddaughter,

Figure 1.7a. Console in the dining room of Giulio Moreschi and Vittoria Cevasco at via Lungotevere degli Anguillara 11, with possible picture of Guendalina Rinaldi hanging on the right. Moreschi-Fellini Archive.

Figure 1.7b. Blurry detail of a portrait of Guendalina Rinaldi. Moreschi-Fellini Archive.

Rita, Guendalina's own son even vacillates between being "adopted" and being simply Moreschi's "son." And the meager state of her survival in the Moreschi-Fellini family archive—or perhaps it is a systematic erasure—only exacerbates the mystery. The archive cannot even claim with certainty to contain a single photograph of her, although survivors believe she is visible in one taken of the dining room at via Lungotevere degli Anguillara 11. The photograph features an elegant imperial-style console (fig. 1.7a) situated before an eighteenth-century gilded mirror and topped with ornate candelabra and a tabletop clock, to the right of which hangs another photo, depicting a woman whose neck is stylishly swathed in a lacy white cowl, her dark hair swept up and knotted with a large piece of jewelry (fig. 1.7b, detail from another image).[19] Who is she, this ghosted woman? And how did the identity of Guendalina come to be ascribed to her? None among the living can say, and no trace of the past will speak about her, much less speak up for her.

Moreschi as Subject of History

Tack backward some forty-nine years and thirty-five kilometers away from Rome to a small Lazian village on its outskirts, where Alessandro's life began on November 11, 1858, not to end until

April 21, 1922.[20] His story is more accessible than those of most other members of his family and circle, yet largely limited to a public profile, since his legacy is virtually devoid of diaries, correspondence, scrapbooks, or memoirs, or what was once there was later lost or sold. What did church politics mean to Alessandro in his teen years? Did he read literature or frequent cafes in Rome? How often did he dine out with friends? Later, did he listen to phonograph records or possess his own gramophone? Or in the grander picture: What were his views on politics, war, art, or the great events and vexations of the day? What did he think of Lombroso's theories of atavism and scientific racism, for instance, if they even appeared on his radar, or the growing scientific racism that would eventually lead to Mussolini's racial laws? What did he feel in older age about the phallic machinery of modernism that so blatantly motored the sound world and imagery underlying a strongly emergent Fascism—of Marinetti's futurist airplane man of 1909 or the futurist noise music explicated by Luigi Russolo in 1913? How did he react to news of the new pseudo-utopia built by Gabriele D'Annunzio after he cantered into Fiume in September 1919, or, much earlier, to the buzz around the gender-bending eroticism of D'Annunzio's wildly popular novel *Piacere* (1889)?[21] What did he think of Italy's shady involvement in World War I and the growing power of the Fascist Blackshirts (Camicie Nere) in Rome, who organized themselves formally in 1919, a year in which Moreschi was involved in a workers' rights group?[22] Or, had he lived a few months longer: What, we might wonder, would he have thought of Mussolini's assumption of power in the coup d'état of October 1922—the infamous "March on Rome" that turned the National Fascist Party into Italy's ruling party?

We know nothing about any of this and cannot even hazard a guess. To judge from the stance of his colleague and superior, Domenico Mustafà (1828–1912), he likely adhered complacently to nineteenth-century church dogma. He was probably not thrilled about the gradual replacements of castrati with unaltered boys in the late nineteenth and early twentieth centuries and the banning of castrati from the papal chapel in 1903. But Sistine Chapel documents show that he dutifully assumed responsibilities as the chapel's *segretario-puntatore* in 1891, maintaining the chapel's daily diaries, and served the next year as *maestro pro tempore*, scheduling rehearsals and meetings and approving absences and leaves.[23] And civil documents, mostly fairly conventional ones, show he assumed full legal responsibilities of fatherhood for his young boy from the outset. From the last, we can infer that before the birth of Giulio, he wanted passionately to have family, something supported by a suggestive comment in the diaries of his 1902 recording engineer, who wrote about the choir: "I particularly remember their rosy-cheeked conductor and solo soprano, Professor Moreschi, whom I then judged to be about sixty but who was amazingly fresh and youthful [Moreschi was actually forty-three at the time] and boasted of a large family, which greatly interested me."[24]

Besides that and the abundance of evidence that he was a highly dedicated musician, all else is mostly anecdote thickly overlaid with the fantasies of contemporaneous critics and travelers and more recent would-be history-makers, people like the storied *New York Times* critic Harold Schonberg, who concluded that Moreschi had no sexual adventures to equal those Schonberg believed true of other castrati and who painted him instead as "a short, plump man" whose "life appears to have been unexceptionable. He sang, he conducted the Vatican Choir, he left a handful of records, and not much more is known about him."[25]

Despite the thin legacy, a fragmentary history survives. Young Alessandro was born to Luigi Moreschi and Rosa Pitolli, the seventh of nine children, and christened Alessandro Nilo Angelo Moreschi. The Moreschi family lived southeast of Rome and just west of Palestrina's eponymous Lazian hometown in the outlying town of Montecompatri in the diocese of Frascati, where Alessandro was baptized by his uncle, Pietro Moreschi, standing in for the priest at the town's parish church of Santa Maria Assunta in Cielo.[26] Located on one of the Alban Hills nestled in the Castelli Romani, Montecompatri in the mid-nineteenth century was still a backward hilltop town with low rates of literacy, no rail transport, and little in the way of modern hygiene. Nevertheless, the town had certain claims to fame, including two churches. One was Santa Maria Assunta itself, a church whose importance rose during Alessandro's childhood when it became too small for the town's populace and talk of expanding it or building a new church was in the air. On August 12, 1865, Pius IX went to Montecompatri to inaugurate the new headquarters of the Municipal Palace and the Clergy. The townspeople reportedly showered the papal carriage with gold coins, though the papacy by then had fallen on hard times since the Papal States had already lost massive amounts of territory to Risorgimento efforts that would soon culminate in a new Italian state. The town's other claim to fame was the church (or "sanctuary") of the Madonna del Castagno. Though tiny, it was a mecca because it housed a cultic, revered image of the madonna and child that drew townspeople and visitors, including popes and high-placed clerics. Situated at the bottom of a hill just below the monastery of San Silvestro, the church had functioned thus since at least the sixteenth century, especially after an 1867 cholera epidemic suddenly came to a seemingly miraculous sudden end when Alessandro was eight years old.[27]

Many years later, in 1914, Alessandro told the Austrian singing teacher Franz Haböck (1868–1921) that he had performed there to great acclaim as a boy soloist, specifically, in the Madonna del Castagno, though he surely performed on high feast days at Santa Maria Assunta, as well.[28] And here things become curious. In 1871, at about age twelve, Alessandro was whisked off to the Holy City. The Italian state had already been in place for about a year by then, and word of the beautiful boy singer from Montecompatri had reached Rome. The papacy used one of its own agents, Nazareno Rosati (1817–1877), to effect Alessandro's removal and relocation. Nazareno, a Minorite friar and high tenor (even alto) soloist much esteemed as a papal singer, had lost his upper register and was mainly working as a composer and teacher by then. None of this would have been documented had Haböck not been writing an ambitious book on castrati, for which he interviewed survivors of the practice in Rome. Rosati "himself," he reported, "had brought [Moreschi] to Rome, where he was accepted into the Scuola dei Carissimi at San Salvatore in Lauro, whose director Fra Vincenzo Torro, together with Rosati, initiated the young singer into an artistic career."[29] Lest there be any question about the accuracy of the account by Haböck (whose factual reports mostly check out), note that the Vatican's expectation to arrange for boys to be located, trained, and later joined to the Sistine Chapel as castrati is documented in papal records dating from as late as 1897, as I explain below.

Thus, we have to wonder whether at a time when castrations for singing had otherwise become very rare, Nazareno was assigned not just to escort Alessandro to Rome, but to see to his castration. More than this, we have to ask whether it's imaginable that the church did *not* encourage and even help organize and attend to boys' castrations, whether in Rome or more likely in their hometowns.

After surgery, a castrated boy would begin tuition-free training at the sheltered church school of San Salvatore in Lauro, as well as gigging in the city's churches, ideally leading to eventual placement in one of its papal basilicas. The school, more precisely, the Schola Cantorum A. Braschi, was run by the religious order of the Fratelli delle Scuole Cristiane and served *in loco parentis*, similar to an orphanage, with all the intensely hierarchical discipline one might imagine. Boys were divvied up into junior and senior classes and further divided by levels, with regular yearly examinations carried out by the chapelmasters of Rome's patriarchal basilicas: Gaetano Capocci, director of San Giovanni in Laterano (the Basilica Lateranense), Settimo Battaglia, director of Santa Maria Maggiore (the Basilica Liberiana), and Salvatore Meluzzi, director of the Cappella Giulia in St. Peters (the Basilica Vaticana).[30] Capocci joined with Rosati in overseeing Moreschi's training, Rosati devoting himself fully to it. Their efforts were repaid in July 1873 when Moreschi made a major debut, only aged fourteen, as soloist at the Lateran, where Capocci was organist and chapelmaster.[31]

A practitioner of neotheatrical styles, Capocci steeped his student in various sacred idioms, always infusing them with then-popular operatic idioms.[32] Unsurprisingly, this aesthetic mixture had already marked a landmark celebration in 1867, staged to commemorate the school's imminent founding on February 1, 1868, prior to Moreschi's arrival in Rome, namely, the humongous performance of Mustafà's motet "Tu es Petrus" for the feast of Saints Peter and Paul. Some four hundred-plus participants from various papal basilicas, plus boy singers — all or mostly all unaltered — solemnized the feast by singing under the cupola of St. Peter's. Boys came from the Collegio Romano, the Ospizio Orfanelli (presumably the Pia Casa degli Orfani), the Seminario di San Pietro (which educated future priests), the Ospizio di Tata Giovanni (an orphanage begun in 1784), the Ospizio Termini, the scuola Notturne Sabini, and the scuola Notturne M. Ricci, converging for a production that Robert Buning aptly calls a "gigantic, quasi-Berliozian performance of a work harking back to the polychoral extravagances of Mustafà's Baroque Roman predecessor Ottavio Pittoni (1657–1743)."[33] Mustafà's biographer, Alberto De Angelis (1885–1965), explains that the choreography of the performance was so bloated that it required choirs placed at either end of the nave, one conducted by Capocci, the other by Mustafà.[34]

Ironically, given the thoroughgoing linkage of the occasion to a prominent castrato, 1867 also marked a new initiative in educating unaltered boys in vocal studies. Through its colossal performing forces and vaunted occasion, the performance operated as Mustafà's own way of saving what were otherwise failing soprano sections in flailing church choirs while addressing the growing reluctance of provincial families to let sons be castrated for the church.[35] It also drove home the hard fact that Rome's papal chapels needed boy trebles and that most of them were no longer going to be eunuchs. In this respect, it marked the true beginning of the end for castrati in Roman churches. And by augmenting the presence of *unaltered* boys, it greased the wheels of the reform-minded churchmen, widely known as Cecilianists, who wanted music to return to the role of serving liturgy through chant and simple polyphony and who also wanted to eliminate *altered* male singers associated with solo virtuosity—a direction that Mustafà paradoxically ended up fiercely resisting while tangling with by-then chapel codirector Lorenzo Perosi (installed in 1898) and finally resigning from his post once and for all in January 1903.[36] To quote Buning again, "Mustafà's success with the performance was unintentionally ironic in that it ultimately enabled Perosi to justify his substitution of boy trebles for eunuch sopranos—just as Baini's work on Palestrina [earlier in the nineteenth century] gave rise to the Austro-German Caecilian reforms which eventually reached Italy and also came to militate against any further use of castrati in the mother-city of Catholicism."[37]

After 1867, uncastrated boy trebles started to become regular features of Vatican and basilican life. As will be seen below, they appeared annually at the Office of Tenebrae at St. Peters, for instance, and continued to be called on for particular celebrations in the 1880s up to and especially after the new constitution of 1891 formally sanctioned their participation, specifically, that of boys from San Salvatore in Lauro.[38]

During the intervening years of 1883 to 1891, Moreschi, already a rising star when Capocci appointed him *primo soprano* at the basilican church of the Lateran in 1873, became the Vatican's biggest vocal attraction. Ten years after the Lateran coup, he carried off a sensational performance of the leap-filled coloratura part of the Seraph in Beethoven's *Christum am Ölberge*, performed in the Italian version on Maundy Thursday, March 22, 1883, during Lent. The next day, he joined the prestigious Sistine Chapel choir as a regular chapel member, still only twenty-four years old and just in time to sing the soprano part in the occult, age-old *Miserere* ascribed to Gregorio

Figure 1.8. Small albumen *portrait d'amitié* of Alessandro Moreschi, one of the earliest surviving images of him. Moreschi-Fellini Archive.

Allegri, thereby avoiding the glacially slow, hierarchical process that usually regulated admission to Sistine ranks.[39] The papal diaries make much of this sudden admission to an exalted post.[40] By virtue of the performance, Moreschi also acquired fame and the epithet of "angel." Mustafà was by then well into his sixties, and the only other Sistine soprano who was both highly regarded and still regularly singing solos was the excellent coloraturist Giovanni Cesari (1843–1904). No wonder one of the earliest images of Moreschi to survive, a small, unknown albumen *portrait d'amitié* from around this time (fig. 1.8), shows him looking well-groomed and buoyant, an air of candid confidence pushing through his youthful gravitas.[41]

Histories of Moreschi have logged parts of these accounts while repeating anecdotal tales of Moreschi's second life singing female arias in fancy salons and hotels. In 1883, he tossed off Gounod's "Jewel

Song" from *Faust* at the salon of a prominent society lady, as noted by the admiring, but disconcerted singer and diplomat's wife Lillie de Hegermann-Lindencrone (1844–1928, formerly Lillie Greenough, later Lillie Moulton).[42] In 1888, according to Gabrielli (active in the Sistine Chapel in the 1920s through the early 1940s), he performed Leonora's mezzo aria "O mio Fernando" from Donizetti's *La favorita* with piano accompaniment supplied by a then sixteen-year-old Perosi, as well as parts of Abigaille's vocally treacherous music from Verdi's *Nabucco*.[43] More public salon performances took place at the fancy Hotel de Russie, near piazza del Popolo, where he shared the bill and quite possibly some ensemble numbers with Verdian superstars—baritone Antonio Cotogni and tenor Francesco Marconi. Luigi Devoti offered the only reference to the event, claiming that "the celebrated soprano [Marie] Durand, whom it was known should have appeared in the concert, did not want to sing, fearing the comparison."[44]

Further evidence of freelancing seems to have gone astray or been occulted by accounts so spare and fragile that they hardly register as evidence of musical or social practice.[45] Only Hegermann-Lindencrone's reports say something more. Writing of salon shows by papal singers, including Moreschi's of the "Jewel Song," she focuses on the hazardous political circumstances that marked the performances and calls out the stakes in Moreschi's semipublic performances of female arias. From her we learn that salons open to both "blacks" and "whites"—respectively, the right-wing religious party of the Vatican and the liberal party of the state—could be hosted by only one Roman household: that of the ultrarich Grace Bristed, aka Grace Ashburner Sedgwick Bristed (1833–1897), daughter of Charles Sedgwick and Elizabeth Buckminster Dwight and second wife of American writer Charles Astor Bristed (1820–1874, hence deceased by the time of Hegermann-Lindencrone's account), whose guests probably cast an inquisitive, if jaundiced eye over the proceedings. The account warrants quoting in full.

> Mrs. Charles Bristed, of New York, a recent convert to the Church of Rome, receives on Saturday evenings. She has accomplished what has hitherto been

considered impossible—that is, bringing together of the "blacks" (the ultra-Catholic party, belonging to the Vatican) and the "whites," the party belonging to the Quirinal. These two parties meet in her *salon* as if they were of the same color. The Pope's singers are the great attraction. She must either have a tremendously long purse or great persuasive powers to get them, for her *salon* is the only place outside the churches where one can hear them. Therefore this *salon* is the only platform in Rome where the two antagonistic parties meet and glare at each other.

We went there last Saturday. The chairs were arranged in rows, superb in their symmetry at first, but after the first petticoats had swept by everything was in a hopeless confusion. Two ladies sitting on one chair, one lady appropriating two chairs instead of one, and another sitting sideways on three. The consequence was that there was a conglomeration of empty chairs in the middle of the room, while crowds of weary guests stood in and near the doorway, with the thermometer sky high! When one sees the Pope's singers in evening dress and white cravats the prestige and effect are altogether lost. This particular evening was unusually brilliant, for the monsignors and cardinals were extra-abundant. There were printed programs handed to us with the list of the numerous songs that we were going to hear.

The famous Moresca [sic], who sings at the Laterano, is a full-faced soprano of forty winters. He has a tear in each note and a sigh in each breath. He sang the jewel song in "Faust," which seemed horribly out of place. Especially when he asks (in the hand-glass) if he is really Marguerita, one feels tempted to answer "*Macché*" [No way!] for him. Then they sang a chorus of Palestrina, all screaming at the top of their lungs, evidently thinking they were in St. Peter's. It never occurred to them to temper their voices to the poor shorn lambs wedged up against the walls.[46]

Hegermann-Lindencrone confronted the experience with her usual attentiveness and wit while advancing Moreschi's age by fifteen years and feminizing his name. She could not separate his emotionality from the dizzying gender inversions of his music-making.

We should take a moment to think about that in view of writings about castrati, still shot through with prurient curiosities. Take

Schonberg's piece, which presupposes sexual excess as endemic to castrati (and is stopped short by its presumed absence in Moreschi), or older ones aghast at men doing vocal masquerades as women. Or think about more recent writings that metabolize Moreschi's "female" performances through gender-bending paradigms. Recently, Nicholas Clapton has been tempted to think in terms of gay camp,[47] but then what exactly does camp mean — a *sensibility* marked by a "love of the unnatural: of artifice and exaggeration," as Susan Sontag had it, and what she called "a private code, a badge of identity even, among small urban cliques"?[48] That seems possible as an explanatory frame for certain off-duty chapel activities, but doubtful for Moreschi, given his marriage and other attempts at normative respectability. More likely, he recognized the irony of impersonating females, not least the irony of Marguerite gazing at herself in a mirror in the "Jewel Song," which so perturbed Mrs. Hegermann-Lindencrone when Moreschi delivered it. If so, it seems likely that his sense of humor was shared by his coterie of peers — used to hearing voices that always already bore marks of difference for outsiders. And then what, too, did such gender mismatches mean in a place like Pisa, where Moreschi toured in 1897, singing the treble part in Rossini's *Messe solonelle*, where the local paper described him as that "excellent *soprano* of the Cappella Sistina"[49] — a common descriptor at the time that naturalized high male voices in a conventional way, euphemizing them in the process and thereby neutralizing the issue.

More famous in its time, and more symbolically potent than any of these, was Moreschi's performance given after King Umberto I of Italy was assassinated in Monza on July 29, 1900, and funerals were held all over Italy. The capital city staged two funerals in Rome's Pantheon, the king's eventual burial place.[50] Correspondent A. Roberto Colombo described performances at both for *La nuova musica*'s September 1900 issue, with two special callouts: one to composer-conductor Pietro Mascagni for the first funeral and another to Moreschi for the second.

> In Rome, the divine powers among the arts mourned with us the sad event that assailed the Italian nation at the Pantheon alongside the venerated corpse of the Martyr. There were two solemn funerals. For the first, the Ministry of Education called Maestro [Pietro] Mascagni, who was able in this painful circumstance to show himself up to his name, giving us new proof of his highly varied talent. . . .
>
> Mascagni's direction was admirable, and equally so the performance by one hundred sixty voices, including the best of our music conservatory.
>
> The second funeral, on the thirteenth, was another worthy commemoration of our unfortunate deceased King. The same choral masses took part, among which were the sopranists of the Sistine Chapel, including the famous Moreschi. This time the direction was entrusted to the maestro Stanislao Falchi (well-known author of the Devil's Trill), who also directed in a magnificent way.
>
> The program consisted of five parts of a Mass by an unknown author from the sixteenth century (Palestrina school), Pitoni's *Dies Irae*, Palestrina's *Peccavimus* and Falchi's *Libera*, also written for the funeral of Vittorio Emanuele II.
>
> Maestro Alessandro Vessella, director of the Municipal Band, composed an elaborate funeral March in those days of suffering.[51]

In recompense for his services and the honor done to the king, Moreschi received from Umberto's son, Vittorio Emanuele III, a gold watch and gold pin—among various items Giulio designated for reverential, perpetual preservation in his will that are now long gone.[52]

Of course, the greatest personal event, as well as the greatest paradox of Moreschi's life, came four years earlier. On April 30, 1896, he was profoundly altered by marrying Guendalina in a union that lasted for eleven years.[53] The marriage certificate sounds conventional enough, except that the couple made no public vows, not even in the chamber of a civil official, but stayed at home, where they had a private wedding. A government official recorded the event:

> Guendalina Rinaldi, having demonstrated with a medical certificate the impossibility of going to city hall to celebrate her marriage, I Esquire Salvatore Bugarini [?] municipal councilor delegated to civil status officer, with my municipal secretary Anastasio Cocchi, went to this house where I found: 1. Alessandro Moreschi, 36 years old [he was actually thirty-seven at the time] and maestro of music, born in Montecompatri, resident in Rome, son of Luigi and of Rosa Pitolli. 2. Guendalina Rinaldi, 23 years old, born and resident in Rome, daughter of Pietro and of Giulia Ferrucci, who asked me to join them in matrimony.[54]

Would that something definite were known of how this came about. Before her death, Rita supplied the following in her *In viaggio con lo zio*, evidently based on oral reports passed down to her (again) by her grandmother Vittoria: "In addition to having an amazing voice my great-grandfather was extremely cultured and refined; his singing career enabled him to travel widely, and his professional achievements gave him tremendous gratification. The only thing missing to make him happy was a family. What he did not dare to do a beautiful woman did: my great-grandmother Guendalina, who asked him to marry her."[55]

What might we make of the notion that by time of Rita's adolescence and young adulthood, Vittoria as the only surviving family memory bank had reported to her granddaughter that Guendalina was audacious enough to co-opt the ritual of the male marriage proposal? Vittoria had married Giulio some eighteen years after Guendalina's abandonment of her husband and son and three years after Alessandro's death, hence her knowledge came from Giulio. Perhaps the proposal was not Guendalina's after all, or perhaps she made it under pressure from her father—according to her birth certificate, a stonecutter (*scalpellino*).[56] Was the marriage an attempt to move the Rinaldi family upward in a rigidly classist world of delimited social and financial possibilities, a strategy that vicissitudes like the king's funeral would have justified, but a highly problematic one for Guendalina? Was the Moreschi family, or at least Vittoria, unable to imagine a castrato proposing or a woman accepting, or was it reluctant to cast Guendalina, who apparently asked Vittoria and Giulio for money for many years, in a less venal scenario?

Whatever the case, marriage changed Moreschi's life profoundly, at least as much as Guendalina's, and in ways that speak to the collision of traditional ways with modern ones. But the radically evolving media environment of the turn of the century transformed his life as well. In April 1902, during Moreschi's married years, the prominent young American recordist Fred Gaisberg captured his voice for a major international label, the famed London-based Gramophone and Typewriter Company, using the latest flat-record technology with horn and cutting stylus shortly after its invention and just before the same team recorded Enrico Caruso. More recordings were made two years later, in April 1904, when the company sent Gaisberg's young compatriot and colleague William Sinkler Darby to record a much more ambitious set of sessions, paying Moreschi a fat advance of 3,000 lire.[57] As exorbitant preservation projects, the recordings recognized the renown and distinctiveness of Moreschi's singing and capitalized on its niche historical value for marketing to new global audiences. Chapter 3 below takes up the nature and impact of those recordings, but here, we should notice the irony of the moment. April 1904 was a half year after castrati were banned from the Sistine Chapel (although Moreschi was grandfathered in until his retirement age ten years later) and less than a month after Giulio was born to Guendalina, auguring a new personal happiness for Alessandro, but intersecting with growing disarray in his personal life.

And then, on June 20, 1905, only a year after Giulio's birth, Pius X disseminated his *motu proprio* titled *Quo Collegium Cantorum Xystini Sacrarii rectius constituitur ac proprio statuto ornatur*, regulating once and for all the rules that ran the Cantoria. By that time, Moreschi's castrato colleagues were basically gone, and Moreschi was helping to raise his fifteen-month-old boy.[58] Just two years later came ruinous upheaval in his home life, culminating in his abandonment and apparent despoliation by his wife. A Roman chapel singer and diarist, alto Luigi Gentili, wrote on June 29, 1907 that Moreschi "could not sing, for he was sick because his wife has fled."[59] The personal history that has been so invisible, forgotten, submerged, and erased contrasts starkly with the recordings that dominate his legacy. Without them, he would never have been emblazoned in the public imagination as "the last castrato," a rubric widely used first on the notes to the 1984 Opal transfers and soon thereafter on the title of a reissue, as I note further in the Epilogue.[60] The moniker has stuck in detailed scholarly studies such as Buning's and more accessible ones such as Clapton's, to say nothing of all the blogs, YouTube posts, podcasts, fan pages, college lectures, and festivals whose flotsam has littered streaming sites and internet highways.[61] Inscribed on shellac, the recordings have also made him *endure* — to harden, indurate, becoming *durable*, or lasting, in that other common sense, which still applies to this day.[62]

The Modern History of Castrati

Let's turn the clock back before Moreschi's time. His transfer to Rome and eventual induction into the pontifical choir flung him onto a career path not unlike his nineteenth-century predecessors': new castrati were added to church rosters after being discovered among or fabricated from carefully selected boy singers found in provincial chapels, mostly on the outskirts of Rome. As in Moreschi's case, they were procured with considerable secrecy by insiders of the papal musical establishment. But contrary to what might be imagined, given their substantial and continuous presence in the chapel through 1903 and beyond, their path was knotty.[63]

The issues had partly to do with procurement, partly with the nature of their status. Not unlike Chinese foot binding, or indeed eunuchs in nineteenth-century imperial China, castrations of boys in the West were largely driven by aesthetic desires — in the castrato case, by the irresistible allure that European listeners found in high, brilliantly resonant voices.[64] Papal documents, reviews, and visitors' accounts reveal those voices as avidly sought after for Roman churches of the *Ottocento*. The whole phenomenon of *castratio euphonica*, exacerbated by the conjoint dilemma posed by the Pauline prohibition on women singing in the church, produced the solution of manufacturing "specialty" eunuchs like those found in societies of ancient and geographically distant worlds, males who were deliberately castrated as a way of forcing them to renounce sex, but who in the Italian case had principally been castrated to preserve their boyhood singing voices. Even if tacit symbolic, cultural, and economic reasons accompanied aesthetic ones, the Italian case differed from many ancient and early modern cases inasmuch as compromised sexual ability was in their instance a secondary outcome.[65]

Regardless of the impetus for and consequence of surgery, it institutionalized eunuchism. Buning argues the point by quoting an eighteenth-century German who recognized the reality by reversing the equation when he called celibate Italian monks "castrati . . . who have not been subjected to surgery,"[66] a witty way of pulling the curtain back on the indirection and obfuscation that was second nature to church ethics. Once castrated—or even when making dubious petitions to *be* castrated, as boys were compelled to do because their consent was nominally required—petitioners produced statements that explained away their actions with the same rhetorical strategies their elders used, especially after the seventeenth century, when modern liberal ideas made castration for singing increasingly anathema.[67] Boys and their handlers and patrons often claimed castrations to be sacrifices to church and God when they didn't ascribe them outright to accidents, or even when they did. The two kinds of claims were often intermixed, since assertions of castrations as sacrifices came to be elided with explanations of them as therapies done to forestall the consequences of physical misfortunes, like falls from horses or trees and bites from wild boars.[68] All such tropes explained away the loss of fertility, which was devastating for Italian males. If Black slave women functioned as what Saidiya Hartman calls "the belly of the world"—a birthing creature who "transfers her dispossession to the child"—the castrate represented their near opposite, the barren of the world, produced by a cut and abjected by virtue of seedlessness, which inverted the condition of a generative, property-owning male mandated for him from biological birth and left him with nothing to transfer in male-to-male "generation."[69] Not only did the church fail to acknowledge such loss, it also failed to acknowledge or deal with its further ill consequences: beardlessness and feminine patterns of fat, but still worse a lifetime of deleterious skeletal deformations, plus physiological disorders such as osteoporosis and physiologically based psychological disorders, above all, melancholia, but also other emotional imbalances. Moreover, the church condoned all this for over four centuries without ever doing so openly or directly. To the contrary, popes such as Alexander VII (1655) and Innocent XII (1691), to take just one slice of historical time, made mention of the existence of castrated singers only to note that they were not to replace falsettists in alto sections.[70]

Indirection hovers everywhere over the earliest papal brief on castrati, the 1587 *Cum frequenter*, issued by the notoriously severe Pope Sixtus V two years after he admitted castrati to the Cappella Giulia.[71]

> Experience shows that *spadones*, though they repeatedly claim themselves capable of coition, together with the women they marry, actually enter into such base unions not in order to live in a sexually disciplined manner, but so that both parties may engage in physically perverse and lewd practices under the outward appearance and form of matrimony. Such unions, which are the occasion of sin and scandal, and lead to the damnation of souls, must henceforth be put aside by the Church, especially in consideration of the fact that eunuch-marriages serve no procreative purpose, but give encouragement instead to the snares of temptation and sexual excess.[72]

Without naming the principal object of the prohibition as *singing* castrati—calling them *spadones* (eunuchs or barren men) instead—

Sixtus V denied them marriage rights, but also the only thing that made up for the lack of marriage rights: namely, their professional identities as musicians.[73] The many castrati who obscured their own castrations necessarily took their lead from Sixtus V and the reams of rhetorical secreting that he and his kind worked to enforce.

And this because for Italy in the seventeenth and eighteenth centuries, and especially in Rome, intense desires for high voices trumped all other considerations. Additionally, since Italian Catholicism prohibited women singing in church, especially in the Papal States, where they were also forbidden from appearing on secular theatrical stages, the main alternative was castrated males. Consequently, castrati dominated the auditory imagination, proliferating on stages and altars not just in Rome, but far beyond, including in the Papal States, where they could be found in such outposts as Perugia, Spoleto, Orvieto, Ravenna, Rimini, and Ancona, located in today's regions of Lazio, the Marches, Umbria, Romagna, and parts of Emilia—all of which had opera houses in addition to numerous churches, many very large.[74] A boom industry in stocking chapel choirs with altered male sopranos and altos resulted, though the system was rarely without signs of distress. Across Europe, philosophes and theologians in the eighteenth century and almost everybody outside the Catholic Church in the nineteenth century launched ethical objections to *castratio euphonica*, which came under repeated attack in the invective tracts of moralists and the poems, plays, and dialogues of satirists, to say nothing of the iconography, often cruel, that marked many visual caricatures.

Still, uses of castrati held up easily in Rome until the 1798 French occupation of the city fractured the system by anticipating the Napoleonic codes (officially installed in March 1804), which forbade both the practice of castration and the use of castrati.[75] The codes were put into effect by making substitutions at Rome's most important public ceremonies and celebrations. At one festivity, at which litanies were performed along the street, held as early as

January 17, 1798, two "'voci virili'" ("manly voices," tenors, in this case) replaced castrati.[76] After the second French invasion, the secretary of state wanted minimally to ban castrati from the presbytery, declaring that their voices, far from being "virile," resembled those of "women and prepubescent boys."[77] Vocal timbre, and not just pitch, was a sonic means through which gender was marked and measured. Given the Napoleonic moral climate, even castrati who were already employed in the papal chapel tried to distance themselves from the practice, as if they had had no part in it.[78]

None of this prevented castrati from continuing to be one of Rome's urban attractions and eventually urban legends, wondrous audiovisual spectacles that could be enjoyed only in Rome's churches, even while they were denigrated in the atmosphere of masculinist revolutionary fervor that marked the Napoleonic years and their aftermath. Musician travelers as illustrious as Otto Nicolai and Felix Mendelssohn reported on them in detail, and expatriates and travelers continued to write about them with stupefied fascination, even after the heyday of the Grand Tour.

Remarkably, the making and use of "*evirati*" went on virtually unabated throughout much of the nineteenth century, despite the challenge of obtaining youths who could be surgically altered, trained, and eventually employed in soprano sections. And contemporary records leave little doubt that church authorities strategized to meet the challenge, especially once the Sistine Chapel suffered the rapid departure of no fewer than three castrati who had been admitted in the years 1816 to 1817. After that, everything hinged on getting hold of more boys. Witness the following supplication, made to Pope Pius VII in 1819, in which a *maestro pro tempore* in the Cappella Sistina joins forces with the soprano castrati:

> The present, and also future, impossibility, of finding sopranos for the service of our church has threatened the Collegio with a crisis. Therefore our maestro, together with the soprano section, supplicates with the Holy Father, that he might wish to deign to admit four castrated youths, to

> be sought throughout Italy, into the venerable Pia Casa degl'Orfani [in S. Maria del Aquiro], so that they might be educated in piety and instructed in music.[79]

The supplicants don't hesitate to blurt outright that procuring four young boys for St. Peter's means averting a calamity. Finding "castrati" for the purpose means "finding sopranos," because using any other voice for high parts is musically unthinkable. The Pia Casa degli Orfani, effectively a small-scale version of the Neapolitan conservatories of the early modern period, though likewise an orphanage in name and practice, expressly cultivated boys to become singers in basilican and other Roman churches.[80] Following the petition above, three boys were brought to the Pia Casa degli Orfani to be taught by a soprano castrato from the Cappella Giulia, Domenico Sgatelli (born 1787), who himself had trained at a Neapolitan conservatory.[81]

Inexorably, we return to the historical questions that bleed through all castrato studies, especially of later times: By what means were boys identified; and when were they removed from their families, and in this instance, transferred to Rome? When in this cycle, additionally, were they castrated?[82] Amazingly, we get no help here from the proliferating news-and-information media landscape that marks the nineteenth century. To the contrary, what's stunning is the church's success at concealment. Still, two clusters of documents let on that the Collegio paid for recruitments, minimally including everything from travel and education to room and board, and raise the question of whether it organized and paid for castrations as well. One involves an allegation by insinuation, made in connection with recruitments of 1861; the other comes straight from the Collegio's mouth in the form of an 1896 resolution, ratified in 1897.

The former, 1861, represents the last time a recruitment of multiple castrati was made (a decade before Moreschi's castration) and included the outstanding Cesari, as well as the much inferior choral singers Giuseppe Ritarossi (1841–1902) and Giosafat Anselmo Vissani

(1841–1916). Decades later, writing in the late 1930s, Gabrielli, still an earwitness to living Sistine Chapel lore, alleges a kind of malfeasance, suggesting that these late recruitments from the poor and illiterate peasantry had something frantic and avaricious about them though he does grammatical backbends to avoid naming the perpetrators.[83]

> The last admission of sopranists *en bloc* was that of 1861. A person having been sent in search of these remnants of barbarism, three of them were found, after patient searches, between Alatri and Frosinone, an area that in the past had provided several of them. . . . All three being illiterate, because they were children of peasants, they were taken to Rome, and interned in the Pia Casa degli Orfani in S. Maria in Aquiro, *at the expense of the Collegio.* They were taught to read [and] to write, and for music and singing they were given to the teacher Gaetano Capocci.[84]

To understand Gabrielli's hedging, it's helpful to make a detour to intermediary writings of the 1910s and 1920s, predating his "Riassunti" but postdating nineteenth-century recruiting efforts, starting with Haböck's reports from his research expedition to Rome. Haböck's firsthand interviews from Easter 1914, together with his assembled secondhand accounts, show surviving castrati still offering reasons for their castrations, but saying nothing about where, when, and by whom they were done.[85] And those reasons reproduce astoundingly traditional, even mythological explanations: because boys had been bitten by wild pigs, or in one case, a wild swan.[86] Haböck's account of Mustafà's castration, for instance, reported to him by a third party, notes that his "fate was allegedly prepared for him in the cradle, when he was attacked by a pig in an unguarded moment—a story shared by the valued Viennese writer and *feuilletoniste* Hugo Wittmann, who at the time would have had a lot of personal conversations with Mustafà in Rome and in Albano during the summer."[87]

This was just one of several tales circulating about Mustafà's castration. (See Chapter 4 below.) It surfaced in numerous variations that reinscribed contradictory truth claims or registered different senses of reality, as myths and fables tend to do.[88] Yet unlike the hints of positivistic approval often given by twentieth-century writers to accounts that emanate from a primary source or someone or something proximate to it, Haböck's account does quite the opposite, mixing reservations with outright skepticism.

> The older soprano [Mustafà] having retired, only three — the last! — Salvatori, Sebastianelli, and Moreschi, remained members of the Cappella Sistina and at the same time of the Cappella Giulia [in reality, Cesari did at least some singing at the Cappella Sistina until his death on March 10, 1904 and Vissani and Meniconi were still unretired then].[89] Salvatori died a few years beforehand; Sebastianelli and Moreschi were still working in the Cappella Giulia at Easter 1914 when I was in Rome for the last time, three months before the outbreak of the World War. Sebastianelli was already in his sixties and no longer did regular choral work.... He too was "bitten by a wild pig" in his youth.[90]

In 1926, the Italian castrato apologist De Angelis repeated some dodgy accounts of Mustafà's castration in his biography of him, but acknowledged the uneven planes of veracity on which they circulated. There were those who claimed, he wrote — "and Mustafà himself never disclaimed it definitively — that he was subjected by deliberate will of his father, desirous of making deliberate speculation out of him, which still toward the end of the last century, and as far as then rarely, used to be practiced by poor and unscrupulous parents on their own sons from whom they wanted to make fortunes as sopranos, on the stage or in church."[91] Mustafà's grandnephews and others contradicted that account, offering up the alternative that a pig had reduced him to that state or that he was born imperfectly, hence had to be castrated for health reasons. Haböck, in his skepticism, called out such ironies, observing drolly that from the time the Papal States fell in 1870, the "'terrible accidents' — bites of the wild pigs, swans, and other animals... which until then had helped many a larynx in Italy to eternal youth — stop completely."[92]

Suddenly, he noted, there were no more attacks by wild boars and swans, and no more need for cures through castration—except, as he knew, Moreschi's, which happened after the fall of Rome.

One way to comprehend these charades and all the quandaries that beset them is through the Collegio's archives, preserved in the Vatican, which provide rather specific, if suggestive evidence—the self-incriminating kind whose preservation might surprise you unless you watched the Nixon administration forced to hand over tapes that documented its own misdeeds in the summer of Watergate (1972) or have followed recent disclosures of rampant pedophilia in the well-oiled silencing machine of the Catholic Church.[93] Dating from 1896 to 1897, the evidence in question establishes the Vatican's rocky, but proactive role in maneuvering to obtain castrati, following several decades during which the Sistine Chapel was continually tensed between two unappealing options: switching to unaltered boys (*fanciulli*), or continuing to procure altered ones (*evirati*).

To appreciate the dilemma, it's helpful to understand that during the whole of the nineteenth century, the Pia Casa degli Orfani had been housing both kinds of boys and routinely advancing both from orphanage living to professional chapel work. As part of their grooming, teachers also prepped both kinds to give periodic demonstrations to chapel members of what they had learned. Out of that process, however, only young *evirati*—and in small numbers, at that—might eventually be admitted to the Sistine Chapel as *soprannumerari* (partially privileged members), and after that as *partecipanti* (fully privileged members), with their years of preparation counted toward retirement.[94] Three were accepted in the years from 1822 to 1831, four in 1852–1853. Admitted altogether later in the century were fewer than ten: Mustafà in 1844 (retired 1902, died 1912), Pasquale Meniconi (educated at the expense of the Sacri Palazzi Apostolici) in 1853 (retired 1905, died at Spello, 1916), Gustavo Pesci in 1855 (retired 1905, died 1913), Giuseppe Ritarossi in 1861 (retired fully in 1901, died 1902), Giovanni Cesari in 1861 (died 1904, before retiring), Giosafat Anselmo Vissani also in 1861 (retired 1905, died 1916), Domenico Salvatori in 1877 (retired after 1903, died 1909), Vincenzo Sebastianelli in 1879 (educated at the expense of the Sacri Palazzi Apostolici as well; retired in 1912, died 1919), and lastly Moreschi, in 1883 (retired 1913, but still singing professionally at least at the Cappella Giulia afterward but more likely occasionally at the Cappella Sistina, almost until he died on April 21, 1922, a day known as the Birth of Rome).[95]

Note, then, that at the turn of the twentieth century, the number of castrati in the papal chapel officially totaled nine, including Moreschi, Mustafà, and Cesari — the three most significant soloists — together with Meniconi, Vissani, Pesci, Ritarossi, Salvatori, and Sebastianelli — a number higher than generally recognized, though after the turn of the century, the numbers dropped quickly and steeply. Salvatori — apparently an uncle of Moreschi's buried in the Moreschi-Rinaldi tomb — was already by then largely relegated to administrative work.[96]

Meanwhile, in the latter years of the nineteenth century, the idea that unaltered boys might sing at the Sistine Chapel had been gradually making its way into papal and indeed Roman consciousness, albeit at a polar pace. Unaltered boys sang there during the 1880s to amplify the soprano section on certain feast days and for significant celebrations, but remarkably, the March 1891 constitution was the first to sanction them for Sistine use and thus disrupt the practice of inducting castrated singers exclusively for the soprano section. The new constitution asserted that it aimed simply to ensure that the Cappella Sistina "be composed of thirty-two singers, or eight sopranos, eight contraltos, eight tenors, and eight basses, as in the past," something it had not fully succeeded in doing at any point in the nineteenth century, least of all as regards the soprano section.[97] One solution involved calling up singers from other papal basilicas, "as practiced in recent years," using the term "cantori" for non-Sistine singers to distinguish them from Sistine "cantori cappellani." Another solution involved using boys as add-ons: "To the thirty-two will be aggregated no fewer than four boys, chosen by preference of the Scuola Pontificia di S. Salvatore in Lauro or an ecclesiastical institution."[98]

What's eye-opening is the immediate prehistory of the decision. The 1891 constitution came about only with strenuous efforts on the part of the chapel's *maggiordomo*, who, as we saw, had to put great effort into getting Mustafà on board with newly incorporating at least some boy singers as reinforcements to the castrati. Let's pause for a moment to think about that: Mustafà, himself a castrato who made bitter remarks about his own castration, was a holdout when it came to eliminating castrati from the chapel in the decade before 1900, once they needed to be replaced—and that includes his objections to substituting unaltered boy singers for adult castrati. In a letter of January 23, 1891, written to Mustafà at his hometown retreat in Montefalco on one of the many occasions when he had temporarily left the chapel in a huff, the *maggiordomo* listed the admission of at least four boys beyond the usual thirty-two singers as one of the reforms that Mustafà himself "had at least in part suggested."[99] If Mustafà actually did so, he must have changed his mind. On February 3, the *maggiordomo* pressed further, reminding him that Palestrina had admitted boys to take part in his own sublime works (when they sang alongside falsettists), and therefore ordering that some be taken from the school at San Salvatore in Lauro to sing at a mass for the dead on February 7.[100] "Perhaps for this 'first time' it won't have the desired effect, but it behooves one to know and feel that the boys are also admitted to sing in the Cappella Pontificia according to the plan of the great Palestrina."[101]

The shift to boys was portentous for later chapel developments, but in the 1890s, not everyone had given up on recruiting more castrati. On April 15, 1896—in the very month in which Moreschi took the stunningly modern step of getting married—the Collegio made a resolution, stemming from Mustafà himself, that solidified a proposal for two more boys to be castrated and cared for *at the Collegio's expense*. Monies were to be supplied to "the *maggiordomo* of the pope . . . to arrange *for the maintenance and religious, literary, and musical education of two castrated boys* [*fanciulli evirati*] who will then have to serve in the soprano section at the Cappella Sistina" (article 7; emphasis mine).[102]

The proposal lays bare-naked the hands-on role of the Vatican in obtaining castrated boys, even at a time when use of boy singers was on the rise and the last castrato recruited had been operated on some twenty-five years earlier. Much of the resolution focuses on the persistent dearth of competent chapel singers. Partial solutions include abolishing the posts of supernumerary (article 3) and substituting at the expense of the Sacri Palazzi Apostolici "cantori estranei" (singers from outside, otherwise unspecified) for those absent because of illness, death, or "legitimate impediments" (article 6), but above all, making "the Collegio di Cappellani Cantori and the Cantori Pontifici" responsible for "the religious, literary, and musical education of the two above-noted boys" (article 8). The article continues: "It remains up to the Collegio to entrust said two boys either to one of the parts of the Collegio or to an ecclesiastical and civil institute of Rome," a stipulation that becomes blatant in article 9:

> A post in the soprano section of the Cappella Sistina being vacated, should one of the two [castrated] youths, in the judgment of the Collegio, be able to take part in the Collegio itself, he will without fail [*senz'altro*] be installed as a substitute in the vacant post of soprano and will receive the 90 lire monthly as [outlined] in article 4. *Should neither of the two youths be judged capable, the vacancy will be provided for in the usual way* (emphasis mine).[103]

The document was signed by the pope and ratified by the Collegio as late as November 16, 1897.[104]

By referring back to article 7 with such dubious rhetorical devices as "fanciulli sopranotati" (above-noted boys) and "detti due fanciulli" (said two boys), the resolution avoided naming the boys for what they were beyond what was absolutely necessary. Apparently, no other boys were ever castrated. But remarkably, in the slippery passage that ends article 9, the resolution avoided closing off entirely the possibility of recruiting still more "fanciulli evirati."

> If no vacancies should arise in the soprano section and meanwhile both [castrated] youths should be capable of singing, they will have to lend their work to singing in the chapel as adjunct singers [*cantori aggiunti*] for only the 50 (fifty) lire already spent on each of them *and consequently no other youths* [*altri giovanetti*] *will be chosen to be educated until such time as the two adjunct* [castrated] *singers should enter the rolls of the Collegio* (emphasis mine).

Left unsaid, or left to the imagination, was exactly what kind of *giovanetti* might be sought if there were to be further vacancies.

Prima facie, it's breathtakingly paradoxical that Mustafà—furious specifically at his father for his own castration, at least by some reportage—was the chief motor pushing the resolution for more castrati at this very late date.[105] The paradox becomes legible only in light of the psychic conditions under which he labored. A castrate who had attained great power and prestige at the tail end of the castrato phenomenon, he represented a major success story. De Angelis, whose life partly overlapped with Mustafà's, thought him the greatest event of nineteenth-century castrati. Besides having become highly literate and skilled in music during his youth, writing compositions and studying composition under Saverio Mercadante (1795–1870), he had taken in some philosophy at Anagni.[106] After being admitted to the Cappella Pontificia as *soprannumerario* in 1848 and promoted to the status of *partecipante* only a year later, he gained celebrity status for his high upper extension, embellishments, and vocal flexibility and was widely sought after for outside bookings in churches and concerts, as well as for teaching. About his singing, De Angelis wrote, "he had the most marvelous soprano voice I ever heard . . . singularly piercing [*squillante*] and resonant . . . [it] echoed from the balcony opposite the papal throne—at times sweet and melodious, at others rebounding with great power through the sacred spaces."[107] His upper register was famously high and easy—something implicit in soprano Emma Calvé's account of learning to sing suprafalsetto tones from him — and he could reportedly carry off Handel and Rossini coloratura with ease.[108] Haböck's Roman informants told him that Mustafà's voice had been "exceedingly powerful and of an exquisite timbre," with "a range from c1` to c3 and a flexibility and ease of production that allowed him to do whatever he wished with it. His coloratura, trills, and messa di voce were exceptional."[109]

Mustafà's success extended to leading roles in the city's musical life. From 1874 to 1884, he served as president of the prestigious Società Musicale Romana, then recently founded, and conducted many large pieces throughout Rome, including Handel's *Messiah* and works by Gaspare Spontini. In his banner years of 1878 and 1881, Mustafà received honors to equal his ego, first being knighted by the Cavaliere dell'Ordine di San Gregorio Magno (Knight of the Order of St. Gregory the Great, hence later references to him as Cav. Mustafà), then being made *direttore perpetuo dei concerti* of the Cappella Sistina. His crowning tribute came on February 12, 1881, when he was named *direttore generale in perpetuo* of the Cappella Sistina, a post he retained for nearly twenty-two years, until January 1903, albeit in an often vexatious manner, particularly in the last four years of his tenure.

And yet Mustafà's castration caused him immense frustrations and anger that fed into his reputation as a high-strung divo. His envious, begrudging nature displayed itself in his stance toward Moreschi, whom he regarded without warmth, though he accepted the need to admit and utilize him.[110] Some saw Mustafà as a powermonger and prima donna — not an irrelevant gender slippage — and resented his exalted appointment.[111] Whether because of the wrongs done to him, his inborn nature, or endocrinological consequences of his castration, he was also notoriously touchy, the victim of what he himself reportedly called "certain quirks and susceptibilities in his character."[112] Repeatedly in the 1890s Mustafà offered his resignation in response to perceived slights, inconveniences, and stresses. And when the arch-Cecilianist Perosi was made codirector of the chapel in 1898, he became cantankerous and capricious to the point of gross dysfunction, tendering his resignation numerous times while fleeing to his hometown in Umbria and neglecting duties in Rome until, finally, in January 1903, his resignation was accepted.[113]

The postunification backdrop to all this bears noting. Mustafà's time as *direttore generale in perpetuo* corresponded to the highly rule-bound reign of Leo XIII. Crowned in 1878, Leo made a strict policy during his pontificate of enforcing the Cappella's constitutions, extending to expulsions of singers for marrying.[114] His policies served up conservative reactions to the 1870 fall of the Papal States and the consequent cloistering of the previous pope in the circa one square mile that makes up the Vatican. Indeed, Leo XIII followed the precedent of Pius IX in circling the pontifical wagons throughout the 1870s, a precedent that started with Pius IX's suspension of virtually all public functions for a couple of years, including musical services, which largely stopped in 1870 when he ended some sixty-eight musical obligations out of pique, excepting those at St. Peters.[115] And Leo XIII continued with a papal politics that corresponded to the "Catholic recovery" sketched in the Prologue. Although in 1878 Leo XIII reinstated some suspended functions, the suspensions had already done their damage, causing singers to be dropped and few sopranos to be added to the chapel.[116] Singers survived the period by taking work at other chapels, but larger problems of staffing and maintaining standards remained. Since the chapel had descended even more deeply than in earlier years into a state of disarray, it fell to Mustafà to restore some kind of former glory by reorganizing it. Given his proclivities, that meant a return to more traditional polyphonic repertories.[117] Most welcomed the reorganization because Mustafà was a chapel member of very long standing and hugely respected for his prestige and musicianship, but his leadership was ultimately entangled with the fate of the castrati, paradoxically both instrumentalizing their end (however inadvertently) and trying to prevent it.

Figure 1.9. Portrait of Lorenzo Perosi, signed to Alessandro Moreschi with "esteem," August 4, 1904. Moreschi-Fellini Archive.

The End of the Castrati

The combination of Mustafà's ambivalences and his entrenchments made it relatively easy for modernist sentiments to take a hard and fast hold against the epistemic disjoint caused by the presence of those Sistine castrati who still filled the rolls of the soprano section toward the end of his tenure. But what concretely spelled their end was the 1898 appointment as cochapelmaster of Perosi, previously chapelmaster of the Cappella Marciana in Venice and an avowed Cecilianist who longed for the simplicity and authenticity of a lost past by way of a return to chant and Palestrina-style polyphony. If Perosi's church and salon collaborations with Moreschi and a portrait signed to him (fig. 1.9) are any indication, he held no personal enmity toward him, but castrati represented for him a general structural and ontological impossibility, expressed in the language of scientific racism. "As soon as I came to Rome, there were so many requests that reached me from abnormal men [*uomini anormali*] to enter into the Cappella that I had the suspicion that there was some ignoble speculation, especially when unhappy boys were presented to me."[118] It's unsurprising that by February 3, 1902, Perosi managed to extract from Leo XIII a papal injunction against recruiting any more castrati, the first formal injunction against their use in the chapel, but not the last.

Definitive change came after Leo XIII died on July 20, 1903, and Perosi's old employer, Cardinal Sarto, ex-patriarch of Venice, was elected as Pius X the following August 4. Sarto sympathized with the whole Cecilianist project and could guarantee Perosi (by then sole *direttore generale in perpetuo* of the chapel) robust papal support. A *motu proprio*—decree by the pope's "own action" (or "papal encyclical")—conveyed that support under the rubric *Tra le sollecitudini* (Among the cares). Delivered on the name day of the patron saint of music, St. Cecilia, November 22, 1903, with sweeping attention to music, *Tra le sollecitudini* declared war on abuses of church music, especially chant.

> Today our attention is directed to one of the most common of [abuses . . .], one of the most difficult to eradicate, the existence of which is sometimes to be deplored in places where everything else is deserving of the highest praise—the beauty and sumptuousness of the temple, the splendor and the accurate performance of the ceremonies, the attendance of the clergy, the gravity and piety of the officiating ministers. Such is the abuse affecting sacred chant and music.[119]

The *motu proprio* went on to trash old customs and assert new principles that would regulate sacred music against "the more common abuses," noting recent progress in Rome and other "nations in which illustrious men, full of zeal for the worship of god," had been working to restore sacred music—an allusion to oltramontane Cecilianist zealots, mostly in France and Germany. Rigorously reworking the purpose of church music, the document avowed that sacred liturgical sounds should do away with all deemed profane, illuminating sacred texts and making music formally subordinate to them in order to move the faithful. The desideratum implicitly elevated chant over polyphony, specifically, the Solesmes redaction Perosi was agitating to have replace the Ratisbon (or "Medicean") one then in general use, as the pope indicated by the phrase "which recent studies have so happily restored to their integrity and purity."[120] Not that Cecilianists meant to make chant completely exclusive in church music. Rather, they wanted it to have scriptural and musical hegemony and for all sacred music to aspire to its condition. Chant became the touchstone and medium for radical claims to a revised papal soundscape.

Therefore, in this return to an "ancient" past, only "classic polyphony" could stand alongside chant. Classic polyphony was permissible—indeed exalted—because it worked to preserve and conjure Palestrina and other music of the Roman school that had "reached its greatest perfection in the sixteenth century." Implicitly, then, the newly acceptable styles extended to the *stile antico* of such sixteenth-century and seventeenth-century composers as Felice Anerio (1560–1614) and Gregorio Allegri (1582–1652), whose admission allowed the church to declare itself an institution that "recognizes progress in the arts." But it drew the line at liturgy, specifically, as liturgy fell victim to nineteenth-century theatrical music. The sound of opera, which had permeated Mustafà's soundscape, became taboo, a site of forbidden pleasure.

> Among the different kinds of modern music, that which appears less suitable for accompanying the functions of public worship is the theatrical style, which was in the greatest vogue, especially in Italy, during the last century. This is of its nature diametrically opposed to Gregorian chant and classic polyphony and therefore to the most important law of all good sacred music. Besides its intrinsic structure, the rhythm of what is known as the conventionalism of this style adapts itself badly to the requirements of true liturgical music.[121]

Pius X's condemnation of modern music sounds like an outright repeat of the Council of Trent. Like the council's fiery proclamations three hundred fifty years earlier, this one opposes music that has "mainly risen to serve profane uses," eradicating it in order to free music "from reminiscences of motifs adopted in theaters." Correspondingly, it demands that performances hew to a temporal and syntactic concinnity between music and ritual, where musical rhythms and pacing closely match the ritual temporalities of chanting, reading, gesturing, moving processually, and taking the sacrament. With these Counter-Reformationist strokes, the church swept away all nineteenth-century Latin-texted repertory, including that by Rossini, Mercadante, and Verdi, much of Baini and Mustafà, and that of minor composers such like Capocci, Meluzzi, Emilio Calzanera, Eugenio Terziani, and Giovanni Aldega, in short, most of the polyphonic repertory performed prior to November 22, 1903, including a good deal of what Moreschi recorded in 1902 and 1904.[122] The proscriptions included non-Latin usages, with exceptions for only a couple of brief motets (one to the Blessed Sacrament after the Benedictus in a solemn mass and one after the Offertory). Also like the Council of Trent, the prescriptions emphasized intelligibility, hence allowed no "breaking" of syllables, but also no "undue repetition." No longer could major components of the ordinary be split up into separate movements, and very little falsobordone would be allowed, nor would concerted psalms, since musical forms of liturgy had to closely cleave to and even mirror textual forms.

All such prescriptions and proscriptions were also tightly imbricated in the new ban on castrati, introduced with the indirect rhetorical device "on the same principle." The pragmatic implications of the phrase were clearer than its muddy rhetoric, inasmuch as the church was already assigning treble parts exclusively to boys (article 5, number 13), allowing castrati to be erased silently without ever being named.

> *On the same principle* it follows that singers in church have a real liturgical office, and that therefore women, being incapable of exercising such an office, cannot be admitted to form part of the choir. Whenever, then, it is

> desired to employ the acute voices of sopranos and contraltos, these parts must be taken by boys, according to the most ancient usage of the Church.[123]

The strangleholds tightened with a decree of January 8, 1904, that banned all the pope's major basilicas, the Lateran included, from performing any "modern" music, with "no exceptions whatsoever."[124]

The nineteenth-century musical excesses that Perosi, Pius X, and other Cecilianists worked to jettison were in one sense stylistic ones, but far more importantly, they were formal, ritual, symbolic, and affective. Throwing away unsafe and indecent elements of romanticism produced austere distillations meant to purify the alchemy of theatrical church styles. The point was to get rid of emotionality and ornament by returning to the severity of the Church Fathers, leaving only what was essential, chiseled, and unadorned.

All this was of course rife with irony. Much as Wagner sought to rediscover a timeless past and to secure it by editing Palestrina's *Stabat mater* (prepared 1848, published 1878), Perosi and Pius X made recourse to a distant past in efforts to locate a new churchly ethos.[125] But if the Cecilianist program personified the church through a quintessentially romantic dream of timelessness, it also chimed with an emerging modernist aesthetics of new and brutal ascetic reduction—a harsh pursuit of the limits of pure plainness, managed by sacrificing what came naturally. In this instance, that meant renouncing emotion-filled operatic vocality in favor of all that was feeling-free, doing so in a search for a (self-)discipline that exceeds whatever is ready to hand, aligning with what Daniel Albright calls the "freakish circumferences of art."[126]

In Moreschi's Wake

All reliable evidence that can be mustered suggests that Moreschi really was the last boy "procured" for castration and grooming by the church, unless there are exceptions that never made it into Sistine documentation. Tallying from 1873, his singing career ended up lasting nearly fifty years, without even counting the precastration years as a boy soloist in Montecompatri. During more than half a century in Rome he sang in papal chapels, indeed, past his official Sistine retirement in 1913 and on virtually until his death.[127]

Meanwhile, Rome was modernizing in contradictory ways that made Moreschi ever more alien to the world around him, even as he also became an object of international media attention through the novelty of the gramophone. After Mustafà's resignation, fifty-four years after he joined the chapel, castrati no longer had a structural hegemony in the Vatican musical establishment, hence the sudden tumble of proscriptions against them. For that most atavistic of institutions, modernization meant converting the all-adult choir with castratos to one with boy sopranos, annihilating in a stroke the arch-Roman tradition that, from Monteverdi to Rossini, had helped lay the foundation for bel canto singing. There was nothing modest about the repertorial suppressions accompanying those proscriptions. The "modern" music exiled included touchstones of the repertory—solo vehicles like Rossini's ornate "Crucifixus" from the *Petit messe solennelle* (1864) that had emerged late in the day from the apex of the bel canto tradition, in turn a product of over two centuries of castrato vocality.

When Moreschi died, he was mourned by Giulio and Amerigo in a notice published on April 22, 1922, in *Il giornale d'Italia* and given a noteworthy funeral on April 23, with of all things, polyphonic music conducted by Perosi. Attending were his student Domenico Mancini, the two Sistine tenor brothers, Ezio and Alessandro Cecchini, the papal singer Albino Gaggi, the papal alto and diarist Luigi Gentili (the same one who recorded the birth of Moreschi's son and his later abandonment by Guendalina), as well as such luminaries as Giuseppe Fiocchi, Eugenio Travaglia, and Alfredo Tamburini, representing the Accademia di Santa Cecilia and various members of the noble Borghese family, all of whom joined the many others who signed a funeral register provided by undertakers M. Moscatelli &

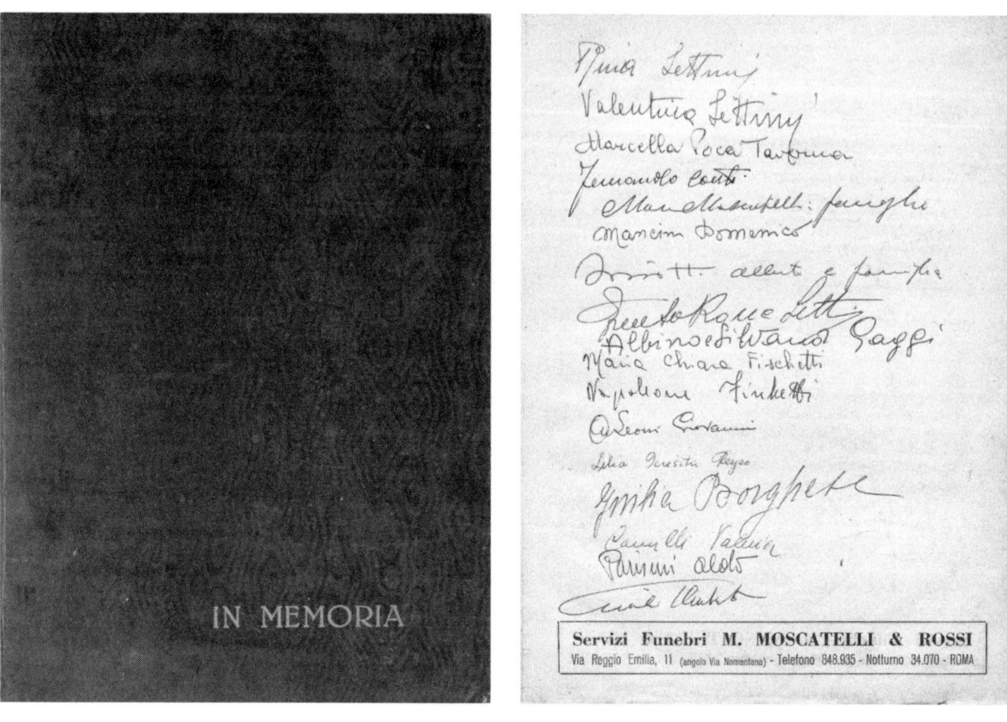

Figure 1.10a. Moreschi's funeral register, cover. Moreschi-Fellini Archive.

Figure 1.10b. Moreschi's funeral register, opening page of attendee signatures, including his student Domenico Mancini, members of the Cappella Sistina, and friends, among them, members of the Borghese family. Moreschi-Fellini Archive.

Rossi of via Reggio Emilia 11 near Rome's Porta Pia (figs. 1.10a and 1.10b) and who were also thanked in a follow-up notice published on April 30 in the *Giornale di Roma*.[128]

The ironies of Moreschi's life and his complicated legacy even before his death add further context to the Moreschi-Rinaldi tomb. A joint tomb meant more than entering into a business contract with another party. By becoming its coconcessionaries, both Moreschi and his father-in-law consolidated the castrato's marriage contractually and legally, but also established a spatial, spiritual, legal, and temporal union between their families. The tomb conjoined them topographically and physically, as well as metaphysically in what was an eternal resting place. Regardless of who shouldered the cost—likely Moreschi—both men exploited available legal and symbolic means to enact their geophysical, familial, and spiritual union.

Over time, however, the tomb proved to be a Moreschi family resting place far more than a Rinaldi one. In 1909, Moreschi's apparent uncle, Domenico Salvatori, was buried there; in 1924, Pietro Rinaldi; and in 1925, Moreschi's nephew, Amerigo, son of Alessandro's brother, Agostino. Others buried there are "Moreschis" too, or affines, including: in 1955, son Giulio; in 1994, granddaughter Alessandra; in 2010, great-grandson Julio—all biological descendants of Guendalina's via Giulio.[129] But Guendalina herself, alienated from the family, is absent from the tomb, as is her second son, Saverio Mancini—maternally a Rinaldi, but also the issue of her presumed marriage to a man named Antonio Mancini. She is thus a mortal cipher, not unlike the archive that has enabled me to write this chapter, a cipher who haunts the tomb.

And yet Guendalina arises after her own death, still hovering mysteriously over family relations, even with a degree of clarity. Fabio still possesses a letter written in 1957 to the Moreschi family by Saverio, then in Thiene, reporting his mother's death. This was thirteen years before he was photographed visiting Alessandra, Rita, and Julio at their apartment in Rome (figs. 1.11 and 1.12).

Figure 1.11. The entrance to via Lungotevere degli Anguillara 11, recently graffitied. Photograph by the author, March 2024.

Enclosed with Saverio's letter was a photograph of Giulio holding the infant Alessandra (fig. 1.13a), a photograph Giulio had sent his mother thirty years earlier with a note on its verso, fictively authored by his infant daughter Alessandra, that reads "Alla mia cara nonna, con affetto, Sandrina. Roma 9 giugno 927" (To my dear grandma, with affection, Sandrina [= Sandra/Alessandra], Rome, June 9, 1927) (fig. 1.13b).

By voicing the dedication to Guendalina from "Sandrina," who was less than nine months old at the time, Giulio was already interpolating the infant as intermediary between mother and son, which is to say between himself and the mother who had abandoned him twenty years earlier. When in 1957 Saverio then returned the photograph to the Roman side of the family, and specifically to Alessandra, two years after her father's death, along with a note giving news of the death of her grandmother Guendalina, he added a

Figure 1.12. Photograph taken in the living room at via Lungotevere degli Anguillara 11. Pictured left to right are Alessandra Moreschi, her uncle, Francesco Saverio Mancini, Rita Fellini, and Julio Solinas Moreschi, June 1970. Moreschi-Fellini Archive.

further note, extending the dedication: "Dopo 30 anni ritorna a te cara Sandra per essere sempre vivo in te ricordo della tua infanzia e del tuo papà. 18/4/57 Saverio" (After thirty years this returns to you, dear Sandra, so that the memory of your childhood and your papa will always be alive in you. April 18, 1957). Saverio's addendum thus offered words of consolation to Alessandra on the death of her father, but not only that. It also reminded her of her uncle and her father's distant half brother—Saverio himself—and thereby, too, of the woman through whom all three were joined.

Figure 1.13a. Giulio Moreschi holding the infant Alessandra ("Sandrina") Moreschi. Moreschi-Fellini Archive.

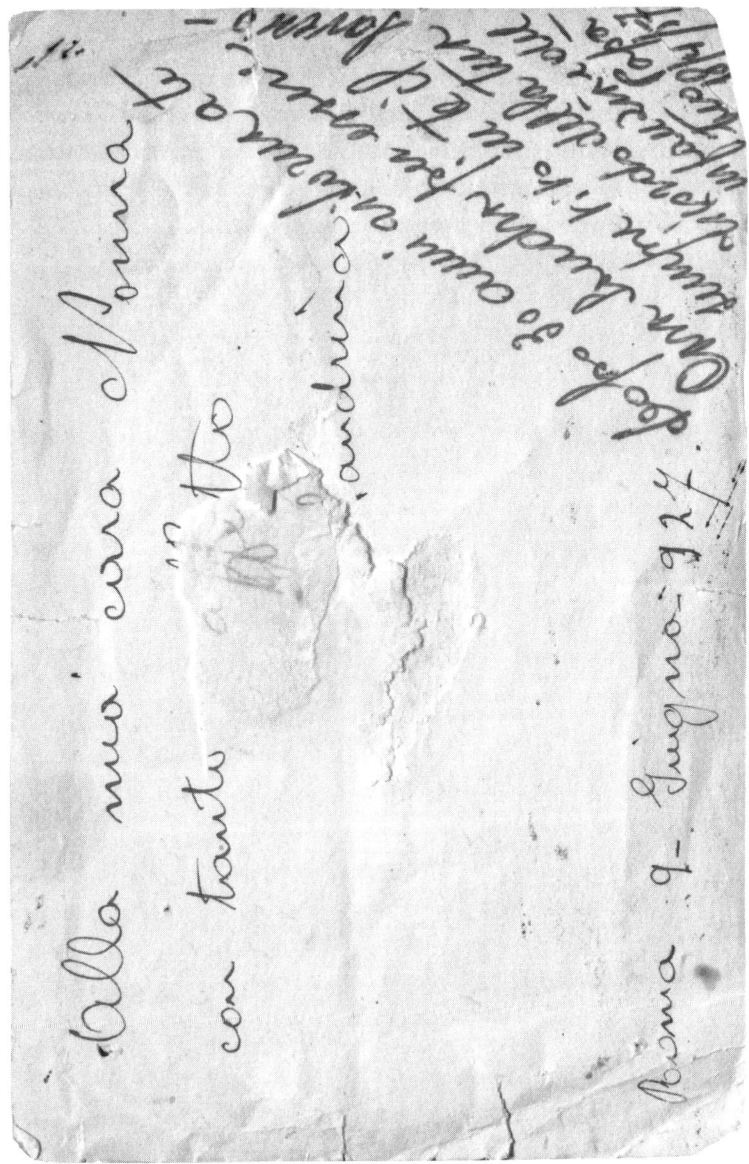

Figure 1.13b. Verso of figure 13.a, including two notes from two different eras. The first, addressed from the infant Alessandra to her grandmother, Guendalina, but in Giulio's hand, reads, "To my dear grandma, with affection, Sandrina, Rome, June 9, 1927." Decades later and nearly two years after Giulio's death, Francesco Saverio Mancini added another note, in blue ink, to the lower right side of the verso when he returned the photo to Alessandra: "After thirty years this returns to you, dear Sandra, so that the memory of your childhood and your papa will always be alive in you. April 18, 1957." Moreschi-Fellini Archive.

Figure 2.1. Film still showing a wooden statue of Jesus in a pose of benediction carried by a helicopter swooping up the side of a 1950s honeycomb apartment building. From *La dolce vita* (1960), directed by Federico Fellini.

CHAPTER TWO

The Sacred Vernacular

Film is a divine way of telling about life, of paralleling God the Father!
—Federico Fellini, *Making a Film*

The Sacred Vernacular

Within the *longue durée* that stretches across Rome's twentieth century, castrati are everywhere enmeshed in what I call the *sacred vernacular*. To think about how it works, picture a suggestive moment drawn from the heart of the Fellini canon. At the start of *La dolce vita* (1960) a large wooden statue of Jesus hangs from a helicopter in a pose of benediction. The plane drifts westward, clattering its way toward the viewer from a long shot as it crosses over a Roman aqueduct, past crowds of running boys, and over stretches of a 1950s apartment block until a shadow of Jesus swoops up the bleached-out side of a honeycomb building (fig. 2.1). A second helicopter comes into view, carrying the journalist Marcello (Marcello Mastroianni) and his photographer "Paparazzo" (Walter Santesso). Two burly laborers cranking a fire hydrant wave their greetings skyward until, abruptly, a bubbly pop song, brightly forward in the mix, replaces the whirr of motors just as the camera pans onto a rooftop decked with bathing beauties who are keen to know where Jesus is going. "To the pope," shouts Marcello, gesturing from his helicopter with "Can-I-ring-you-up?" motions before trailing Jesus into a crowded St. Peter's Square.[1]

The scene, one of the best-known in film history, borrows from a 1956 iteration of the May Day festival held annually by the Associazione Cattolica Lavoratori Italiani in honor of Italy's workers and celebrated that year by gifting a statue of Christ likewise delivered to St. Peter's via helicopter.[2] The inspiration is unmistakable, but other vernacularisms come in its wake. For one, the Felice aqueduct visible near the very start of *La dolce vita* runs adjacent to a soccer field not far from Cinecittà, where Fellini made most of his films in the famed Studio 5. For another, the women's radio blares out the dance song "Canzonetta."[3] And most conspicuous of all, Christ arrives not with a herd of sheep or on a mule or an oxcart, but hanging from a rattling aircraft and pursued by a seedy paparazzo and his womanizing journalist.[4] The moment is not so sacred as to prevent Christ from swinging from a flying machine or to dispense with the scopophilic gapers and media-giddy tourists who throng to meet him. It's not so unadulteratedly sacred as to stop Marcello from trying to put the make on the young women and definitely not sacred enough to prevent the filmmakers from suddenly abandoning the bustling crowds and clanging bells of St. Peter's by way of a sudden fast cut from the Vatican to an exotic nightclub show.

Setting the viewer's first sights on a kitschy Christ figure and its herdish devotees amid a clutch of new machines and new media was Fellini's way of signaling the entanglement of the church with the popular and the modern, but also signaling the contingency of grace. Those who first glimpse the statue are laboring, working-class males from Rome's scruffy periphery, recently settled by immigrants mostly from the impoverished south, and only then the tony girls nearer the Vatican. Straddling a range of ranks and genders, the people's class differences matter, but so does the fact that despite them, everyone confronts the statue with a mixture of bedazzlement and easy familiarity. Domesticated tokens of the sacred constantly tease the edges of their daily worlds. Fellini was the master critic of such edges, indeed, an inveterate maker of what we might call *boundary figures*, constantly meandering through spaces at once numinous and grotesque, forbidding and homespun. Think of the giantess and her dwarves in *Fellini's Casanova* (1976), or Giulietta Masina's beleaguered clown, Gelsomina, of *La strada* (1954); or think of the endless parade of zaftig and eccentric women epitomized by Saraghina in *8½* (1963)[5] (figs. 2.2, 2.3, and 2.4).

While Fellini's boundary figures help work through psychic and moral dilemmas, they always carry the risk of indulging viewers in the same profligacies the film critiques. Where in *La dolce vita* are the lines between innocence and decadence, the sacred and the everyday? Fellini, who thrived on ambiguities, had no interest in clarifying them. His ubiquitous threshold figures move seamlessly between religious and mundane worlds, between purity and corruption, producing an array of sacred kinds, even sacred monsters. Boundary figures are disturbing, often horrible, but they also endear others who regard them as essential to life, especially Roman life, as beings who enjoy special access to intimacies of the heart and psyche. Besides the giantess, dwarves, and clowns, there are the petty tricksters, con men, and madmen, prostitutes and sex goddesses, all figures to whom Fellini's populaces are much attached and whom they tend to greet with blithe, easygoing acceptance, even anticipation.

Arguably the most sensational and sensationally incarnate of Fellini's boundary figures is the chief female protagonist of *La dolce vita*, the overwhelming Sylvia (Anita Ekberg). Though nobody's first idea of a sacred figure, Sylvia gets a starring role at St. Peter's early on when she ascends an immense staircase to the top of the cupola and emerges on the balcony in a then-fashionable dress that mimics the cassock and collar of a priest (fig. 2.5).[6] Catholic critics and censors thought this blasphemous, but for Fellini, it underscored, ironically, Romans' casual way of imbricating the profane in the sacred, manifest in the contradictions of the massive ecclesiastical

Figure 2.2. Film still of the giantess and her dwarves, from *Fellini's Casanova* (1976), directed by Federico Fellini.

Figure 2.3. Film still of the beleaguered clown, Gelsomina (Giulietta Masina), from *La strada* (1954), directed by Federico Fellini.

Figure 2.4. Film still of the zaftig Saraghina from *8½* (1963), directed by Federico Fellini.

Figure 2.5. Film still of Sylvia (Anita Ekberg) talking to Marcello (Marcello Mastroianni) after climbing the stairs up to the cupola at San Pietro. She wears a dress fashioned after a priest's cassock and collar. From *La dolce vita*.

establishment that dominates their landscape. Even so, Sylvia troubles all this. Always literally larger than life, she is not just the unattainable diva-woman of exaggerated features and physical proportions — a deliberate Rita Hayworth, as affirmed by a scene of her watching Hayworth in a movie theater with Marcello — but a primordial maternal goddess, moving seamlessly between human and animal worlds, like the goddess Diana. As a "pagan goddess," or what Alessandro Carrera calls "a figure of "irrepressible, 'inhuman' joy because . . . more-than-human,"[7] she is perfectly objectified to ignite male sexual fantasies.

Carrera also reminds readers that the iconic Trevi Fountain scene serves as a sort of Christian baptism and conversion, connecting to the "miracle scene" that comes later in the film, when two children claim before television cameras that they've seen the Virgin Mary.[8] Is this a hoax of theirs, a hoax of the television producers, or a prank of Fellini's — a kind of hypernarrative *mise-en-abyme*?[9] Or is it Fellini laughing at the gullibility of onlookers, who fall prey to organized religion? Is he telling us that religious sentiment, with its compulsion to theatricalize popular beliefs and make appeals to the divine, is just "self-fulfilling," thereby drawing attention to the complicity of religion with the spectacularizing technomediations of modern life? We can't help but wonder, because scenes like these force us to confront fantasies of age-old religion (Catholic, in this case)—its codification and the consolidation of religious beliefs that are always already mediated, narrativized, and mediatized in the same ritual acts that instantiate them. Fellini wants to force the issue, to ask how we can take comfort in religion when new, twentieth-century media have already traversed our fantasies of it and hystericized it, causing the buried pathological feelings it causes to be somatized through endless repetition and reproduction.[10]

Celluloid Angels

Such questions entangle the late castrato as a liminal and transitional figure who is also a ghostly one. I raise them while calling attention to Fellini's brew of sacred vernacular tropes in order to think backward to the last castrato and his predecessors and forward to the Italy and especially the Rome that Fellini and his contemporaries inherited. Paramount among the angels who inhabited their world was the real-world Giulietta Masina. Not only did she play that role in Fellini's life, she also played it in the lives of Moreschi family members, serving as intermediary, intercessory, touchstone, witness, and guardian angel. Often a clown, she was also a figure of grace and redemption.

Before turning directly to Giulietta, I want to think with the angels in Fellini's early films more broadly. In his marvelous essay "Autobiography of a Spectator," Italo Calvino writes: "Fellini has stated that a spiritual, magical form of knowledge and religious participation in the mystery of the universe runs counter to cold, intellectual rational lucidity"—this about a director who acknowledged as much many times.[11] "Cold, intellectual rational lucidity" lurks in the subterranean quarters of Fellini's cosmopolis, most memorably in *La dolce vita*'s Steiner, whose sterile disillusionment with the world leads him to kill his two children and then himself. Creative souls, alive to mysteries, register as Steiner's opposite. For them, the route to understanding comes not, or not only, from the intellect, but from the outside, especially from outside the decadent city, which is often encountered upon approach from the provinces. Thus (per Calvino again), "the biography of the Fellini hero, which the director goes back to and starts over again each time," involves a young man who leaves his small town, goes to Rome, and goes to the other side of the screen, makes movies, becomes cinema himself."[12] This is the story of Fellini's autobiographical *Roma* (1972), and it's implied in his quasi-autobiographical *I vitelloni* (1953). Or if the young man doesn't make movies, he often becomes grist for them. Such a path is possible only because Fellini, like the diva Sylvia, is a kind of anarchist (as Gianfranco Angelucci writes), if an order-loving anarchist, hence always apt to see the dynamism in his characters.[13] But it is also possible because Fellini makes repeated recourse to an angelic liminality, to figures that guide the transition between inside and outside and represent the transformability in what I am calling the sacred vernacular. A transgressive kind, the Fellinian angel, and angels generally, are at once trustworthy and disobedient, hence inexorably drawn to the borderlands of ontology and social acceptability. Inherently anarchic, angels have avatars in phantomic castrati, each of them caught up in Fellini's self-described "dialectics" as opposing forces that struggle between bourgeois snares and bourgeois defiance, between enchantment and disenchantment, ghostly presences and earthly ones.[14]

Fellini did not put any castrati in his films until *Casanova* (1976), where they are sheer farce, but other angelic kinds repeatedly visited his films, especially early on, when they took conventionally Christian forms.[15] In his first solo feature, the comedy *Lo sceicco bianco / The White Sheik* (1952), a Bernini angel holding a garment, identified as a shroud or vestment, positioned at the north-central

Figure 2.6. Film still of an angel, designed by Gian Lorenzo Bernini and located at the north-central part of Rome's Ponte Sant-Angelo, who oversees Wanda (Brunella Bovo) as she makes a farcical attempt to drown in the Tiber by suicide; from *Lo sceicco bianco* (1952), directed by Federico Fellini.

portion of Rome's Ponte Sant'Angelo, stands at the ready when the female lead makes a weak-willed, farcical attempt at suicide by landing a pratfall in a muddy puddle by the Tiber while holding her nose (fig. 2.6).[16] In his second feature, *I vitelloni / The Young and the Passionate* (1953), two callow youths try to peddle a life-sized gilded angel, stolen by night from an antiquities shop, to a nun before a village madman adopts it (fig. 2.7) and proceeds to carry it around, worshiping it as the Madonna. Other angels, embodied in human or quasi-human forms, accompany outlandish capers and misadventures. The eponymous sheik played by Alberto Sordi in *The White Sheik* steps literally out of the pages of fantasy, specifically, the then-popular *fotoromanzi* (comic books or *fumetti* using photos, instead of drawings), to appear before his female admirer dressed in white and winging his way earthward on a swing that dangles from the treetops (fig. 2.8).[17] And yet, the angelic sheik is not just the stuff of dreams, fantasies, and fantastical carnivals, but a comic means of

Figure 2.7. Film still of the village madman who adopts the gilded angel stolen from an antiquities shop by two callow youths and venerates it as a Madonna. From *I vitelloni* (1953), directed by Federico Fellini.

Figure 2.8. Film still of the sheik (Alberto Sordi) appearing to Wanda, angel-like and decked in white while descending from treetops on a swing; from *Lo sceicco bianco*.

exposing the ever-present potential life holds for trading in misprisions and outright deceit while returning the errant heroine to her conventional marriage.[18]

To see further into Fellini's angelic signs and icons, consider what has motored angels for millennia in such archetypes as the cherubim, the seraphim, or the archangels Gabriel, Michael, and Raphael and what links them together typologically. All these figures mobilize journeys beyond earth, acting dynamically as intermediaries between realms visible and invisible, earthly and divine.[19] Angels may come endowed with visible forms, but they do not classically provide concrete knowledge in sensory ways. Instead, they act as emissaries for what cannot otherwise be seen, moving between divine realms to which they travel and then bear witness on their return to earth. In that role, they serve as signs of higher authorities with whom they have contact. They take many visible guises and assume many different traits — noble, abject, comical, reticent, vain, strident, mysterious, impish, martial, or childlike (or several of these combined) — always haunted by the paradox of being somehow tangible, yet vanishingly elusive.[20] They incite the imagination of humans who finally intuit their importance, but only despite definite limits to their external forms and their very palpability, for their value inheres in crossing thresholds and cloaking the mysterious dominions to which they have access. As Massimo Cacciari notes, they veil truths by withholding direct verbal or sensory knowledge of distant spheres, failing to provide knowledge of them in properly physical or human ways.[21] Hence, the wings on which they so often fly, birdlike, are not just iconic symbols, purely visual figurations, but the means to propel their spiritual mobility and freedom from earthly bounds. And only because of that can they aid observers in rebinding or consolidating their relationship to God in a process that Sofia Gubaidulina famously called "re-ligio."[22]

Such conditions relate intimately to associations of angels with sonorous musical realms that themselves carry traces of the divine and inspire feelings toward it. Hence the so-called "Angelo di Roma," Alessandro Moreschi, who induced rapture by giving voice to the part of the Seraph in Beethoven's *Christ on the Mount of Olives*, or (to cite one more example from among innumerable others) the castrato Mariano's singing of the *Miserere* reported on by Sievers: "he sang with a sweetness, a portamento and a purity of tone compared to which every voice I ever heard before seemed to be but bawling of the roughest, moist untutored kind. . . . I would have taken the singing of Mariano for the voice of an angel descending from the clouds."[23] But hence, too, the anarchy and abjection that lurked. While Moreschi's angelic singing conveyed an ineffable sense of the divine, he was also subject to abuse and invective: by the petty Vatican chapelmaster-composer Salvatore Meluzzi (see Chapter 4), by the decades-long indifference, if not downright resentment, of his castrato superior, Mustafà, and by the unchecked, sometimes rude curiosity of various onlookers.[24] Angel figures are not immune to abuse; witness the angel in Gabriel Garcia Marquez's "A Very Old Man with Enormous Wings: A Tale for Children."[25] Indeed, they are common victims of it. And this because the angel, as Cacciari insists, exists in the realm of human desires, above all, those navigated by fantasy and imagination.[26] One thing we learn from Fellini's films is that angelic-human figures participate in an economy of abuse by suffering harm for others—precisely what the angelic Giulietta Masina does in all three of her most important Fellini features: *La strada* (1954), *Le notti di Cabiria / Nights of Cabiria* (1957), and *Giulietta degli spiriti / Juliet of the Spirits* (1965).

How exactly does the angel function in Fellini's earliest solo features?

Notably, in order to effect what was to become the stereotypical Fellinian arc of the provincial who goes to Rome, both *The White Sheik* and *I vitelloni* require the angel, even though they also trouble it. In *The White Sheik*, a newlywed couple from the outlying Lazian city of Viterbo roars into town on a train to meet the groom's relatives and have an audience with the pope (fig. 2.9). No sooner do they arrive at the hotel than, in a send-up of celebrity culture, the starry-eyed wife, Wanda (Brunella Bovo), wanders off in search of her mythical divo-idol from the *fumetti*, the White Sheik ("Fernando Rivoli") and gets inadvertently cast in a new magazine issue. Thus begins what Stefania Parigi calls the film's "ramshackle carnival."[27] After arriving in Rome with her husband, Ivan, Wanda—assonant with *vagando*, straying (or even, as in English, wandering)—secretly makes her way to the offices of Incanto Blu, publisher of her favorite *fotoromanzi*, to the allusive accompaniment of church bells. Already while conversing with the magazine editor, Wanda is swooning over images of her adored sheik (fig. 2.10). Her conflation of fantasy and reality has just begun, but it is already challenged with the departure of the actors and crew for the beach at Fregene, colorfully described by Fellini's contemporaneous biographer, Tullio Kezich:

> An extraordinary scene unfolds in front of Wanda in the courtyard of the old building at via Maggio 24. The pageant is the debut of Fellini's ragtag cinema world. A procession of costumed characters descends the stairs of the building. There's a March [by Nino Rota] playing in the background.... There is Felga, the mysterious Greek woman; Omar, the Bedouin; and a clutch of black men. People scurry around [a]waiting trucks; orders are shouted—this is the underbelly of filmmaking. In a trancelike state, Wanda boards a truck and follows the crew to Fregene, where they are going to shoot an adventure sequence. The young bride is captivated by the new world, which is fabulous to her eyes, but actually revealed here in all its grotesque squalor.[28]

The scene, heavily classed and racialized, is given the savor of a freak show, but rather than being an instance of "grotesque squalor," at least in Wanda's eyes, it's her first hint that the fantasy she's about to traverse is just that. It covers over a seedy reality that is hardly exotic in the ways she imagines, but rather in a way that she misses. Before she knows what's up, she gets herself into deep waters, riding out of Rome in the crew's old jalopy for a photo shoot with hollered freeze-frame commands barraging her from all

Figure 2.9. Film still of the newly wedded groom Ivan (Leopoldo Trieste) arriving in Rome on a train from outlying Viterbo; from *Lo sceicco bianco.*

Figure 2.10. Film still of Wanda swooning over the sheik at the offices of Incanto Blu, publishers of her favorite *fotoromanzo*; from *Lo sceicco bianco.*

sides. Meanwhile, the swing-borne Sheik appears to her alone, in subjective close-up, delivered as if straight from the sky, so magically it makes tears roll down her cheeks (figs. 2.11a and 2.11b).[29] By now, Wanda has been inserted into the cast as the slave girl Fatima, draped in a gauzy slip finished off with costume jewelry, and then sculled out into the Mediterranean, where the Sheik/Rivoli tries to seduce her in a first real test of her fantasy-romance. Once rebuffed, Rivoli quickly rows them back to shore, where he meets the fury of his brawny wife, looming viciously in an exaggeratedly low angle-shot. The wife assaults Wanda and gives her husband an unvarnished piece of her mind, exposing Wanda's idol as a deceitful, blubbering mamma's boy (fig. 2.12).[30]

While Wanda's angel is crashing to earth, her husband, Ivan (Leopoldo Trieste), searches for her frantically, making up one outlandish subterfuge after another to explain her absence to his Roman relatives. Careful editing depicts Ivan's progress in parallel montage with Wanda's misadventure. A memorable fast cut to the

Figure 2.11a–b. Film stills of a) a close-up of the sheik leaning toward Wanda from his swing, and b) close-up of Wanda crying at the sheik's divine appearance; from *Lo sceicco bianco.*

opera has him and his in-laws watching Don Giovanni try to despoil Zerlina in "La ci darem la mano," just as Rivoli tries to "force a kiss" on Wanda.[31] By nighttime, Ivan, desperate, is found by two prostitutes, including the good-hearted Cabiria, played by Masina in a part that anticipates her role in *Nights of Cabiria.* In less than five minutes, Cabiria visits Ivan in good-fairy form, warding off his despondency while participating in the movie's carnivalesque spirit. Before they meet, Ivan spies Cabiria in extreme long shot cheerfully showing her companion how to do a lively dance. She notices him, wondering aloud whether he might harm himself, and, reassured, sits herself down to wipe away his tears while munching greedily, open-mouthed, on his packet of sugared almonds (fig. 2.13). Drawn from the pages of Fellini's pageant, Cabiria ministers with a full, lusty spirit. For all her kindness, she is not innocent of the world, but only innocent as a human being—she has cousins who went to see the pope, she boasts naively (as Ivan and Wanda were to have done)—and is otherwise frank and knowing.[32]

Over time and place, many angels, like Cabiria, have been drawn from lowly underworlds or bizarre upper worlds. The figure who

Figure 2.12. Film still of Wanda fighting with the sheik's brawny wife as he turns into a blubbering mamma's-boy type; from *Lo sceicco bianco.*

Figure 2.13. Film still of Cabiria (Giulietta Masina) wiping away Ivan's tears while she munches on sugared almonds; from *Lo sceicco bianco.*

announced to the very old and barren Sarah that she would soon be great with child and birth the infant Isaac made her erupt in laughter, much as the elephantine man with enormous wings of García Márquez's story causes villagers to throw things at it and laugh. Nor are angels, Cabiria and others, far from all that is unruly and kitschy. They easily make their way from pagan motifs and folklorish tales to Judeo-Christian ones and back, often turning up in mercantile sites or outright schlock—think of fairies and angels finding their way to the tops of Christmas trees and onto an infinity of Hallmark cards in 1980s America or their many equivalents in postwar Italy.[33] Or for posher, more bourgeois iterations, take a look at the ornamental cherubs that hailed visitors on arrival at the Moreschi/Cevasco household (fig. 2.14).[34]

Even when angels invite laughter, they function like human-made saints. The statue of the saint on which the camera settles at the end of *The White Sheik* (fig. 2.15) is synonymously called an angel in the published screenplay ("Ivan turns to look at Wanda, but his face darkens again as he sees her gazing blissfully at something. He follows her eyes and finds that the object of her gaze is . . . the statue of an angel atop the colonnade").[35] The saint/angel confusion only proves that what matters is not the literal origin of the figure, but its function: Ivan and Wanda can make their transition to the married life that should have begun the day before because it is blessed by a saint or an angel or by both. Effectively, as Giorgio Biancorosso points out, they can remarry in what might be thought of as a comedy of remarriage.[36] And thus, too, they can exit the comical envelope that enfolds the bulk of the film.[37]

Throughout it, and through all its escapades and capers in and out of the hotel, the desk clerk—played by none other than Giulio Moreschi himself—reappears regularly, periodically sidling up to his madcap guests like a revolving animatronic figurine in a toy carrousel to ask if they want to buy a postcard (fig. 2.16).[38] By the time this was filmed, Giulio had greatly expanded in girth, and his leering attempts to sell Roman postcards to provincial guests make good fun of the Fellinian trope of the provincial in the city, or what

Figure 2.14. Ornamental cherubs at via Lungotevere degli Anguillara 11. Moreschi-Fellini Archive.

Figure 2.15. Film still of the saint on which the camera settles at the end of *Lo sceicco bianco*, called an "angel" in the published screenplay.

Figure 2.16. Film still of the hotel clerk played by Giulio Moreschi, described in the credits of *Lo sceicco bianco* as one of several "nuovi attori," here shown asking guests if they want to buy a postcard.

Aldo Tassone summarized when he wrote that "province and city become 'a provincial in the city' in all the films of Fellini."[39]

Like *The White Sheik*, Fellini's next feature, *I vitelloni*, set in a small town reminiscent of Rimini, entwines the provincial who goes to Rome with the sacred vernacular, despite vast differences of plot, genre, and character. The film features five aimless, middle-class young men, a gang of lazy layabouts, who perform a fictive version of Fellini's youth while performing some more or less explicit version of themselves. Or add the diffident, feckless Riccardo Fellini to volcanic Federico, and the film is almost a double (auto)biography, staged as a reminiscence about the escapades of young provincials relocated in the subjunctive mood as collective symptom of the authorial self Federico and his ego opposite, Giulio and Vittoria's son-in-law, the tenor "Riccardo."[40]

Thus seeded in patches that multiply Fellini's status as autobiographical auteur, the film is an early incarnation of Calvino's observation that with Fellini, "the concept of autobiography has become the concept of cinema."[41] Fellini explained how this relates to a Fellinian youth.

> I left Rimini when I was seventeen. I really didn't know the young men who hung around the street corners, the "lady-killers" I portray in *I Vitelloni*, but I would observe them. They were older than I, so they weren't my friends, but I wrote about what I saw of them and their lives, and what I imagined. For a young man in Rimini, the life was inert, provincial, opaque, dull, without cultural stimulation of any kind. Every night was the same night.
>
> These overgrown calves, which is what the title means literally, haven't been weaned yet, but they are already wonderfully able to get into trouble.[42]

The film, made over a decade after the brothers' move to Rome, is hardly a diplomatic copy of their lives, but a rather an "invenzione," based on blurred and partial memory and "real" only in the sense Fellini intended in declaring to his fellow scriptwriter, "What we've invented is all authentic."[43] Even the small town depicted, filmed in a series of different locations (Florence, Ostia, Fiumicino, etc.) both *is* Rimini and is a *projection* of it. In that imagined space, a gang of five girl-chasing, prank-pulling, troublemaking young men is caught in the present progressive (and regressive) of lazy seaside summers, idle do-nothing big shots too big for their britches.[44] Only for those who are not permanently stuck in the provinces can a mythological Fellinian arc uncurl, taking the provincial to the new space-time of the city. Hence, the film ends with the most contemplative and least deluded of the *vitelloni*, Moraldo (Franco Interlenghi), carrying his baggage to the train station,[45] though not without the supplement of the sacred vernacular. Where the castrato, many years beforehand, had received the sobriquet of "angel" after arriving in Rome, Moraldo departs for Rome with the blessings of one — a blessing that lets him begin shaking off the official church under which the *vitelloni* are continually buckling.

Early on, the film revisits this persistently middle-class religious vernacularism when the leader of the gang, Fausto (Franco Fabrizi), tries to run out on his pregnant girlfriend, Sandra (Eleanora Ruffo), who is also Moraldo's sister. Sandra's predicament echoes that of Sandra (Alessandra) Moreschi nine years earlier, in June 1944, when she married Riccardo Fellini at age seventeen (apparently not yet pregnant, but very soon to be).[46] And Riccardo, like the other *vitelloni*, will stay in the provinces because he is one of them, one of the "nobodies," as another *vitellone* Alberto (again played by Sordi) puts it when he laments "We're all nobodies."[47]

And yet, what proves fatal are the compulsive attempts by the most reckless nobody, Fausto, to realize the fantasies of the Latin lover. Early on, while Fausto is packing his bags to make his escape from a shotgun wedding, his father gets wise to what's happening and comes down on him like a jackhammer: "You scoundrel! I swear on your poor mother's grave that this is the last dirty trick you'll pull! That girl's father is a gentleman like me! He worked all his life... to support his family with honor! I'll drag you to church myself. [*almost sobbing*] You'll see, I'll kick you there myself."[48] With vein-bulging, working-man's wrath, he orders Fausto to stay and make things right, for in traditional Italian society, "official" sex is designated for marriage, and any sex destined to become visible should redound to the honor of the Catholic family. The scoundrel slinks outdoors, where he's consoled by his pals—all but the clownish Alberto, who is convulsed in rude laughter.

Cut to the "matrimonio riparatore" where the narrator—Fellini himself—announces in voiceover, "So they got married, and it was a lovely wedding, if readied a bit quickly. Riccardo sang Schubert's 'Ave Maria' and made everyone cry." Making everyone cry is what mobilizes the machinery of the sacred vernacular. And just then, floating out of the organ loft, is the same tenor Giulio had trained to sing with what Hegermann-Lindencrone called "a tear in every note and a sigh in every breath."[49] Fellini again gives the backstory:

> I sang until my younger brother, Riccardo, started school. He sang much better than I did. He had a truly beautiful singing voice. It was a gift. The teachers all exclaimed, rightfully, about how wonderful it was....

> ... he used his gift to sing at our friends' weddings, as he does at the wedding in *I Vitelloni*. His voice brought him pleasure, but I think because singing came so naturally to him, he didn't value it enough. He was good enough to sing professionally at the opera instead of just at the weddings of our friends, but he didn't have that kind of drive.[50]

Riccardo's singing wafts over the scene during a classic Fellinian backtracking shot that passes from the bride's mother weeping into a handkerchief to the groom's father looking somber and disgraced. The camera settles on the altar, where the kindly small-town priest blesses the newlyweds with cloying sincerity: "You cannot imagine with what joy, in this moment, I join you in matrimony, you dear Fausto and you dear Sandra" (fig. 2.17).

Sympathetically, Fellini takes aim at all the churchly doings that stifle the town's youth. Exiting the ceremony, Alberto crowds the bride out of the photographer's view when he moves in to congratulate the groom (fig. 2.18), a suggestion that he and the other *vitelloni*, far from being saved by the church, are forever doomed to their small-town hijinks, failures, and disappointments. Ultimately, only Moraldo can escape, by deploying what Fellini calls "drive." An early confirmation of that comes in the wedding scene, when he's shown in a deadpan close-up, gazing upward at Riccardo's angelic voice, already a sentient observer (fig. 2.19).[51]

Before Moraldo can realize that drive, the film involves him in a last bit of the tragicomical mischief that ends with a failure of will that marks the *vitelloni* through and through. Enter the life-sized gilded angel that functions as a recurring motif in the diegesis. It first appears after Fausto—now married to Sandra and working a patronage job as a sales assistant selling angels and other upscale tchotchkes in an antiquities shop owned by a friend of his father-in-law's—gets himself fired for trying to seduce the boss's wife, to the fury and shame of his in-laws. Soon afterward, Fausto gets the idea of retaliating by spiriting the angel from the shop's attic storage with Moraldo's help. He tries to palm it off on a convent

Figure 2.17. Film still of the cloyingly sincere small-town priest who marries Fausto (Franco Fabrizi) and his pregnant girlfriend Sandra (Eleanora Ruffo) in *I vitelloni*.

Figure 2.18. Film still of Alberto (Alberto Sordi) crowding the bride and groom out of the photographer's view in *I vitelloni*. Riccardo (Riccardo Fellini) appears on the left.

whose young novitiate is enamored with it, but who declares, a bit blasphemously, "We already have enough angels"—whereupon it ends up being venerated by the madman as the Madonna.

In the film's final episode, Moraldo, irremediably tired of his dead-end life, finds himself walking to the train station at the liminal hour of dawn. En route, he encounters the angel once again and lifts it up in a recollection of Fellini's frequent assertion that the provincial who leaves the motherland will nevertheless remain caught in the trappings of a vernacular Catholicism that is Italy. Now a sacred medium of transition, the angel takes on a propitiatory function, capable of delivering Moraldo to a new life. Like countless other angels, this one tacitly embodies sacred knowledge and wisdom while offering protection. Moraldo will soon encounter a dizzying plentitude of such angels: beneath Roman rooftops and eaves, on bridges and colonnades, in churches and paintings, at souvenir stands, on frames, clocks, and timepieces, dressers and consoles, cradles and armoires. But his is nevertheless

Figure 2.19. Film still of Moraldo (Franco Interlenghi) gazing up at the choir loft as Riccardo (Riccardo Fellini) sings Schubert's "Ave Maria" in *I vitelloni.*

Figure 2.20. Film still of Riccardo sleeping through Moraldo's departure in *I vitelloni.*

a crucial pilgrimage that lies beyond the reach of the other *vitelloni*, who sleep through his departure, including Riccardo — along with Moraldo, one of the two most directly (auto)biographical characters in the film, according to Fellini.

"Weren't you happy here?" asks the young boy, Guido, on the railroad platform in a shot–reverse-shot sequence that ends with Moraldo suddenly turning to the sleepy city in a contemplative point-of-view shot. His look toward the screen is a look at the suspended life he is leaving. One after another, the camera pans in medium to extreme long shots (fig. 2.20) across each *vitellone* lying in that most liminal of states, asleep as if in a dream.[52] Or as Federico said of the Riccardo in *I vitelloni*,

> Riccardo wants to be an operatic singer, but he never practices except when he's performing at parties, like my brother, Riccardo. Leopoldo thinks he wants to be a writer, but he is easily distracted by his friends and the girl upstairs. Only Moraldo, the observer, does something about his somnolent existence. He makes the only choice possible for him. He leaves, with the

> unanswered question he has just been asked still in his ears—"Weren't you happy here?"—as his early morning train seems to pass through the bedrooms of the people he leaves behind. With his departure, he will no longer be part of their lives, as they will no longer be a part of his. They continue sleeping as Moraldo wakes up to life.[53]

At last, Riccardo is Riccardo Fellini, just as Moraldo is Federico, who said point-blank, "When I left Rimini, I thought my friends would be envious because I was leaving, but far from it. They were perplexed."[54]

Eternal Vernaculars

The sacred vernacular described thus far, eternally satirized by Fellini, is his antagonistic love object, the object of his comedy and the object of his baroque mannerisms. As Calvino notes, what I call the sacred vernacular is elaborated in Fellini's "repressive school-church"—think of *Roma* again, and especially of *Amarcord* (1973)—as well as the "more vague church that functions as a mediator between the mysteries of nature and those of man."[55] Both of these Fellini considered as *his* church, an Italian birthright that carried rights of ambivalence. "Yours is a great responsibility. You can either corrupt or educate millions of souls," says the Monsignor in *8½* (1963)—a film that begins with the image of Guido (Marcello Mastroianni) panicking in a traffic jam and then escaping up into the air with arms outstretched in benediction (fig. 2.21), not unlike the rising Christ dangling from the helicopter in *La dolce vita*.[56] As Carrera points out, the Monsignor's intervention is unsurprising since clergy in the 1940s and 1950s were busy approving, disapproving, and censoring films while trying to woo directors to their creed. Nor is there anything surprising about Fellini's depiction of himself as a kind of heretical believer:

> I believe in Jesus: that he is not only the greatest person in the history of the human race, but that he continues to live on in anyone who sacrifices himself for his neighbour. I know little about Catholic dogma, and I may be a heretic. My Christianity is rough and ready. I don't go to the sacraments,

Figure 2.21. Film still of Guido (Marcello Mastroianni) flying upward out of a traffic jam, arms outstretched in a Christlike way. From *8½*.

> but I think that prayer can be thought of as an exercise to bring us closer and closer to the supernatural.[57]

Irreverent at the very least, the words characterize Fellini's attitude toward sacred tropes, but also those of compatriots who accommodated them with casual familiarity.

Not all were forgiving, and not all for the same reasons. In his (in) famous essay "The Catholic Irrationalism of Fellini," the Marxist writer and filmmaker Pier Paolo Pasolini succeeded in insinuating a critical perspective that permanently marked Fellini as both a neorealist auteur and a neodecadent one.[58] It did so in response to the immense worldwide reaction to *La dolce vita* by glossing Fellini's peculiar brand of Catholicism. Issued in *Filmcritica* in February of 1960, the essay worries over the unexamined life of the mind that Pasolini perceives in Fellini, his inattention to his own ideologies, which therefore slip in and out of the viewer's consciousness unmarked and ultimately slip right by. Hence the label "decadent" that Pasolini slaps on Fellini's tacit ideologies.[59] "Decadent" here denotes intentional exaggeration, amplification, caricature, and *bizzarrie*. It accounts in Pasolini's thinking for the contortions to which professional actors are subjected, as well as the cinematic conditions of nonactors "taken from reality . . . as if in a bare documentary, who are grafted onto the complex organism of Fellinian language with the violence of the most extreme naturalism."[60] It also accounts for something of *La dolce vita*'s "customs and environments," overblown, immoderate, eccentric, or wretched, specifically (to cite one example), in such scenes as "the stupendous images of the miracle with the lights and the umbrellas under the pounding rain."[61]

For Pasolini, actors, episodes, and ambience are all tarnished by these jarring juxtapositions of realism and decadence. Nor are the formal elements of Fellini's filmmaking divorced from them. Pasolini points to how abruptly and extravagantly Fellini's camera moves, from long leisurely takes to fast cuts, from contemplative, lyrical montage to jerky splices, from syntagmatic phrasing to sudden parataxis. As he writes, elaborating the idea through the supple figure of a diaphragm,

> The framing of the scenes and the movements of the camera always create a kind of diaphragm around the object which complicates that object and renders in the most irrational and magical way its insertion and its concatenation of relations with the surrounding world. At the start of the episode the camera is almost always in motion and its movements are never simple. They are *paratactic*,[62] as one would say when speaking of literature. It frequently happens, however, that in the midst of the camera's sinuous and parenthetically subordinated movements, the most simple kind of shot will be brutally inserted—almost in documentary fashion like the quotation of a spoken language.[63]

Nothing, in short, is purely "functional." All is "excessive, overcharged, lyrical, magical, or too violently veristic" and "semantically amplified."[64]

In the next chapter, I return to this notion as it relates to what I've come to think of as *the veristically tinged phonic excess* in Moreschi's singing, a sacred vernacular mode of vocality that is hybridized in multiple castrato traditions as they intertwine with various nineteenth-century operatic ones, specifically, with the newer, emotionally exaggerated tendencies of verismo.[65] The question for now is what makes Fellini's excessive overchargedness not just "irrational" and magical, but Catholic. And the answer, for Pasolini, has to do with the refusal of reason and, above all, the refusal of ideology. Fellini's world is regulated not by any "dialectical" relationship between sin and innocence, Pasolini insists, but by grace. "It is by means of this Catholic, and in a certain sense, naive, almost infantile irrationalism that there appears in Fellini that style which we have called frontal—without internal perspectives and without gradations of moral values."[66] Pasolini cannot accept what he calls "the binomial ideological base of provincialism/Catholicism under whose sign Fellini works," an "absolute product of Catholicism," notwithstanding the grace that marks that world, a grace that has "almost always descended already and is circulating from person to person, from act to act, and from image to image."[67]

Responding to the trouble he got into with Pasolini for being a "Catholic" director (code for "apolitical" and to a degree "*not* neorealist") Fellini intermittently conceded, saying, as we saw, that he was religious in a "rough and ready" way, that he loved Jesus, or that prayer brings people closer to the supernatural, proclaiming his wife the epitome of true Catholicism for her ability to love selflessly or describing the innocent baby-faced smile of Pope John XXIII (reigned 1958 to 1963) as one that simple people could immediately see as "the essence of goodness."[68] Later on, he mischievously parried charges of being anti-Catholic by picturing Catholicism as a ritual comfort, valuable precisely for its capacity to prod its adherents into defiance.

> Being born in Italy how could I have chosen any other religion? I love its choreography, its changeless hypnotic scenes, its precious settings, its gloomy songs, the catechism, the election of a new pope, the sumptuous machinery of death. I have a feeling of gratitude for all the distortions, the obscurities, the taboos which have created an immense body of dialectic as a basis for life-giving rebellions.[69]

In truth, of course, the church represented both the strictures that beset hearth and home and a certain cozy bourgeois comfort. Fellini attested as much in his record of a dream, set down in 1961, where he fawningly asks Cardinal Montini, later Pope Paul VI (reigned 1963 to 1978), whether he trusts him (to which he gets a resounding no) and whether he believes he is religious:

> "Oh, religious yes. . . . You can see in your face that you're religious."
>
> "What stupendous eyes you have. Cardinal," I say, a little coyly.
>
> Now we're at home, my mother and father are both there, it seems like Cardinal Montini has forgotten something and we're waiting for him to show up from one moment to the next because he's coming back to pick it up.

Fellini's "expressionistic amplification of customs and of environments," as Pasolini called it, was thus indivisible from the church side of his Italy and his sacralization of larger-than-life characters.[70] Italy in Pasolini's account is a swampland, persistently sinking its natives into a mire of their own making, one that is ideologically senseless, filled with negligence, the unconsidered life, and saved only by grace as an unthinking set of forbearances and absolutions. And yet most have seen *La dolce vita* as a film that does far more than indulge in hedonism or careless grace. They have understood it as worrying over and finally damning the inability to live unthinkingly or love selflessly, as approving of grace while ultimately being troubled by it.

At the same time, we should note that grace is the very quality that marked the figure who is both missing from *La dolce vita* and most closely associated with Fellini as well as with the Moreschi family that Fellini so often ignored.

Graced by Giulietta

In a vivid photograph from Rita and Fabio's wedding reception, Fellini's wife, Giulietta, strides across the terrazzo floor with a gait of easy self-possession (fig. 2.22). Someone you would choose to brighten up your party, she is the very picture of openness, vivacity,

Figure 2.22. Giulietta arriving at the apartment at via Lungotevere degli Anguillara 11 for the wedding reception of Rita and Fabio, September 14, 1973. Moreschi-Fellini Archive.

Figure 2.23. The principessa Cecilia Borghese, Giulietta Masina, and Vittoria Cevasco have a drink and a smoke at the wedding reception of Rita and Fabio, September 14, 1973. Moreschi-Fellini Archive.

refinement, and emotional intelligence, limbs sleekly muscled, ready to greet the world, her quiet incandescence flaring with life.

A man watches her discreetly from behind. People are always watching, but Giulietta, coifed to perfection and turned out in a chic, slim-fitting frock set off by an elegant purse and gold lamé mules, enters the room with a brisk sense of purpose. To guess from additional photos, she's looking for the bride's grandmother, Vittoria, and the Principessa Borghese, a family friend, with whom she settles down to aperitifs and a smoke (fig. 2.23). It is September 14, 1973. Giulio has been gone for some eighteen years, and Alessandra, following the ceremony at the Campidoglio earlier in the day (fig. 1.3), seems no longer in evidence.[71] Vittoria, now seventy-four, is instead the constant stream that runs beneath the Moreschi family, whose plights Giulietta knows well. It's Vittoria's apartment at via Lungotevere degli Anguillara 11, bought with money from her Genoese uncle (owner of a tanning factory) and long "defended" by her "against speculation and debt," where the reception is held, across from the Isola Tiburtina.[72] The warmth Giulietta feels for Vittoria is palpable. It brings to mind her earlier ties to her much-loved and likewise formidable Aunt Giulia, with whom Giulietta lived in Rome as a high school girl and who later attended her tiny wartime marriage to Federico, joined by Giulio and Vittoria, Alessandra and Riccardo, on October 30, 1943.[73]

Federico often commented that no human being epitomized grace as thoroughly as his wife. After featuring her as Cabiria in *Le notte di Cabiria / Nights of Cabiria* (1957), he wrote a famous open letter to a Jesuit priest, first published in German by a Zurich newspaper in the year of the film's release.

> Cabiria, my most recent creation, is fragile, tender and unfortunate; after all that has happened to her, and after the collapse of her naive dream of love, she still believes in love and in life. A lyrical, musical outburst, a serenade sung in the woods ends this last film of mine (which is full of tragedy),

> because in spite of everything Cabiria still carries in her heart a touch of grace. We must not try to discover just what is the nature of this grace; it is kinder to leave Cabiria the joy of telling us, at last, whether this grace is her discovery of god.[74]

Later, when asked by a filmmaker who of all people he most admired —and after unspooling a list that mixed a variety of notables with clowns and prostitutes—he named those he had left off the list because he admired them so "constantly, lastingly": his grandmother Franzscheina and his "lifelong companion," Giulietta.[75]

How exactly Fellini expressed this admiration cinematically has generated much discussion. Carrera calls Cabiria a Franciscan and the "only true Christian character" Fellini created.[76] At the end of the film, there's a moment when all seems lost. Indigent, having been bilked out of all her money by a con man, but still making her way, she suddenly finds herself walking out of the woods to a street where smiling young people with mopeds are dancing and singing, "innocent as angels," as Carrera writes.[77] It is the lyrical moment of Cabiria's final serenade. And then suddenly great sunbeams flood her with light. Giuletta, at her most iconic, her mascara-stained cheek dampened with a clown's tear, makes a fleeting glance outward with a tear-soaked smile (figs. 2.24a and 2.24b). This is also the Giulietta of *Giulietta degli spiriti / Juliet of the Spirits* (1965), where the eponymous Giulietta epitomizes goodness, despite a deceiving, philandering husband and a set of depraved friends. And there again, we see her at the end, even more disconsolate than Cabiria, but still forbearing, with a tear rolling down her cheek (fig. 2.25).

For Federico, Giulietta was not a stereotypical Christian angel, but a real human being navigating between mundane and religious worlds, always with a touch of comedy. "With her clown-like gift for mimicry, she embodies in our relationship my nostalgia for innocence. When I was in the States with her, after *La strada*, people didn't know whether to smile at her or kiss the hem of her garment. They saw her as someone halfway between St Rita and Mickey

Figures 2.24a–b. Film stills of the tears of Cabiria (Giuletta Masina): a) in oblique perspective and then b) in direct address and extreme close-up, with her smiling faintly, from the end of *Le notte di Cabiria* (1957), directed by Federico Fellini.

Mouse."[78] Liliana Betti, one of Fellini's collaborators in her various roles as secretary, assistant director, second unit director, and casting director, expressed something of the same. Her brilliant interpretation of Giuletta's role in the marriage with Federico appears in a chapter of her 1976 book on Fellini: "For an essentially voracious and eccentric nature like Fellini's, Giulietta is the solid nucleus, the axle guaranteeing its integrity."[79] But this must be read in conjunction with Betti's depiction of Giulietta as a complex and nuanced figure in ways that eluded the minds of less subtle observers:

> Petite as she is, Giulietta has a bizarre temperament, whose contradictory and dynamic alchemy suggests the endless rippling of water, its infinite refraction. She is extroverted, vivacious, melancholy, sensitive, thoughtful and euphoric, sensible and unpredictable, sentimental and comical. The element amalgamating these often contrasting features is a curious imperceptible absence, the slightest shadow of a trance. Giulietta has always reminded me of another person closely linked to Fellini: Nino Rota, who has composed the music for all his films. When I found out that music would have been the most authentic vocation for Giulietta too, the association I made struck me as less irrational.[80]

Figure 2.25. Film still of Giuletta's tears at the end of *Giulietta degli spiriti* (1965), directed by Federico Fellini.

Betti pinpoints antinomies — sensible/passionate, thoughtful/comical, rational/intuitive, devoted/dreamy (with the "shadow of a trance") — that subtend Giulietta's role in the extended family. In a series of photographs, Giulietta holds Rita's hand on arriving at and departing from Rita's confirmation, assuming a maternal role that supersedes that of Alessandra (who takes a back seat), providing a stalwart presence at the ceremony (see Appendix 1: Photo Essay nos. 15, 16, and 18). The photographs confirm Rita's dolorous claim in her unpublished memoir *In viaggio con lo zio*, which fleshes out her relationship with Aunt Giulietta, that she and her mother — a detached, retiring presence pictured with white hat and bag in the same photographs — never loved each other.

One chapter of the memoir recounts Rita's return from London at about age nineteen or twenty with "a new haircut and more than one miniskirt" in her suitcase, noting that she had to "be careful not to wear them in front of Aunt Giulietta" who, though not a prude, nevertheless attended dotingly to the proper appearance of her niece.[81] There were reasons to be concerned, one of which was surely Rita's troubled, broken relationship with her mother.

Another was her premature entry into the world at birth, with serious respiratory issues and no assurance of survival and at precisely a moment that was one of acute sadness in Giulietta's own life. Rita was born on March 20, 1945, Giulietta and Federico's baby Pierfederico (Federichino) two days later. Afflicted with encephalitis, he died the following April 24.

Afterward, Giulietta fixed her attention on her nieces and nephews and put her charitable impulses into other young people through a variety of good works.[82] An amazing episode in chapter 16 of *In viaggio* fleshes out the protective and altruistic sides of Giulietta's character. One day in the early to mid-1960s, Rita, by then in her early twenties and employed as a psychiatrist's receptionist, puts on a flared, polka-dotted minidress and skips over to a nearby auto repair shop to meet her boyfriend, a mechanic she met when her father, an aficionado of cars, brought her along there. Approaching, she hears agitated voices in the back and soon realizes that one of them is Aunt Giulietta. She hides, crouching down low between vehicles, because, as she writes, "Had my aunt seen me, I would not have been able to justify my presence in that place." Just then, she hears the voice of a man and sees the feet of the same man in blue overalls along with the feet of a girl in flats and those of her aunt:

> Crawling, I tried to get as close as possible. Now I was able to pick up whole passages of the conversation. Aunt Giulietta's tone of voice was hard, dry, strange for her, and the man's no less so. I was scared at how arrogant his voice was. This was not the way to talk to my aunt. The girl was silent. I moved a little closer. Now I could understand the full meaning of the discussion. The girl (I could not figure out who she was) must somehow have been a ward of my aunt, who at this moment was fiercely defending her virtues and merits, presenting her as a real catch for the man who might marry her. I felt an unexpected sense of envy for that stranger, but immediately I had to change my mind. The man replied with a coarse laugh. I just couldn't understand who the girl was, because my aunt never named her, but spoke of her using terms like "the girl," "this young woman," "this creature," without ever saying her name.

I was dying of curiosity, but couldn't get any closer. I was sure the girl was under the protection of Aunt Giulietta, who was very involved in various kinds of charitable works, so basically there was little that was surprising had it not been for the peculiarity of the scene I was witnessing. The man continued to use a very contemptuous tone every time he addressed my aunt. Then suddenly, one sentence revealed to me the whole morass. The girl, however shielded, had managed to get pregnant by the man in the blue overalls — no doubt after having taken them off I thought in a sarcastic burst of hostility towards this *incognito*. Far from assuming his responsibilities, the man threw the situation onto the [plane of the] obscene and grotesque. In fact, more than that: he was threatening and asking for money in order to make the situation right by marrying the girl. Or else for a good abortion.

Rita goes on, explaining Giulietta's resolve in the midst of an increasingly tense situation.

The tone had become even more threatening, Aunt Giulietta even firmer and more resolute, the girl exhausted by the tension, lost her pee, which ended up on the garage floor two meters from my face, then burst into tears hysterically. She must have been exhausted with fear and shame. Honestly, I would not have wanted to be in her place, even if I felt envy for her for her at first for having somehow stolen from me the affection of Aunt Giulietta. I wanted madly to get out of my hiding place to defend my aunt and see what that girl looked like. The fight ended there and the three of them left the garage. Crawling out from under the car, I shifted my gaze and saw [my boyfriend] Claudio on the other side of the garage, likewise under a car. He had listened to everything too, and with a finger on his lips was signaling to me to keep quiet. The man in the overalls was the owner of the garage, and Claudio knew about the whole affair. I felt full of anger and sadness, sad for Aunt Giulietta and how she had been treated. Then I understood some of her silences, the reserve that surrounded her and Uncle Federico, the fear of being constantly approached by strangers — though this anxiety about privacy had made them distance themselves a little from the rest of their family.[83]

Rita's text registers an ambivalence about family that had affected both Federico and Giulietta while also marking Giulietta as a she-bear mother type, much as she described herself in an account given directly to Tullio Kezich, likely in the 1980s. Below, she explains how she differs in this respect from her husband and how she developed her character through a precocious upbringing that had her living from a young age in Rome with Aunt Giulia, far from her nuclear family:

> I continued to adore my family without reserve, perhaps I even idealized papa and mamma because I didn't live with them full time. In this I am utterly different from Federico, who hates any kind of obligation, starting with those toward relatives. Papa and mamma never deserted me, mind you. They simply wanted to offer me an opportunity that my siblings did not have. Because of the education they gave me, I have always considered them perfect. I have never heard sermons [lecturing] at home. Indeed, they may have spoiled me, as did my siblings. They kept saying to each other: Giulietta is with us so little, let's let her do what she wants. And being in Rome and the elder sister, I soon became very mature. I was everyone's mother.[84]

That motherliness was an "axle" for the Moreschi branch of the Fellini family, much as it had been for Federico, the girl in the garage, the readers of Giulietta's monthly advice column, and many others.[85]

The Angel of Rome

Of all the angels encountered above (guardian angels, angelic mother figures, angel figurines) only one person was nominally christened an "angel." After Moreschi received the moniker during Lent 1883, following his ravishing performance as the Seraph in Beethoven's *Christ on the Mount of Olives*, it blanketed his reputation, calling up iconic, gestural, and sonic associations that proliferated in Rome in the forms of visual iconography, sounds, and rhetoric, including prayers, figures of speech, wood and stone carvings, porcelain figurines, and music for the liturgy and rituals. Of course, angels also proliferated everywhere on the peninsula, but they were nowhere so ubiquitous as in that mother city of a global Catholicism that Rome had become.

It's unsurprising that the ascription of "angel," indefinite in gender and a mediating figure—should have stuck to Moreschi and become embedded in his living body. Nor is it surprising that he was epitaphed "L'Angelo di Roma" (fig. 2.26). The panoply of funeral rituals that marked Moreschi's passage from life to death included a small art-deco-styled card, preserved in the Moreschi-Fellini Archive, that repeated the sobriquet for funeral attendees who gathered at S. Lorenzo in Damaso to hear a requiem mass conducted by Sistine chapelmaster Lorenzo Perosi and accompanied by numerous Roman chapel singers. As they did so, they could read on the card that Moreschi "departed at age 64, having lived for music through his angelic voice, admired and lamented by all on the seventh day after his death" (April 28, 1922). And they could see on the card's verso an angel writing on a large tombstone the motto "La mort est la resurrection" (Death is resurrection) (figs. 2.27a and 2.27b),[86] a reprint of a French religious engraving that carries the caption (attributed there to the preacher Père Lacordaire, aka Jean-Baptiste Henri Lacordaire, aka Henri Lacordaire), "Toutes les separations du temps / ne sont qu'un rendez-vous pour l'étérnité" (All the separations of time are but an appointment for eternity).

Death turned Moreschi's body and voice into an assemblage that haunts us the way the prospect of death haunts us, as something anticipated, but also bygone that accompanies us in the present, recalling an ambivalent past marked by secrets and misdeeds and auguring a disturbing future. Rather like Walter Benjamin's famed account of the "Angelus Novus"—the figure drawn from Paul Klee's image that stands as the frontispiece to the *Theses on the Philosophy of History*, Benjamin's last work before his suicide and the subject of the ninth thesis—this angelic Moreschi is a figure we might perceive as pointing both forward, toward an unknowable future, and backward, toward a partly painful past. He was remembered in his time for creating raptures, but ones that inevitably conjured

Figure 2.26. Stone that reads "L'Angelo di Roma," laid over Alesandro Moreschi's tombstone by an unknown party. Photograph by the author.

Figures 2.27a–b. Card of April 28, 1922 for Alessandro Moreschi's funeral: a) The recto states that he "departed serenely at age 64 on April 21, having lived for music through his angelic voice, admired and lamented by all"; b) The verso shows an angel who writes in French on a large tombstone "Death is resurrection" (La mort est la resurrection). Moreschi-Fellini Archive.

his violent misfortune and could hardly augur happy futures, blowing listeners "backward into the future," as Susan Handelman says movingly of Benjamin's angel.[87] Nor is the Moreschi angel one made of nothing but lovely airy spirit, like an Ariel. His epithet is founded on a highly charged and eerie body, what Lesley Stern evocatively describes (in a different context) as the site of an "uncanny exchange between body and phantom, flesh and memory, image and flesh."[88]

Of course, the angelic castrato hardly begins *ex novo* with Moreschi. Throughout different times and places, high voices have stood in for angels, hovering, as Freya Jarman notes, between the divine and the mundane,[89] and castrati have had a special place among those stand-ins. Their bodies, like Christ's, were mortified in sacrificial acts of bloodshed that made them unsuited to the business of procreation practiced by unaltered men, but well suited to practices of heavenly musical worship.[90] For that reason, too, physically altered thus, their voices developed as high, pure, and piercing, sonically connotative of angels, even as they "register[ed] negatively racial and sexual difference" and as they bore terrible physical aftereffects. No wonder Richard Wagner thought of Domenico Mustafà for the part of *Parsifal*'s magician Klingsor, self-castrated to suppress his sinful desires for women.[91]

What the angelic meant to Moreschi's contemporaries emerges in writings by the renowned tenor Giacomo Lauri-Volpi (1892–1979), who encountered the castrato voice via a quasi-autobiographical tale by Enrico Panzacchi entitled "Cantores" (1885) that I take up in Chapter 4. According to Lauri-Volpi's paraphrase of it, borrowed virtually without attribution, the castrato

> emitted in his immobility and serenity a fluted voice, light, spontaneous, immune to forcing and debasement,[92] as if pressed out of feeling made sound. Neither [Erminia] Frezzolini nor [Adelina] Patti, two great sopranos of the nineteenth century, had completely satisfied the desire of Panzacchi, who felt that they fell short in the face of insurmountable limits. Instead, this magical soprano, who drew to the vertices of aesthetic emotion a highly sensitive writer of highly modern taste like Panzacchi, ascended with his

> high voice the barriers of the human; he rose towards the infinite with abandon, the ravishment of his whole being transporting souls upon hearing it, all [of whom were] suspended on the thread of this voice).[93]

Although, as I argue, the voice Lauri-Volpi read about in Panzacchi was, if not completely fictional, then at least more likely closer to that of castrato coloratura Giovanni Cesari (1843–1904) than to Moreschi, it still aligned with Roman mythologies of Moreschi, whose voice assumed the propitiatory powers of an angel.[94] In 1918, when Lauri-Volpi unexpectedly passed by Moreschi one day on a street between the Corso to the west and via del Babuino and piazza di Spagna to the east, he interpreted the incident as a portent of good.

> I encountered the sixty-year-old Moreschi in via Belsiana at the same moment in which I was about to sign the very first contract of my career with the theatrical agent Storti. People turned around to look at him. And I heard someone who said, "That's Moreschi." He was an ordinary man, of medium stature, his lips parted in a lovely smile. He would have seemed one of many had his beardless face not been reminiscent of something that, given the profession he practiced at the Sistine Chapel, recalled those curious anomalies who for two centuries had produced voices of unheard-of beauty.
>
> The encounter with the possessor of the famous voice seemed to me a good omen, my having to start my lyric ascent with *I Puritani*.[95]

In my earlier book, I tried to rethink the angel-and-monster ascriptions that have surrounded castrati from the sixteenth century onward. I made recourse there to humans' encounters with various farmyard animals, from the bloody castrations routinely done to produce barrows, steers, and capons, to spectacles of caged beings displayed for rough-hewn, rubbernecking customers, to wider affinities from ancient times to present ones between men and beasts, the metonyms of feathers and wings, and to the elisions manifest in the iconic symbols of eggs, cats, armadillos, pigs, and monkeys. García Márquez's story "A Very Old Man with Enormous Wings: A Tale for Children," which features a "flesh-and-blood angel" viewed by its captors as a "fugitive survivor of a celestial conspiracy," hence dangerous, but paradoxically curative, as well, with the power to heal a sick child, was particularly suggestive for that rethinking.[96] Such powers, I argued, carried redemptive capacities for larger groups, who understood them through tropes of sacrifice evocative of the passion of Christ. And sacrifice, central to Christian and especially Catholic tropology, was also crucial to the repertory of explanations for castration used by castrated singers, who often invoked the need to make bodily offerings to god, church, and prince, even as, in order to justify and excuse their bloody operations, they interwove them with fantastical accounts of injuries that had necessitated them.

What's striking for the more "rational" modern era of the last castrati is that far from abandoning such explanations, they became even more inventive.[97] Confabulations strayed far from explanations for celibacy made by other kinds of celibates (who, if they had cause to mourn, had no need to confabulate), whereas the explanations of late castrati hearken to a more distant castrato past, including superstitious or Galenic medical explanations that had long been common to castrati, especially those from rural origins.

Historically, the precise circumstances of castrations for singing have always been opaque. Hence, it should come as no surprise that how Moreschi's "sacrifice" came about remains a cipher. His native village of Montecompatri, a mere thirty-five kilometers from Rome, might as well have existed in another century, outside of time and place, having been joined to Rome by railroad only in the mid-nineteenth century. Some 2,259 souls strong in the census of 1859, Montecompatri probably had only a small percentage of literate residents during Moreschi's childhood years, and its local traditions were emphatically, resolutely religious, even if mixed with pagan superstitions. Besides the usual daily and weekly observances, religious practices included a liturgy of devotions centered on adoration of the Madonna del Castagno (Madonna of the Chestnut Tree), performed in the tiny chapel residents called

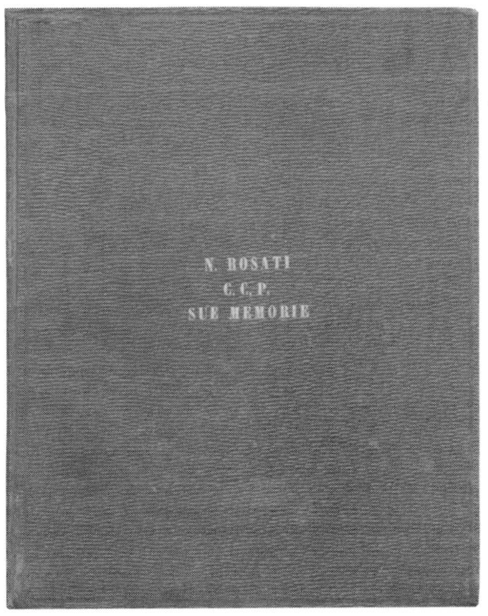

Figure 2.28. Cover of Nazareno Rosati's scrapbook containing his newspaper clippings among other items, left to Alessandro Moreschi. Moreschi-Fellini Archive.

the Santuario della Madonna del Castagno.[98] The town revered the Virgin for her role in sparing its residents from the cholera epidemic in summer 1867, nine years after Moreschi's birth, a commemoration celebrated with a prayerful procession of thanks held every first Sunday in September.[99] And the Madonna made the town a pilgrimage site for visitors attracted by her salvific powers and the sounds of chapel singing—especially of the boy singer.

Until Moreschi left Montecompatri with Nazareno Rosati as Vatican agent and chaperone, seeing to his training and placing him at the church school of San Salvatore, all of this formed part of life as Moreschi knew it. What's unsaid in documentary history, but is, I think, likely, as I suggested in Chapter 1, is that Rosati coordinated with the Vatican in seeing to his castration. Afterward, he continued to play a big part in the boy's life[100] and apparently left him a prized object on his death in 1877: his handsome collection of *notizie* (newspaper clippings of printed notices), hand-annotated and pasted into a large linen-bound album (fig. 2.28), an object that remained in family hands.[101]

The long-term damages caused by castration — bone ailments, mental anguish, moodiness, and melancholia — were compounded by the elimination of castrati from lines of filiation. From that perspective, Moreschi's familial and hereditary strategies read as courageous, optimistic adaptations. His marriage to Guendalina and his arrangement with her father, Pietro, to become coconcessionary of the large tomb at Cimitero del Verano four years later testify to that. Marriage, an elegant tomb, posh housing, and fancy outings added up to bourgeois respectability, consolidated by Moreschi's high standing as a singer. He could look forward to life with a family to whom he could make important bequests. But then came the disturbances, disappointments, trauma, grief, and shame that mark his middle years, which in hindsight seem inevitable.[102]

A State Apart

Given all this, Moreschi might seem to align with what the ancient Romans called *sacer*: sacred in the sense of being set apart, consecrated, and hallowed, yet thereby accursed. And although he was sacred, in various ways and even embodied aspects of what Giorgio Agamben calls "bare life," he was quite unlike the ancient Roman figure of the *homo sacer* whom Agamben famously (and not uncontroversially) took up, a figure who could be killed by anyone, but not offered in sacrifice.[103]

What's nevertheless striking, I would argue, is that both figures were marked by difficulties and paradoxes wound up in the dialectical machinery of sovereignty — something Agamben analyzes in connection with the *homo sacer* and that I've analyzed in connection with castrati.[104] Consider that even after papal sovereignty collapsed formally in 1870, sovereignty continued to exert itself during Moreschi's early years through the new Italian state, which collaborated intimately with the Catholic Church and sanctioned it socially and legally. Not only that, but it was precisely within the post-Risorgimento orbit of the state apparatus that the last castrati functioned. Even as they were increasingly absorbed into everyday life, especially after 1891, they were nevertheless subject to the operations of a *state machine* that assigned them existence in something of a *state apart*, not unlike Agamben's widely cited "state of exception." Where that "state apart" marked their relationship to the world around them, the state machine produced and regulated it, even regulating the politics of memory that eventually consigned castrati to a decades-long near-oblivion.

To think further about their abjection in the face of state machinery, it will be useful to make a brief detour to a tale told by Agamben in chapter 9 of *The Open: Man and Animal*. The tale recounts how in 1874, a prominent German naturalist philosopher proposed (in his *Anthropogenie*) that "man" evolves from apes, albeit *without languages*, as a kind of *ape-man* (*Homo alalus*), but how in 1891, an equally prominent German linguist inverted the terms, claiming that man originally evolved *with language*, as a kind of *man-ape* (*Homo glalus*). The story smacks of the age-old contest over what determines humanness, one in which language wins out, because more than anything else, it predicates humanness on a belief in the exceptionalism of "man." But the moral of Agamben's tale is something else. By being proposed first as a languageless "ape-man" who precedes humans evolutionarily, as the naturalist Ernst Haeckel had it, but then being changed to a "man-ape" in the Darwinian reckoning of linguist Heymann Steinthal, humans of these two kinds became part of the same dialectic. Although superficially different, both were made to function within a single evolutionary and conceptual system.

The takeaway for our themes lies in the fact that since both Stein thal and Haeckel were wedded to nineteenth-century humanist anthropologies, both had to judge humans as derived from and partially akin to a *cognate nonhuman*. It hardly matters whether what's privileged is a speaking ape who is really a man or the man who speaks like an ape—not only because (as Agamben rightly says) "the animal-man and the man-animal are two sides of a single fracture," but above all, because what counts in both versions is the requirement that the category of the human contain an alien and repudiated part.[105] Neither can do without this irremediable fracture, produced by what Agamben names an "anthropological machine."

For our purposes, I would also stress that their historical situatedness is highly relevant: both adduce their visions in later nineteenth-century Europe. The problematic of the man-ape/ape-man figure emerges at the same time that castrati are under near erasure, a time that coincides with Lombroso's devastating scientistic criminal anthropology, which is not divorced from the state machine insofar as the state deals with the criminals that Lombroso's theories set out to finger. What matters is that castrati are lingering and then passing out of existence at the very historical moment when terrible anxieties arise over the epistemological and bodily zones of indeterminacy in which humans reside—one where humans in the by-then more epistemologically precarious Global South are apt to occupy a less stable place than in the Global North.

Here it's useful to extend Agamben's dialectical thinking, for this is a zone in which his notion of an *outside*—in our case, what's "captured" and castrated, but then *prohibited, discounted, or eliminated*—can explain its very exclusion by an *inside*, namely, what's *counted, sanctioned, and embraced.* In the present context, we can conceive the "inside" as consisting of unaltered boys and men, but moreover of the papacy and the state that desperately and rather suddenly come to need those unaltered males to replace altered male sopranos, thus excluding this terrifying outside.[106] By this means, we also can start to approach the logic of the outsider, exemplified paradigmatically not by the late castrato, but by the mid-twentieth-century Jew who, by being ingathered and consumed in the murderous "capturing" projects of Hitler and Mussolini, comes to epitomize bare life.[107]

The adjacency of castrati to Jews, animals, Blacks, foreigners, and other outsiders, partial though it may be, hardly needs explanation and indeed has been noted elsewhere.[108] But what of the role of the sovereign and of the state of sovereignty with respect to such figures of alterity and precarity? Move closer to our time, and we go from what seems superficially to be a harmless discovery of paleontology to the malicious turning of the Jew into what Agamben deems the ultimate "non-man produced within the man." In this gloss, the human produces the inhuman, historically in the forms of slaves, "foreigners," and "barbarians" and nowadays in the forms of prisoners, refugees, trafficked women, and caged and maligned immigrants, all of whom are oppressed by sovereign others.

The condition of the late castrato cannot be assimilated to such figures except in one important sense: namely, that the castrato emerges at the point where the fully human person ought to exist, but where instead, to quote Agamben, "there is only the place of a ceaselessly updated decision" in which breaks in the chain of connection from animal to human are "always dislocated and displaced anew."[109] What *fails to belong* and *cannot belong* in this neither-this-nor-thatness is not human life exactly, nor is it animal life, but rather a distinctly reduced life obtained by bloody means. Like clowns and prostitutes — but perhaps even more invariably bloody in his emergence than they — the castrato, I would argue, was quite literally born out of his relegation to such a state through *othering, displacement, and Catholic sacralization* (reworked as sacrifice) that is also an *abasement, (de)privation, and accursedness.*

In Moreschi's time, that relegation was enacted by the Catholic Church as sovereign through the state's approbation of the papacy, even after the pope was formally deposed on September 20, 1870, the day when the Papal States under Pope Pius IX met with definitive defeat and the Italian peninsula was unified under King Victor Emmanuel II of the House of Savoy, effectively ending the Risorgimento.[110] And yet even in the face of such inauspicious developments — the dissolution of the Papal States and a pope turning himself into a prisoner in the Vatican palace while desperately trying to hold onto power — both church and pope retained considerable power and distinction, far more than either may have feared.[111]

Indeed, in 1871, papal sovereignty was still strong enough to accommodate a castration. It was strong enough that the church could exercise what Michel Foucault, Agamben, and others have called *biopolitical power*, that is, political power over life, and what elsewhere, following Achille Mbembe's notion of necropolitics, I call *castropolitical power*.[112] That means not the power to kill (as in Mbembe's "necropolitical power") but to *castrate*, a right that the church clearly, but secretly arrogated to itself. By the early to mid-nineteenth century, the deployment of that power had reverted from other parts of Italy and other sovereign bodies or their proxies and settled exclusively in the papal see as heart and motherland of the Catholic Church, whose power over life cannot be pried apart from this particular category of the sacred.[113]

On this view, the castrato is not just Other, but the Other inside us. He exists at the border between noise and song, exotic others and civilization, mythical notions of bodily integrity and equally mythical notions of bodily damage. Historically, he had also resided geographically between an imagined Mediterranean and an imagined Atlantic, or more specifically, as Bonnie Gordon (partly following Serena Guarracino) has argued: between Italy and the "torrid zone."[114] This explains why when choral "clerics" who were members of the Cappella Sistina, including castrati, were newly allowed to marry in 1891, they were in a meaningful sense *desanctified*, made formally speaking less sacred or unsacred. That desanctification was likely the reason Moreschi's marriage was possible at all, even in the quasi-clandestine form in which it took place, at home, rather than in church or even in a civil office. And it certainly explains why Moreschi wanted to modernize his condition thus, making his status sacred, but normative, through marriage, and also in a sense vernacularizing it. Paradoxically and poignantly, it explains why the late Roman castrato could no longer be part of a pervasive sacred vernacular tropology, which hinged on tokens of the familiar—innocuous comforts that would not threaten the "inside," but rather console it.

CHAPTER THREE

Haunting Voices

Moreschi represented the most suggestive phenomenon of a whole epoch, for he had an unmatchable expression, albeit in the midst of chaotic forms of art where the choicest classical music was confounded with the most vulgar baroquisms. Can one speak of white voices without mentioning the most beautiful voice that perhaps nature ever deepened with such riches in the human throat?

—Private communication from Giovanni Gavazzi
to fellow falsettist Alessandro Gabrielli, April 18, 1918

To perform in the glare of arc lamps while simultaneously meeting the demands of the microphone is a test performance of the highest order. To accomplish it is to preserve one's humanity in the face of the apparatus.

—Walter Benjamin, "The Work of Art in the Age
of Technological Reproducibility"

Phonographic Loss

Few voices in the history of Western singing have so disarmingly sounded the past or haunted the present as those of castrated males. Reports on castrato voices are overrun with tropes of loss and haunting.[1] When Rossini famously lamented, "Alas for us, we have lost our bel canto," loss of bel canto served as an alibi for loss of castrati.[2] Moreschi's contemporary Vernon Lee (Violet Paget, 1856–1935) repeatedly voiced her obsession with the aural specters of past castrati: "Sometimes the vague figures of those we have never heard, and never can hear, will almost haunt us."[3] One singer who particularly did so, long gone and totally inaudible, loomed large in her imaginings: "And of all these dim figures of long-forgotten singers which arise, tremulous and hazy, from out of the faded pages of biographies and scores, evoked by some intense word of admiration or some pathetic snatch of melody, there is one more poetical than the rest — for all such ghosts of forgotten genius are poetical — that of Gasparo Pacchierotti, who flourished just a century ago."[4] Her Pacchierotti, like the castrati Rossini pined for, was a site of yearning, of insatiable longing for something exquisite and uncanny in its very lack of presence.

Lee lived outside Florence from 1889 onward, but had visited Italy more than once beforehand. As a child of twelve, in about 1870, she heard Pacchierotti's living avatars during Christmas festivities at the Sistine Chapel, as Jessica Peritz notes. The passage that reveals this, recounting the interminable wait after arriving at the church, is worth quoting at length. The wait began with

> hours that seemed an endless dream under the immense cupola, shimmering blue and white and gold, where the sunbeams, through the haze of incense, struck upon the huge gold letters "Tu es Petrus". Endless, endless; until at last there echoed through the vastness of the place the quavering notes of singers, the shrill blasts of trumpets; and there became visible, moving above the heads, above the sheen of the bayonets and the halberts, the great fans of ostrich feathers, the golden tassels and the gently swaying throne, the white splendor of the pontifical robes and jewels. The trumpets shrilled through the cupola, the incense rose in great blue wreaths. . . .
>
> From that moment everything seemed changed. I was wild to be taken to all the ruins, where, among the vine roots and the dry thistle flowers, I hunted for bits of porphyry and *giallo antico*, for scraps of scarlet and blue plaster hidden under the rubbish and weeds. I was wild to be taken into those dark, damp little churches, resplendent with magic garlands and

> pyramids of lights, and full of long, sweet, tearful, almost infantine notes of voices, whose strange sweetness seemed to cut into your soul, only to pour into the wound some mysterious, narcotic balm.[5]

If she went to those churches to hear sweet, tearful, infantine voices, she never wrote about them again. Too alive, too wholly present, one imagines; too liable to spoil her reveries by undoing the sounds she cradled so lovingly in her mind. As Peritz shows, Lee often remarked that empathic connections in art are formed from memories of what one yearns for, and not from what *is*, not least in her musings on Pacchierotti. Indeed, her aesthetics of music came to be premised on what Peritz describes as "the interplay between bodily sensations, affective memory (if not yet so-called), and historical knowledge."[6] Yet accordingly, her aesthetic writings also hanker after tangibles mobilized by what Bonnie Gordon calls (playing on Derrida) a "case of archive fever."[7] Archive fever pushed her to search continually for a not-thereness that inevitably left her "troubled," since it was a mirage that she was seeking.

Later on, another witness did go to Rome and the Vatican and for the express purpose of hearing Moreschi. It's time to turn for a close look to Franz Haböck, Austrian son of a senior postal worker who studied medicine before dropping out to follow his passion for music and become a respected singing teacher. Haböck married a PhD mathematician and became an esteemed board member of the Viennese Society of Friends of Music (Gesellschaft der Musikfreunde in Wien). He was not just a practitioner, but an astute listener, a person of learning who held further memberships in the Viennese Music Society (Wiener Tonkünstlerverein) and the Austrian Society for Experimental Phonetics (Österreichischen Gesellschaft für experimentelle Phonetik), among others.[8] In the course of his scholarly career, he published various papers, a book on the physiological foundations of singing, and an edition of Farinelli's arias (widely circulated), as well as preparing the large tome on castrati—mostly, but not only seventeenth-century and eighteenth-century—posthumously edited and published by his widow, for which he's well remembered.[9]

Finding himself at Easter 1914 face to face with Moreschi (whom he'd first heard only in 1911), by then going on fifty-five years of age, Haböck was overwhelmed by his luminous sound. Mere description could not convey the intangible feelings it aroused, feelings Haböck pressed into a sensory and pointedly metaphorical account: "When one wants to describe the sensual impression a voice makes, one might say that it has a golden or silvery sound or feels warm or cold. Moreschi's voice can only be likened to the clarity and purity of crystal." Anatomizing it, he added:

> The absolute evenness and timbral unity of his sound, its unusually powerful, clear, transparent, and sweet tone, completely different from a woman's or boy's voice, the complete effortlessness with which, because of his apparently inexhaustible air supply, one almost physically empathizes [with it] all awoke in me a compelling impression of the most beautiful wind instrument ever given life by human breath.... When his voice rose above the choir in a crescendo, it overpowered the boy sopranos as completely as a searchlight outshines a little candle.[10]

However powerful, the encounter did not prevent Haböck from craving the sounds of a castrato past, especially since his interlocutors took pains to impress on him the marvels that he could no longer access acoustically: "All my informants agreed that Moreschi's voice in its heyday had been of a beauty and power that they had never heard in a male or female voice."

Like Vernon Lee, Haböck was late to the party, but all the more enraptured for that. And like her texts, his are rife with contradictions. Moreschi had never possessed "the right flexibility for coloratura singing, nor did he have a trill," Haböck claimed, yet he wrote of Moreschi's *Swellton* or "swell"—probably meaning both gradual crescendoing and descrescendoing and including the *messa di voce*, which does both on a single pitch—"was always incomparable." The account has an air of authority, including a scientistic, objectifying feel, but if Moreschi's *Swellton* was literally "incomparable," the equal, say, of the seventeenth- and eighteenth-century voices of Baldassare Ferri or Farinelli, could it really have exceeded theirs, and did it exceed Cesari's and Mustafà's in the experience of Haböck's informants?[11] Tellingly, Haböck alleges Moreschi's bygone *Swellton* as something wonderful, heard by other people before him who continued to lament its passing. The whole collage of words, tropes, and memories rests on anecdote destined to stir up longing and nostalgia. The obscure object of desire is best not experienced in its fullness and presence, the better to project fantasies about it while still anticipating their failure. Ambivalent experience of the present folds over into fantasies of the past, pushing toward a time of "this has been" (present progressive continuous) to which Peritz calls attention in Lee,[12] accompanied by similar misprisions and hyperbolic embroideries. Which suggests that for Haböck, Moreschi may have *had* to lack a trill (though we know that without one, he could not have sung Gounod's "Jewel Song," as Mrs. Hegermann-Lindencrone reported he did) because the trill that *never was* hedges his bets against dreams of bringing the past back to life.[13]

If Haböck inevitably fails as an unmediated source concerning literal events, and even remembered ones, he succeeds at reporting on Moreschi's voice as a subjective shaper of history and memory. It's the combination of audible and remembered voice — voice as remembered by others — that compels him to conjure a mythical past, sketchy as phenomenon, but rich in delineating the overlaps that articulate relationships between voice and memory. Haböck's account reminds us that (as Lee thought) divorcing the two is impossible, especially in the case of the castrato; for the same desire, the psychic lever that propels the conscientious witness toward the present and the *real*, finds the same witness pining anxiously for days gone by.

Prima facie, the complicities between voice, nostalgia, and memory ought to be rendered superfluous by the material fixity of the recordings that captured Moreschi's singing in 1902 and 1904, but theorists of early phonography agree that recordings tend to produce the opposite. Even after fragile, ephemeral formats were replaced just at and after the turn of the century with more durable ones, with improved fidelity, greater technological stability and sustainability, and new capacities for mass reproducibility, recordings still brought with them associations with death and new forms of alienation, especially vocal recordings. Tom Gunning offers a compelling explanation of how recordings were thus allied with voice: "if the technology of recording serves to preserve the voice, it also transforms it fundamentally, not the least through its power of abstracting it from its embodied instance. Separated both from its human bodily source and the moment of its origin, the recorded voice becomes an alien entity, free-floating and re-playable, belonging in effect to no one, or perhaps clinging to whomever hears it."[14] Phonography of whatever era both produces the sounds of voices and causes a divergence from them by removing sound from source in the effect called "acousmatic" by theorists from Michel Chion, Steven Connor, and Mladen Dolar to Brian Kane.[15] The scope and nature of the acousmatic are widely debated, but the hard material fact is that sound recording eliminates direct visual, haptic, olfactory, and gustatory sensory perception from listening experiences, together with much historical context related to sound sources.

Perhaps, then, we should speak of early recordings in relation to a kind of sensory or contextual death. Jonathan Sterne shows specifically how new capacities to reproduce sound using stable, nonephemeral mechanisms were wielded at the turn of the century to preserve the voices of those who would eventually (often soon) be gone, or to preserve them before their decline. The vanguard of this preservationist era in sound recording was about 1900–1901, when flat shellac records in ten-inch formats could newly permit recordings of circa three minutes, made using horns and cutting styluses, replacing wax cylinders and other ephemeral technologies with more durable ones just before the first Vatican recordings.

As newfound abilities to reproduce sound stabilized and became the norm, they aligned, Sterne shows, with nonsonic technologies of preservation.[16] "New, innovative recording equipment and media were developed with the specific aim of producing longer-lasting recordings. In this respect, sound recording followed innovations in other nineteenth-century industries like canning and embalming."[17] Sterne pursues this line of inquiry not as a technological determinist in the manner of Friedrich Kittler—not, for instance, to claim that our neuropathways were remade in the process—but as a historian observing the material genealogies of preservationist tendencies in heaps of documents, contemporaneous with those of early recording technology, about preserving voice as a way of contravening its ephemerality. And he does so for an era when sound was starting to be thought of as an archive, reminding us that "for its early users, death somehow explained and shaped the cultural power of sound recording."[18] Embalming or "canning" the voice in some way forestalled death or redeemed it by allowing for repeatability of a kind deemed desirable to the new consumer culture while slowing the decaying process so the voice would stay fresh, "keeping" for future listenings by future generations.

In these ways, sound preservation and the separation of sounds from source look forever forward, going beyond the oft-cited modernist capacity of sounds to travel on their own. What is modern is less that separability per se than the sense that the voice *must* be objectified in order to be conserved, archived, and reproduced on new and different machines by different persons in different, sometimes far-flung places—indeed, to be turned into capital. In 1896, a Victorian commentator put it this way: "The great speakers, singers, actors of to-day have it in their power to transmit to posterity all the excellencies they are so richly endowed with. Art in its perfection need no longer be lost to succeeding generations, who now shall be able to enjoy all its benefit by setting in motion the wheels of a simple machine."[19] Sound reproduction, now understood as (among other things) an extension of oratory, could be stored away, to be consumed by future buyers and other listeners operating in the most varied circumstances.

A new kind of presence might be reclaimed as one prize of phonography, despite the presumed alienation of acousmatics, but if so, it's a prize that comes with a price. Phonography, by claiming presence while delivering sound without its visible source, offers acoustic presence—a vivid record of an auditory fact and even an amplification of it—in exchange for a lie that covers over loss. Not the loss of fidelity exactly (not something early phonography could easily lie about), but the loss of the real, of a here-and-now immediacy of the live, never to be regained or perhaps never having been truly accessible in the first place.[20] Recording in these ways also wedges itself between the "real" and the mediated, becoming only more so with the aftereffects of distribution, circulation, replay, archiving, collecting, remembering, remediating. Strangely, then, phonography and vocality are haunted by much the same paradox.[21] Or to think of it another way, recordings of the voice, thrilling, magical, and eternal though they may be, will tend to haunt already haunted objects. Thus, what phonography promotes are not just memories of live audition or imaginings of the voice, but the elliptical assemblage of practices situated between performing, sounding, listening, and remembering.

The many recordings made to preserve the voice artifactually before death also underscored their precarity and turned phonography itself into a kind of death knell. Standing on the other side of a divide from living sounds, phonographic records become present by virtue of their brute thingness, their irrefutability as objects, and by the avid collection and circulation of them in circuits of listening in which they invade retail shops, barbershops, homes, and libraries, devouring space. And yet early shellac recordings were fragile, difficult to store, and often all but impossible to preserve over time. How many have been consumed by fires, damaged in moves, or flooded in basements? How many libraries have deaccessioned them? How many families, businesses, and collectors have seen passions for old records wane with successive generations; how many have been too pressed for space or funds to keep them and so left them in junkyards or alleyways as their technologies became obsolete?

Just such dilemmas shadow a passage written by Giulio Moreschi dictating last instructions for his estate. Ten months and eighteen days before he died at age fifty-one of complications from diabetes, he wrote out a will specifying how his possessions at the apartment that he and Vittoria shared at via Lungotevere degli Anguillara 11 were to be distributed (figs. 3.1a and 3.1b):

> All the photographs of artists displayed in my studio and the autographs of Maestro Perosi that are in a box in the library should be forever displayed to the everlasting glory of my father Alessandro Moreschi, just as his phonographic records should be preserved in the best possible manner in order that the children and all descendants of Rita may know the artistic glory of my father, about whom there is also a scrapbook with all the newspaper articles and notices of his life.[22]

Of this entire legacy, only one fragmentary autograph score of Perosi's and six signed artists' photographs can be traced to the family archive.[23] The scrapbook of Alessandro Moreschi's life and work has long since vanished, seemingly without a trace, along with the family's entire collection of fourteen of his 78s.[24]

A sad irony hangs over these losses. All that Giulio attended to with such loving care, made, and later collected in a spirit of preservation as warrants against loss—the loss of a voice, a maestro, a colleague, a life story, a father, a fleeting encounter with greatness, a memory—all those were the very things that were *not* kept and did not finally prevent the loss of family memory. They went on their errant way, even if the inheritance, including all that's missing, has nevertheless played a meaningful part in the family's legacy.

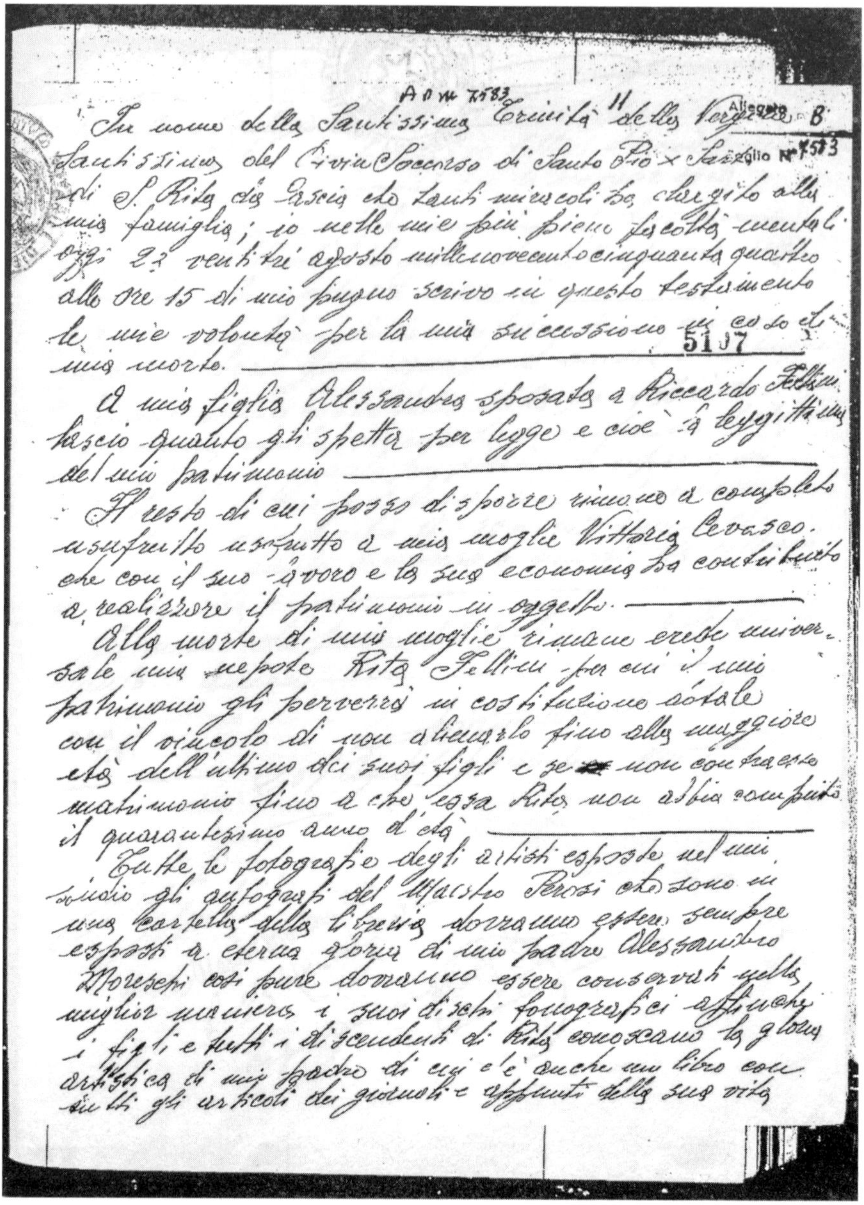

A. Not. 7583

Allegato B

Foglio N° 7583

In nome della Santissima Trinità della Vergine Santissima del Divin Soccorso di Santo Pio X e di S. Rita da Cascia che tanti miracoli ha elargito alla mia famiglia; io nelle mie più piene facoltà mentali oggi 23 ventitrè agosto millenovecentocinquantaquattro alle ore 15 di mio pugno scrivo in questo testamento le mie volontà per la mia successione in caso di mia morte.

5107

A mia figlia Alessandra sposata a Riccardo Pellini lascio quanto gli spetta per legge e cioè la legittima del mio patrimonio.

Il resto di cui posso disporre rimane a completo usufrutto a mia moglie Vittoria Cevasco che con il suo lavoro e la sua economia ha contribuito a realizzare il patrimonio in oggetto.

Alla morte di mia moglie rimane erede universale mia nepote Rita Pellini per cui il mio patrimonio gli perverrà in costituzione dotale con il vincolo di non alienarlo fino alla maggiore età dell'ultimo dei suoi figli e se non contrae matrimonio fino a che essa Rita non abbia compiuto il quarantesimo anno d'età.

Tutte le fotografie degli artisti esposte nel mio studio gli autografi del Maestro Perosi che sono in una cartella della libreria dovranno essere sempre esposti a eterna gloria di mio padre Alessandro Moreschi così pure dovranno essere conservati nella miglior maniera i suoi dischi fonografici affinchè i figli e tutti i discendenti di Rita conoscano la gloria artistica di mio padre di cui c'è anche un libro con tutti gli articoli dei giornali e appunti della sua vita

Figures 3.1a–b. Holograph will of Giulio Moreschi, August 23, 1954, Archivio Notarile di Roma, notaio Alfredo de Martino, Repertorio no. 15297, Raccolta no. 7583.

la spilla e l'orologio del Re Umberto e Vittorio Emanuele
III Re d'Italia con le relative lettere d'accompagno
andranno sempre conservati con la maggior cura
e se Rita avrà un figlio maschio che battezzerà
col nome di Giulio il giorno che egli sposerà avrà
tutto per un regalo di nozze.

Nomino esecutore testamentario il mio carissimo
amico Umberto Giuli esempio di onestà e rettitudine

5118

Le mie esequie siano fatte nella forma più semplice
e economica mentre sia curata la confezione della
cassa di zinco e quanto più possibile le riparazioni
della tomba al Verano di Roma dove voglio riposare
accanto a mio padre Alessandro l'uomo che
più mi ha amato compreso e educato sia nell'arte
che nella vita

In nome del padre del figliuolo e dello Spirito
Santo. Amen

Aristide Moreschi

AAM 7583

23/Agosto/1954 – ore 15.45

Maria Mariani teste

Lucia Marcante teste

Mechanizing the (Castrato) Voice

A spirit of preservation also drove both Vatican recording sessions, of April 1902 and April 1904, in which Alessandro Moreschi was featured literally objectified, that is, made into an object so as to permit new subjective experiences in future times. The history of the recording sessions that were Moreschi's most important music-historical legacy has occasionally been told elsewhere, most significantly in Robert Buning's outstanding thesis on Moreschi's recordings and voice, though widespread misunderstandings about them persist.[25] Jerrold Northrop Moore's biography of recording engineer Fred Gaisberg (1873–1951) briefly recounts the part of the history that leads to the 1902 sessions.[26] Gaisberg traveled extensively with his brother, Will, persuading singers to be recorded for the sake of their fame and posterity, most especially where prospects included commercial gain for the London-based Gramophone and Typewriter Company Limited for which they worked, including niche market opportunities. There was an unforgettable trip to Milan and La Scala in 1899, where Gaisberg was floored by Verdi's favorite tenor, Francesco Tamagno, in *Trovatore*, after which an "enthusiastic mob" "carried Tamagno to his hotel and demonstrated until he appeared on his balcony and sang [the *cabaletta*] 'Di quella pira.'" The young engineer sat dazzled, watching Verdi, Puccini, Leoncavallo, Mascagni, Giordano, and Tamagno stroll by from his perch at Café Biffi in the Galleria.[27] July took him to Paris, August to Madrid, September to Belfast and Dublin. Only a couple of years earlier, Gaisberg had been photographed in Washington, DC, with Emile Berliner and a crew of young hotshots, what today we'd call audio geeks, including William Sinkler Darby, who later recorded the 1904 Vatican sessions.[28] And the travels continued: Saint Petersburg in 1900 and 1901, where they had to record a poor comic singer, an underwhelming balalaika player, and a harmonium player before Fred realized he had to become an entrepreneurial talent scout and lit upon a prodigious bass named Feodor Chaliapin, whom he would return to record more than once.

The 1902 Sessions

In March 1902, Fred and Will set out for Milan with assistant William Michaelis, joining up with company agent and representative Alfredo Michaelis to form a small party of G & T associates. The group had its sights set on opera and especially Caruso, hence, their Italian sojourn began at his La Scala performance. Thunderstruck, Fred resolved to record him, undeterred in the face of the company's balking at Caruso's hundred-pound fee. Since the tenor was unavailable during his run, Michaelis secured permission through a well-placed Swiss guard to capture the sounds of the Cappella Sistina and above all the voice of the nonagenarian Pope Leo XIII (born 1810, reigned 1878 to 1903).[29] The party made a detour to Rome, where Fred and Will set up their equipment in a large salon of the Vatican Palace covered with Titians, Raphaels, and Tintorettos and were photographed beneath the cantoria at St. Peter's (fig. 3.2, left to right: William Michaelis, Moreschi, and Fred Gaisberg).

Capturing the papal voice proved impossible, but they were able to immortalize the voice of the last castrato and his Sistine colleagues, bringing us to the moment the machine enters the life of what Boston's *Musical World* dubbed the choir's "prima donna," whose encounter with the new medium was given form in experiences recounted in Gaisberg's diaries.[30] After their sojourn in Milan, he writes, "We next went to Rome, where we remained five days. During this time we made records of the Sistine Capella [sic], the celebrated male choir of the Pope. The soprano voice parts are all sung by men who have been operated upon in their youth."[31]

This frank account of the sopranos' origins—"men who have been operated on their youth"—comes from a passage of Gaisberg's diaries that was not published in the unexpurgated form quoted here until 1981. An earlier publication, from the September 1944 issue of *Gramophone* magazine, is what Robert Buning aptly describes as "bowdlerized and padded out."[32] Cleaned up for public consumption, it was replaced with a dodgy account of the sopranos:

Figure 3.2. Below the cantoria at San Pietro, left to right: William Michaelis, Alessandro Moreschi, and Fred Gaisberg. April 1902. EMI Archive Trust, Hayes, Middlesex, England.

> The practice of obtaining male sopranos for the choir was discontinued after Leo XIII, and those who formed our choir were simply carefully selected males with natural soprano and alto voices. Well, the choir arrived and made record after record. I particularly remember their rosy-cheeked conductor and solo soprano, Professor Moreschi, whom I then judged to be about sixty but who was amazingly fresh and youthful and boasted of a large family — which greatly interested me. I also remember the haunting beauty of the ageless Gregorian Chants as they were perfectly intoned in those surroundings. My brother Will and I worked fast and furiously packing the waxes as quickly as they were recorded.[33]

Several aporias mar Gaisberg's 1944 revision. For one thing, when Gaisberg made the recordings in April 1902, Pope Leo XIII was still alive, and it was the "men who had been operated on in their youth" referred to in his *actual* diaries whom he recorded, men who still exclusively sang soprano parts in the Sistine Chapel choir. They were not those described above as "simply carefully selected males with natural soprano and alto voices." Only the alto voices were "natural" in the sense Gaisberg means to convey here — that is, unchanged from their condition at birth — while the soprano voices had still all been produced through prepubertal surgeries. For another, the "amazingly fresh" Moreschi was not "about sixty," but only forty-three, though he may well have looked much older, since deprivation of testosterone often led to premature wrinkling. And finally, as for Moreschi's "boast" of a large family, commentators have been understandably bewildered, though the comment begins to make sense in light of the history delineated here.

What's equally interesting, coming from an engineer specialized in sound and acoustics, is the otherworldly quality that (immediately after his 1944 reference to Moreschi's boast) Gaisberg ascribes, enraptured, to the choir: "I also remember the *haunting beauty* of the ageless Gregorian Chants as they were perfectly intoned in those surroundings." A previous comment prefaces that quote with a little historical sketch of the choir's makeup in times past.

The latter starts with an account of how they managed to get in to record it:

> William Michaelis, through his friend Capitano Pecci of the Swiss Bodyguard, the Pope's nephew, had involved himself in a tangle of complicated wire-pulling, the result of which was the acquisition of records of the famous Sistina Capella [sic] (private choir of the Pope dating back to the fourth century) and perhaps the voice of The Pope (Leo XIII) himself. The Sistina Choir then consisted of thirty-two choral chaplains who sang at the services officiated over by the Pope. It was noted for preserving the music of Palestrina and for the beauty of the singing, due to the male sopranos, which dispensed with boy sopranos, thus adding solidity to the singing.[34]

We are supposed to read this believing it's a description not of the male sopranos Gaisberg actually recorded, but of those of Sistine choirs past. Via a narrative sleight of hand, the once-fourth-century-choir slithers magically into one made up of thirty-two chaplains, or singers, of Leo XIII's time who preserve Palestrina in the most beautiful way by "dispensing with boy sopranos" in favor of "male sopranos," reservoirs of acoustical heft that Gaisberg glosses as "solidity." Those male sopranos — castrati, in today's common parlance — whom he claims *not* to have recorded were precisely those men he *did* record and knew he had recorded. And with respect to 1902, their solidity was precisely *not* of their then past, but of their then present.

What's ironic here, of course, is that the truth inhabits a lie. What Gaisberg presents as second-hand knowledge of a time gone by is in fact first-hand knowledge of a certain unique physico-acoustical beauty, narratively displaced to a past Gaisberg never actually experienced, rather than being avowed as the one he did — a truth he acknowledges only in his unexpurgated diaries.

The beauty in question has an objective cause. Since the larynx is highly susceptible to hormonal environments, it remains small and supple when a boy is castrated testicularly before puberty, the laryngeal vocal cords being even shorter than a woman's and situated high in the throat. Once a castrated boy attained adulthood, his lungs, by contrast, would be the size of a grown man's, or even larger, owing to the deprivation of the growth hormone, which often failed to regulate fusion of the bones. As the "power source" for a singer, the lungs therefore ejected air that pressed forcefully against the cords of the larynx (the singer's "sound source") to generate laser-beamed tones of unequalled focus, strength, and ductility. Furthermore, high pitches emitted by the cords upon emission resounded in a man-sized vocal tract, mouth, and nose (the "sound modifiers"), which again could be even larger than that of a typical adult male, owing to a jaw enlarged by failure of bones to have fused properly in the growing cycle.[35] Another correspondent for the *Musical World* noted the consequence of all this (alongside a picture of Moreschi with the misleading caption "Leader of the Papal Choir at the Vatican"):

> In "length of breath" the old male sopranists unquestionably excelled. Imagine a singer with the large chest of Myron Whitney [American bass (1836–1910)] and the small larynx of Adelina Patti [legendary Italian-American soprano (1843–1919)]—a big air reservoir with a small faucet. No wonder they sang long phrases.
>
> In combining beauty of tone with power the artists of the old school were possibly better, though history tells us that some of the greatest of them had imperfect voices. (Pacchierotti's, for instance, was often uncertain and nasal.) I doubt if the difference was great. There is nothing in the florid music of the old school that modern sopranos cannot do except the extremely long phrases and there is some question as to whether the old singers were able to sing chromatic passages rapidly.[36]

Since unsurprisingly, the G & T Company appears to have made no contract for the 1902 sessions with Moreschi (or other singer), we can only suppose that Moreschi not only became their chief soloist, but (because of his celebrity) came to be the only castrato Gaisberg remembered by name in his diaries. Moreschi's solo numbers total four: a romantic art song, "Ideale," by Paolo Tosti, two pieces by now-forgotten nineteenth-century composers of church music Luigi Pratesi and Salvatore Meluzzi, written in the romantic theatrical style soon to be banned from the chapel, and Rossini's "Crucifixus" from the *Petite messe solonelle*, which counted in the same vein.[37] An attractive tenor named Primo Vitti got two solos, a Latin-texted theatrical number by Moreschi's teacher Gaetano Capocci and an Italian rendering of Georges Bizet's "Je crois entendre encore" as "Mi par d'udir ancora" from *Les pecheurs des perles*.[38] A much inferior high tenor/alto, Antonio Comandini, interesting only for his vocal relationship to Moreschi, plowed drearily through four ten-inch sides of a Capocci setting of "Laudate pueri Dominum," accompanied by a piano and a boy choir.[39]

Altogether, the Gaisbergs cut nineteen sides, all of Sistine soloists and choir, fifteen of them eventually published, including three of the rarer seven-inch disks and twelve ten-inch ones. Other Sistine castrati, Giovanni Cesari, Domenico Salvatori, and Vincenzo Sebastianelli, are probably just barely audible in choral numbers, if hard to make out, but notably, Perosi is nowhere to be found—Perosi, whose fanatical opposition to nineteenth-century church music was already oppressing the choir and who essentially forced out castrato codirector Mustafà.[40] All this nineteenth-century repertory—exactly what Perosi wanted gone—emphasized the theatrical a year and a half before the pope issued his crushingly zealous reform encyclical *motu proprio*. And neither were any of Moreschi's gender-bending solo arias in evidence.

Besides the failed quest for the aged voice of the ninety-three-year-old pope, the 1902 recording project emerged as a technological ghost of the Grand Tour, not unlike the exoticizing impulse that motivated Italy's special commissary for fine arts to try to interest the Chicago and London world expositions of 1893 in booking the Sistine Chapel.[41] In Gaisberg's case, the impulse merged with a peak point in ethnographic recordings, a moment when both recording companies and ethnological institutes sought out the exoticist feel of the Grand Tour via a technological ethnography.

That impulse also skirted the edges of the colonialist ones that marked the Gaisbergs' work farther abroad, undertaken shortly after the Vatican sessions. On September 28, 1902, Fred set sail for Asia on a ship loaded with enough recording equipment for a year. He joined a group of passengers his diaries describe as "tea planters, railroad and mining engineers and managers, departmental managers," as well as some young women looking for prospective husbands among the men who were making parasitical money on the Indian subcontinent, where the ship was headed. Events on board included "fancy-dress" balls, to one of which Gaisberg went as a Japanese man, his assistant as a "white-eyed Kaffir"—a reference to the music hall comedian and musician, British G. H. (George) Chirgwin (1854–1922), routinely billed as "the White-Eyed Kaffir" in his wildly popular and blatantly racist minstrel act for which he painted one eye with a white diamond over his blackened face.[42]

Once the ship reached Calcutta, Gaisberg discovered the English there had no interest in Indian music. Again, he took on the task of recruiting talent, but in a frame of mind shocking to most twenty-first-century ears:

> Our first visit was to the native 'Classic Theatre' where a performance of *Romeo and Juliet* in a most unconventional form was being given. Quite arbitrarily, there was introduced a chorus of young Nautch girls heavily bleached with rice powder and dressed in transparent gauze. They sang 'And Her Golden Hair Was Hanging Down Her Back', accompanied by fourteen brass instruments all playing in unison. . . .
>
> We now proceeded to attend a dinner party and Nautch dance in the home of a wealthy *babu*. We elbowed our way through an unsavoury alley, jostled by fakirs and unwholesome sacred cows, to a pretentious entrance. The host and his native guests eagerly welcomed the brave band of *pukka* [genuine] Anglo-Saxons who bestowed such honour on his house. No native women were present excepting the Nautch girls, who had lost caste. We Europeans ate at a separate table; not even our host sat with us. After a rigidly European dinner we retired to a large salon and were entertained by the Nautch girls.

> At this particular dinner we heard two popular dancing girls, one of them named Goura Jan, a Mohammedan, rather fat and covered with masses of gold armlets, anklets, rings, pearl necklaces, heavy earrings hanging from about ten piercings in each ear. Her crowning adornment was a diamond fastened on the side of her nose. Her teeth were quite red from betel-nut chewing. Her chewing habit necessitated the presence of a bearer following her about with a silver cuspidor into which she would empty her mouthful, much to the distraction of her charms. She terminated each song with a most cleverly executed muscle-dance. The lady gets 300 Rupees an evening, and can often be seen driving in the Miadern in a fine carriage & pair.[43]

Gaisberg's "Nautch girls," properly called "tawa'ifs," were courtesan performers, many of whom had lost status after moving from court to urban theater and salon in a time of colonial rule beset with Victorian moral judgment and hypocrisy.[44] Tawa'ifs of lesser status were constrained to entertain in commercial theaters wearing skimpy garb and doing virtual "whiteface" impersonations, unlike elite counterparts, who performed for British male spectators.

Gaisberg implicitly assimilates the leading tawa'if performer, the one he describes as a betel-nut-chewing-and-spitting "Nautch girl," to other spectacles that revolt him—"unwholesome" sacred cows and begging Muslim fakirs—though soon enough, he would capture her on phonograph and (one assumes) on camera, as did he did others he called "nautch girls" (figs. 3.3a and 3.3b).[45] Widely celebrated under the name Gauhar Jaan (1873–1930), she was renowned, after moving to Calcutta from Benares with her Armenian mother, for dancing the virtuosic style of kathak at elegant courts and singing in up to ten languages. Her first performances happened in Calcutta in 1896, and her first recording, a khayal for Gaisberg, was made in November 1902, six months after the Vatican recordings of Moreschi and the Sistine choir.[46] On records and in performances, she also popularized a number of other genres of Hindustani classical music, mastering the art of reducing the lengthy forms to circa three minutes for recording purposes.[47] Not least, Jaan served as a

Figures 3.3a–b. a) "Nautch girl" (Figure 3.3a), captured on camera by Fred Gaisberg. b) Gauhar Jaan (1873–1930). EMI Archive Trust, Hayes, Middlesex, England.

principal inspiration for the legendary mid-century Hindustani classical singing star Begum Akhtar (Akhtari Bai Faizabadi), so-called queen of ghazals.[48] Whether Gaisberg ever sensed the immensity of her importance to the culture and history of Islamic South Asian performance is hard to know.

Over the span of a year, further travels took Gaisberg to Tokyo, Shanghai, Hong Kong, Singapore, Bangkok, and Rangoon (modern-day Yangon in Burma, or Myanmar) in East and Southeast Asia, among other places, and in 1907, he journeyed to Egypt.[49] On his trip east, he worked with his usual "Trojan" energy, Yankee ingenuity, and arch-positivistic determination to document musical sounds in the most unmediated way possible. In stark contrast to his famed mid-century disciple, Walter Legge, who worked to shape the performances he recorded, Gaisberg told colleagues he saw his task as capturing as many "sound photographs or gramophone disc sides" with as much accuracy as possible during any one session.[50] The idea was to enhance sounds recorded through ceaseless toil, capturing them in their ideal form and thereby perfecting the art of recording itself. Recording would thus serve to make the truest possible copies of existing sonic realities with maximally little interference. In this, Gaisberg reveals himself a descendant of nineteenth-century observational science and a staunch early-twentieth-century modernist, aspiring to Lorraine Daston and Peter Galison's ideal of "objectivity" characteristic of scientific and technological currents in which objectivity is achieved by strenuous labor unmarred by human judgment or intervention.[51]

The 1904 Sessions

By April 1904, musical realities of Sistine church life had shifted radically. With the *motu proprio* of November 22, 1903, now in effect for nearly six months, the recording sessions developed along lines ambitious enough to accommodate the aspirations of the reforming Cecilianist church by capturing the largest possible numbers and kinds of artists and genres, sung and spoken. The upshot was fifty-five mostly Vatican-related matrices cut in ten-inch and twelve-inch formats, only a few of which failed to be issued (though mysteriously, various matrix numbers did go unused). By any reckoning, the sessions must also have taken three times as long to record than the 1902 ones, perhaps even more, considering that this time, Darby as engineer took advantage of the rich Roman music scene to add in several non-Vatican musicians.

Signs also point to longer, more intense preparation for the 1904 sessions than those of 1902, which had a seat-of-the-pants quality to them. A contract with Moreschi, drawn up by the director of the "Gramophon Company (Italy) Ltd.," Alfredo Michaelis, on March 1, 1903, stipulated a number of conditions (fig. 3.4): 1) Moreschi would be obliged to execute with "some singers of the Cappella Sistina, assisted by other professors of the patriarchal basilicas of Rome, twenty disks, repeating some already made, to be recorded on Gramophone Monarch," the new "sister label" of Gramophone Concert Record, used for higher-end classical releases on twelve-inch records;[52] 2) in return, Michaelis, as representative and director of The Gramophone Company (Italy) Ltd., would pay Moreschi 3,000 lire, about $17,400 in today's currency;[53] 3) Moreschi was obliged "for the duration of one year, to begin on 1 March 1903 and extend through all of March 1904, not to execute under his direction and not himself to sing into any talking machine in general, and for such obligation [would] receive the sum of 1,500 lire, already included in the 3,000 as in article 2"; 4) upon signing by Michaelis, Moreschi would receive 500 lire as part payment of the 1,500 lire for the engagement, being paid the remaining 1,000 lire "within the month of April of the current year" (1903); 5) the pieces were to be executed within the month of March 1903; 6) "in case of an impediment on one side or the other, the disks would be executed at a time to be established within the year"; 7) payment of the 1,500 lire for the execution of the disks would be paid upon their being made.[54] The singer put his signature to it: "Alessandro Prof. Moreschi."

There was nothing overly cautious about the company procuring an exclusion clause to prevent Moreschi from recording in the months the contract covered since by 1903–1904, Italian singers were making disks at an astounding rate and, by serendipity, he had already entered the pantheon of international recording artists. Yet new G & T recordings with Moreschi failed to materialize during that year, meaning that the company failed to honor the dates specified in article 6. Sessions were pushed back to coincide

1442

Con la presente scrittura privata da valere quale pubblico atto tra il Sig.r Alfredo
Michaelis quale direttore della The Gramophon
Company (Italy) Ld. ed il Prof. Moreschi Alessandro si è stabilito quanto segue: ——
1°. Il Prof. Moreschi Alessandro si obbliga di
eseguire con alcuni cantori della Cappella Sistina coadiuvati da altri professori delle Pa-
triarcali Basiliche di Roma Venti dischi
ripetendo alcuni già fatti da fissarsi nel
Grammofono Monarch. ——
2°. Il Sig.r Michaelis quale rappresentante
e direttore della The Gramophon Company
(Italy) Ld. si obbliga corrispondere Lire Tremila (Lire 3000) come esecuzione ed ingaggiamento.
3°. Il Prof. Moreschi Alessandro si obbliga per
la durata di un anno da incominciare dal 1°
Marzo 1903 a tutto il Marzo 1904 di non fare
eseguire sotto la sua direzione e di non cantare
lui stesso in altre macchine parlanti in genere
e per tale impegno riceve la somma di Lire
Millecinquecento (Lire 1500) già comprese nelle Tremila lire come nell'articolo 2°. ——
4°. All'atto della firma il Sig.r Alfredo Michaelis verserà al Prof. Moreschi Alessandro Lire Cin-

Figure 3.4. Contract made between the Gramophone Company (Italy) Ltd. and Professor Alessandro Moreschi in Rome, March 1, 1903. EMI Archive Trust, Hayes, Middlesex, England.

quecento (Lire 500) in acconto delle Lire Mille cinquecento (Lire 1500) per l'ingaggiamento versandogli la rimanenza cioè Lire Mille (Lire 1000) entro il Mese di Aprile del corrente anno, tenendosi sciolto qualora non avvenisse detto pagamento. ———

5°: I pezzi saranno eseguiti dentro il Mese di Marzo corrente ———

6°: In caso di impedimento da una parte o dall'altra i dischi si eseguiranno in epoca da stabilirsi entro l'anno. ———

7°: Il pagamento delle Lire Millecinquecento (Lire 1500) per l'esecuzione dei dischi sarà fatto all'atto della suddetta. ———

Roma 1 Marzo 1903 ———

Alessandro Prof. Moreschi

with the thirteenth centenary of the death of Pope Gregory the Great, conducted with maximum pomp on April 11, 1904, as climax to a Gregorian Congress at which numerous Cecilianist luminaries gathered in Rome from across Europe. According to *The Times* of London, "The Pontiff was carried into the Basilica [of St. Peter's] in the Sedia Gestatoria [portable ceremonial throne], and with the customary pomp and procession."[55] Reuters estimated that seventy thousand people attended the ceremony and *L'Osservatore romano*, the official mouthpiece of the Vatican, reported that mass was sung with a choir of 1,210, including choristers drawn from the different seminaries and patriarchal basilicas of the city.[56] Performers included the Schola Cantorum of the Benedictines, the religious of various orders and congregations, and alumni of the seminaries, together with foreign ecclesiastical residents in Rome. And in keeping with the Cecilianist agenda, the repertory consisted solely of plainchant, together with so-called classic polyphony by Palestrina, Viadana, and Gabrielli.

Coincident with the shift from affectively charged, often melismatic theatrical music to syllabic music of monophony and restrained polyphony was one made, "on the express recommendation of his Holiness,"[57] from ceremonies involving mass public shows of emotion to a new "absence of any applause or demonstration" from the masses, who were now to display "greater reverence in [their] behavior" (as reported by *The Times* of London). No longer allowed to cheer while the procession passed, onlookers resorted to silently fluttering their handkerchiefs.[58] The new regime of decorum was ritually combined with a new regime of sound through ceremonies that pretended to vaunt Pius's new sacred music as a way to venerate Gregory. By introducing the Solesmes usage in the presence of its Cecilianist promoters, including the Benedictine Solesmes monks themselves, the event could elide Pius with Gregory as dual makers of church music. On a quasi-revanchist side of the historical divide, doing so also doubled the valence of script. *Scripting* inevitably meant both *dictating* immutable verbal texts and musical notes and *pre*-scribing them, including in the sense of commanding a priori that new rules and norms be put in place and followed. On the more modernist, progressive, and industrially advanced side of things, scripting and dictating also meant *inscribing* those texts, notes, and rules not just on paper, but on shellac.

None of these inscriptive forms was wholly separable from or opposed to the others, above all because inscription entailed a reversion to recent, now-exiled traditions in order to preserve them while simultaneously acknowledging new, Cecilianist traditions that harkened back to a Counter-Reformational past.[59] In all cases, inscription also meant making it possible for "the literal Voice" to be "heard in the land," as a 1904 ad in London's Burns and Oats put it.[60] A robust lineup of dignitaries and seminarians participated: Dom André Mocquereau, promoter of chant rhythms derived from neumes and initiator of the famous *Paléographie musicale* facsimiles; Dom Joseph Poithiers, author of the *Mélodie grégorienne d'après la tradition* (1880) and advocate of oratorical rhythms for the performance of chant; the Jesuit priest Angelo de Santi (1847–1922), founder in 1910 of the Scuola Superiore di Musica Sacra; the Baron Rodolfo Kanzler, architect, musical director, and later protocineaste (and as of April 25 a member of Pius X's newly founded commission on the Vatican chant edition); Antonio Rella, director of Gregorian chant at the Vatican seminary and a fanatical Cecilianist; and Henri Laurent Jannsens, Benedictine priest, theologian, musician, and translator, who conducted the Benedictines of San Anselmo during the mass.

In light of all this, it's surprising that the repertory recorded by Moreschi and the Sistine choir hardly differed in kind from that of the 1902 sessions. Darby launched the enormous enterprise by cutting five Moreschi solos, the first a redo of Rossini's "Crucifixus" that recalls the phrase in article 1 of his contract stating that he could execute "twenty disks repeating some already done." Moreschi had probably been aching for a redo since the earlier recording started out well, but ended up in a train wreck, whereas the 1904 take is studiously, almost painfully correct. Following it was a pair of romantic-theatrical liturgical pieces, Ignace Leybach's "Pie Jesu" from the *Dies Irae* and Eugenio Terziano's "Hostias et preces" from the Requiem offertory. Another Tosti art song followed, the religious "Preghiera," and then the Bach-Gounod "Ave Maria" (*Meditation sur le Premier Prélude de Piano de S. Bach*), all with piano accompaniment, plus added organ on the Terziani and the traditional violin obbligato on the "Ave Maria."[61] The net effect was to have captured Moreschi more or less in his natural habitat, insofar as he emerges here as a first among equals, fully prepared to ignore the reformational restrictions in a preservation project not thought answerable to the same strictures as music for ceremony and worship.

And yet what next happened complicates the story further. After Moreschi's solos were finished, the makeshift studio welcomed the starring operatic tenor Fiorello Giraud. In later March and April 1904, Giraud was singing Cavaradossi in a revival of *Tosca* at the Teatro Costanzi (nowadays the Teatro dell'Opera), an opera about which the Costanzi could feel proprietary, not only because it's set in Rome, but because it premiered there in 1900.[62] Included in the 1904 cast were Romanian prima donna Hariclea Darclée from the original production and Roman baritone Antonio Magini-Coletti, a standby who appeared often at the Costanzi over the course of decades.[63] Earlier in the season, in February and early March 1904, Giraud had been singing *Lohengrin* there, and before that, starting on December 26, 1903, Tristan (in *Tristano e Isotta*), including in the presence of the king and queen. Giraud was a big-voiced Wagnerian, what Italians call a *tenore robusto*, but his contributions to the 1904 sessions ranged from Wagner and the veristic Giordano to another Tosti art song, "Oblio." Understanding these different Tosti performances happening side by side, Moreschi's and Giraud's, reframes the castrato, situating him in collegial relation to operatic figures and turning Moreschi into less of a twilight figure and more of a contemporary, sharing repertory, venues, technologies, and engineers with numerous other artists who were drawing on the same repertories on session after session in the early Italian years of acoustic discs.[64]

In further appearances, Moreschi switched hats more than once —doing the solo plainchant "Incipit lamentatio," directing a chorus of men and boys in a "Gloria," and taking a solo part in Capocci's trio "Laudamus te" with added boys choir and two soloists (tenor Cesare Boezi and bass baritone Paolo Dadò). All the while, Tosti remained the red thread that ran through the sessions. Two other opera singers interpolated Tosti songs alongside other songs and opera arias: the lovely, little-known lyric soprano Bice Mililotti, who followed Perosi, and the still lesser-known tenor Aristide Rota. Surrounding a recording of Vittoria's *Improperia* conducted by Kanzler, Mililotti offered a typical mixture of aria and salon song with the flower aria from Mascagni's *L'amico Fritz* and Tosti's "Seconda mattinata," while Rota did Neapolitan songs plus the tearjerker "Il tuo pensiero" by the obscure opera composer Augusto Rotoli. Not to be left out, Rota also recorded Tosti's "Sogno."

Distinct from all this were several "discorsi" (lectures) made on twelve-inch disks, most of them intermixed with cuts of chant, but also an additional three cuts by Mililotti, with "Dopo" as the requisite Tosti song.[65] Kanzler's *discorso*, the first, was, of all things, a celebration of the gramophone record and company entitled "Il Grammofano applicato alla divulgazione ed alla tradizione del Canto Gregoriano" (The gramophone applied to the dissemination and tradition of Gregorian chant), otherwise labeled "In lode del Grammofono" (In praise of the gramophone). Rella's "Preliminary to the practical course for teaching of Gregorian chant" held forth on the teaching of Gregorian chant, ending with his intoning an antiphon.[66] The obsessionally ascetic and reformist De Santi, one of the crafters of the 1903 *motu proprio* along with Perosi, recorded a lecture on the opening of the Gregorian Congress ("Discorso di apertura del Congresso Gregoriano").[67] Pothier made a cut titled "The fundamental character of liturgical chant ("Le caractère fondamentale du chant liturgique") and Mocquereau "The Gregorian School of

Solemnes" ("L'École Grégorienne de Solemnes").[68] When all was said and done, those who were deeply invested in the Cecilianist reforms could celebrate their victory over past trespasses by returning to music as the ultimate register of Roman Catholic ideology and morality.

Presumably, they nonetheless listened to prereformist Moreschi during the congress, at minimum with the Sistine choir, since he was grandfathered and not up for retirement for nearly another decade. What they heard can be gleaned from the recordings, to be dealt with anon. But the groundwork for them was already in place decades earlier in the singing Moreschi did as a young adult in Rome during the 1870s and 1880s.

Moreschi's Vocality, Prerecorded

Many listeners describe their first experience of Moreschi's singing in a language of dysphoria, hearing a voice of unplaceable timbre and a delivery filled with bizarre catches and flourishes and disorienting registral shifts. Like his uncanny body, his singing was as strange to most as the Indian subcontinent was to Gaisberg.

Dysphoric audition of castrato voices has a long history, of course. The late eighteenth century was already hissing with their "supernatural" and "superhuman" sounds,[69] and by the nineteenth, they had turned into psychic phantoms. And as we've seen, Vernon Lee wrote explicitly about castrati as revenants, focusing on ones that could invade her mind's ear because they no longer existed.[70] Thus, it was not by accident that Pacchierotti came to life when Lee stumbled on the garden of his villa, nor that in her 1891 story "An Eighteenth Century Singer: An Imaginary Portrait," the singer took a tangible, if ghostly pseudonymous shape as "Antonio Vivarelli."[71]

The year 1891 was the same one in which the great French diva Emma Calvé (1858–1942) made the psychological trope explicit when she described the voice of Mustafà, then sixty-two, who would soon become her teacher as she noted in a somewhat confabulatory memoir:

> During my sojourn in the Holy City, I often went to hear the choir of the Sistine Chapel, which at that time was under the direction of the last of the eunuchs, Mustapha, a Turk, like all his companions. He had an exquisite high tenor voice [sic], truly angelic, neither masculine nor yet feminine in type—deep, subtle, poignant in its vibrant intensity. He sang the church music admirably, especially Palestrina. He had certain curious notes which he called his fourth voice—strange, sexless tones, superhuman, uncanny!
>
> I was so much impressed by his talent that I decided to take some lessons from him.[72]

Calvé's stumble over the provenance of Mustafà and his colleagues bears the mark of what Jacques Lacan would have described as a hitch in causality, something that limps, breaking the chain of psychic causes because it doesn't work.[73] The giveaway is her depiction of Sistine castrati as an explicitly oriental alterity, woven into a narrative of origins redolent of eunuch guards and Ottoman harems.

Calvé had her predecessors. About a decade earlier, Lillie de Hegermann-Lindencrone noted in her witty memoir, *The Sunny Side of Diplomatic Life*, that she would sometimes sit at St. Peter's "entranced, listening in the deepening twilight to the heavenly strains of Palestrina, Pergolesi and Marcello. Sometimes the soloists sing Gounod's 'Ava [sic] Maria' and Rossini's 'Stabat Mater,' and, fortunately, drown the squeaky tones of the old organ. A choir of men and boys accompanies them in 'The lnflammatus' [sic], where the high notes of M[oreschi]'s tearful voice are almost supernatural."[74]

And yet, creaky organ or none, hearing Moreschi sing Rossini's operatic "Inflammatus et accensus" from the *Stabat mater* (1831–1841) when he was all of twenty-one or twenty-two transported her. Imagine its umbral C minor hurtling along in double dotted notes and landing the soloist's first cadence on a long-delayed tonic (m. 23) in a single, grandly theatrical sweep, or the chorus pedaling away for six whole bars on unison C before giving way to the E-flat dominant and a choral-accompanied cantilena solo in the relative major. Imagine the charge she felt on hearing Moreschi staged in those two big gestures, C minor to E-flat major over the course of that showy A–A' form, her emotion as the movement closed with its triumphant C-major coda, dusky and lamenting at first and then furiously Rossinian as Moreschi dug into his low c's and fired off batteries of trills running up to high c's.[75]

Like other numbers from his youth, the "Inflammatus" speaks to Moreschi's ability to cross over and combine mechanically different vocal functions, including a high and flexible lyric soprano and a dramatic mezzo. It's precisely what characterized a number of female bel cantists of Rossini's time who emerged under the influence of castrati. One of these "multifunction" singers, Giulia Grisi (1811–1869), had actually premiered Rossini's *Stabat mater.* She and others were living and dying by the inheritances of castrato stars such as Farinelli and Pacchierotti, both of whom were known for coloratura, high-pitched and low-pitched, as well as expressive legato in slow arias and strong lower extensions.[76] And all such registral mixing was adopted for a variety of soprano voice types by the likes of Giuditta Pasta (1797–1865, a mezzo student of castrato Girolamo Crescentini), Rosamunda Pisaroni (1793–1872, who went from soprano to contralto), and Maria Malibran (1808–1836, versatile soprano virtuosa and sister of Manuel Garcia, Jr.).[77] They both adopted the castrato's multirange, multiregister singing and in some cases (Giuditta Pasta's and Benedetta Rosmunda Pisaroni's among them) inhabited castrato roles as male characters, recalling a past of cross-dressing that in years gone by had often been forced on castrati.[78]

Nor is the "Inflammatus" the only number Moreschi performed in the 1880s that filtered older castrato singing through early nineteenth-century females. In other numbers, Moreschi impersonated female characters vocally. Most gender-bending was Gounod's "Jewel Song" from *Faust*, "Ah! Je ris de me voir," performed at the house of American society lady Grace Bristed (Mrs. Charles Bristed) of New York, as reported in 1883 by Hegermann-Lindencrone.[79] Its protagonist, Marguerite, newly bejeweled, gazes at herself in a mirror provided by the malevolent Mephistopheles, who plots to enchant the figure of Faust, whom he's turned into an attractive young man. Even such a fan as Hegermann-Lindencrone, on hearing Marguerite emanate from a castrato, found it too much to bear, as we've seen.[80]

Like the "Inflammatus," the "Jewel Song" requires a winning ability to bounce sound nimbly across registers and keep the melodic line up in the air. Notably, it's a vocally flirty number, unsingable without the persuasive trill required from the very beginning of the aria, when the singer has to trill on b' for ten and half beats before swirling up to g" and then trill again on an f-sharp" that spirals up to b" at the end—*pace* Haböck, who (as we saw) said Moreschi never had a trill.[81] No wonder that in the same year that Hegermann-Lindencrone wrote about Moreschi's "Jewel Song" he was also swept into full membership in the Sistine Chapel, following an outstanding performance of the Seraph's part in Beethoven's *Christum am Ölberge*. Different from the "Jewel Song," the Seraph's aria "Preist der Elösers Güte" sung by Moreschi in Italian depends not on lyrical agility so much as on breath control and a four-square, instrumental type figuration in running sixteenths. Among its earlier, albeit far more extreme precedents, one might note the extravagant instrumental coloratura sung by certain female sopranos—Constanze's "Martern aller Arten" from Mozart's *Die Entführung aus dem Serail* (1782) and the Queen of the Night's arias in *Die Zauberflöte* (1791)—but here without their screechingly high or highly acrobatic arpeggios; or earlier still, we might think of the highly figurative coloratura pulled off by such castrati as Farinelli, Ferdinando Mazzanti, Antonio Bernacchi, Farfallino (Giacinto Fontana), and Luigi Marchesi. The Moreschi examples are milder than the storied ones sung by late eighteenth-century sopranos and eighteenth-century castrati, but they share certain vocal demands and cognate effects: florid passages stretched over long spans of time and wide tessituras, held up by the breath on high pitch peaks.[82] They all require stretching and pulling the vocal

Example 3.1. Florid passage with rising trills from Ludwig van Beethoven's Seraph's aria "Preist der Elösers Güte" from the oratorio *Christum am Ölberge* (1803), mm. 82–89. The aria, sung in Italian by the Sistine Chapel Choir with Alessandro Moreschi as soprano soloist, was performed on Maundy Thursday of Lent, 1883. Transcription and reduction by Mark Yeary.

apparatus to its limits, especially for those singers of the Beethoven aria who opted to hazard the *ossia* pitches in example 3.1. (There is no way of knowing if Moreschi did.)

One of Moreschi's disciples we encountered in Chapter 1, the Sistine falsettist Alessandro Gabrielli, points to an aria Moreschi sang a few years later, at age twenty-nine or thirty, that showcases quite a different voice. "In 1888, at the Associazione Artistico-operaia [the Artist Workers Association], he sang the aria 'O mio Fernando' from *La Favorita* [by Donizetti], accompanied at the piano by a young man—that young man being a sixteen-year-old Don Lorenzo Perosi."[83] Leonora delivers the aria in act 3 during a heated moment when she realizes she must tell her true love she cannot marry him. While technically difficult, the aria demands none of the lyric coloratura of the "Jewel Song" or figurative passagework of the Seraph's aria. It's meant for a dramatic mezzo of a kind known from recordings of singers from the early to mid-twentieth century—Ebe Stignani (1903–1974), for instance, or Giulietta Simionato (1910–2010). And in fact, the original version, from *La favorite* (Paris, 1840), was sung by Rosina Stoltz, who had only a two-octave range, from a to a'', but "vocal colour and [a] broad palette of timbres."[84] To make it work—whether the whole scena, with recitative-cavatina-recitative-cabaletta sections, or just the cavatina—a singer has to give it dramatic sweep by coloring its full range. Even failing that, Moreschi could not have carried it off without negotiating multiple registers while holding the melodic line up in the air. A singer working in 1840, not long after the time when castrati reigned in the opera house, would have acquired that kind of skill directly from castrato teachers or else from others who had studied with them and passed down their craft. For Moreschi to make recourse to a Stoltz bel canto aria in 1888 was to act as a kind of spirit guide, connecting backward to the older world of female sopranos and mezzos, who themselves drew on still older castrato singing traditions, all perpetuating their castrato heirs.

Verismo Reengendered

But Moreschi is also up to something different here. Although he spent part of his youth extending earlier castrato traditions as a multivoiced, virtuosic singer who could carry off trills, elegant crescendos and decrescendos, and *messe di voce*, who could shift registers with ease, and who could color his voice with nuance, he also relished a late nineteenth-century emotionality.[85] The recorded corpus helps very little to provide a vocal archaeology of those earlier years when he sang female arias and virtuosic showpieces, for by 1902, Moreschi's voice had wandered into repertories better suited to a prematurely aging physical instrument, with a lower register and a less elastic technique than he'd previously had. What the recordings can teach us about is the feel and style of his delivery, how he shaped performances, and how he used his vocal mechanisms—things accessible to the ear only through the whirring of the gramophone.

To be sure, the recordings may disappoint at first (as they did me), but they force a *volte face* in conceiving how castrato vocality stood in relation to late nineteenth-century singing, perhaps more specifically, Roman singing. The residue that sounds in 1902–1904 smacks, it seems to me, not just of the nineteenth century generally (which it certainly does), but of the 1890s, embodied in an intense expressivity of tears, sobs, gasping *h* sounds, scoops, and glottals. Although various contemporary recordings by female sopranos show touches of something akin to that, the full package is rare, pronounced to a Moreschi-like degree above all in verismo lodestone Eugenia Burzio (1872–1922). Famed for her performances in Mascagni's veristic *Cavalleria rusticana*, with libretto based on the archverismo poet Giovanni Verga, Burzio was in fact, as William Ashbrook writes, a "belcantista with a verista's emotional instincts" (something we might indeed say also of Moreschi). Continuing, he notes, she could "sail not quite imperturbably through complicated *gruppetti*, yet her attention to the significance of the text is exceptionally insightful. It seems as though she is always singing in italics."[86] And indeed, the CD transfers made by Ward Marston make her verismo bonds stunningly clear.[87]

Moreschi may never have heard Burzio live before 1911, but her passionate delivery reverberated around Italy from the time of her 1899 Turin debut as *Cavalleria rusticana*'s Santuzza.[88] On recordings, she regularly reaches blood-curdling extremes that move her into a universe wholly different from Moreschi's, and yet Moreschi has the sobbing in spades. When he sobs the line "Una novella aurora" at the end of his very first solo matrix, the humble seven-inch of Tosti's "Ideale," it's hard not to hear verismo impulses, and the same goes for moments recorded by his contemporaries Giraud and Vitti.

The ramifications of this unexpectedly deepened in one of my talks with Moreschi's great-grandson-in-law, Fabio, whose conversations with me have returned repeatedly to Guendalina's abandonment and financial ruination of the family. In one of these refrains, Moreschi and his wife emerged as regulars at the opera, at least in their sunnier days—something unaccounted in literature about him.[89] A family tale has it that when the castrato and his wife appeared there, people would ask who was more beautiful, the queen or Guendalina, for she was so covered in the fine jewels that had been given her by her husband. On this account, they had to have been attending the Teatro Costanzi, which was regularly attended by royalty. According to the chronicler Matteo Incagliati, on one special night, St. Stephen's Day, December 26, 1903, the king and queen "brightened" the great hall, making it look "magnificent, ablaze with light, all the tiers of boxes packed, and a select and elegant public on the parterre."[90] Whether the Moreschis were there that night, visible in the blazing light, no one knows, nor would Incagliati have reported it. Least of all would he have reported that on that evening, when bright light made everyone visible, the castrato's wife was in her third trimester, great with child.

But what of the shape-shifting thought that while visiting that most profane shrine of hyperemotion, Moreschi was imbibing a certain veristic version of *romanità* by hearing the likes of *Cavalleria rusticana* (premiered in Rome, 1890) and *Tosca* (also premiered there, in 1900)? What if we think that thought together with the image of him singing opera arias publicly at the Hotel de Russie alongside Mascagni tenor Francesco Marconi and baritone Antonio Cotogni—both major opera stars and favorites of Verdi—as Gabrielli reported in an account that explains the presence of Cotogni in the photo in figure 6.1?[91] Taken together, these reports might transform how we hear his singing. They might also shape how we view photographs (previously unknown) signed to Moreschi between 1897 and 1903 by famous singers and composers, some of whom were outright verismo artists whose images figure among the few traceable to the ones Giulio displayed in his studio with such pride. "To the Illustrious artist Alessandro Moreschi, Enrico Caruso. Rome 1903," reads one (fig. 3.5). "To the most dear professor Alessandro Moreschi, with esteem and affection. Mascagni. Rome, 1898," reads another (fig. 3.6). "To the distinguished artist Signor Alessandro Moreschi, Memento of Puccini. Rome, Puccini, 16 [?] 1900" yet another (fig. 3.7).[92]

And yet, as I suggest above, it's not just verismo mannerisms that are at issue. Moreschi's pervasive habit of embellishing scores with octave scoops and fast, anticipatory glissandi of different intervallic

Figure 3.5. Portrait of tenor Enrico Caruso (1873–1921), signed "To the illustrious artist Alessandro Moreschi, Enrico Caruso." Auctioned to a private anonymous owner by Casa d'Aste Babuino in late 2010 or early 2011.

Figure 3.6. Portrait of verismo opera composer Pietro Mascagni (1863–1945), signed "To the most dear professor Alessandro Moreschi, with esteem and affection. Mascagni. Rome, 1898." Hanna Holborn Gray Special Collections Research Center, University of Chicago.

Figure 3.7. Portrait of Giacomo Puccini (1858–1924), signed "To the distinguished artist Signor Alessandro Moreschi, Memento of Puccini. Rome, Puccini, 16 [?] 1900." Auctioned to a private anonymous owner by Casa d'Aste Babuino in late 2010 or early 2011.

spans—effectively "acciaccature"—echoes down a long corridor of castrato singing (though not only that). In my hearing, the habit culminates in veristic sounds, but does not exclude earlier castrato practices. Instead, the two reach us as intermingling traces. I've listened to recordings by about seventy different opera singers Moreschi might have heard live at the Costanzi between 1880 and 1904. Astoundingly, those recordings account for about two-thirds of the singers who performed there in those years. A few date from as early as 1897 with Bettini cylinders. Others start to proliferate in 1901 and 1902 after the introduction of flat-record shellac technology and ten-inch formats, and many others date from later years. Curiously, not one of them exhibits upward scoops with anything like the ubiquity and clarity of Moreschi's. If Moreschi's glottal mannerisms and scooping overlap with the verismo glottals and outright sobs (*singhiozzi*) of contemporaneous opera singers, they do so mostly through the technical mechanism required to execute them. The net result may be an expressive overlap, but the practice of contemporaneous opera singers is not identical to Moreschi's, which written evidence suggests relates to the centuries-long castrato propensity for bounding easily across registers and moreover of making frequent upward ornamental lifts, often from chest to head, on accented notes. Redeployed by Moreschi, who makes them recurrently, they take the form of tiny emotional charges—mini cousins to verismo sobbing, but only occasionally manifest as that itself.

I wonder, therefore, whether a certain vernacularization of emotional church singing, manifest in sacred idioms and half buried in disparate vocal genealogies, "stencils" something "real" off the past, like Sontag's photographs—something real, yet vanished. Even though earlier upward-shooting glottals may have been less pronounced than Moreschi's, as the recorded evidence suggests, a related practice can be tracked backward to early nineteenth-century Sistine singing. Its most vital witnesses are two: Giuseppe Baini (1775–1844), composer, papal singer by 1802, and chapelmaster by 1814; and Felix Mendelssohn (1809–1847) who, during his travels to Rome in 1831, wrote up detailed reports of papal music for Holy Week to his older friend Carl Friedrich Zelter (1758–1832).[93] There are later witnesses, too, as well as substantially earlier ones, but we can start with these two.[94]

During the French occupation of Rome and the Papal States, Baini was recording certain practices of papal chapel performance to preserve them against French invaders, specifically, in his manuscript "Regole circa il modo di cantare le lezioni, le lamentazioni ed i capitoli, e di intuonare il canto gregoriano secondo lo stile osservato dai cappellani-cantori della Cappella pontificia: Epilogate da uno de'cappellani suddetti l'anno 1806" (Rules about the way of singing lessons, lamentations, and chapters, and of singing Gregorian chant according to the style observed by papal singers in the Papal Chapel: Summed up by one of the above-mentioned choristers in the year 1806), a manuscript annotated and later posthumously printed by his student Adrien de la Fage (1801–1862).[95] In part 2, "On the way of singing Gregorian chant," Baini divides into a series of regulatory "premises" those so-called "traditional" practices of ornamentation ("girelli") that he claimed had gained the "approbation and applause of listeners" and that particularly distinguished pontifical singers.[96]

What Baini there calls the "*appoggiatura*" (example 3.2) is mostly consistent with what the term means today (not all sources use the word this way, as we will see)—that is, a note that descends by step after the essential note is approached by a rising third, fourth, or even fifth. (In the examples that follow, ornaments appear as diamond-shaped notes.) Yet importantly, "appoggiatura" turns out to be something of a catch-all for four different types of related ornaments. A second type, "vernacularly called a *zampetto*," descends from ornamental to essential note by third.[97] A third, the grace note called a "*mordente*"—confusingly, nothing like our modern "mordent," but most relevant to Moreschi's vocality—leaps up to the essential note by fourth, as in example 3.3 (see the part marked "Si canta" meaning how the notated example should be sung), although it can also leap up by third, sixth, and other intervals.[98] Coming fourth is the "trillo," which denotes precisely what we moderns understand to be a trill (Baini notates it more than once).[99] By way of summation, Baini provides an example showing all four types of ornamentation with the rubric: "One can recapitulate in a single example the appoggiatura, the zampetto, the mordente, and the trillo" (example 3.4).[100]

Further on, Baini adds a rueful cautionary to the whole discussion. These notes are "declaimed in a way that's not at all clear in writing." Instead, he writes, they entail "an aspiration made with energy" (*impeto*) on the pitch in question, rather than being a "real note," adding: "So if knowledge of it were lost, I don't know how it could be regained; I posted it here because it's sung, but I'll repeat again, how to perform it I can't explain."[101] Because this is the stuff of oral transmission, Baini must do his best to inscribe it, of necessity rather artificially, in order to hedge against its loss.

Little could he have imagined the sonic inscription that would preserve it acoustically, or something like it, on Moreschi's recordings. Baini's "mordente" proliferates in Moreschi's singing well beyond the single chant he recorded. On both recordings of Rossini's "Crucifixus" from the *Petit messe solonnelle*, for instance, he delivers multiple upward grace notes that rise up a full octave. That light fleck upward before the essential pitch is characteristic of his practice, but it doesn't always occur at the octave; the one that starts the Bach-Gounod "Ave Maria," for instance, consists of an upward-leaping major sixth, and others proliferate at other intervals.

Somewhat confoundingly, Mendelssohn, in his extraordinarily meticulous notes to Zelter, says that the Italians call these upward-leaping ornaments "appoggiaturas," a word he seems to have borrowed from Roman chapel musicians as a generic coverall, though there is no mistaking what he means by it, nor is he alone in his usage. He goes on to illustrate them by providing examples at the intervals of fifth, sixth, and third, noting: "I was struck with the meaning they attach to the word appoggiatura. If the melody goes from C to D, or from C to E, they sing thus, and this they call an appoggiatura"

> *Premessa prima.*—L'*appoggiatura* ha il seguente segno se voglia indicarsi ◆, e significa che dee aggiungersi con buona maniera leggermente una nota nel luogo dove è posto il segno. Si suole l'appoggiatura usare nel salto di terza che sale, onde si prende con l'appoggiatura il salto di quarta; alcune volte anche si pone fra due note di grado se salgono, per farvi il salto di terza, se scendono per ripetere la prima; anche (ma di rado assai) si pone nel salto di quarta prendendo coll' appoggiatura il salto di quinta.

Example 3.2. Explanation of the appoggiatura by Giuseppe Baini (1775–1844), originally part of his *Regole circa il modo di cantare le lezioni, le lamentazioni ed i capitoli, e di intuonare il canto gregoriano secondo lo stile osservato dai cappellani-cantori della Cappella pontificia: Epilogate da uno de'cappellani suddetti l'anno 1806* (Rules about the way of singing lessons, lamentations, and chapters, and of singing Gregorian chant according to the style observed by papal singers in the Papal Chapel: Summed up by one of the above-mentioned choristers in the year 1806), but here given as annotated and later posthumously published by his student Adrien de la Fage (1801–1862) in his *Essais de dithphérographie musicale ou notice, descriptions, analyses, extraits et reproductions de manuscrits relatifs à la pratique, à la théorie et à l'histoire de la musique* (Paris: O. Legouix, 1864), p. 455. The explanation clarifies that the appoggiatura "must be added lightly with good style" to a note in the place where a diamond-shaped sign appears, continuing: "It is customary to use the appoggiatura in the leap of third going up, where the leap of fourth is taken with the appoggiatura." The upward appoggiatura is thus a kind of upward scoop.

> *Premessa* 3ª.—La proprietà del *Mordente*, il quale si suol segnare sopra la nota così *m*, è di mutare quella nota stessa su cui è segnato e portarla una quarta sotto, si suol mettere alla seconda di due note che salgono di grado :

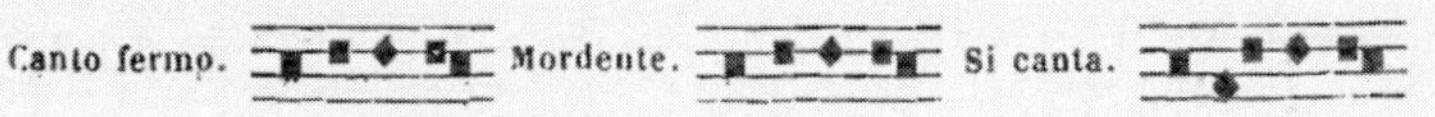

Example 3.3. Baini's demonstration via La Fage of what he calls here the upward-leaping "mordente," shown with the diamond as what "is sung" ("si canta"). La Fage, *Essais de dithphérographie musicale*, p. 455.

> Si epiloga in un solo caso l' esempio dell' appoggiatura, del zampetto, del mordente e del trillo in fine :
>
> App. Zamp. mord. Trillo.
>
> Canto fermo. Si canta.

Example 3.4. Baini's demonstration via La Fage of his four types of ornamentation, furnished with the rubric: "One can recapitulate in a single example the appoggiatura, the zampetto, the mordente, and the trillo." La Fage, *Essais de dithphérographie musicale*, p. 456.

MUSIC OF THE HOLY WEEK. 

183

and this they call an *appoggiatura*. Whatever they may choose to designate it, the effect is most disagreeable, and it must require long habit not to be discomposed by this strange practice, which reminds me very much of our old women at home in church; moreover the effect is the same. I saw in my book that the "Tenebræ" was to be sung, and thinking that it would interest you to know how it is given in the Papal chapel, I was on the watch with a sharp-pointed pencil when it commenced, and send you herewith the principal parts. It was sung very quick, and *forte* throughout, without exception.

Example 3.5. Felix Mendelssohn's description and transcriptions of "appoggiaturas" at the fifth, sixth, and third (i.e. upward appoggiaturas) that he heard at the Sistine Chapel. From Felix Mendelssohn Bartholdy, *Letters from Italy and Switzerland* (New York: Frederick Leypoldt, 1865), p. 183.

(example 3.5). No fan of them, he adds, "Whatever they may choose to designate it, the effect is most disagreeable, and it must require long habit not to be discomposed by this strange practice, which reminds me very much of our old women at home in church."[102]

The practice had evidently been in vogue for a long time, certainly among castrati, among whom it can be traced back more than a hundred years before Mendelssohn. The principal singing pedagogue of the first half of the eighteenth century, the castrato Pierfrancesco Tosi, in his *Opinioni de' cantori antichi e moderni* of 1723, provides a whole chapter on appoggiaturas, mostly ignored by commentators, that spells it out. Tosi claims the appoggiatura need not move only by step, but "may . . . pass from one distant Note to another, provided the skip or interval be not deceitful."[103]

Tosi's view was echoed by members of the Italian school who preceded and overlapped with Mendelssohn. Tenor and singing teacher Domenico Corri (1746–1825), a product of Nicola Porpora's (essentially) Neapolitan school, provides numerous examples of upward appoggiaturas in his undated volumes published as *A Select Collection of the Most Admired Songs, Duetts, &c. from Operas in the Highest Esteem . . . in Three Books*, probably in the early 1780s.[104] His "Directions to Singers" there explains that "the Grace of more intervals [i.e., greater than a second] always ascends" and should be "taken lightly" and "leap into the [essential] note rapidly" (example 3.6a). His later four-volume anthology, *The Singer's Preceptor* (1810), again contains numerous examples, always leaping upward in the way of Mendelssohn's "appoggiaturas," although in the first section on the "Grace" from lesson 8 on the appoggiatura, Corri names them "Leaping Graces" (example 3.6b).

Especially notable are examples in the *Select Collection* that showed users the ornamentational dexterity and nuance of star castrati who thrived during Corri's earlier years, not least their command of the upward appoggiatura. Buyers who read through "Deh, placatevi con me" from Christoph Willibald Gluck's famed reform opera *Orfeo ed Euridice* (1762) (example 3.7a) could "hear" Gaetano Guadagni lean into his heartrending pleas to the Furies with full-octave leaping graces—Mendelssohn's "upward appoggiaturas" and Baini's "mordenti"—and could try to copy them themselves.[105] Arias from Metastasian *opere serie*, as sung by Giuseppe Millico (example 3.7b) and Gasparo Pacchierotti (example 3.7c), similarly provided written records of moving and extraordinary castrato vocality that call to mind what Shane Butler has glossed as the "ancient phonograph"—precursors, we might say, to Moreschi's G & T inscriptions and ones designed to satisfy local amateurs and melophiles who might sing them, "listen" to them, or just show them to others.[106]

EXPLANATION of the GRACES.

All Ornaments, as Graces, Cadences &c. in this work are diſtinguiſhed by the ſmall notes, which are alſo mark'd according to their exact duration.

The Aſcending Grace of one interval, is expreſsed ſoftly, and its ſtrength encreaſed gradually up to the Note.

The Deſcending Grace of one interval, is a degree ſtronger than the note and gradually ſoftened into it.

The Grace of ſucceſsive intervals, is rather of a rapid execution and encreaſes its ſtrength as it riſes.

The Aſcending Turn, begins ſoftly, and encreaſes its ſtrength as it riſes, then gently again ſinks into the note.

The Deſcending Turn, begins ſtrong, and decreaſes its ſtrength as it falls, then riſes into the note ſtrong again.

THE FOLLOWING GRACES being of a different nature from any of the above, a ſeparate explanation of them is neceſsary.

They are not to be conſidered as forming any part of the air; but are only intended to give to certain notes a particular emphaſis or expreſsion. The execution of them, Therefore, ought to be ſo rapid, that, while the effect is felt, the ear ſhall yet be unable to determine the character of the ſounds or to diſtinguiſh them from the predominant note by no effort whatever indeed can they be rendered totally imperceptible, or if they could, they would not then exiſt. But the more imperceptible they are, the more happy is the execution, the more perfect the union, and the more delicate the effect, whereas, by an execution which renders them diſtinctly perceptible, they would loſe their nature and inſtead of the adventitious graces now under conſideration, become part of the melody itſelf.

or or The Grace of more intervals always aſcends. It is to be taken ſoftly, and to leap into the note rapidly.

The Turn Grace is to be taken ſtrong, and melted into the note.

This Grace cloſe after a note is to ſhow that the time neceſsary for its execution is to be deducted from the laſt part of that note, Example this is equal to this

As this has the peculiar property of uniting two notes of any intervals, in executing it, it is neceſsary to ſwell the note into the Grace, and the Grace muſt melt itſelf again into the note following.

Example of one Interval — Note ſwell into the Grace melt into the Note

Example of more Intervals — Note ſwell into the Grace melts into the Note

NB. Theſe Graces if properly ſung, are the higheſt ornament of an Air: but if not executed with great nicety and taſte, they are rather detrimental to it, and therefore the performance of them may be conſidered optional as they are in reality no part of the melody.

Example 3.6a. "Explanation of the Graces" from Domenico Corri's *A Select Collection of the Most Admired Songs, Duetts, &c. from Operas in the Highest Esteem... In Three Books* (Edinburgh: John Corri, n.d. [1782–1783?]), p. 8.

Lesson VIII

Appogiatura

The Grace

This is the most expressive ornament of Vocal Music and appears to have been the origin of all the other embellishments, as Turns, Shakes, &c. (see page 2)

These Graces are of different descriptions, as in the following Example, but that which we term the superior, without doubt, is the one dictated by nature, while all others are the mere production of art.

The distance of the intervals of Graces of all descriptions, should be consonant with the Key, and, as the modulation varies, so the Graces must be regulated, as the incidental alterations may require.

The length of time to be given to Graces, altho' in general marked, yet never can be given so accurately as to direct the true expression of the words, which must be therefore regulated by the judgment, taste, and feeling of the Singer.

Exapiple

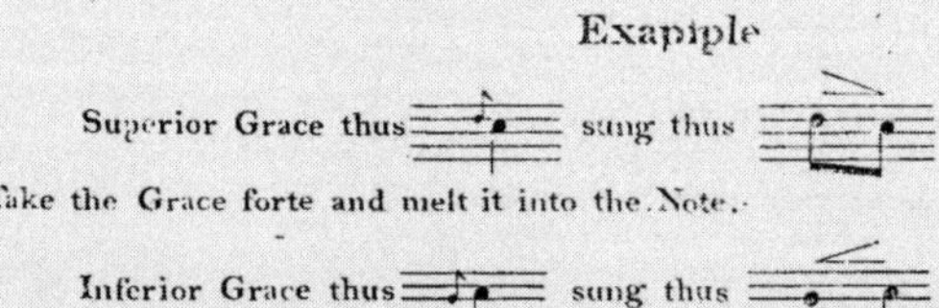

Take the Grace softly and force it into the Note.

This Grace is similar to those above, but has this distinction, that the strength necessary to it's execution must be regulated more or less according to the distance of the Intervals.

In descending, drop the Grace into the Note, and in ascending, swell the Note into the Grace.

Double Grace thus — or — sung thus — or

Begin soft, gliding with crescendo into the Note.

Example 3.6b. "Leaping graces" as notated among other types of graces under the rubric of the appoggiatura, in lesson 8 of Domenico Corri's *The Singer's Preceptor, or Corri's Treatise on Vocal Music*, 2 vols. in 1 (London: Mr. Silvester and Messrs Longman, Hurst, Rees & Orme, 1810), p. 32.

3.7a

Examples 3.7a–c. Domenico Corri, in *A Select Collection of the Most Admired Songs, Duetts, &c. from Operas in the Highest Esteem . . . In Three Books* (Edinburgh: John Corri, n.d., vol. 1 (Edinburgh: John Corri, [1782–1783?], exemplified many of these. Example 3.7a shows castrato Gaetano Guadagni's leaping graces at the fourth and at the octave in "Deh, placatevi con me" from Christoph Willibald Gluck's famed reform opera *Orfeo ed Euridice* (1762), where they have a wailing effect (p. 42, see arrows); example 3.7b shows castrato Giuseppe Millico's leaping grace at the fourth in Tommaso Giordani's collaborative opera *Artaserse* (p. 1); example 3.7c shows castrato Gasparo Pacchierotti's leaping grace at the sixth in a cantata on *L'olimpiade* (p. 25).

3.7b

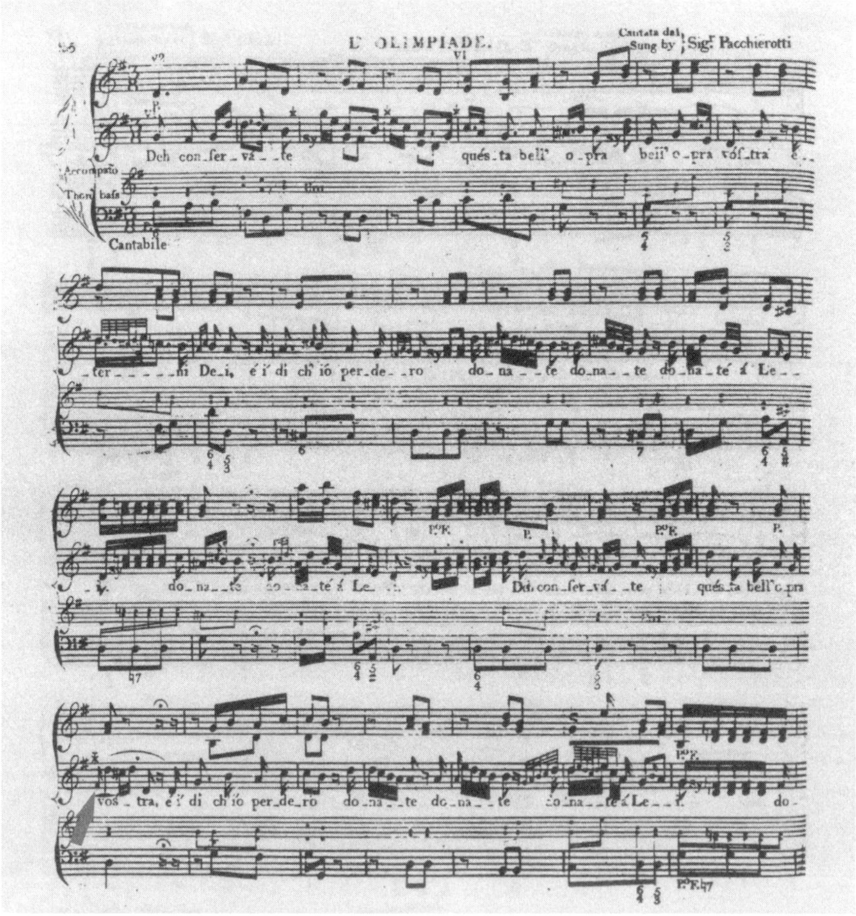

L' OLIMPIADE.

Cantata dal
Sung by Sig.r Pacchierotti

Acompto
Thoro bass
Cantabile

Deh con_ser_va_te questa bell' o_pra bell' o_pra vos_tra e_ter_ni Dei, e i di ch'io per_de_ro do_na_te do_na_te do_na_te a Le_i. do_na_te do_na_te a Le_i. Deh con_ser_va_te questa bell' o_pra vos_tra, e i di ch'io per_de_ro do_na_te do_na_te do_na_te a Le_i. do_

3.7c

One castrato, chronologically proximate to Mendelssohn, became the exemplum of the technique in a way that was apparently all but inimitable. Superstar Giovanni Battista Velluti (1780–1861), who flourished in the first third of the nineteenth century, surfaces in numerous prints and manuscripts, including commemorative ones, that provide ornamentational scripts for his performances. One was famously recorded by the great singing pedagogue Manuel Garcia, Jr. (1805–1906) in his *Traité de l'art du chant* (1840 and 1847) to showcase Velluti's art, not least his prolific "upward appoggiaturas" (examples 3.8a and 3.8b), namely, Francesco Morlacchi's "Caro suono lusinghier."[107] Velluti's art also circulated in numerous manuscripts.[108] In the Grand Scena of Rossini's opera *Aureliano in Palmira* (1813), in which the castrato played Arsace, the composer even made the clarinet and oboe imitate Velluti's upward appoggiatura (example 3.9).[109]

Velluti engaged the practice not as an outlier or an innovator, but as a preserver of tradition who saturated it almost to a sinking point. By his time, fears of the castrato body had led to its exile from the stage.[110] Velluti's aspiration-filled singing, rife with upward appoggiaturas, can be stitched to the late nineteenth-century Vatican practice of soprano castrati, even mediated by a mid-nineteenth-century non-Vatican castrato named Paolo Pergetti. Obscure apart from his notoriety as an avatar, Pergetti appeared after the sun had already set on castrati outside Rome. In his small *Treatise on Singing Forming a Complete School of the Art in 3 Parts*, published around 1850 in London, where he seems to have been a mere curiosity, he included a number of upward appoggiaturas at the fourth, fifth, sixth, and octave (example 3.10) as a kind of portamento effect in the "light" style. Ghostly echoes of castrati past.[111]

Support for the idea that these ornamental and expressive practices survived and increased among late nineteenth-century castrati exists in Sistine scores contemporaneous with Moreschi, treated by Graham O'Reilly in his book, *"Allegri's Miserere" in the Sistine Chapel*, and realized in his ravishing recording of Mustafà's 1892 manuscript

3.8a

3.8b

Examples 3.8a–b. The renowned singing teacher Manuel Garcia, Jr. (1805–1906), showcased castrato Giambattista Velluti's art in his *Traité complet de l'art du chant en deux parties* (Paris: Chez L'auteur, 1847), including the "upward appoggiaturas" that proliferated in Velluti's singing of Francesco Morlacchi's "Caro suono lusinghier." These are shown in example 3.8a at the fourth and in 3.8b at the sixth and the seventh. Other examples displayed Velluti's command over the leaping appoggiatura at the octave and ninth.

Example 3.9. In the Grand Scena of Rossini's opera *Aureliano in Palmira* (1813), in which Giambattista Velluti played Arsace, Rossini had the clarinet and oboe imitate the castrato's upward appoggiatura. Gioacchino Rossini, *Aureliano in Palmira: Dramma serio per musica in due atti di Giuseppe Felice Romani*, ed. Daniele Carnini and Will Crutchfield (Pesaro: Fondazione Rossini, 2019).

552
139
Ars.
-mè! lon - ta-no dal-le u-ma - ne vi-cen-de in se-no a vo - i vo-lon-tie - ri trar-re - i i
I
Vni
II
Vle
Vc. e Cb.
143
Ob.
I Solo
Cl. in Do
I Solo
Fg.
I Solo
Ars.
po - chi gior - ni mie-i;
pizz.
I
Vni
II
pizz.
Vle
Vc.
Cb.
pizz.

3.9 (cont'd)

38 PEL LEGGIERO. THE LIGHT.

Nel Leggiero, al contrario, si anticipa la nota o sillaba.— Il Portamento è il colorito espressivo dei nostri affetti tristi o leggieri: quindi si deve fare attenzione di non confondere le due maniere, che produrrebbe un cattivo effetto.— Nel Portamento non si deve strascinare la voce, che n'è l'esaggerazione del medesimo: Vi sono dei casi, come quello d'orrore, o di dolore, ove lo striscio fa effetto perchè esprime la situazione.

In the Light style, on the contrary, the note or syllable must be anticipated.— The Portamento is that colouring which is expressive of our sad or joyful feelings: hence it is requisite to pay great attention not to confound the two styles, as it would produce a very bad effect.— In the Portamento, the voice should never be dragged which would be an exaggeration; though there are cases such as of horror or excess of grief, &c. in which it is effective, because it assists in rendering the situation.

Example 3.10. Castrato Paolo Pergetti's *Treatise on Singing Forming a Complete School of the Art in 3 Parts* (London: Robert W. Ollivier, n.d. [ca. 1850]), p. 38, showing numerous upward appoggiaturas at various intervals. Image courtesy of the Bibliothèque National de France. Reproduced by permission.

version.[112] O'Reilly shows that Mustafà's *Miserere* is largely based on the 1711 version by Tommaso Bai, tailored to Allegri, but distinct from it and richly ornamented for Holy Week Tenebrae services.[113] Example 3.11 shows the extent of Mustafà's expressive markings, ornamentations, and other specifications in a document that in O'Reilly's word "micromanages" the performance while seeking to preserve it for posterity at a fragile moment in the life of the chapel, much as Baini had done during the Napoleonic occupation. Expressive directions along the lines of "dolciss[imo]" (first measure of example 3.11) appear throughout the manuscript in such words as "tranquillo," "ondeggiate," "sensibile," and "risoluto," even down to borrowing Verdi's famous "un fil di voce" (the thread of a voice) from Macbeth's sleepwalking scene and the end of Violetta's "Addio del passato." "Portando" markings also proliferate, matched by a glut of gruppetti and appoggiaturas, notably including upward ones, all this being just what Mustafà himself had sung in decades past.[114]

Some of the portamenti help the first soprano bound up the gamut. The ossia marking scored with a slur (example 3.11, top right) lets soprano 1 shoot up to the stratospheric heights of a high C, or as the inserted note puts it: "N.B. If it should better suit the first soprano to support the high C, he can take [the syllable] 'me-' on C [above middle C] before taking the high C."[115] No one but Moreschi could have sung the high C, and in fact, it was Moreschi who sang it at age twenty-five when Mustafà's *Miserere* was first rehearsed on March 24, 1884, and performed at the Tenebrae services on the following April 9–11—Moreschi, whose voice was what a French observer called "powerful and agile" with a "penetrating sweetness."[116]

Who, then, would have partnered with him, singing soprano 2? An intriguing question, inasmuch as soprano 2 often joins soprano 1 a third below. My best guess is Giovanni Cesari, notwithstanding Buning's conjecture that his voice had dropped by then, for by turns, soprano 2 often also sticks together with the lower soloists who yielded to Moreschi. The score's instructions to the lower voices makes the matter clear. As soprano 1 came off the high C, their

Example 3.11. Excerpt from the so-called "Allegri *Miserere*" as rewritten by Tommaso Bai in 1711, reworked in a performance version by castrato and Sistine Chapel Director Domenico Mustafà in 1884, and finalized by him in written score in 1892. The soprano 1 of Mustafà's version, extant in the Biblioteca Apostolica Vaticana, Fondo Cappella Sistina, MS 375, as shown here, was sung by Alessandro Moreschi. Reproduced by permission of the Biblioteca Apostolica Vaticana.

underlying notes were to be "held" until the soprano 1 concluded his freely rubato coloratura descent, marked "a piacere" (see the designation of "tenuta fino alla risoluzione dal 1° soprano" on the lower parts).

O'Reilly makes the priceless observation that Mustafà's score is "as close as we can get on paper to any aural recording."[117] How fascinating to see that at this labile moment in the history of sound and other instances of technological reproduction, as well as the history of the church, Mustafà should have worked to get that "close" to a sound recording.

Vocal Tattoos (the Sob and the Catch)

Most accounts of Moreschi connect him vocally to a crepuscular Sistine tradition. Without disavowing that, I propose to link him both to the past and to a more modern and secular strain of Italian life and practice, a castrato tradition that is thoroughly interlaced with the operatic. Moreschi's participation in it made him frankly unreformist with respect to the church, and local events made it more so. Recall that the matrices he cut at the outset of the 1904 sessions—five, mostly gooey sacred solos—happened right up against a sixth matrix that captured the big-voiced operatic tenor Giraud singing Tosti's "Oblio."[118] As early twentieth-century singing goes, Giraud's performance is not particularly demonstrative, but it leans toward the vocality explored above, even including a hint of a sob.

I want to pause here over the sob, specifically, over Giraud's final words "our eternal love" ("il nostro eterno amor"), but more generally over the sob as a kind of tattoo written over and through the work of Primo Vitti, Giraud, and a vast and forking tradition that extends backward in time long before them and forward to their contemporaries—what Garcia conjured when he wrote the words "Sob. Inhale with excitement" over a fleeting moment in Velluti's "Caro suono lusinghier" and moreover when he represented Velluti's performance with a proliferation of leaping graces (example 3.8b). At work here are complex genealogies that resist disentangling, but some distinct threads are suggestive.[119] Vitti's Bizet and Giraud's Tosti both show something of a high romantic idiolect. Moreschi partook of it with everything from robust sobs to slight laryngeal catches that verge on them. In both, emotional conviction settles in the throat to produce an unpitched phonation upon attack and a persistent array of glottals, aspirates, and upward scoops as large as an octave or a ninth,[120] heard clearly in Moreschi's delivery in Tosti's "Ideale."

As we've seen, these upward-shooting aspirates go back at least to the early eighteenth century. What matters are the technical continuities between Moreschi's sobs and his upward grace notes, as well as the sonic and historical-performative continuities of those grace notes themselves; for continuous vocal lineages find Moreschi's sonic present haunted by a past that vests the emotional in the physical. The ubiquitous crackly sounds Moreschi used for launching upper notes represent a physiological cognate to the sob produced by the veristic body in pain, a pain that is at once somatic, affective, and broadly cultural. To assuage any lingering doubts about this, listen to a bit of Moreschi's Bach-Gounod "Ave Maria," stippled with upward scoops, or to the first measures of either of his Rossini "Crucifixes." Or listen to the start of his rendition of Giovanni Aldega's "Domine salvum fac." The list goes on and on. All these perform an enhanced affect — the poignancy of an aching vocalic body. They manifest a long-lived *melo*-dramatic body of Italian vintage, one of musical excess and overstatement.[121]

Had I not learned from Moreschi's descendants that he and Guendalina were regulars at the opera, where they had a kind of celebrity status, I would have been somewhat mystified by the extent of this in Moreschi's own singing. Learning it sent my imagination careening backward, not as far as castrato inheritances circa 1680–1830, but to those of the Roman opera houses of Moreschi's time. Granted, he gained the right to go the opera only after the 1891 constitution that effectively secularized Sistine chapel singers, lifting bans on celibacy and participation in secular public life.[122] But even assuming chapel singers actually observed bans on theatergoing before 1891, they had endless other ways to absorb operatic vogues.

An explicit one from just before Moreschi's time revolved around his teacher Gaetano Capocci (1811–1898; see figure 6.1, standing in the middle): a Roman composer; organist at various churches, starting in 1830 with Santa Maria in Vallicella (also the "Chiesa Nuova"), and in 1839 with Santa Maria Maggiore; and from 1855, *maestro della musica* at San Giovanni in Laterano.[123] Like the church works of other nineteenth-century composers, Capocci's were highly theatrical—exactly what was to be banned in 1903. More than that, part of his compositional activity in the 1860s and probably beyond involved "rifacimenti," a term applied to operas converted into sacred dramas by replacing original texts with new ones in the way of contrafacta and then further adapting them for all-male casts. Capocci seems to have specialized in them. Like other composers, he also made *pasticci* of operas outfitted with new religious texts or created dramas with altogether new words and new music. Effectively, what Capocci and other Roman composers were making were (semi)staged oratorios that included travesty parts. Some men played male roles and others female—whether with out-and-out cross-dressing no one seems to know. Mustafà likely participated in an adaptation of Rossini's *Semiramide*, and if so, almost certainly took the title role. As De Angelis put it, Capocci

> enjoyed great popularity thanks to his talent and activities, and to some extent thanks to those curious musical evenings he organized at the Oratory of San Filippo. Before 1870, operas were performed in this Oratory, drawn from among those most in vogue, and were reworked [or reduced: "*ridotte*"] in such a way that they could be sung entirely by men. The curious results included Rossini's *Semiramide*, whose female parts were interpreted by two singers from the Sistine Chapel. At other times newly written libretti were set to music, or else selections from a mixture of operas were adapted from libretti to create an original piece. Capocci was often the author of these centonized works, and it is easy to understand how priests who were

> forbidden from attending the theaters adored Capocci and came gladly to his evening gatherings. In truth, it should be remembered that, for San Filippo, the Roman maestro expressly composed two much-admired oratorios, *Il Battista* and *l'Assalonne*.[124]

Bear in mind that clergy, including papal singers, had been forbidden from attending theater since the bans made by Pope Benedict XIV (reigned 1740 to 1758), even though many did. Earlier evidence shows, moreover, that all-male performances of theatrical works by the likes of Rossini, Giovanni Paisiello, Pasquale Anfossi, Pietro Alessandro Guglielmi, and Ferdinando Paer were reset to sacred texts as *rifacimenti* in the late eighteenth and early nineteenth centuries and also performed surreptitiously, hence late at night, as German travelers reported after hearing them at St. Filippo Neri's oratories during the 1820s and 1830s.[125] In this sense, *rifacimenti* done closer to Moreschi's time—in *accademie* and *saggi*, at schools and oratories, with boys and men performing operatic solos and ensembles—extended earlier practices, reiterating their clandestine nature.[126] According to early biographers, the fabulously famous baritone Cotogni even seems to have made his debut in such an oratorio, alongside Mustafà and Nazareno Rosati.[127] But while there were no consequences for him, for chapel singers there could be. As late as 1895 Moreschi was even denied authorization to participate in a "paid *accademia*" (a commercial, paid salon or concert appearance), though he was allowed to take part in private musical performances.[128]

Returning to the opera house of Moreschi's Roman years, the effects of an operatic argot are clear. Just listen to some of the stars born only a few years after Moreschi who sobbed much as he did (links and track numbers in notes). Ernestina Bendazzi-Garulli (1864–1931) performed Rossini's *Stabat mater* at the Costanzi during Lent of 1884 to wild acclaim, and likewise Bizet's *Pearl Fishers* in 1886.[129] In a Pathé recording, probably from 1903, she can be heard delivering a great sob at the end of Manon's farewell to the humble domesticity she has shared with Des Grieux, "Addio mio picciol desco" ("Adieu, notre petite table" in the original), from Jules Massenet's *Manon*.[130] Later, during a more certain period of Moreschi's operagoing, Cesira Ferrani (1863–1943) — the eponymous prima donna in the premiere of Puccini's *Manon Lescaut* (Turin, 1893) and his first Mimi in *La bohème* (Turin, 1896) — performed Mozart's *Requiem* at the Costanzi in 1892, together with the Pergolesi *Stabat mater*, performances Moreschi could well have attended.[131] Her own "Addio mio picciol desco," recorded for G & T in Milan during December 1902, also ended with a great sob, if a more singerly and metrical one than Bendazzi-Garulli's.[132] Or take Gemma Bellincioni (1864–1950), whose premiere performance as Santuzza in Mascagni's *Cavalleria* came with a searing "Voi lo sapete, o mamma." Her sobs were more restrained than either Bendazzi-Garulli's or Ferrani's, to judge by a 1903 recording done for G&T in Milan, where she produces the requisite dip into chest on "io piango!" ("Lola e Turridu s'amano, io piango, io piango!" [Lola and Turridu love each other, I weep, I weep]) to make what's nevertheless a searing, sobbing cry.[133]

And then there was Calvé, born the same year as Moreschi. In 1891, she was not only learning from Mustafà how to sing stratospherically high and supposedly castratoesque flute tones, but was singing the premiere of Mascagni's *L'amico Fritz* at the Costanzi.[134] Her recording career began about seven years later with a Bettini cylinder, probably made in 1898, and in February 1902, she made several Mapleson cylinders in New York City of numbers by Mascagni, Bizet, and Gounod. Later the same year, like many others, she cut a G & T disk of *Cavalleria's* "Voi lo sapete" in London and went on to make at least two more, including one for Zonophone in Paris in the fall of 1902 and one for Victor in Camden, New Jersey, in April 1907. On all those, she never failed to sob.[135] The last of them went for broke, exploiting the golden opportunity Mascagni provided with a deep dive into her robust and dramatic chest.[136]

What's fascinating is that sobs are not just inventions of an archveristic, so-called "realism" (an oxymoron if ever there was one). In 1807, the obscure singing pedagogue G. G. Ferrari invoked related mechanisms in a little treatise that links them with heightened emotionality by labeling them "piagnistei." There, the Italian is translated into English as "shrieks" (example 3.12), though the word is more commonly translated as "moans," "whines," or "cries." "Piagnistei" as Ferrari intends them assault the ear sonically and emotionally by shooting quickly upward on accented notes. They are upward appoggiaturas (or upward "leaping graces") that we might well regard as aesthetic and physiological precursors of the sob. They could even be heard as what Amy Skjerseth, following sound scholar Seth Kim-Cohen following anthropologist Mary Douglas, calls sonic "matter out of place," or what we could reframe in this lyric environment as "noise . . . out of place"—something alien to music, polluting to music *as* music, and intentionally so.[137]

Repetition and Event

All these elusive practices circulate in the written material forms of treatises, musical scores, and recorded anecdotes, but reside acoustically as *aural* tattoos of early phonography—which is to say, etymologically and theoretically speaking, in *writing* of the *voice*. Angels who appear on the labels of early flat disc records, which revolutionized the possibility of permanency through their newfound capacity for preservation, put the work of inscription on display.[138] By virtue of its inscriptive powers, the phonographic angel might be named *the writing angel*, one who informs the viewers' records that what is etched on them is dependable because uniform, regular, and reliably repeatable. Yet the angel's marks cannot also help but signal a failed permanence: the transitory character of the gramophone, subject to changing technologies, marked by missing subjects (speakers, singers, and listeners), and liable to be strewn about in broken replicas.[139]

Given the paradox of writing the voice, perhaps I can be forgiven the irony of turning to a voice demoter, Jacques Derrida, and to his late essay "Typewriter Ribbon," for some reflections on

Example 3.12. The obscure singing pedagogue G. G. Ferrari, in his treatise *Breve trattato di canto Italiano* (London: Schulze & Dean, 1818), adduced mechanisms related to so-called upward appoggiaturas that he called "piagnistei." These are given as "shrieks" in *A Concise Treatise on Italian Singing, elucidated by rules, observations, and examples. . .*, the English translation by William Shield (London: G. Schulze and J. Dean, 1818), p. 1, ex. 5. Reproduced by permission of St. Andrews College Library.

the meaning of phonographic circulations.[140] Of course Derrida, deconstructionist and antimetaphysician, spent a lifetime dismantling presence in order to refocus language around writing and *away* from voice, both of which phonography involves. And he did so by discovering absence and heterogeneity in the operations of written language as a play of difference. Those operations, in turn, bring into view the *trace*, that ineradicable yet intangible remainder of difference, which is always marked by a temporal dimension since signifiers do not just *differ* from their signifieds, but are famously *deferred* from them *in time* — hence Derrida's neologism *différance*.[141]

Of interest here is that the resultant traces, though thin and fragile, provide an off-ramp from otherwise closed linguistic systems. Traces are what make it possible for utterance to go beyond those places where the ink stains the page, to places *beyond writing*, or very simply put (for present purposes): to *performance*. By virtue of the trace in *différance*, writing is always under erasure. And even the trace itself must be forever subject to erasure, to being crossed and blotted out.

How might the Derridean trace exist in the acts of recorded performance to which I've been calling attention here? Indirectly, "Typewriter Ribbon" provides a clue at a moment when Derrida distinguishes, but then productively confuses two kinds of operations or "agencies" as he looks to envision a future in which human events and machinic operations participate in the same logics. Before such a time, there lies on one side the operation he calls the *event*, which is to say something singular that happens just once. On another, there lies *automatic repetition*, a phenomenon that is endlessly iterable. Phonography, though not the object of Derrida's attention, notably consists of both a singular performance, essentially unrepeatable (at least in its nuances), and a machine that mechanically records that performative event for keeps, to be ceaselessly reproduced, replicated, and reheard.[142]

We know where this will eventually lead. For Derrida, no operation will ever be pure — neither the event nor automatic repetition.

The one always "infects" the other. Hence *différance*. Hence the ubiquitous trace.

Perhaps the future that Derrida tried, presciently, to envision in "Typewriter Ribbon" had already arrived decades earlier. For if we take the event to be performance, roughly speaking, and take automatic repetition to refer to technologies of reproduction, then another difference arises: between animacy and inanimacy, and relatedly between the subject who makes the thing and the reproducible object thus produced, which in its turn is also infected. For Allen Weiss, that difference emerges almost imperceptibly when "the 'I' of writing (active subject) [is] insidiously and immutably transformed into the 'I' of text (inanimate object)."[143] Another form of infection of one by the other.

Attending to Derrida and Weiss, we might infer a material meaning of trace as it relates to repetitions, replications, copies, and inanimate objects, but also to the *phonic* dimensions of singing and voice itself. Indirectly, Michel de Certeau's writings on phonic, sounding voice provide some help here, even if "trace" is not his word. In his much-read essay "Vocal Utopias: Glossolalia," wordless utterance (glossolalia) stands as a vocal antonym to language. Glossolalia, to quote Certeau, "pushes up through the cracks of ordinary conversation" by such means as "bodily noises" and "fragments of others' voices [that] punctuate . . . sentences with breaks and surprises."[144]

Bodily noises, fragments of others' voices: In glossolalia, Certeau finds a way to put his finger on the embodied materiality of voice, a materiality that signifies through nonsemantic noise and other material borrowings. His interest lies in how such effects emerge and circulate, in how vocal effects skirt formal signification even as they exceed it. For Certeau the babble of glossolalia represents a kind of "secondary vocalization" to which I'd add such wordless or quasi-wordless cousins as aphasia, hiccupping, groaning, grunting, sighing, and gasping, all of which are opposed to what Certeau calls "the major voice," the supposed "messenger of [specified] meaning."[145]

And how about sobbing? How about catches in the throat during the otherwise mostly lyrical, mostly ordered, and mostly texted vocalizing that we call singing? For Certeau, the only way utterance could ever immunize itself against the messiness of dialogue would be to omit all such wonderful "secondary vocalizations" and instead confine itself to dull "*propositional* discourses." Think of announcements and reports, or still more so, of edicts or theses, genres that tend to circumvent the Other as addressee by delivering messages devoid of emotion or persuasion.[146] To conceive utterance in such a reduced way helps clarify exactly what singing *doesn't* do and doesn't *want* to do. By contrast with propositional utterance, singing opens itself to the noises and aggravations of otherness by choking up, sighing, bursting forth, and crying wordlessly or, musically speaking, by producing melismas, vocalises, and (to return to Moreschi) catches in the throat, upward appoggiaturas, leaping graces, and verismo sobs.

Although for Derrida the trace marks *all language* all the time, singing—differently from persuasive or propositional utterance—makes itself available to others in special ways. It's helpful to think of the overlapping traditions, multiple stainings, and myriad forms of appropriation that circulate around and within Moreschi's world as forms of *contamination*. Doing so gets us out of old-fashioned histories and positivist analyses of influences, allowing us to think more subtly about the elisions between opera arias, secular art songs, and theatrical religious songs. It allows us to conceive them as zones of erratically, unsystematically, irregularly shared practice and experience. If we could hear Moreschi's performances of opera arias from the 1880s and 1890s, we would undoubtedly hear leaping appoggiaturas from much earlier Sistine and even castrato practices going back a century or two, as well as sobbing catches in the throat heard in the contemporary opera house. There would be no way to discern an absolute divide between these sounds and the traditions intermixed in them or to establish clearcut lines of development—divides and developments that surely don't exist in any strict forms and surely never did. This is precisely what Carolyn Dinshaw attempts to get at in her explorations of temporal folds between medieval and present-day lives and scripts.[147] Which is not to say that just any kind of operatic idiom could be taken over into Sistine practice. The shouts and silences of verismo opera would hardly do in the chapel, for instance, and outright spoken passages of vendettas and curses hurled across the footlights had to remain in the strict confines of the opera house. When the sobs that verismo opera made explicit were transported to Sistine singing, they seem to have been tempered and blended with a nineteenth-century lyricism and sentimentality, which merged with touches of a verismo idiolect to form part of what I've been calling a "sacred vernacular." Only very partially could verismo be incorporated into the soundscape of the Roman church. It remained an alien Other to Sistine singing, yet one that stained the church as a memory, a trace, partly blended, partly on the escape. When the right moment struck, it could jack up the emotional side of things.

The *event* that interests me in all of this is above all the recording session because it consists of both the singularity of performance and its production as *automatic repetition* through the inexorable work of the horn and cutting stylus and the reproductions that follow. Walter Benjamin's iconic essay "The Work of Art in the Age of Its Technological Reproducibility" famously called attention to that fact in the epigraph already quoted above: "To perform in the glare of arc lamps while simultaneously meeting the demands of the microphone is a test performance of the highest order. To accomplish it is to preserve one's humanity in the face of the apparatus."[148] In combining both of these — the humanity of the performative event and the fearsomely inexorable technology of automatic repetition — recording constitutes itself as a triumphant, but quintessentially impossible phenomenon, and it will enter into and combine with many other events and repetitions over the course of its long life.[149]

Still, on rare occasions — not so very rare on the earliest recordings, whose high cost made retakes prohibitive and whose novelty, as Will Crutchfield shows, often took performers by surprise—the *eventness* of the recording explodes into view. Listen to the latter half of Moreschi's "Ideale," now easily available on streaming sites, and you will hear this. As the performance works its way up to and past the climactic sob that starts at 2:18, it drives home the precise paradox into which the sob and the upward appoggiatura have stumbled, landing in this endlessly iterable, automatic record of performance and yet reminding us eternally, again and again, that it is just that, a performance, hence iterable only because it is replayable.

But what specifically happens here? Like Moreschi's "Ave Maria," his "Ideale" mixes castrato vocality with verismo conviction, filling the song with glottals, aspirates, *h* sounds, and scoops as large as an octave or a tenth—perhaps what Garcia intermittently calls the "petite note inférieure."[150] Moreschi's rendition lacks the heroism of Caruso's 1906 recording, but puts in its stead an animated, sometimes *affrettando* impatience alternating with *ritardando* romanticism.[151] Most striking to me is a sobbing anticipation to "una novella aurora" in the second stanza. But then, after all that, the song having finished, along comes an unguarded, disarmingly transparent and fleeting moment when Moreschi, having finished the performance, follows it with a barely audible gasp of "ehe" (something like "oh my"). It is an expression of wonderment, but also disconcertion in the face of the machine that he has just survived. Clamorous volleys of applause and shouts of approbation by his colleagues follow. Domen Marenčič points out that all this may well have been orchestrated, notably by the recording engineer. But whether that's the case or not, is its affect and effect any less "live," even spontaneous, for that?[152] Suddenly, we listeners hear something that is no longer Derrida's automatic repetition, no longer Weiss's "'I' of text," but rather an event. A performance after all.

Voicing Remains

The entire enterprise that has become this book started out with a letter to Maria Rita Fellini, spurred on by my search for the castrato voice. I was after a vocal genealogy—something like the one I recounted in *The Castrato*, traceable, if hardly in a Derridean way, from castrato Girolamo Crescentini (1762–1846) to his pupil soprano Isabella Colbran (1785–1845), wife of Rossini, to the premier nineteenth-century singing pedagogue, Manuel Garcia, Jr., which then leads to his late nineteenth-century pupil Matilde Marchesi (1821–1913). Marchesi's studio produced many of Moreschi's operatic contemporaries, some of whom taught her methods to others, including the Spaniard Melchiorre Vidal (1837–1911), who taught such Italian bel cantists as Lucrezia Bori (1887–1960), Rosina Storchio (1876–1945), and the Spanish soprano Elvira de Hidalgo (1891–1980). During the Second World War, it was De Hidalgo's fortune to be in Athens, where the teenage Mary Kalogeropoulou (1923–1977) studied with her, after which, newly renamed Maria Callas, she landed like a rocket ship on the stage of La Scala.

Are Maria Callas and Giulio Moreschi both descended from castrati?[153] In my wide-eyed thinking during the winter of 2010—not baseless, as it turns out—it seemed that something like the Crescentini-to-Callas genealogy should have been traceable from early nineteenth-century castrati and their pupils to Alessandro Moreschi and from him to his students and followers. Giulio was chief among the latter, not just a son, but a product of Alessandro's studio. But there were others, including his student, falsettist Domenico Mancini (1891–1984), and additional singers he taught or influenced, among them falsettist Alessandro Gabrielli and alto Luigi Gentili.[154] In this thinking, Giulio's practice would lead to his own students Riccardo Fellini and, according to Fabio and Rita, his bosom buddy Alberto Sordi, plus the whole cohort that studied with Giulio from about the mid-1920s until his death in 1955. By tracking down Riccardo's voice and its pedagogical origins, I hoped to place one more pebble on the paths that meander into the studios of singing teachers and thence to stages, salons, and churches, not in straight lines, but through the crooked passageways that run from castrated singers to their vocal successors, by which time voices are routinely being "captured" as the lingo has it, not just in prints and manuscripts and through anecdotes, but on cylinders and disks and materially reproduced with ever greater precision and stability.

On a certain reckoning, all this was of course a fool's errand. The brute materiality of the trace and its peregrinations, especially the sonic trace, will always elude our grasp. And yet contemplating its journeys, through bodies, passions, and institutions, fleshly production, practice, and experience, has its own payoffs: new and different traces; new ways of listening; new modes of encounter, including ethnographic ones. I would not have dreamed that Alessandro Moreschi's disciples would sing like castrati, but two falsettists do, both of them audible on rare, mostly one-on-a-part choral recordings. One of them, Alessandro Gabrielli, sounds so much like Moreschi that on first encounter I took him for one myself; the other, Domenico Mancini, was taken for a castrato by Perosi.[155]

Mancini came to Rome from Civita Castella, in the same province of Viterbo that brought us the guileless couple in Fellini's *Lo sceicco bianco*. In about 1968, he recorded in his thick Lazian accent a charming, candid report on his career that briefly recounts his lessons with Moreschi. Its refrain, reiterated in a flurry of rhetorical variations, is that singing is learned by *imitation*.[156] I translate the commercially released portion of a longer interview below, dividing Mancini's comments into three successive sections, with quoted parts blocked and italicized:

Part 1

As a child I had a good voice to be sure, and I was already singing at my church, the Cathedral of Civita Castella. And an aunt of mine, coming for the holidays from Rome, said "Oh, what a beautiful voice this nephew has, we could have him study formally." So she went to San Pietro and seeing all those singers, she approached Moreschi (because he was easily recognizable). Moreschi accepted me for an audition.

I came to Rome on November 14, 1904, and on the 17th of that month, [with] Moreschi returning from his holidays (because November 18th is the feast of the consecration of St. Peter's), I had an audition. He listened to me and he began to give me lessons. Of course, those lessons were superlative. It was he who sang all the time [the phrase "era sempre *lui* che cantava" enunciated with great authority and emphasis] *and I had to imitate him, because singing, like anything, like any other profession, is acquired by means of imitation. It was marvelous. I was enchanted by his incredibly beautiful voice, and I tried to imitate him as a boy who had a great passion for singing would do. I began studying with Moreschi, imitating him, and I imitated him with the voice that I had, since it hadn't yet changed.*

Everything, in sum—the whole enterprise of teaching and learning to sing, hence *becoming a singer*—rests on copying a master.[157] The account, revolving around Mancini's status as novice in a master/apprentice relationship, hardly differs from what one would expect from a seventeenth-century or eighteenth-century singer. The pupil sings like the master because it's axiomatic that the master sings in the best possible way, with insuperable beauty, correctness, and authority, and because imitation is the only way to ever do likewise. The presumptions that underlie Mancini's tale could hardly be further from liberal and neoliberal ideologies associated with "finding one's voice"—precisely what modern-day students typically expect teachers to help them do, driven by ideals that, as James Q. Davies has argued, have pervaded vocal pedagogy since at least the mid-nineteenth century.[158]

The thirteen-year-old Mancini starts off by imitating using "the voice that [he] had" because his voice had not yet broken.

Part 2

So I sang like him in my chest voice, and then I added my head voice. But then, around age fourteen [laughs] *you know, you get a man's voice. And then I started singing with the falsettists. I started to acquire my head voice again—the head voice that all we men have. Of course, you have to practice with it in order to use it, because it's a voice that comes from practice, and by means of musicianship. You need to be a musician to sing falsetto.*

Instead of [attending] the school of Perosi, who didn't want me in his school, because since I studied with Moreschi, Perosi thought I was a castrato.[159] *So he didn't*

> *want me.* [interviewer asks why] *Because remember, the motu proprio had come down that eliminated the voices of castrati from the choirs. Those who had already been there were kept on until their contracts were over [and they reached retirement], but if they were young ones, they weren't admitted. And Perosi got the impression that since I sang in the style of Moreschi, that I was one of those voices. And so afterward, Moreschi had me sent to the school of San Salvatore in Lauro. And there I did everything. I completed primary school, which I had previously left, and then I went on to the conservatory and studied double bass. I graduated and I still play the bass at age seventy-six.*

It wasn't just Mancini's young mind that was adaptable to Moreschi's lessons, but his still-prepubescent physiology, which for a brief time still resembled that of Moreschi, whose own larynx had stopped growing and toughening once he was castrated at around age twelve.[160] Like Moreschi, with his essentially unchanged vocal folds, the young boy Mancini could therefore sing higher in chest (i.e. in "modal" or "natural" voice) than a noncastrated adult could do. Indeed, as I've argued previously, both the unaltered boy and the castrated man were able to sing more or less up to the octave that rises up from middle C to an octave above (c' to c") without shifting registers.[161]

What exactly prompted Perosi to reject Mancini out of hand is hard to say, whether it was his prejudices, combined with his ever-worsening mental state—afflicted with the paranoiac schizophrenia that dogged him all his life and may have made his Cecilianist aversion to castrati particularly toxic—or whether he was actually misled by the exactitude with which Mancini imitated Moreschi.[162] Perosi's thinking, like his listening, stands beyond our epistemological reach, nor can the recordings close the gap. In what follows, Mancini himself explains something of how the perceptual split between performer and listener can mislead and how the trickiness of the apparatus can alienate performer and listener alike. The perceptual split defeats the possibility of knowing one's own voice. The apparatus inevitably confounds the listener who enters the varied perceptual fields it opens up. To start out, Mancini offers a quasi-Kantian observation:

Part 3

There are always a lot of people who pay me compliments, but you can't really know the effect your voice has from the audience's perspective. So when I went from Switzerland to Milan, thanks to a friend of mine, I wanted to go to one of those recording studios to hear how my voice sounded. That's what I did, as a souvenir. It's a souvenir of the time, of an era, but it's not very presentable. Because I am a musician, after all, and the adjustments I had to make in order to record, all of it affected my intonation, which I didn't notice at the time, but which is so evident upon listening to the recording. And it's not presentable, really. Well I mean the technique is the same, because I had to imitate Moreschi, I had to imitate everything completely, just the way he did it. And that was how he taught.

How to make sense of Mancini's acoustic relationship to Moreschi's oralities from these anecdotes, so suggestive, but lean? And how to listen from the haze of scratches, pops, and cracks, limited frequencies, and sometimes wobbly placement of Moreschi's solo recordings to Mancini's choral, yet clearer electrical ones, the earliest from 1936?[163] Some resemblances strike the unsuspecting ear. Mancini's falsetto on Mozart's "Ave verum corpus" sounds as robust as any that one could hear from a falsettist, and the same is true on a "Benedicta es venerabilis" by Armando Antonelli. He omits his teacher's rapid upward appoggiaturas, but his vocal production, including gliding scoops, is familiar. The breathy, hooty timbres common to many countertenors of the last half century and more are nonexistent. And there's that Moreschian operatic quality that ghosts everything.

Listening to the powerful emission of soprano falsettist Gabrielli and alto Luigi Gentili compounds the impression.[164] But sonic genealogies throw up barricades as soon as one sets out to follow them. Here's another one. Moreschi's chief pedagogical legacy, his son Giulio, left not a single sonic trace. Insofar as his voice lived on, it was solely through the raft of students trained in his studio between the mid-1920s and 1955, starting with his wife, Vittoria, whose concert at the Hotel Plaza was packed with difficult verismo numbers (fig. 1.1b). Moving to the 1930s and 1940s, before and after the war, a handful of aspiring stars and starlets are traceable through the Moreschi-Fellini Archive or through oral history. Besides Riccardo, there was Sordi.[165] And there was the Parisian Noëlle Norman (née Simone Denise Bruleport, 1921–1985) (fig. 3.8), who started out doing small parts in four French films in 1938 and 1939, appearing with Vittorio De Sica in the musical comedy *Finisce sempre così* (Italy, Cinecittà, November 29, 1939), where she may have encountered another of Giulio's students, the Russian/Ukranian Assia De Busny (1906–1990), who had a bit part in it (fig. 3.9).

Then the war changed everything. Norman played in *Dopo divorzieremo* (Italy, September 21, 1940, directed by Nunzio Malasomma), but being French, hence a national of the enemy country, she left for France around the time war broke out, returning only in 1947 for her first top billing, in *L'ebreo errante* (January 24, 1948).[166] De Busny also decamped to Paris, where she recorded some French cabaret-style numbers on Columbia 78s. Her specialty became wartime songs of longing, waiting, loneliness, and loss by the likes of Paul Durand and Willy Engel-Berger, delivered with an attractively light lyric voice and a quick, old-fashioned vibrato.[167] Like other pupils, she regularly sent fond remembrances to Giulio, including in the form of annotated photos of herself and her young family.

Sordi and Riccardo Fellini may have kept going to the studio during the war or have gone there when times were safe for moving around the city. Like them, many of Giulio's students who crop up in the archive were centrally involved in cinema, too. Of these, only one, Theodora (Teddy) Getty Gaston, committed to a career in opera, left a surviving account of the studio, the one adduced in the Prologue above. Figure 3.10 shows her in a photo from 1939 on her terrace in Rome holding Giulio's hand, her teacher surrounded by her and another apparent student.[168] That was many decades before her hundredth birthday, when she published her recollections in a memoir about life with the miserly J. Paul Getty, whom she married in Rome that year.[169] Her memories document the devastating transformation of Moreschi's studio from its lively prewar heyday

Figure 3.8. Portrait of French singer-actress Noëlle Norman (1921–1985), signed to Giulio Moreschi, "with whom I worked with all confidence and hope." Moreschi-Fellini Archive.

Figure 3.9. Portrait of Russian/Ukrainian singer-actress Assia De Busny (1906–1990), signed to Giulio Moreschi "with all my gratitude." January 20, 1940. Moreschi-Fellini Archive.

Figure 3.10. Giulio Moreschi with two young women, marked "Tedi" and "Titti" and dated 1939 on the verso in the hand of Vittoria Cevasco. Tedi was Theodora (Teddy) Getty, née Lynch (1913–2017), later Getty Gaston, an aspiring opera singer and wife of J. Paul Getty, who was stranded in Rome during the war where she had stayed to study opera with Giulio. The identity of "Titti" is unknown. Moreschi-Fellini Archive.

to its sorry state once international students quickly fled following Italy's entrance into the war. Giulio had regularly welcomed students into an extended *famiglia* that included members of his own household. Dinners out on the town often brought the day's work to a convivial close. The first time Teddy sang for Giulio — before her husband went off to pursue business travels, leaving her at the nearby Ambasciatore Hotel — she and her husband celebrated the beginning of Teddy's studies with Giulio and Vittoria at Alfredo's, where Giulio declared he would get her concerts and an opera debut with a small company in "no more than three months."[170] They left the restaurant with Giulio singing Salvatore Cardillo's "Core 'ngrato" "like no one since Caruso."[171]

Teddy became close enough to the family to know something of its musical lineage, but apparently not its real secrets — only that Giulio was "the son of one of the last great singers of the nineteenth century, a male soprano."[172] Her studies lasted a few months, spent going to daily lessons, memorizing parts, studying history and literature, and thinking about opera roles. On some nights, she joined the Moreschi family and Giulio's students at the Cisterna in Trastevere, near the Moreschi-Cevasco home, where they would all sing.[173] But the threat of war hung in the air. Teddy gives a harrowing account of the day Italy entered the war, when Maestro Giulio and other pupils were celebrating their last rehearsal with drinks at the Ambasciatori before leaving on a little concert tour. The party ended up seated nerve-rackingly near Mussolini's son-in-law, Foreign Minister Count Gian Galeazzo Ciano, whom everyone knew was playing a key role in determining Italy's future.[174] They left, moving on in Teddy's car, but got caught in piazza Venezia, where Mussolini was shouting his declaration of war on France and England from his infamous balcony, with hordes of Blackshirts going "absolutely wild, yelling themselves hoarse." When they finally reached the Moreschi house, they were met by Alessandra and Vittoria, "crying hysterically '*Julio, Julio [sic], siamo in guerra.*'" All at once, the long assault of nightly blackouts, alarms, quaking

Figure 3.11. Film still of Teddy Getty Gaston as the opera singer in Billy Wilder's noir classic *The Lost Weekend* (1945), directed by Billy Wilder. Uncredited.

Figure 3.12. Portrait of a student of Giulio Moreschi's, possibly a Greek tenor, signed from his "most affectionate alumnus," here presumably playing Cavaradossi in an Athens production of *Tosca*. Moreschi-Fellini Archive.

buildings, and blasting antiaircraft guns began, quashing Teddy's dreams of a future in opera, along with the prospects of Moreschi's other students.[175] As hopes for concerts were put off indefinitely, Giulio's studio shrank to just a few. "The war had robbed Moreschi of his livelihood, and he was suffering, as were all the artists, painters, and scholars, for Rome was empty of gaiety, the people disheartened, and there were no foreigners who wished to study or to buy. All that was left was the daily sickening infiltration of the Nazis, who virtually took over the Italian government—their secret police everywhere."[176]

Teddy stayed on for a while, having to declare herself of the Ayran race and becoming a journalist, which got her put into jail and then under house arrest until, after some time, she made it out of Rome and, in 1945, was cast as an opera singer in Billy Wilder's *Lost Weekend* (fig. 3.11).[177] Other students simply had to leave the city as fast as possible, including a tenor, possibly Greek, who is pictured in figure 3.12 playing Cavaradossi in an Athens production of *Tosca*.[178] Ethi Junger, by that time married to an Englishman and hence in peril, remained, as did Riccardo and Alberto, then dodging the draft, but there's no trace of others.[179]

CHAPTER FOUR

Masculinities and Hermaphrodites

> Mustafà, gifted by nature with a superb physique — imposing stature, nice features, lively, penetrating eyes — was never reconciled to his disgrace; and to the perennial and burning memory of this he wanted to attribute the cause of certain quirks and susceptibilities in his character. . . .
>
> . . . Nor is there any testimony that Mustafà was tied to his father by constraints of affection. I was also told at Montefalco that when his father went there to pay him a visit, Domenico Mustafà was ashamed to present him to his friends and kept him hidden in a house for the whole time of his stay and worried about getting him to take off as soon as possible.
>
> — Alberto De Angelis, *Domenico Mustafà*

Anecdotes of almost preposterously Freudian character and no little violence swirled about Moreschi's castrato superior, Domenico Mustafà, who was said to have harbored the deepest resentment toward his father for the injury done to him and the venality that motivated it. Alberto De Angelis published one such anecdote, collected from the Perugian nobleman Gino Monaldi (1847–1932), who managed Rome's Costanzi and Argentina opera houses from 1891 to 1893 and who long afterward, in 1920, published his fatuous, error-ridden *Cantanti evirati celebri del teatro italiano* (Celebrated castrato singers in the Italian theater). In De Angelis's words: "One day (Gino Monaldi narrated to me), during a meal, someone having made an indiscreet allusion to the imperfect physique of the singer, he suddenly climbed up, holding a knife to peel a piece of fruit, and in furor exclaimed 'if at this moment I were to learn that it was my father who diminished me thus [*ridurmi così*], I would kill him with this knife.'"[1]

De Angelis reported another tale that circulated from Gaetano Capocci to the Vatican archeologist, church reformer, choral director, and photographer Baron Rodolfo Kanzler (1864–1924). "For his part, the Baron Rodolfo Kanzler recounted to me that once Mustafà attacked his own father with a double-barreled shotgun, accusing him of having had him castrated for speculative ends. This was told to Kanzler by Maestro Capocci, who, present at the scene, interposed himself to impede Mustafà from putting into action a tragic plan."[2] Not every account was so theatrical, and some came straight from locals in Mustafà's Umbrian hometown, but all have the flavor of an inside scoop.

How many other tales, how much more blather and gossip eddied around castrati still living in Moreschi's time? And then, too, how much paternal resentment — or was De Angelis slipping into a quasi-psychoanalytic account under the influence of early translations and glosses of Freud? It's hard to say, except that by 1926, when De Angelis published his biography of Mustafà, the Italian reception of Freud, still in its infancy, had already begun to penetrate Italian intellectual life. A translation, *Sulla psicoanalisi: Cinque conferenze tenute nel settembre 1909*, edited by the general psychiatrist Marco Levi Bianchini, was published in Naples in 1915 and six years on an Italian translation of Freud's theories of sexuality.[3] By then the still-early dissemination of Freud's ideas was being led by Edoardo Weiss, a more influential and far more reliable figure than Levi Bianchini and one whose professional formation was closely tied to Freud, having produced an early translation and introductory writings on him.[4]

This chapter begins by broaching psychoanalytic matters in a quest for the Italian male, from Moreschi to Fellini and back, across the

Ariadne web that stretches across this book. It finds that where emergent ideals of masculinity haunted Moreschi and his colleagues around the turn of the century — ideals that by the time of Mussolini's *ventennio* had exploded into the Fascists' bellicose images of masculinity, marked by colossal statues, powerful engines, and barbarous shouting — such specters had become objects of suspicion for the postbellum, post-Fascist generation of Fellini, no longer besotted by them. By the 1950s, popular imagery was instead making room for masculine countertypes: antiheroes, inept men, good and innocent types, and sentimental characters. By the early 1960s, satires of normative Italian males abounded in film and other representational forms.[5] All in all, we might say that the postwar take on the Italian male was critical and ambivalent, even as it was also endlessly forgiving.[6]

In what follows, I confront nearly a century of views, from the 1880s to the 1960s, through a series of readings, rather in the manner of an omnibus film, starting with a 1961 essay on the Great Mediterranean Mother by Fellini's German-Jewish Jungian psychoanalyst Ernst Bernhard (1896–1965), who fled Nazi Germany for Rome in 1936. From there, I move backward to the dilemmas posed by the castrato in liberal Italy, reading the ecstatic and fantastical experience of a castrato voice recounted by the minor literato Enrico Panzacchi (1840–1904) in his 1885 story "Cantores!" Even before Panzacchi idealized the castrato voice, Moreschi, already an object of intense melophilic desire, had been called out to Vatican authorities for divalike behavior by a prominent chapelmaster and labeled a hermaphrodite. What the epithet says about the status of the castrato drives the penultimate section, pursued first through Alberto Savinio's 1918 metaphysical novel *Hermaphrodito* and then through the episode of the hermaphrodite in *Fellini Satyricon* of 1969. In between, I enlarge on the union of Alessandro Moreschi and Guendalina Rinaldi, a union that veered far from prevailing marital paradigms that situated males as generative patriarchs, even as it tried to accommodate them.

My goal is not to chronicle instances of Italian maleness as contrasts to a defective, anachronistic castrato, but to bring out the ontological stakes in evolving gender differences that the castrato disturbs but also clarifies, differences that have shadowed a family history phantomatically over the course of a century and a half. The figure of the hermaphrodite proves useful in this task because its condition assumes a shape-shifting, quasi-Ovidian function, from the hermaphrodite who is *imputed from the outside* (in Moreschi's case), to the ones that are *staged as quasi-religious icons* (explicitly in Fellini's *Satyricon*), to the one *imagined as a metaphysical being* (in Savinio's novel, founded throughout on the metaphor and metaphysics of the hermaphrodite)—all of whom, I argue, do their work of shape-shifting through the voice.

In the last regard, it's well to remember that like earlier castrati, late Vatican ones sound otherness by continually functioning as embodied and sensible because audible boundary crossers. In one sense, Moreschi senior was a man of the church, but in another, a highly secular man, a man who went to the opera, got married, sang arias and opera ensembles in hotels and salons, probably participated in clandestine reworkings of secular operas (*rifacimenti*), as Mustafà and others had, and certainly dressed like a dandy, collected autographed opera portraits, and went on to make commercial recordings, including of secular and semi-secular songs, as well as raising a child who grew up doing most of the above and more. He almost certainly went to the movies, too, not just to the religious magic lantern shows put on by the Baron Kanzler and movies in the religious cinematic vein with which Kanzler was associated, but worldly movies, given that by 1917, his nephew, Amerigo, was operating a movie theater just off piazza Venezia, the Cinema Venezia.[7]

Moreschi, in sum, was very much a boundary crosser, and not just an embodied, but a specifically sonic, musical one. For above all, he was a man of song, with its own ramifications for Italian identity.

The Church and the Great Mediterranean Mother

Ernst Bernhard moved to Italy permanently with his wife, Dora. after being refused asylum in Britain. Some parts of their Italian residency gave them a bumpy ride. In 1938, Italy implemented Fascist racial laws. By summer 1940, the Bernhards were imprisoned in the internment camp Ferramonti di Tarsia in Calabria soon after it opened, remaining there for over three years, until the camp was liberated by the Allies in September 1943.

Seventeen years after the Bernhards' release, in 1960–61, Federico Fellini found his way to the doctor's Roman office at via Gregoriana 12, apartment 15, above the piazza di Spagna, to begin what turned out to be a four-year-long course of sessions.[8] Chapter 5 takes up some fascinating outcomes of those sessions in the form of Fellini's dream books, where Riccardo Fellini features far more often than the amount of contact sustained between the brothers might forecast.[9] During the start of Fellini's sessions, Bernhard also produced his Jungian essay on the Italian psyche as an object of psychoanalysis, "Il complesso della Grande Madre: problemi e possibilità della psicologia analitica in Italia" (The complex of the Great Mother: Problems and possibilities for analytical psychology in Italy). Originally (and, given his history, somewhat ironically) written in German, the essay theorized the existence in the Italian family of a long-standing Jungian archetype[10]—a "Shadow" that Bernhard refers to throughout not just as The Great Mother (as in the title) but the Great *Mediterranean* Mother. In his account, the Great Mediterranean Mother haunts Italian life and especially the psyche of the Italian man, marking him with traits with which he's often caricatured: untrustworthiness, lack of principles, hypersexual compulsions, vanity, a spoiled and sentimental nature, and generally impulsive behavior.[11]

The merest brush with such notions makes obvious how the prominence in the Vatican of castrated men could agitate the Italian psyche, particularly at this moment in history. Suzanne

Stewart-Steinberg has argued that what the postliberal moment produces is an "anxious" Italian ego, something sentimental, unruly, ungovernable, and (in sum) childlike. Indeed, in the myth of Italy, our own moment still does so, casually perpetuating such ideas in current-day popular culture. But Stewart-Steinberg also wants to add a significant historical corollary, arguing that the childlike male emerges in the context of Italy's comparatively late industrialization, modernization, and national integration, to which we could add: its new class mobility, growing numbers of working women, and new colonial and imperial projects, particularly in the lands now called Ethiopia and Eritrea (and later including Libya), all of which were components of a country stubbornly adhering to "prototraditional and protoirrational political structures."[12]

With this in mind, we might return for a more granular look at Bernhard's essay, which posits the Great Mediterranean Mother in a Jungian vein as the "key" that makes it possible to "unlock the enigma of the Italian *anima*," a type that for Bernhard has loomed for millennia, often pathologically (as with Circe, said to have made men lose their heads and to have turned them into purely instinctual beings). Bernhard goes so far as to claim that the Great Mediterranean Mother, who stands in mythically for the Italian woman, manifests in all persons and all aspects of society. The Great Mediterranean Mother lives hidden within every Italian woman, each housing the former as the protagonist in a network of relations.[13] On his account, since attitudes surrounding her extend infinitely through mechanisms of projection, the needier the child—especially a male child—the more she springs into action, perpetuating lack of reliability and punctuality in her offspring. But Bernhard goes further still. Because he assumes that the Italian male is dominated by her, he also assumes that the Italian male lacks capacities for abstraction and manly discipline, instead succumbing inexorably when he comes into conflict with her or her proxies.

Reading Bernhard's essay, it's hard not to think of Alberto Sordi in *Lo sceicco bianco* as the sheik who disintegrates when faced with his domineering wife, or of Alberto (Sordi again) crying on his mother's apron in *I vitelloni* when he learns that his older sister whose earnings have been keeping them all afloat has eloped—a popular type for Fellini years before he met Bernhard and well worth laughing at in celluloid comedy. For Bernhard, behaviors like these always come from a maternal source, expressed in the constant Italian refrains of "Poveretto!" and "Pazienza!" that convey the mother's endlessly introjected unconscious as she assumes the role of the great consoler.[14] Hence Bernhard's presumption that the Italian man's leniency toward his own faults and foibles was learned at his mother's bosom, to be cyclically repeated as he counts on the mother's continual protection.

As Bernhard's analysis develops, the Great Mediterranean Mother quickly goes from being a Jungian archetype to a hardened stereotype—a dialectical one, yet with devastating effects. The more she excuses her children, he claims, the more dependent they become, until inevitably, her excuses backfire, and the same dynamic that caused her to be venerated transforms her into her maternal opposite: a devouring mother type, a trope Bernhard delivers with unabashed confidence. This underbelly of the Great Mediterranean Mother is moreover taken to account for negative complexes and dangerous neuroses that lurk around her living and breathing manifestations.[15] The actual mother, Bernhard asserts, represents the undifferentiated Shadow side to whose influences the Italian man is easily exposed through identification because of his relatively weak ego (an identification that, on the good side, also tends to make Italian men rather maternal). But then the essay throws up another negative dimension in the person of the father, taken to represent something like the Freudian superego, bound up with rights and duties, in contrast to a maternal brother or an uncle who might step in to soften the father's role.

The upshot for Bernhard is no less than an Italian man of compromised morals. While often the ideal lover, he runs the constant risk of experiencing passion as a symptom and turning jealousy into a tactic since his passions dispose him to fixation, obsession, and even actual "crimes of passion," deemed natural by public opinion and therefore excused.[16]

Most strikingly for my themes, Bernhard's mother figure impedes her children's independence precisely because she is the pillar of religion. In particular, his essay depicts the male child not just as a mamma's boy to his own mother, but as a *puer aeternus* vis-à-vis the church, which Bernhard understands as a fundamentally conservative institution functioning to promote and make manifest arrested societal development. Once again, a dualistic nature marks Bernhard's analysis.[17] The *puer aeternus* so produced may be driven by "creative intuition, and a sense of adventure," but he also reacts against the church, much as he reacts against the mother, becoming (not unlike *I vitelloni*'s Fausto) rebellious, impulsive, overly excitable, and daring to the point of being foolhardy.

Such oppositions will not surprise followers of Fellini, given his complex views on Italian religion (recall Fellini's ironic "gratitude" to the Roman Catholic Church "for all the distortions, the obscurities, the taboos which have created an immense body of dialectic as a basis for life-giving rebellions gratitude to the church").[18] The church's age-old attraction to ancient Etruscan elements, which intensely preoccupied Fellini in the 1960s, gave Bernhard grist for his mill. To the occult, the otherworldly, miracles, and magic Bernhard ascribed the ongoing popularity and power of the church in the twentieth century in arguments that lie surprisingly close to those of certain scholars of Catholic modernism. John Pollard and Darrell Jodock, for example, both stress the remarkable post-1870 rebound the church made after the fall of Rome by vernacularizing itself among the populace. Others, notably David Kertzer, underscore the church's sustenance of Mussolini.[19]

Unsurprisingly, Bernhard discovers the popularity of the church in its power to manifest itself in each individual as something distinctly patriarchal, yet also to show itself as ennobled and spiritualized by the Virgin in a personal, matriarchal vein. Hence, for him, matriarchy persists in tension with a patriarchal shadow—the flip side of churchly beneficence, whose "dual aspect" becomes the central problematic of Italian neuroses. And this is key: Bernhard's bad, all-consuming mother, who necessarily exists alongside a beneficent one, is not a figure the church can escape, even as it bestows the Great Mother's blessings: "Her genial system of caring for souls is at the same time a rigorous system of control and a cruel system of punishment, which for centuries became in literature and art a gymnasium of sadistic fantasies. Since [there are] those who are not or do not want to be her children, she strictly excludes them from her graces and condemns them to the eternal punishment of Hell."[20]

Bernhard's solution to this massive psychocultural dilemma was of course Jungian psychoanalysis, with its promise to make the light and shadow of the Great Mediterranean Mother visible. For Bernhard, judging from a point of view that does justice to the matriarchal type meant not relegating it to a Shadow position, but rather bringing it out into the open, whether in conscious or unconscious experience. Only in that way could the Great Mother live in her proper place and dispense all her benefits harmoniously.[21] Beyond that, Bernhard supposed that Italians could contribute to the world by adumbrating and expanding on the Great Mediterranean Mother. Attempts at patriarchal oppression (as happened, he noted, with Fascism) would always, to the contrary, be marked by the exaggerated character of adolescence and would eventually have to submit to the Great Mediterranean Mother, as occurred by the end of the war.[22]

All this reverberates with Fellini's personal journey and creative output, markedly in the postwar period, a time that Bernhard himself experienced and later influenced. But in my view, there is something in it that precedes those years as well, thinking especially of the postliberal moment experienced by Mustafà, Moreschi, and the papal chapel after the fall of Rome—the years of "Catholic recovery," 1870 to 1914, when Italy was struggling to pinpoint its national identity and character and laying the sorry ground for its surrender to Fascism.[23] It was a time of impotence for Italian intellectuals, including, not much later, such an important Marxist as Antonio Gramsci (1891–1937), as well as other precarious left-leaning critics, who could write and speak to great everlasting effect, but not effect external change, hence being relegated to a time of colossal defeat.

One of the most trenchant analyses of those earlier decades, Stewart-Steinberg's *The Pinocchio Effect: On Making Italians (1860–1920)*, aligns to a surprising degree with what we've seen in Bernhard, in her case supported by a literary-historical optic trained on earlier generations. *The Pinocchio Effect* sees the kinds of failures noted by Bernhard as having been vouchsafed by late nineteenth-century and early twentieth-century writers who associate certain traits of *italianità* with "superficiality, rhetoricism, absence of essence, and a childlike nature."[24] To unfold its argument, the book makes recourse to Carlo Collodi's Pinocchio as an ambiguously complex, unpredictably nuanced, but invariably childlike figuration of Italianness operating along two main fronts. On one front, children become the focus of Italian educational ideologies and programs, famously, Maria Montessori's, in a world in which Italians themselves were often regarded as children.[25] On another, grown Italian men come to be conceived as preternaturally impotent. Both phenomena relate dialectically to women's strong role in resuscitating the post-1870 church (without their being assigned official roles in it, of course) — a church that affirmed the value of womanhood and motherhood at the same time as writers were highlighting a "crisis of the paternal function, and hence . . . a crisis of male performativity."[26]

The arguments are both provocative and disorienting for thinking about castrati, who inhabited a force field littered with cognate anxieties. Mustafà's refusal of his father notwithstanding — and notwithstanding a host of countermanding tactics, including Moreschi's marriage and fatherhood, designed to subvert the fates predestined for castrati and the ambivalences and aversions observers projected onto them — castrati themselves often bought into those fates.

How, we might ask, were different cultural types, technohuman and transspecies, produced within what were basically the same historic matrices? One of those cultural types is the stringless, animated, dancing, darting, magic-and-animal-engaging puppet Pinocchio around which Stewart-Steinberg's argument turns. Another is the early modern comic character Pulcinella, whose uncanny origin myths and myths of kinship got bound up with those of castrati. Like Pinocchio, Pulcinella, the half bird, part castrato comedian prevalent in Italian festive life, was a highly transformable figure.[27] Whereas the manmade Pinocchio first entered literary collections in the same year of 1883 in which Moreschi became a *partecipante* in the Sistine Chapel, Pulcinella emerged centuries earlier around the same time castrati did. Running through both Pinocchio and Pulcinella is a constant performativity, always veering toward iconoclasm and insubordination, including affinities with Carnival and a susceptibility to riotous social and symbolic reproduction.

There the affinities wane, but don't end. Folk tales, satires, and visual iconography prolifically depict Pulcinella in the out of doors, often in multiples — whole families or clans of Pulcinellini. Thoroughly theatrical and castratolike, with a high cackling voice, sexual deficiencies, and a womanish figure, Pulcinella might be thought of as quintessentially early modern, prone to bizarre forms of procreation, amphibious, androgynous, and affinal to animals. He was yoked to the animal world through his very name, evoking the *pullus*, or chicken, and endlessly paired with other domestic fowl as well as mammals, including dogs, cats, pigs, and donkeys.[28]

However partial and provisional Pulcinella's affinities with castrati, they didn't pass unnoticed. The castrato Filippo Balatri produced writings elaborating the correspondences, joking in his satirical pseudoautobiography in verse *Frutti del mondo* (1725–1732) about having been brought into life by a rooster-surgeon specialized in castration of boys for singing (a "norcino"), much as Pulcinella had been brought to life in certain earlier texts and images.[29] By brooding and hatching male-soprano chicks, Balatri's cock became a maker of castrati within a larger mythical order in which males reproduce males. Indeed, Balatri's tall tale would not have been possible but for Pulcinella's endless reproduction in the form of triplets, quadruplets, quintuplets, squadrons, entourages, armies, charioteers, revelers, feasters, *burattini* (puppets), and above all, whole bands of families. One eighteenth-century caricaturist underscored the castrato-Pulcinella connection by depicting a castrato watching a pair of Pulcinella puppets perform in a Venetian window during Carnival, effectively deploying the same poetic tropes that poets and comics played with, according to which males castrate other males to make Pulcinella types.[30]

What's notable across these different scenarios is that, more broadly, males repeatedly produce other males. Making males was the very business of a church that effectively cranked out castrati, or at minimum deployed them, for centuries in tandem with, and very often in cooperation with, princes, fathers, teachers, and other paternal figures. In modern times, making males was also the symbolic and pragmatic business of schools, churches, and government bureaucracies. Hence Stewart-Steinberg's argument that Pinocchio, as a product of the later nineteenth century, was not just manufactured mechanically, but reproduced in ways that figure the modern Italian man. Whether a "puppet" of early Novecento state apparatuses or a puppet "strung together" via ideology (as she would have it), Pinocchio figures as a pawn who lacks agency.[31] Strikingly, too, Pinocchio, like Pulcinella, is an Italian man-child who is inherently reproducible, but who also, in his case, displays elements of looseness, what the late nineteenth-century Neapolitan writer Pasquale Turiello called *scioltezza*, implying tendencies to push against collectivities in favor of individualism while manifesting difficult dialectics between them, as Stewart-Steinberg quickly points out—tendencies to both accept and resist the limits imposed by strong men in cults of power.[32]

If Pulcinella and Pinocchio represent different stages and incarnations of an "Italian man," it's unsurprising that both are also reminiscent of Freud's band of brothers in *Totem and Taboo*, "in revolt against a ruthless and cruel father," manifested in Pulcinella's case by birthings and hatchings aided by feckless, reckless males and domineering females and in Pinocchio's by Fire-Eater's theater.[33] We might think back, too, to the anecdotes about Mustafà's resentment of his father which echo the disturbing recollection Balatri made in 1725 of his father's call for his castration.[34]

The "castropolitical power" briefly discussed in Chapter 2 meant that those who were powerful—above all, monarchs, including the papal monarch—maintained political control over bodies, including the right to order castrations (even if it was a right to which they did not lay formal claim and one for which they generally did not take responsibility).[35] The papal monarch thus maintained biopolitical power. And that power aligned, even as it contrasted, with late twentieth-century and early twenty-first-century cartographies that map again onto other power hierarchies: those that stand at the intersection of human and animal as drawn up by Donna Haraway, for instance, and those that stand at the intersections of sex and gender as drawn up by trans philosopher Paul B. Preciado.[36] Even after the papacy lost "necropolitical power" (the right to kill) in 1870 by losing the territories known collectively as the Papal States, it continued to exercise castropolitical power, most probably seeing to Moreschi's castration the following year or at minimum exploiting it thereafter. That meant that the papacy did not just suddenly revert from temporal sovereignty to spiritual sovereignty—nor, indeed, was any such absolute opposition possible—but went on using a degree of temporal sovereignty after the fall of Rome. Then, as late as 1897, as we saw in Chapter 1, it resolved again to use its temporal powers on more boys, or at least to get hold of any castrated boys it might by some good fortune "discover." We might say, then, that while the rest of Western Europe went from being a "sovereign society" to a "disciplinary society" around 1800, as Michel Foucault argued, papal Rome did not. Rome never fully emerged from the grip of papal rule except in formal governmental terms. And between 1902 and 1904, it only partly gave up power over castrati, expelling them from its choirs after most had already died or retired, but utilizing those who remained. All to say that while time marched onward in the West, it folded in on itself in the Vatican. At the same moment that the demands of modernity seemed a sine qua non, even in Rome, the papacy lagged behind, remaining glaringly premodern. If late castrati thus exemplify the condition of papal time as time displaced, they also index epistemic shifts in the political terms of Europe, exemplifying the same ongoing power of sovereign biopolitics that they resist.

How does all this tie the castrato to problems of manhood and *italianità* that Pinocchio raises for Stewart-Steinberg, a puppet who is delinked from religious categories and distantly echoes a rebellious, infantile, and sexually deficient early modern Carnival character elided with the pagan, the gluttonous, the scatological, and even the obscene?[37] Before taking leave of Stewart-Steinberg, let's read her gloss of the late Ottocento literary scholar Francesco De Sanctis, who called on Italian poets to help shape Italy's future:

> De Sanctis consistently relates . . . insincerity as a lack of interiority to a feminized and feminizing sentimentality, to a rhetorical quality of Italians that severs their relationship with the word and catapults them into the melodramatic world of music and opera. The word is extremely powerful, he states, when it comes from the soul, but when interiority is nonexistent or empty, it becomes insipid and boring. In Italy, the word had become a sound; literature had become music and song. Hence "melodrama and musical drama are the popular genre, where scenery, mimicry, song and music work on the imagination far more powerfully than an insipid word, a vacuous sonority, which has turned into a mere supplement."[38]

De Sanctis's reservations were hardly new, nor was the battle between linguistic content as essence versus sound and music as supplement, surface, or ornament. The battle goes back to Cicero, whose ideas were rearticulated with startling clarity during his sixteenth-century reception by Italian humanists and literati, who grounded their debates on the Italian language (the *questione della lingua*) in a set of oppositions: between the relative merits of Ciceronian rhetoric, driven by the force of eloquence, argumentative, gestural, and sonic, as compared to those of Scholastic philosophy, driven fixed principles and formal logic.[39]

By no coincidence, castrati emerged not in the "less enlightened" Middle Ages, whose values were inscribed in syllogisms, axioms, *questiones*, and soliloquies that turned around logic, but in early modern times, specifically, the second half of the sixteenth century, whose values were embedded in the persuasive force of rhetoric. The later sixteenth century also witnessed steep rises in capital accumulation, colonial domination and extraction, mercantilism, urban expansion, and (indivisibly) explosions in the trafficking of bodies, especially of slaves. In Italy, these developments were closely tied to economic instability. Indeed, the entire advent of castrati coincided with the advent of patrilineal devolution and descent based not on horizontal clans, but direct vertical descent through male lines, in turn a way of correcting for declining wealth, since thin vertical lines of descent could secure what wealth existed within nuclear families whose goal was to protect their capital. Most women of station went to convents, while most cadets went to the military or the priesthood in a world in which only first sons were privileged with rights of primogeniture.[40] Boys who were neither first sons nor noble were not infrequently castrated.

The historical situation thus coincided with what Bonnie Gordon in *Voice Machines* identifies as violent colonial fantasies of exploration and migration that cannot be pried apart from castration itself. Gordon understands the castrato as a technological means by which those fantasies were realized at home and abroad: "The timeline of the castrato phenomenon centers on the period that Anglophone historians think of as the early modern," which, "uniquely, both *produced* a caste of technologically altered male singers and reinflected the nature/art, techne/nature differences that it inherited from ancient and medieval times." To establish how this happened, Gordon "attends to the ways that early modern inventions and encounters participated in making castrati" and thinks about how "settler colonialism, emergent racialized worldviews, the printing press, gunpowder, and the telescope" all played a role in making castrati.[41]

A Castrato Fantasia (on Maleness and Voice Love)

A special kind of melophilia has much to do with the explosion of castrati in early modern Italy and their sustenance into modern times. Without intense desire for ravishing high voices, the symbolic, economic, and pragmatic vicissitudes that brought about castrati and sustained them over centuries would have been impossible. Francesco De Sanctis, notably, found the Italian love of sound deeply and disturbingly gendered. For him, sound itself was feminizing, and relatedly, sound was almost tantamount to voice, specifically, female voice. Had anyone asked, De Sanctis would surely have said that Italian love of voice even made room, shockingly, for an altered, sexually compromised caste of male sopranos to endure in the Roman church.

Mladen Dolar's influential Lacanian book on voice, *A Voice and Nothing More*, riffs on this problem in order to bring out the often troubling disjuncture between vocal meaning and vocal sound. The book begins by telling a joke about a group of Italian soldiers reacting to an order to attack. Their response underscores the supposed Italian love of sensuality, expressed in their attachment to beautiful voice.

> In the middle of a battle there is a company of Italian soldiers in the trenches, and an Italian commander who issues the command "Soldiers, attack!" He cries out in a loud and clear voice to make himself heard in the midst of the tumult, but nothing happens, nobody moves. So the commander gets angry and shouts louder: "Soldiers, attack!" Still nobody moves. And since in jokes things have to happen three times for something to stir, he yells

even louder: "Soldiers, attack!" At which point there is a response, a tiny voice rising from the trenches, saying appreciatively "*Che bella voce?*" "What a beautiful voice!"[42]

Prima facie, what we have are soldiers more smitten with voice than disposed to battle. But it isn't just voice that's at stake in the joke, and not just *Italian* voice, but Italian masculinity, including all the issues surrounding the voice/gender relation raised by the prospect of soldiers so enamored of voice that they fail to attack when commanded by a superior, even under threat of bodily harm. Love of sound is emasculating and reduces national interest to the superficial, the sensual, and the aesthetic.

Here, I want to turn to a story that has often been cited in literature about castrati, but not closely studied: Enrico Panzacchi's "Cantores!" first published in his *Racconti incredibili ed credibili* in 1885 and later republished in editions of 1889, 1890, 1894, and 1900. (See the text and translation of Panzacchi's story in Appendix 2.)[43] Panzacchi was an emphatically minor writer and critic, given to a kind of literary braggadocio, if lacking the literary gifts to fully carry it off. His story, staged in quasi-autobiographical terms, collapses author and character, encouraging the reader to identify the author's first-person invention with the author himself.[44] We first encounter him heading to St. Peter's on Ascension Day after a leisurely lunch and finding himself entranced by the voice of a castrato. The story has entered the annals of castrato literature because it contains one of the most pointed depictions of a castrato voice to be found anywhere, a voice described as high-pitched, mellifluous, exquisitely refined, as sweet as a flute and as light and untrammeled as a skylark, with a perfect intonation and an effortless passaggio from one register to the next.

Although the mise-en-scène for the story is St. Peter's, its focal point is instead the cantoria, whose choir stalls were of course still then stacked with eunuchs. Panzacchi immediately announces his approach to St. Peter's in the proleptical terms of an unnamed "desire that's at first glance inhuman, grotesque, odd, and a bit monstrous [*teratologico*]," yet not out of keeping with "a high sense of truth." The revelation is presented, brinkmanlike, by a man on the verge of a fall. As he enters the church at sundown, with the great shadows of the colonnade settling onto the square, he finds a mix of natives, tourists, religious people, and gapers all heaped together in a peculiarly Roman anthill, lost among the great naves and pylons of the church, then apprehends a sound of inexpressible, unearthly beauty.

> Was it an instrument? Was it a human voice? At first I could not understand. . . . It was the sound of an unusual timbre and height, very fine,[45] yet vibrant for this vast space in a way that seemed to fill it completely. After taking a few steps in the basilica, I heard distinctly notes of a phrase from a biblical verse reach my ears. So without doubt it was a human voice.
>
> And what singing, signora! Imagine a voice that combines the sweetness of the flute and the lively mellifluousness of the human larynx, a voice that rises, rises light and spontaneous, as a skylark flies through the air when it's inebriated by the sun; and then when it seems that this voice must be poised on the highest vertices of the topmost range, takes further flight, and rises and rises, always with equal lightness, equally spontaneous, without the least expression of force, without the slightest hint of artifice, of searching about, of effort — a voice that, in sum, gives you the immediate sense "of feeling made sound" and the ascent of a soul toward the infinite on the wings of that feeling.[46]

Musicologists have previously been drawn to Panzacchi's tale for its apparent close listening to a castrato voice.[47] But here I want to think about it somewhat differently. Whether or not the voice described is that of a specific singer heard by the author and then elaborated in his tale, it aligns with other descriptions of castrato voices well enough to suspect the author modeled it on them. In the end, though, the voice matters not as empirical or historical evidence, but as the index of a (masculine) relation to the Other, specifically to the voice of the Other. "For Cantores!" is ultimately a love story braiding voice tightly within it, one that, like many other love stories, is finally about self-love. As the listening author, fictive or real, encounters the castrato voice, what he hears is not an alien Other, but himself. The Other excites him mostly because he enables the author's trope of himself as prone to, indeed victim of, bizarre, illicit impulses, far from the bourgeois norms that sharply differentiated men and women in his time, not least in the church. Springing from the castrato voice, then, comes Panzacchi's telling of his dissolute and disorderly passions, clumsily tethered to his supposed access to higher truths inaccessible to conventional beings.

For those familiar with the work of artists and writers known as the Scapigliati (literally, Unkempt or Disheveled Ones), whose movement (Scapigliatura) flourished around the 1810s to 1870s, Panzacchi's pseudobohemian style will be familiar, even if doctored with bits of earthy verismo.[48] But it's the voice of the castrato that counts—a proxy that impels the protagonist to a zone of dangerous self-discovery motivated by passionate attraction. The castrato does not merely enable Panzacchi's strange passions, however. He also furnishes him with a way to stage himself as a man driven by necessity.

All this is conveyed to a skeptical auditor, a disapproving, but mysterious (because absent) lady friend whose regard Panzacchi laments he may have lost ("I do not think, my sweet friend, that I have been unworthy of your esteem"). As with much else in the text, which is filled with allusions and gaps, we know Panzacchi's addressee, his "dolce amica," only elliptically, via his reference to a (missing) letter to which he responds by attending to her withering contempt for his weird, outsized passions. Nor do we understand why he's unready for the day, why he's unaware that it's the feast of the Ascension, and why he's therefore unprepared to find thronging crowds at St. Peter's ("I believed that as usual I would find the great church empty at that hour, but I was mistaken").

This thwarting of signs through hints, circumlocutions, and mistaken pathways is part of what makes "Cantores!" a *racconto incredibile*, as the expanded 1885 edition of the anthology has it, and "unbelievable" in a way that already suggests a sly intertwining of veracity with make-believe. Thwarting conventional signification also puts the reader hand in hand with the author in an instant when something takes total possession of him. That something is not just music, although music is its trigger, but a vocal sound that agitates him so thoroughly as to change his status as a human being, causing him finally to object that his obsessive preoccupation with a castrato has not meant that he has "ceased to be a man!" but rather added to his manhood. Notably, Panzacchi enters St. Peter's at the witching hour, in the shadow of Vespers, and exits in love with a castrato's voice, a product of his imaginings that constitutes a being in love with himself. The castrato's sound bewitches, seduces. It is irresistible—something outside the ordinary sphere of sounding and hearing. For the body to submit to such forbidden pleasures requires the vast exterior mysteries of the Vatican piazza and the interior mysteries of the Sistine Chapel, haunting in their disclosure of a voice that is "feeling made sound," and one that plunges the listener apprehensively, but immediately and inevitably, into love and self-loss with a sound that's at first obscure: "As I pushed open the heavy curtain of the door a musical sound suddenly struck me. Was it an instrument? Was it a human voice? At first I could not understand."

The voice exceeds words, even though words alone can ensure its humanness. As if listening to a recording, Panzacchi notes: "After taking a few steps in the basilica, I heard distinctly notes of a phrase from a biblical verse reach my ears. So without doubt it was a human voice." And once our hero finds it, he also finds a voice worthy of the term "soprano" by natural and divinely ordained right, unlike what applies to the venal women who populate the operatic stage.

> Finally I had heard the true voice of the soprano. May the female sopranos who usurp this name hide themselves! We will call them "soprane" [a made-up feminine form of soprano] if they like; but it is to be hoped for the sake

> of the art of singing, which is greatly declining, that they once again abstain from the wretched ambition of rising through the efforts of their larynx to certain diatonic vertices only legitimately permitted to true [male] sopranos, to sacred sopranos, to sopranos by divine right.

The passage molds to a psychoanalytic reading almost too well in its gloss on the operations of voice. Voice here is a crucial remainder, beyond words and beyond phonology, a remainder that cannot be incorporated fully into the subject who experiences it as an "object" in the peculiarly Lacanian sense of something that disturbs the psyche. Music may try to domesticate the object with its irresistible qualities—its luxurious sounds and harmonies, entraining feel, and seductive timbres, which capture the attentions of Panzacchi—but the musicking castrato voice will remain forever troubling, hence prone to being fetishized as it opens up disconcerting, inexplicable gaps in the listener.[49]

Enter love in the form of self-love. The voice adored and idolized here is narcissistically so. As Dolar and Shane Butler point out, such a voice summons in memory the narcissism of the eponymous Ovidian character Narcissus, in his affair with the nymph Echo, to whom he speaks, but only to hear his voice return to him, devoid of new words and meanings, yet filled with entrancing sounds.[50] Panzacchi's narcissism fails, like that of Narcissus himself, because the voice of the Other is (to borrow Dolar's word) "intractable," and Narcissus would rather die than abandon himself to it: "at the very core of narcissism there lies an alien kernel that the narcissistic satisfaction may well attempt to disguise, but which continually threatens to undermine it from the inside."[51] And indeed, as Butler insists, the key figure in the Narcissus myth ought to be Echo, who signifies the hollowness of unfulfilled longing that never comes back with real meaning. Echo merely repeats emptily the sounds she hears to the one who, as an expression of self-love, adores her.[52]

This problem of self-recognition emerges starkly in Panzacchi's story. After voicing his excited admiration for the castrato whose voice he purportedly hears, he races away from it, galloping finally into a mad phantasmagorical fantasy of merging with this strange, seductive Other through a kind of paraphilia located right in the holy grail of Catholic sanctuaries that is St. Peter's. Witness the following, still addressed to his elusive lady friend:

> In the heat of my enthusiasm, I pronounced to myself a mad wish that I had the candor to express to you and which threw your expressions of horror onto me.
>
> What do you want me to tell you? During that motet of Allegri's a strange change occurred in me, and it seemed that suddenly a great light shone in my soul. In that light I saw a bizarre vision—the ancient Corybantes who, with gestures and cries of ecstatic people, led around a vertiginous dance, and in the middle of that welter I saw rising up the weighty and serene figure of Origen who, extending a hand with his eyes straining toward the stars, was exclaiming: "Blessed!"[53]... At the same time, certain words came to mind with which the Duke of Richelieu thanked the divine goodness when he realized that he had reached the end of his career as a man—not meaning the diplomatic or the military one, of course.
>
> And I thought: when this young man is further along in years and one day notices himself no long having a voice suited to a mystical office... with what words will he thank God for the career he has completed?... my mind went clambering up through the perilous and splendid spire. I felt chords and dissonances ring in my ears and vibrate throughout my whole being, full of strange, voluptuous pleasures.... I raised my eyes and it seemed to me that even the Evangelists, from the gigantic plumes of the vault, were nodding to me with their heads that I was right. I must have been mad, if you like, but I was proud and happy.[54]

Caressing and invading his ears, Panzacchi's aural sensation turns into a "mad" castration desire that seemingly gestures toward the ritualized moment when the choir would sing the most mythologized of all Vatican repertory, Allegri's *Miserere*—although the allusion, if it's meant to be that, is a shabby one, since Allegri's *Miserere* was strictly for Tenebrae services during Holy Week, not for Ascension, when Panzacchi says his outing took place.[55] What matters more is that Mustafà's surviving score for the work was performed in the late nineteenth century with a hyperexpressive romanticism.[56] Instead of feeling ambivalent, much less ashamed that the Vatican (and tacitly, Italy) is still making castrati, the author/character feels excited by their romantic expression, proud of his countrymen who castrate young boys to make them into glorious singers, and happy for the rapturous fantasies that allow him to imagine himself as one with them — precisely what most Romans were no longer proud of. At one moment, we might be reading Hegel or Schopenhauer, at another Freud, but the pro-creator and keeper of the phenomenon is the Catholic Church, which in 1885 was still closeting any reservations it might have had about helping to butcher boys for the papal choir.[57] Its stewardship alone allows this enrapturing sound to fall upon the soul like a "heavenly dew."

It matters that Panzacchi gets to this end stage not through vision, but through a combination of seeing and hearing. At first, his encounter is blind, his gaze severed from his eye, but he pursues the voice, pushing across the crowded church, body by body, until he's staring straight up at the cantoria. And what he then sees above him is his double, the creature who has invaded his ear and will disrupt his sense of everyday reality. Panzacchi hears and finally sees himself in the castrato, but the sensations come hauntingly and troublingly from inside. To think with Dolar about this dilemma: "As soon as the object, both as the gaze and the voice, appears as the pivotal point of narcissistic self-apprehension, it introduces a rupture at the core of self-presence."[58] Music and voice lie at the heart of this rupture. The danger, especially of voice — and the central conceit of Panzacchi's tale, which has him giving himself over to that danger — is to try merging with the castrato's vocalic body, in which Panzacchi thinks he discovers himself.

And again: it's by virtue of this maneuver that Panzacchi genders the voice.

Of course, music in the papal church was always already in a fix because its cadre of castrati was radically outmoded and threatening to the social and even political order, even if still deemed politically necessary from a reactionary core within. By 1898, when Perosi entered the picture, correcting voice and body had become an urgent task. We've seen that just after the turn of the twentieth century this meant excising castrati, a task Perosi, always encumbered with precarious mental health, claimed to have taken very much to heart, not least because the male body is endangered by social corruption that involves capital—in short, dirty money:[59] "The substitution [of boys for castrati] has cost me more mental strain than all the music I have composed. But I insisted on it for grave moral reasons, since shortly after my arrival in Rome, so many requests to join the choir began reaching me from abnormal men that I suspected some ignoble speculation behind them."[60]

Inextricably, correcting voice and body also meant confining the voice to the *letter* of the liturgy. Once the encyclical of November 22, 1903, was put in place, insisting that each note take just one syllable, words could also no longer be broken up, and texts of the mass could no longer be arrayed in multiple, separate movements. The voice had to carry the word not in the lively and sensuous way that Monteverdi and his brother intended with the *seconda prattica*, but in the withering, dehydrating way the Council of Trent intended when it demanded that voice and verse march to the tune of the symbolic order. So while the Sistine Chapel began marching that way once again, the voice of the castrato would soon stop marching altogether. There would be no more rapturous, lyrical flights, no more ravishing coloratura, no more Rossini, no more castrati.

Excursus: The Moreschi Marriage

Some castrati, as we know, went on singing in the papal chapel past November 1903: Cesari until his death in March 1904 and Moreschi in the Sistine Chapel beyond his retirement in 1913, at least occasionally, and above all in the Cappella Giulia almost until his death in 1922. Beforehand, Moreschi had begun building a secular life for himself, starting with his marriage to Guendalina in April 1896 and the birth of a son in March 1904.

To judge from what survives, Moreschi hardly recognized these acts with his own written words, except for making a holograph will stating his postmortem wishes in the briefest of terms (fig. 4.1):

> Wanting to make a public declaration of gratitude to my beloved wife Guendalina Rinaldi Moreschi, I name her my universal heir, commending her piety and religion in support of my soul.
>
> Rome, December 14, 1896
>
> Alessandro Moreschi[61]

Aside from official diary entries Moreschi made while serving as *segretario-puntatore* of the Cappella Sistina in 1891, and apart from a few signatures on other documents, these words, registered and preserved at the Archivio notarile distrettuale di Roma, are unique, among the few to survive in his own hand and certainly the most personal, if also official.

Why this declaration of gratitude, and why his wife as universal heir? Designating Guendalina universal heir prevented anyone else from laying claim to Alessandro's estate, of course. But more than avowing fealty to his spouse, as wills do, Moreschi's made a total financial commitment. Did the Rinaldis expect Alessandro's will to satisfy the terms of a bargain that had allowed him to secure a young, beautiful bride in a way that, given his condition, was unprecedented? Did the document register transactional terms of a marriage that were prearranged? To think about those questions, we have to add to the mix that Guendalina's father, Pietro, was a stonecutter (*scalpellino*), a skilled artisan, but an artisan all the same. At the time of Guendalina's birth, the family was living at the respectable address of via Monterone 82 in the parish of Sant'Eustachio near piazza Navona and the Pantheon.[62] And yet Pietro worked with his hands. However respectable, he was a kind of laborer.[63]

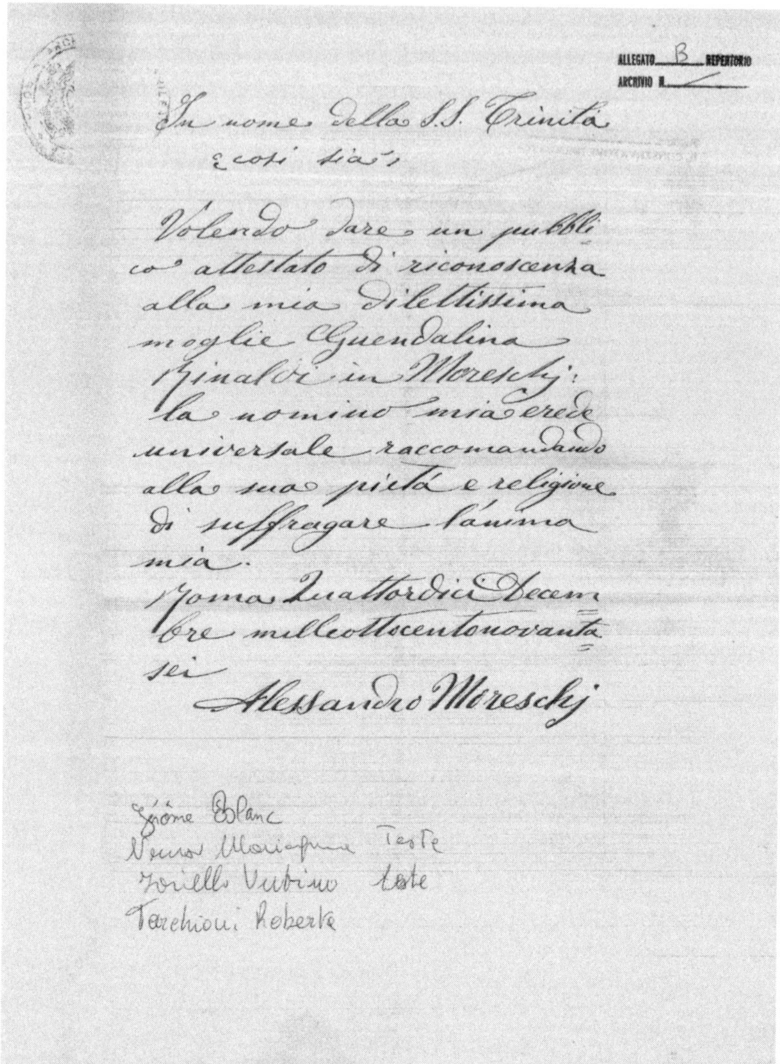

ALLEGATO B REPERTORIO
ARCHIVIO N. —

In nome della S.S. Trinità
e così sia.

Volendo dare un pubblico attestato di riconoscenza alla mia dilettissima moglie Guendalina Rinaldi in Moreschj: la nomino mia erede universale raccomandando alla sua pietà e religione di suffragare l'anima mia.
Roma Quattordici Decembre milleottocentonovantasei
Alessandro Moreschj

Jérôme Blanc
[illegible] Teste
[illegible] teste
Tarchioni Roberto

Figure 4.1. Will of Alessandro Moreschi. Archivio Notarile Distrettuale di Roma, atto notaio Balsi Matteo, December 30, 1896, Rep. n. 18.

In this light, the joint establishment by Pietro and Alessandro of a fancy tomb and nice-sized burial plot at Cimitero di Verano in 1900, four years after the marriage, speaks further to the weight of Alessandro's actions. For Guendalina to marry a castrato in a Catholic country where such marriages were otherwise unheard of surely meant upward financial and even social mobility for the Rinaldi family, which the tomb and Alessandro's testament ensured, indeed, ratified.[64] But there's reason to wonder about the nature and financial implications of this briefest of all wills, as well as the timing. December 1896 was half a year after Alessandro married Guendalina. We've seen that the marriage certificate (much longer than the will) suggests affairs were carefully managed to stage the wedding at home, as a civil affair, avoiding the disapproving gaze of unwanted onlookers and certainly of the church. Here is the full text:

> On April 30, 1896, at four pm, in the house located at Via Corso V[ittorio] Emanuele 187. Guendalina Rinaldi, having demonstrated by means of a medical certificate the impossibility of going to the municipal house to celebrate the wedding, I, the lawyer Salvatore Bugarini [?], municipal counsel appointed to office of the Civil State, went to this house with my municipal secretary Anastasio Cocchi where I found 1. Alessandro Moreschi, a thirty-seven-year-old music maestro, born in Montecompatri, resident in Rome, son of Luigi and of Rosa Pitolli; 2. Guendalina Rinaldi, twenty-three years old, born and resident in Rome, daughter of Pietro and of Giulia Ferrucci, who asked me to join them in marriage. To this end they presented me with the documents described below and from the examination of these and those produced in the publications, as I found nothing to hinder marriage, I read articles 130, 131, 132 of the civil code to the spouses; [and] when I asked Alessandro Moreschi if he intends to marry Guendalina Rinaldi and to the latter if she intends to marry Alessandro Moreschi, and each having answered yes, in the presence of the witnesses described below, I have pronounced in the name of the law that they are joined in matrimony. At this marriage were present Ottaviano Agostini, fifty years old, an office worker, D[on] Giovanni Giancinquanta, fifty-nine years old, [and] Domenico Salvatori, a 41-year-old singer, and D[on] Salvatore Langeli, 41 years old. The

documents presented are the certificate of the publications carried out in Rome on the 19th and 29th of April 1896 and the certificate of Doctor Glori.

[signed]
Alessandro Moreschi
Guendalina Rinaldi
Giovanni Giancinquanta
Salvatore Langeli
Domenico Salvatori[65]

During the whole swath of time encompassing the marriage, the making of the will, and establishment of the tomb, from 1896 to 1900, Alessandro and Guendalina were cohabitating. From at least 1900, they were living by the Pantheon on via della Palombella (see fig. 1.4), where they remained until at least 1906, adding baby Giulio to the household on March 15, 1904. Who fathered the baby no one knows, at least not for certain, but when it came to declaring its birth, Alessandro took matters into his own hands, apparently assuming full rights and responsibilities (fig. 4.2), to judge from the birth record:

March 19, 1904 at 7:10 pm in the Casa Comunale. Before me, Cavalier Vincenzo Capo Sernone[?] Stefanelli — Officer of the Civil State of the Municipality of Rome designated by the Mayor on March 10, 1897 by means of an approved deed — Alessandro Moreschi, 38 years old,[66] a vocal artist domiciled at via Palombella 38, appeared and declared that at 2:30 am on the 15th of this month, his wife Guendalina Rinaldi, cohabitating with him, gave birth to a baby boy to whom he gave the name Giulio Maria Pietro Luigi and whom he does not present to me. Antonio Davanti, 52 years of age, and Amerigo Moreschi [Alessandro's nephew], 22 years of age, both residents of this commune, were present as witnesses to the above and to this deed. The birth and the sex were verified by the midwife Maria Moreschi; the presentation of the newborn was foregone for health reasons. Having read this deed, the interested parties sign before me:

Signed: Alessandro Moreschi, Antonio Davanti, Amerigo Moreschi.[67]

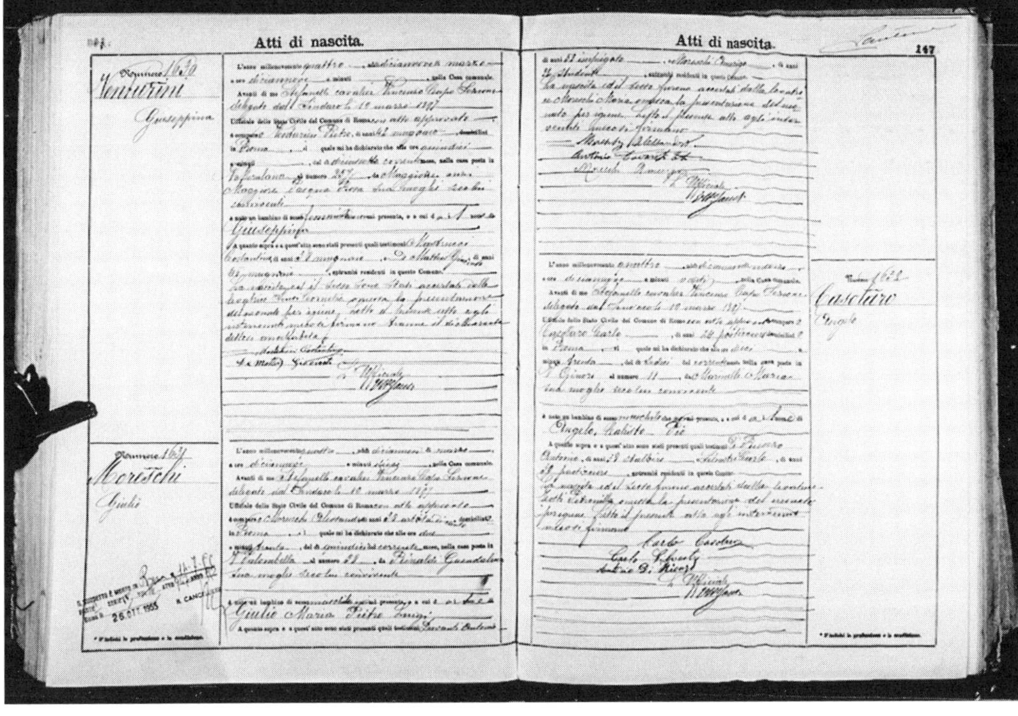

Atti di nascita.

Atti di nascita. 147

Figure 4.2. Municipal act by Alessandro Moreschi declaring the birth of his son, Giulio Maria Pietro Luigi Moreschi. Archivio di Stato di Roma, Stato Civile Italiano, Atti di Nascita, 1904, vol. 3, part 1, series A, pp. 146–47, n. 1631. Reproduced by permission, with protocol 2226-P.

There's not a hint that the child is anything but his, but notably, Giulio was not named principally after his paternal grandfather, Luigi, nor after Guendalina's by-then seemingly estranged father, Pietro, although both names are included in the long string that includes middle names (see fig. P.1). His Christian name seems instead to have honored Guendalina's mother, Giulia, deceased since 1899.[68] Just as the couple had not presented themselves publicly when they married, the child was not presented physically when his birth was recorded.[69]

Or Is It a Hermaphrodite?

Two months before Moreschi rose to the post of *partecipante* in the Cappella Sistina, but while already a regular in the Cappella Giulia, he was called out for divalike behavior in an official complaint lodged by the Cappella Giulia's chapelmaster, Salvatore Meluzzi (1813–1897) and slapped with a nasty label. A minor composer and cleric with a fairly powerful position, Meluzzi claimed that Moreschi

> sang on Wednesday in the venerable Chiesa del Sudario in splendid vocal condition: the next day, Thursday, he could not make himself available in San Pietro for the feast of St. Peter's Chair on account of a rather sudden vocal decline; today, in a most splendid vocal state, he was able to perform a funeral mass at the Chiesa di San Carlo al Corso [the Basilica dei Santi Ambrogio e Carlo al Corso]. Monsignor de Nekere has described this perfectly. Excuse me for the trouble I put you to with this disagreeable tale. It does not seem proper to me that the Vatican Chapter should be dictated to by the whim of a hermaphrodite.[70]

Meluzzi's slur might provoke thinking about gender differences that marked a castrato in the masculinizing decades of the late Ottocento and early Novecento and even its more distant prior history. The epithet implies an amalgam, an amphibious creature that is neither this nor that, one nor the other, what Peter Stallybrass and Allon White named a "threshold creature."[71] For people of a certain educational background, it might have recalled the quasi-homosexual origin story of humankind told by Aristophanes in Plato's *Symposium* that has Zeus dividing the rebellious human race by cutting every human being into two halves and causing like halves to fall in love ("those split from males pursue males," and so on), turning a physiological condition into an amorous one. More likely, it recalled one of the offspring of Venus and Mercury, or even Apollo's clairvoyant prophet, blind Tiresias, who spent seven years transformed as a woman.[72] What it would have conjured for anyone — and what's immediately striking about Meluzzi's cruelty — is his determination to turn Moreschi's gender into something monstrous because compound and therefore untrustworthy. His language made Moreschi the site of an unstable, abhorrent multiplicity.

Any disturbance that provokes such a venomous urge to disgrace another might also invite archaeological thinking about the castrato's ontology. In what follows, I explore it in two objects at two different moments in the twentieth century: first, early twentieth-century Savinio's *Hermaphrodito*, and then the episode of the hermaphroditic demigod in *Fellini Satyricon*. In both, albeit very differently, the hermaphrodite to which Meluzzi sutured his young castrato soprano emerges as a figure of radical alterity who upsets the unconscious and the viscera of its observers along with their quasi-conscious sense of identity.[73]

Alberto Savinio (1891–1952), futurist author, pianist, composer, painter, playwright, set designer, and critic, was the brother of the more famous metaphysical painter and writer Giorgio De Chirico. Born in Greece to Italian parents, Savinio grew up in Athens, along with his brother, but the two returned to their heritage country following the death of their father. At an early age, Savinio, after using his birth name of Andrea Francesco Alberto De Chirico, took the assumed name of Alberto Savinio to remove himself from the shadow of his brother. In the course of things, through various byroads, the two made their way to Germany and thence to Paris, where they settled as young adults and where Alberto became a favorite pianist of the surrealist circle cultivated by André Breton and Apollinaire.[74]

Savinio's novel *Hermaphrodito*, parts of which saw print as early as 1916, at the height of futurist writings, traces the hopeless attempt by the soldier/protagonist Nivasio Dolcemare (the Christian name is a revealing anagram of "Savinio") to journey back to Greece after the war.[75] The novel points homeward without ever finding home, or, as Franco Baldasso puts it, it's about "impossible homecoming." Dolcemare is an obvious projection of Savinio, the artist/writer/musician who had long since left Athens and returned in 1917 as a soldier stationed in Thessaloniki on the Macedonian front. Through enigmatic byways and strange feints of language, a flurry of macaronic tongues combined with extravagant jokes, puns, riddles, parody, pastiche, scatological tropes, and linguistic misunderstandings (*equivoci*), Dolcemare makes his way toward home. Yet home always eludes him.

In all this, there looms what Keala Jewell calls an "ontology of multiplicity" for which the hermaphrodite is both the principal figuration and its embodiment.[76] The hermaphrodite is also the site of a corresponding existential dilemma linking the impossible journey to a futurist postmetaphysics that embraces a broad spectrum that runs from reason to unreason.[77] These impossibilities play out in language, where linguistic plays and unreason form the philosophical basis for challenging an originary, linguistically unified world, a world Baldasso sees as preceding the Tower of Babel, and replacing it with a Nietzschean etymological genealogy of humankind inspired by Nietzsche's endlessly plural, fragmentary, equivocal, and nondialectical *Genealogy of Morals* (1887).[78] On this view, Savinio's literary project utilizes the hermaphrodite — container of all that abhors unity, system, and singularity — to figure the continual existence of difference and lack of system, a place that utterly resists order and synthesis. Only the hermaphrodite can enable the protagonist's errant journey and his errant discoveries.[79] There is more than a trace of a Derridean trace here, one that also encompasses his critique of originary language and the many mother tongues.[80] And there is certainly a move from the medical and material hermaphrodites of medieval and early modern creation to a psychological and even nationalistic one.

Yet Savinio's protagonist, Nivasio Dolcemare, is perhaps above all about morphology, ontology, and the human. Dolcemare uncovers errancy at different levels and in different registers over the course of *Hermaphrodito*: in the great diversity of languages that proliferate throughout the text and the varied and rather chaotic, purposely undisciplined uses to which they're put; in the protagonist's protean and wayward encounters; in the mixture of epochs and spaces invoked, from an archaic, ghostly past to a bewildering present; and, not least, in the assemblage and trajectory of the novel's loose diegesis.

Its penultimate part, a fifty-plus-page-long section called "The Departure of the Argonaut" (La partenza dell'argonauta), finds the antihero Dolcemare traveling from Italy to Greece. He arrives there, Jason-like, but not in search of any Golden Fleece or royal road to understanding. Rather, he looks for provisional knowledge about personal identity, world history, and human existence, none of which turns out to exist except in disconcertingly manifold and partial forms that provide no final answers.[81] Hence, the last leg of his journey unravels in four endings. It includes a long *epilogo* (epilogue) that leads finally to a last section called "Oration on the Roof of the House" (Orazione sul tetto della casa), divided into three parts: "The political man," "The religious man," and "The lyrical man."

The first part anticipates the second through reference to a so-called Jewish city and "the captivating warmth of Jewish character," though no actual hermaphrodite appears until later "as the religious man." When he finally appears, as the Jew, he manifests the condition of the outsider. Not by chance, what Dolcemare also seeks are the city's synagogues. Once there, he approaches the Jewish hermaphrodite in the open air, from outside the built world,[82] whereupon, reaching the gates, he encounters the Jew building his home. At first, the protagonist derides the edifice, along with the strident, multivoiced proclamations the Jew makes from his unfinished rooftop, delivered as if to a crowd, but in fact to no one in particular. But he soon comes to admire both home and voice. The passage merits quoting at length.

> In one of my earlier forays, I had pushed to the gates of the city where houses are cropping up.
>
> There I stumbled upon a Jew who had finished building a brick cuboid for himself,[83] with three openings and a wedge-shaped roof from which a pole was raised that stood there with the apathetic imbecility that a wooden lightning rod can have.
>
> The roof was as yet uncovered and revealed the bare pyramid of architraves on which two tree branches fluttered.
>
> The Jew climbed up onto the summit and opened his arms like a joker king. His dry and piercing voice cried out into the twilight the grateful prayer for his finished work.
>
> Proclaimed in the open air, what was spoken by him were not words scattered in the wind: he pronounced them with care and vigor that gave them the weight of metallic drops falling into a solidifying cauldron.
>
> Although I was alone with my snout raised in front of his skeleton-house and my presence had not yet struck him, he spoke with far-reaching energy and seemed to harangue large masses of people gathered beneath him.
>
> I am used to processing with my whole cerebral plexus, acquitting it with praise or else condemning it irrefutably; so I risked compromising myself in the face of my conscience such that at first I judged the oratorical efforts squandered by the homunculus as a flagrant indication of his idiotic vanity. But in time, I recognized my error and corrected it: I will consider the example for the alternating events of acts to come and compose my mind so as to be ready for a jet of heroism out of the seemingly more trite and idiotic phenomenon.
>
> As far as I was aware, the Semitic builder, with every one of his voices, was tightening a knot around a long mystical ring in which he was enveloped

as in a rosary of sausages, gathering around him a column of men, past, present, and future, that spanned the centuries from one darkness to another.

In that man's incomprehensible Sanskrit, I understood that he was carrying in himself and in that house of his all the fossils through which he had taken his entry into this crooked life, while he was also engendering around himself and in the house he raised up around himself all the zoids that would sprout from his seed.

He was a strange man, a true world machine and worthy of demonstrating his ancestry better than the Colleoni of Venice and the Tricouillard of France.

As I carefully examined him, he exposed the terrible fecundity enclosed in his worm-ridden body.

I divined in him a mixture of the two sexes, with evident androgyny and a calculus of patromaternity. I guessed he was ill with a double genital motor and suffering from both his ovaries and his testicles.

Although his genital membering [*membratura*] showed the travail of a progressive chachexy [cachessia, debilitation or wasting], the mark of infallible generation was engraved upon it — in observance of the law that multiplies the fermenting of the germ up from the coagulated/clotted worm [*vermina raggrumata*].[84]

He was devoted to procreation and to the consequent problem of childbirth, which he would have resolved on his own.

My summary of the diagnosis gave me the following revelation:

pregnant over a period of nine days and breasted like a Tiresias, the man on the roof dumps grape-like clusters of flesh from the stinking meatus [*meato*] that twist on the ground, then raise themselves up and walk, and from there grow vigorously — blown up/inflated by a dilating/swelling heat — and finally serious men and doctrinarians in morals are made.[85]

Note that the Jewish hermaphrodite, a lone being, holds the power to edify the protagonist and even chasten his intellectual arrogance, although nothing in the text clarifies just what kind of power makes that possible.[86] A sovereign, yet abject, even comical figure — at once a Joker king and a "homunculus" — the hermaphrodite has an almost limitless capacity for procreation, extending from the present back to ancient times. Not only is he is said to have been knotted into a "long mystical ring" and to carry fossils within him, for centuries he has solved the problem of childbirth, engendering all manner of zoids. On examining him closely, the protagonist finds an androgynous mixture of sexes that make him both father and mother by virtue of a "patromaternity."

But existing in that state means living life in a roiling crucible. For although his body constitutes the site of an overwhelming fecundity and "infallible generation," his multiple genitals suffer from malnutrition and degeneration, and worm-ridden waste infects his Tiresias-like breasted body.[87]

Paradoxically, serious men who grow up to specialize in morals nevertheless issue as progeny from this bizarre mixture. They cannot escape their grotesque origins since their profound ethical knowledge is birthed from the anus—and not in the form of ready-made humans, but in the defecated form of excrement that has been rotting in the intestines as *vermina raggrumata* before the body expels it. Such procreation goes beyond earlier examples of cloacal parturition (of whatever sexual kind). The anus here does not just function as the portal for issuing new life; rather, it births new life in the form of feces. In this respect, it exceeds the anal birthings of Pulcinellini associated with Pulcinella (which I discuss in connections with castrati elsewhere),[88] resembling instead the obscene scatological descriptions in Latin macaronic hexameters of Teofilo Folengo's *Baldus* written about by Barbara Spackman and noted by Jewell as a strain of the Italian humanist tradition on which *Hermaphrodito* calls.[89]

Furthermore, and unremarked in literary analyses of Savinio's text to date, is that the hermaphrodite's corporeal hybridity includes a startling voice set in a cacophonous soundscape. His multiplicity of vocal registers, timbres, and identities forms a piece with vocal signifiers noted by recent voice theorists, especially in deaf speakers and singers, transsexuals, Black and Latinx singers, and other voices of alterity, as well as in the voices of extraordinary divas, including travesty females, trans singers, and castrati.[90] It's a voice whose multivocality conjures the divine. As such, it endows the hermaphrodite with a certain otherworldliness that vouchsafes his capacity to move between worlds. It lingers in the listener's consciousness, archaic and haunting, yet piercing, and with a sturdiness like "the weight of metallic drops falling into a solidifying cauldron."[91]

In the last section of "The Departure of the Argonaut," "Il lirico," when the protagonist is still searching for home, we get purchase on what this amounts to:

> No matter how far I walked, I could not get rid of the voice of the strange hermaphrodite, who cut the epochs from one end to the other.[92] And yet it was in vain that I wanted to erase the brick house: I always saw it, and still I see it.
>
> The house, friends, the house!
> Who among us will know how to dissolve
> the enigmatic knot of stone?[93]

The hermaphrodite's voice persists in the present, connecting him to a distant past. Though critical writings on *Hermaphrodito* have not made voice and sound their focus, they seem to me to relate to Baldasso's observation that "in his own body, the Jewish hermaphrodite conceals the most profound of genealogies. He *is* genealogy."[94] In the final paragraphs of "Il lirico," genealogy extends, lamentingly, to the sounds of voice and the sounds of time the world over. Shortly before the book ends, the protagonist nails his glove to a wall, where it hangs, "a corpse of a hand," evoking the empty hanging glove surrealistically painted in 1914 by Savinio's brother, De Chirico (fig. 4.3), with its musical title of *Le chant d'amour*—metaphysical love represented with a Greek bust, a surgeon's glove, a rubber ball, and the outline of a train passing noisily through a voided, empty city.

Hermaphrodito sounds both noisily and lyrically throughout, often unnaturally so, as with De Chirico's lyrical love song jarringly

Figure 4.3. Giorgio de Chirico, *Le chant d'amour* (The song of love), oil on canvas (1914), 73 x 59.1 cm. Museum of Modern Art, New York City, Nelson A. Rockefeller Bequest. Object no. 950.1979. Artwork © 2024 Artists Rights Society (ARS), New York/SIAE, Rome. © The Museum of Modern Art/Licensed by SCALA/Art Resource, NY. Published by permission.

juxtaposed with the locomotive. Pigeons sing like the grieving Ariadne. Invisible choirs ring out. An African expedition intones a hymn to Tripoli. And frequently, "The Departure of the Argonaut" breaks into song, notably, "It's a Long Way to Tipperary," an anthem of the Great War. When a riot of languages is interrupted with a "metallic glissando" (*ligatura metallica*), it's given onomatopoeically as "Gluc! Cip! ... gluc! gluc! cip! cip! cip!" / "Gluc! Cip! ... gluc! gluc! cip! cip! cip!" A "canto di pianto" (weeping song) attaches to suicide, slow songs and solfeggi reverberate, metallic alarms go off to the "hysterical song of the locomotive," and again and again, our raucous hero cries out. "I want to tune my future song to the sound of the shofar," he declares in "L'ora ebrea."[95]

These constant cries, noises, and songs anticipate the Jew's irresistible voice as part of a new-world ontology that figures a new utopia, though a dissenting utopia, to be sure.[96] And then at last, the text ends with a boisterous, clamorous circus, barking trombones and women squealing in the orchestra stalls, a juggler–tightrope walker slinking about in a skin-tight shirt as the protagonist laments that "with a tragic twirl," all this "will fall into the sawdust of the track, like a summer star."[97]

It will also leave the hero finally with neither song nor drama —which is to say: still without home. Which is also to say: still hermaphroditic.

Remarkably, though Nivasio Dolcemare, who is of course Savinio, disdains the odd hermaphrodite on first encounter, the hermaphrodite never induces any obvious castration anxiety. Instead, he expresses a world-historical ontology better than conventional discourses can, whether philosophical or historical. And he embodies a world-historical ontology that produces better *morals* than do its alternatives. The ontology of the hermaphrodite may be monstrous and uncontainable, multiple and multivoiced, but for that very reason, it is generative, even genealogical. The hermaphrodite traces history and time, procreating and enabling procreation.

What to make half a century later of the hermaphrodite that enigmatically appears as an albino in the middle of *Fellini Satyricon*, a hermaphrodite nowhere found in Petronius's satirical, picaresque first-century CE novel on which the movie was very loosely based? Apparently the hermaphrodite was Fellini's invention, or perhaps his joint invention with cowriter Bernardino Zapponi.[98] Broadly speaking, it fit into the film's dreamscape of antiquity, following the peregrinations of the young and beautiful, but impotent Encolpius (Martin Potter). Although Encolpius sleeps with the sorceress Enotea (Donyale Luna) near the end of the film, the numerous disconnected episodes before that fade in and out like so many mirages of the unconscious, always with Encolpius postulated as an ego figure on a sex/gender axis with little stability. Encolpius first shows himself a figure of mourning, pictured before a wall of illegible graffiti, lamenting that he's sold himself as a woman even when approached as a man, that he acted as a *puttana* in prison, that his own mother convinced him not to act as a man, that he loves the girlish boy Gitón (Max Born), and that (by implication) he is no longer a man. Sexual inversion is posed as a kind of pollution. Almost immediately, we're whirled onto a stage set where slaves parade around in masked animal heads and a boy offered for sale is touted because he "plays female roles well."

Since sex is also power, everyone is implicated in an endless series of tawdry power struggles. In many of them, Encolpius competes with his friend, Ascyltus (Hiram Keller), for Gitón's love; in others, the viewer is taken into the decadent theatrical worlds of Trimalchio ("thrice king," Mario Romagnoli, listed as "Il Moro" in the credits), the old poet Eumolpus (Salvo Randone), and others.

In short, *Satyricon* stages a dreamworld governed by currencies of money, greed, and lust, and a depravedly transactional one. From this dystopia, the episode of the hermaphrodite (Pasquale Baldassarre) wafts into view,[99] prefaced with a monologue in broken Italian delivered to Encolpius by a servant woman. Encolpius listens as the camera lingers with sly and suggestive intermittency on his cunning smile.[100] "Do you know the Hermaphrodite? He's a little girl, but also a boy, performs a lot of magic and cures people with plague, predicts the future. He's up there in the old temple of Ceres. One time he punished a city that was bad to him . . . changed it into a chicken coop, all the people were like chickens [imitates the clucking of chickens]."

Figure 4.4. Film still of the fragile hermaphrodite in *Fellini Satyricon* (1969), directed by Federico Fellini. An old man lifts him up while exposing his breasts and penis to adoring beholders, who regard him as a semidivine healer.

Turning a city into a chicken coop and its inhabitants into chickens requires a richly inversive politics. Not just hermaphrodites, but castrated men—sexually multiple and ambiguous, and moreover altered by other men—were often assimilated to capons, roosters, and other fowl, and indeed, the very word "castrato" conjures certain edible meats for Italian ears.[101] But then, all is inversive in the unstable universe of this film. Encolpius and Ascyltus are next seen in Ceres's temple, which teems with desperate mothers, the blind, the infirm, and the raggedy poor, some of whom lay down offerings to plead for cures. An old man lifts the fragile little hermaphroditic creature up and parts a gauzy covering to reveal its breasts and penis to the adoring beholders (fig. 4.4). Soon enough, though, the old man is run through by a robber's sword. Encolpius and Ascyltus join forces with the robber, abduct the creature, and steal their way into an imaginary desert landscape. Carrying the hermaphrodite in a wooden cart, they descend a craggy hill onto parched earth where it moans in a thin high voice, lips crinkling from thirst until it dies.

A bloody fight ensues between the friends and the robber, who gets killed in the struggle.

The episode of Fellini's albino hermaphrodite makes up what Alessandro Carrera calls the missing "psychical stratum" holding together memories "submerged by millennia of other myths, other forms, other stories."[102] Commenting on the present, the episode brings to the surface an always unraveling, death-dealing, soulless world in which the liminal, unstable creature is curative, yet always a victim. Being a demigod, not fully of this world, Fellini's hermaphrodite intervenes in the "natural world" via transformative deeds, including mysterious, but good ones: divination and healing, for instance. Yet what makes it a remediating figure also attaches it to troubling genealogies, not unlike Savinio's Jewish hermaphrodite. How old is Fellini's hermaphrodite? And where does he come from? What is his genesis? A small, high-voiced, vulnerable, dejected, whimpering, and ageless creature, wrinkled but young, young but wise, the hermaphrodite of *Satyricon* is a kind of elderly child, like the wrinkled young Vatican sopranos whose progression to physiological adulthood earlier in life had been literally cut off by castration.[103]

To highlight all this, Fellini makes use of numerous signs and media, among them the hermaphrodite's (empowering) stigmata of sexual ambiguity, weakness, and albinism, all expressed in a pallor that pervades its world. Indeed, as Stephen Snyder has argued, the episode of the hermaphrodite involves a larger formal scheme that governs the film, as different stretches of it emphasize different colors, from the redness that dominates the dinner at Trimalchio's estate and Licha's ship to the whiteness expressed via overexposure of color and lack of pigmentation in a snowstorm, a white-out, suicide, and death.[104] Pallor, premature wrinkling, and melancholy were all marks borne by castrati that had a specific hormonal etiology in the deprivation of testosterone before puberty, the same deprivation that caused abnormal growth patterns, small, undeveloped penises, and reduced (if not nonexistent) erectile function.

Perhaps, then, it's of interest that, as Snyder also notes, the pallor of Fellini's hermaphrodite has sonic associations. In the sequences dominated by whiteness, air is the most pervasive of the four elements. It is manifested especially in the sound and action of whistling wind, but also manifested in the whining of supplicants and in the whimpering expiration — literally, the exhaling — of the hermaphrodite as it breathes its last.[105]

Once a cartoonist, Fellini famously turned Petronius's text into near comic book cinema, assimilating its fragmentary, open nature to that of Italy's popular *fumetti.* And although *Satyricon* is an intensely visual film, Fellini described it in sonic terms that are vividly alive. His diffuse, messy book *Fare un film* on filmmaking — his own — includes fragmentary records on *Satyricon*'s camera work, direction, and editing in which rhythm, tempo, timbre, and voice are all conspicuous. Take the following, outlining his desiderata in cursory, disconnected notes:

> ARHYTHMIC — FAINT — INDIRECT — UNPREDICTABLE.
>
> Exasperating slowness, the speed of microbes.
>
> ACTED POORLY, with extremely long periods of silence, faltering language. Broken, hesitant; an impersonal dubbing, detached like the voices for news on the radio. Dubbing that's technically incorrect, with voices that finish before their lips do or continue afterward: enough to horrify sound technicians and above all the Americans who, in front of a shot filled with thousands of angry, mutinous sailors, would take the trouble to avidly spy during a tempest at sea so long as the orders the admiral shouts coincide with the movement of his lips.
>
> A great, suggestive & mysterious fable. A film made up of fixed, immobile frames, without dollies or other movements of the camera. A film to contemplate, similar to dreams: and it leaves you hypnotized. Everything will be disjointed, fragmentary. And at the same time strangely uniform. Every detail will stand out; isolated, enlarged, absurd, monstrous: like in dreams.[106]

Fellini's montage, drawing together of strands of unconscious, dreamlike material and disconnected myths, woven into intensely expressionistic imagery, resonates with the kinds of castrato hauntings I've tried to characterize in this book. The albino hermaphrodite lacks the robust voice of Savinio's hermaphrodite — its voice is the very opposite of it — but it shares with him a debilitated body and a certain innocent, childlike character that roams over the Roman psyche and worries it.[107] Both figures constitute the site of a paradoxical convergence, one that lies at the heart of Fellini's film, where abjection and infirmity pair up with powers of prophecy and healing and with Jewell's ontology of multiplicity.

The film also concerns itself with the themes of plundering wealth by killing off what lies close to godliness. Within the span of a mere few minutes, the plunderers first worship the hermaphrodite and then treat it as loot while letting it die of thirst. The atavistic creature is consigned to endure such paradoxes — something it has in common with the castrato. Significantly, both are also avatars, divine reembodiments who circulate in productive, even magical ways, but problematically so, because viewed as wretched and therefore open to abuse and despoliation. Despoliation comes in profane forms, as the grime of capital makes painfully clear.

Let's listen to what the novelist and journalist Alberto Moravia (1907–1990), himself a Roman of half-Jewish descent, had to say about the hermaphrodite of *Fellini Satyricon* in his famous *New York Review of Books* essay of 1970, relating it to the idiosyncratically syncretic religious strain that runs throughout Fellini:

> To understand Fellini's special kind of religiosity, we believe that the greatest importance must be attributed to his manifest preference for the monstrous and impure. In *Satyricon* the monstrous and the impure regularly take the place of the ugly and the beautiful. The monsters are the old, the sick, the infirm, the unattractive; the impure, the young and the beautiful.... The hermaphrodite is not by chance both monstrous and young, beautiful and impure. One does not have to make a great effort of the imagination to

> trace back this preference for the monstrous and impure to a fascinated and funereal moralism. Fellini is attracted by antiquity precisely because he sees it as corrupt and moribund.[108]

Moravia's goal was to bring out Fellini's attraction to decadence, much as we saw Pasolini assert in Chapter 2. "There is in . . . [Fellini] a decadent who is magnetized by the most celebrated and most historic of all decadences."[109]

The interlocking triad of capitalism, abjection, and decadence is everywhere overwritten on castrato history, shaping a kind of castrato ontology. Before the second quarter of the nineteenth century, many castrati, "though always Italian-made," thrived on an international stage. Once they withdrew to Italian churches and quickly to Rome and the Vatican around 1830 to 1850, they became stand-ins for the Roman Catholic Church, signs of a reactionary institution clinging to an antiquated past widely seen as brutal toward boys. Yet eventually, that same church turned out to be not reactionary enough. By the time Moreschi joined the Sistine Chapel in March 1883, he and his colleagues were already radically out of place. Casting him as a hermaphrodite, as Meluzzi did, effectively acknowledged that he was angelic, a quasi-divine divo in the Vatican imaginary, even before he rose to become a Sistine regular. But it also retaliated against the angel-castrato by spewing invective into official channels, invective that surely fell short of the still worse nastiness Meluzzi would like to have spewed. Fellini shows us that abjection always opens itself to this dynamic of desire and repulsion, shape-shifting in unpredictable ways. And castrati, however formalized their appointments, remained Agambean outcasts, invited into the pope's inner sanctum, but outsiders within it, like the pasha's eunuchs. They preserved a distant past, but got pushed out when Cecilianism moved in to reclaim a still more ancient past by adopting Council-of-Trent-like strictures in the 1903 St. Cecilia's Day *motu proprio.*[110]

Moreschi would hardly have been out of place in a parade of Felliniesque Romans. Think not just of Meluzzi dubbing him a hermaphrodite, but another calling him a "peacock" when he double-booked himself at two different churches on the same evening.[111] Or think of Haböck's disconcertion at his high speaking voice, as if he'd met someone miming a female.[112] As Marguerite Waller says of the critical reception of Fellini's hermaphrodite—that he was "banished to sideshow liminality"—Moreschi, vain and divalike, even as he tried to accommodate to patriarchal norms, overran the boundaries of masculinity and inevitably ended up at its liminal edges.

And yet at last, what Moreschi wanted was a bourgeois life. His wish came true when he entered the legal institution of marriage to become part of a larger political system of sociality. But he fit into it awkwardly, a conformist unable to avoid challenging the sexual politics of his time, despite what seems to have been his largely docile, compliant, and conservative nature. Was he victimized by his wife's infidelity, or did he orchestrate the addition of a son to his family, perhaps even through the blood and thus bloodlines of his nephew? Who could ever know?

CHAPTER FIVE

Secrets, Phantoms, and Crypts

Vittoria was the one who knew everything, but she didn't speak easily because of her character, which was very reserved. When I met her she had already undergone an operation that had ruined her vocal cords. So she spoke with great difficulty at a very low pitch. But it's thanks to her that I came to know all the goings-on of the family, the habits of Alessandro Moreschi, signor Giulio, and then of his death, of the life of Alessandra and Riccardo Fellini (although they lived in a different house for a period of time). She was a person who had been very much tested by life; in addition to the impairment of her voice . . . a very rich uncle who had a tannery in Liguria had raised her and then furnished her with a dowry with which she bought the apartment at Lungotevere degli Anguillara, an apartment that she had always defended against speculation and debt, even though later, for love of her daughter, she mortgaged the apartment. In the end, the daughter would sell it. Alessandra would sell the apartment. And Vittoria would die in an old age home, surely not what she would have wanted from life, a life that had scarred her, that had put malice and hard times before her at certain moments, in certain respects, though she had confronted the difficulties with strength, with the character of Genoese sailors, one could say. Hence the impression that I had of her, which stayed with me, was that of a woman who had sweetness under a hard rind. I repeat, the family was one that had passed through highs and lows, many difficult moments, squabbles, hence she, too, was embittered by all this.

—Fabio Panconesi, March 23, 2015

> I am convinced that the dissipation of a single "phantom" is capable ultimately of modifying the structure of the grand abominable Truth.... Each time a small victory is won over Death for Love.
>
> —Nicolas Abraham, psychoanalyst, April 1974 and March–July 1975

Over the generations, strong-willed women—reserved, like Vittoria, or demonstrative, like Guendalina and Alessandra—dominated the Moreschi family. Alessandro's status as a castrato and his later abandonment by his wife led to a family history that functionally inverted the lexes "father" and "mother," especially once he assumed a maternal role for three-year-old Giulio. And yet the family also placed a high value on masculinity. Alessandro himself cemented the structural place of "il padre" and "il maschio" by asserting himself as Giulio's father before the law, a claim Giulio renewed and fortified in the next generation.

Most strikingly, Giulio did so by writing out his own will in such a way as to ensure that well after his death, male descent would govern the devolution of the part of his estate that comprised his father's material legacy. Made up when Rita was only nine years old and signed on August 12, 1954 (see Chapter 3 above), the will made decidedly paternalistic provisions to guarantee that Giulio's inheritance from Alessandro would survive intact, specifying that if Rita should have a male child and baptize him with the name Giulio, then, and only then, upon that child's marriage would he receive the entire legacy as a wedding gift. The bequest was fundamentally patriarchal in that it presumed male preeminence in matters of family devolution and governance, which it also reinforced. But it was also patrilineal inasmuch as the legatee looked, indeed longed, to leave the family's treasures to a male heir within the direct family line, one who was married and therefore presumed to be procreative. Its dictates allowed for only a single exception, namely, that if Rita's first male child were to come of age without marrying, then Rita, on reaching her fortieth birthday, would inherit everything—a stipulation that not only hinged on the fate of her first male child, but assumed she would have children in the first place, which she did not.[1]

Like many wills, this one has a certain spectral frisson. By prescribing how his patrimony was to be preserved—as it happened, a year before his death at age fifty-one and already looking ahead two generations—Giulio was orchestrating, via a male line, his own return to the living. He was dreaming of himself as a revenant, specifically, a patriarchal revenant. To imagine such a return was possible not only because his bequests and provisions could be made as blunt material facts, but because Giulio believed that exchanges effected in the forms of gifts, donations, and legal transfers of ownership could extend family relations after death, shaping futures and elongating them while reserving in them a critical place for him and his single most cherished forerunner.[2]

In all this—and to return to the phonographic traces explored in Chapter 3—a distinct place was reserved for Alessandro's sound recordings. Being owned, cared for, cherished, played, and replayed, by themselves and for others, which is to say, being *shared*, were all acts that mediated (literally) their capacity to serve as proxies for the dead, promoting the dead as revenants with respect to the living. Replay of the records, here intended in its broadest meaning as essayed by Rebecca Schneider as a kind of reenactment that can affectively resuscitate those no longer living, revived the past in such a way as to resurrect the dead.[3] In this case, it could eventually resurrect Giulio, too, as the one honored with preserving the sounds of the dead, thereby allowing him to return with his father to the living.

Transgenerational Haunting

A chasm separates Giulio's wishes from later developments. For a variety of reasons—the vagaries of time, the vicissitudes of family life, and the fortunes and cares of various descendants—his testamentary provisions had little material bearing on later settlements.

By the time Rita turned forty, in 1985, she and Fabio had already left via Lungotevere degli Anguillara 11 a year beforehand, and Vittoria, who died that year, had been placed by Alessandra in a home for the elderly that same year. As seen in Chapter 3, the collection by then had probably already been reduced to a fraction of its former glory, with the recordings, gifts from the king, and a scrapbook, plus many photographic portraits of singers and much else having gone astray. Losses that were equally psychic and material thus colored the story and consciousness of the castrato's great-grandchildren.

Indeed, Rita and Fabio's very spotty knowledge about the generation of Moreschi senior merged with their sense of the present, exposing features of what French psychologist Anne Ancelin Schützenberger (1919–2018) calls "the ancestor syndrome" in a book they had encountered in Italian translation when it was issued with the following blurb: "We are simple links in a chain of generations and we often become victims of events and traumas already experienced by our ancestors. It is the familiar unconscious: the story that others have written for us. Anne Ancelin Schützenberger, therapist and analyst with over fifty years of experience, in this book explains her original psycho-genealogical approach, namely, how to reconstruct the genealogical tree of the family psyche."[4]

Already at our first meeting in 2010, Fabio told me about having read *La sindrome degli antenati* and discussed it with Rita. He also exemplified its dynamic by sketching for me an embryonic "genosociogram," depicting family members relationally over generations through ties that were both genealogical and social.[5] Such a mapping, locating Rita and him as a present-generational collective ego, had long since ignited questions in them about private family traumas, losses, and quarrels that have reverberated over four generations.

After speaking with Fabio about this during a period in which Rita was ill and therefore reclusive, I read *The Ancestor Syndrome* the way you might watch a movie wondering what your companions are thinking. Before turning to its core concepts, I want to make note of repetitive naming patterns in the Moreschi genealogy (fig. P.1), traceable to Alessandro, which are of course commonplace among Italian families. Rita's mother, Alessandra Moreschi Fellini (the castrato's granddaughter), along with Rita and Fabio's nephew, Alessandro Carlo Leone Solinas Moreschi (2006–) — great-great-grandson of Alessandro Moreschi, grandson of Alessandra, and son of Rita's half brother, the late Julio Salvador Solinas Moreschi and his partner, Emanuela Dessy Saddì — are both named after the castrato. Their names pay homage to their castrato ancestor while perpetuating his lineage beyond biology through nominal revenants. A Giulia/Giulio cluster, traceable to Guendalina's mother, Giulia, extends forward to the Giulio birthed by Guendalina and raised by Alessandro senior and reappears as "Julio" (= Giulio), born in the wake of Alessandra's presumed remarriage in Mexico about 1960 or 1961 to Giovanni Antonio ("Chico") Solinas, following her separation from Riccardo Fellini some years earlier.[6]

Current-day analysts would largely resist seeing homologies between naming practices and psychic structures, yet most would likely agree that where such practices prevail, naming adumbrates affective and material economies that knit descendants together with ancestors. Theories of "ancestor-syndromes" have tended to see naming as entangled with emotional bonds and family histories, often problematically so. In this thinking, names intersect with unbalanced emotional ledgers that haunt families through negative expressions of loyalty, repeating destructive behaviors, for example, or otherwise causing family members to experience "repercussions" as payback, unless debts are somehow settled psychologically, a view accented by Ancelin Schützenberger.

Such perspectives sit more or less adjacent to Freud's "uncanny," where those who are subject to eerie sensations experience what should feel familiar as instead feeling strange. Freud himself, in his famous 1919 essay on the subject, "Das Unheimliche" (literally, "The Unhomey" but also meaning "uncanny" in German and routinely translated thus into English) was tempted to conclude that what is "uncanny" is frightening precisely because it is *not* known and familiar, but only seems as if it should be. It seems so because it is "forgotten" through repression.[7] Hence the uncanny, creeping along the edges of the strange and the familiar, involves not just repression per se, but often secreting in the sense of keeping secret. As Nicholas Royle notes, while any notion of the uncanny will be caught up in crises over what is proper—personalities, property, and indeed names, for instance—and will involve disturbances to things that should feel familiar but don't, Freud's uncanny specifically turns on mysterious feelings of being at odds with one's environment and moreover with *oneself*—of feeling split, doubled, and strange. These fundamentally spectral feelings are often irreconcilable and thus irresoluble by the psyche precisely because they cause one to "lose one's bearings . . . [as one finds] oneself immersed in the maddening logic of the supplement."[8]

My initial conversation with Fabio and Rita already made it clear that the family's past has been pervaded with sensations of the uncanny. Most particularly, Guendalina's actions have never ceased to haunt the Moreschi family, not least because soon after her alleged theft, it became impossible for the losses ever to be recovered, especially in Fabio's recollection of Vittoria's account, which tells of Guendalina liquating valuables straightaway and quickly letting her lover lose everything at the gaming tables. Whatever the case, financial losses evidently injured the family with a material violence on top of the emotional one, something particularly difficult for an Italian family to suffer in a society where family wealth is critical not just to well-being, but to patrimonial status and dignity.[9] Reverberating through the generations, Guendalina's theft seems to have turned from a trauma into what psychoanalysts Nicolas Abraham (1919–1975) and Maria Torok (1925–1998), to whom Ancelin Schützenberger's account is markedly indebted, call a "founding silence," something rarely mentioned that haunts the family as a psychic "phantom" or ghost, producing ripples and repetitions over time.[10]

It's worth reading Abraham and Torok closely, not to endorse their theories, much less to psychoanalyze the family, but because their views, as mediated by Ancelin Schützenberger, have resonated with the castrato's descendants, who have seen in them balms and possible cures.[11] They help contemplate the various byways prompted by family members in this book, especially those that have emanated from conversations with Fabio and with Rita's memoir *In viaggio con lo zio*. In what follows, I therefore take up the relevant core concepts in Abraham and Torok's writings, considering them in relation to those of Freud and Derrida before moving on to the figure that serves as a hinge between the Moreschi and Fellini families, Riccardo Fellini, especially as he appears recurrently and problematically in Federico's famous dream books.

Both Abraham and Torok were Hungarian-Jewish survivors of World War II and émigrés to Paris, albeit in different years. Together, they produced the most prominent psychoanalytic account of transgenerational haunting to their time, one that evolved out of their collective and separate work on metapsychology, mourning, melancholia, secrets, and crypts. By the time of Abraham's untimely death in 1975 at age fifty-six, all these were tied to notions of the phantom.[12] In their analysis, as captured in Abraham's late essay on the subject, a phantom will haunt descendants, yet is wholly psychic, "nothing but an invention of the living." It is something a person summons to "objectify . . . the gap that the concealment of some part of a loved one's life produced in us."[13] In that sense—and here I return to my third sense of the term "phantom" as delineated in the Prologue—the phantom points not solely to the fact of individual psychology (as Freud's fundamental notions of transference and the libido largely do, for instance), but to elements of a psyche that operate guilefully within a broader multigenerational framework.

To explain its existence, Abraham and Torok conjure as core metaphors the shell and the kernel, first elaborated by Abraham in his 1968 review essay of Jean Laplanche and Jean-Bertrand Pontalis's encyclopedic handbook of Freudian psychoanalytic terms *The Language of Psycho-Analysis* (*Vocabulaire de la psychanalyse*).[14] There, Abraham delineates the philosophical implications of Freudian psychoanalysis while dilating on problems of the (in)coherence of the self, revealing what the couple's editor and translator, Nicholas T. Rand, calls a "general theory of the genesis of phenomena" that departs from Freud and attracted the likes of Jacques Derrida.[15] Abraham's theory of the "shell" (shared with Torok) more or less parallels Freud's ego, the anxious operator that balances superego and id, while his "kernel" more or less parallels Freud's id, the site of pleasure. But as Christopher Lane explains in his skeptical review essay of Abraham and Torok, where Freud's id designates a site of organic pleasure that produces sexuality as an enemy destructive of happiness, Abraham and Torok's kernel designates a set of impulses they claim can be discovered and treated reparatively.[16] The telos that informs their theories ultimately consists of cures that rescue the imperiled self through utilitarian forms of therapeutic intervention. Lane parses this difference in terms of the unconscious: where Abraham and Torok "see the unconscious as an aberration designed for remediation," Freud sees the unconscious as "irrevocably 'alien' and antipathetic to conscious thought."[17]

Secrets and Crypts

To explain the phantom's incursions into psychic life, then, Abraham and Torok turn, contra Freud, toward the concrete phenomenon of secrets. Secrets are what chiefly explain for them the phantom's intrusions as they cause psychic gaps and breaks—incoherence—that cannot otherwise be accounted for. How might this way of thinking help account for issues encountered by the four generations of Moreschis who range between the covers of this book? It seems they might be understood as *casualties* of quite specific secrets, three main ones: first, the secret of who fathered Guendalina's first child; second, the secrets that cluster around

Guendalina's flight, including the reasons she abandoned her son and husband and the circumstances surrounding her theft and squandering of family money; and third, but not least, the constellation of secrets surrounding Alessandro as castrato, including how the decision was made to castrate him, by whom, who carried it out, and when and where, which in turn are embedded in a long history of secret-keeping by the church, as well as by singing teachers, parents, patrons, chapelmasters, agents, and so on.

Of course, things would be simple if nothing were needed to heal all wounds but the unveiling of external facts. What's secreted, by contrast, always situates itself between the real and the phantasmatic, presence and absence, operating in a state of continual recursion and deferral that recalls Derrida's *trace*. And indeed, threaded throughout the arguments Abraham and Torok published, particularly between 1968 and 1973, is the belief that locked up somewhere in victims of mourning and melancholia, including in libidinally charged fantasies about the dead, are secrets that function less as specific instances of concealment or denial than as internal splittings of a subject resulting from trauma and silence, if a silence that always threatens to secrete what is secreted. What separates them from Freud is that for Abraham and Torok, an individual might literally become two or more persons psychically in much the sense popularly described as "split" or "multiple" personality, however perilous and suspect, even corny, the idea might sound today.[18]

What matters here are not just these internal splittings, but the "real" consequences of secrets in the ordinary sense. Following Abraham and Torok's arguments will tend to lead to the conclusion that what affected Alessandro's descendants were secrets surrounding his adult life or secrets surrounding his castration as a boy. But there was also a cognate secret *about* those secrets, a kind of second-order secret that was kept by Vittoria in later times. It turns out that Vittoria relegated Alessandro's very status as a castrate to a domain of "we don't talk about it." Hence, during the first eleven years of Rita and Fabio's marriage, from 1973 to 1984, when the couple lived at Lungotevere degli Anguillara 11, although Vittoria spoke often of her husband's father, she never mentioned that he had been castrated, at least not to her grandson-in-law, Fabio. According to Fabio, she even declined to refer to Alessandro with such polite language as "cantore evirato."[19] By suppressing the very matter of his having been castrated, she participated in the wider repression of castrato memory perpetuated by church and state and indeed by Italian musicology, which hardly took up castrati as objects of historical study until the advent of the early music movement in the 1980s, after which, euphemisms continued to prevail into the present century, when exceptions have often crept in, secrets being secreted (accent on the second syllable) as they seep out.[20] Not only that, but like the recording engineer Fred Gaisberg when he published his expurgated diaries in 1944, Vittoria avoided all the mysteries in which Alessandro's castration was embedded by declining to acknowledge the very fact of what he was. Instead, she only allowed as how Alessandro was not Giulio's biological father and speculated, as we saw, that Giulio's biological father may have been a nephew of Alessandro's—though on what authority she said so, and, if true, with what effect on the uncle-nephew relationship remains unclear.[21]

Given that Vittoria's suppression took the tangible form of a secret, it would have fortified subjectively (and intangibly in the analysis of Abraham and Torok) a *crypt*, "an isolated region within the psyche in which an experience that is shameful, and therefore unspeakable, has been 'buried alive.'"[22] The crypt works here as a metaphor for how secrets are squirreled away. Insofar as they produce psychic gaps, they also, for Abraham and Torok, create sites of unfinished business that are inevitably left open and therefore fall prey to the phantom's intrusion. The phantom invented by the living will objectify a gap, turning it into something concrete that takes the form of psychic figments and remnants, hence the need, however problematic, for a psychic crypt in the first place.

And yet Abraham and Torok would maintain that gaps are never consciously created. To the contrary, the phantom "ghosts" the psyche as a roving unconscious presence — indefinite, meandering, and elusive — and therefore malicious. Nor is the phantom real in the sense common to spirits, specters, and ghosts in many cultures, ancient and modern, that hold them to be family familiars, avatars, or antagonists.[23] To the contrary, Abraham and Torok's phantom lacks all material presence in the physical sense. In the words of Colin Davis, what they call a phantom is instead

> the presence of a dead ancestor in the living Ego, still intent on preventing its traumatic and usually shameful secrets from coming to light. One crucial consequence of this is that the phantom does not, as it does in some versions of the ghost story, return from the dead in order to reveal something hidden or forgotten, to right a wrong or to deliver a message that might otherwise have gone unheeded. On the contrary, the phantom is a liar; its effects are designed to mislead the haunted subject and to ensure that its secret remains shrouded in mystery.[24]

Nevertheless, and despite Abraham and Torok's best efforts, it's hard for them to avoid personifying phantoms. Veering toward agency, their phantoms often recall living creatures, even though they are not meant to and are not themselves capable of revealing secrets. For therapeutic reasons, the secrets Abraham and Torok associate with phantoms can and should for them be revealed through discovery or "unvaulting" of the crypt by those who stash them away, only to be haunted by them. In that way, love can assuage mourning and melancholia, ameliorating the forces of death and loss.[25] And this because the secret consists of what Davis calls "a productive opening of meaning rather than a determinate content to be uncovered." The secret furnishes its heirs with work to be carried out, as if the afflicted were their own analysts, finding their own cure.[26]

The wounds of those who inherit secrets will emerge as whatever has allowed founding silences to be formed in the first place, pathologies that keep repeating themselves in endless variations, repeating lies and prevarications, harboring enigmas, and thereby producing similar symptoms in victims, the result of the errant pathways that silence and obfuscation are bound to take as they twist and turn mischievously over time. Above all, it's founding silences that push the psyche into habits that Freud called *repetition compulsion*—except that for analysts in the Abraham-Torok vein, it's not just an individual who is compelled to keep repeating traumatic, troubling circumstances, tendencies, and events, but whole families, whose repetitions reverberate over several generations. This is the kind of repetition Fabio and Rita discussed with each other and conveyed to me, following Ancelin Schützenberger's following of Abraham and Torok: repetition that manifests *transgenerationally*; repetition compulsion in a familial and multigenerational key.

As such, it differs fundamentally from Freud's famous account of the "return of the repressed" since indestructible memory traces in the Abraham and Torok view are not located solely in the individual unconscious.[27] Rather, as their late work (especially Abraham's) describes the phantom, a collective transgenerational memory is encrypted in each psyche. Encryption constitutes the means by which victims stash the past. Their take on things puts Moreschi history in a striking light, inasmuch as information about Giulio's biological father and his mother's transgression was apparently secreted enough to become quickly lost to intergenerational knowledge, along with family genealogies themselves, yet was still troubling to family psyches. In fact, the "I" word, *illegitimate*, hovered over speech and action surrounding Giulio, but was evidently never uttered or written (and, indeed, seems to have been legally averted four days after Giulio's birth by Alessandro's declaration of himself as father to the authorities; see Chapter 4 above).[28] And the "A," word, *adultery*, though it loitered in the ruins of Guendalina's life, seems not to have been uttered aloud either, certainly never by those I encountered. Voiced instead were other wrongs and other consequences: a thieving wife, an abandoned child, the melancholia of a mourning father, as well as general family woes memorialized in Rita's *In viaggio con lo zio* and in the tiny handwritten annotation of the Sistine Chapel diarist who noted in June 1907 that Moreschi was out sick because his wife had fled.[29]

Françoise Meltzer writes that a central problem of Freudian psychoanalysis lies in its insistence "on transference, and perhaps even more significantly, on displacement as fundamental principles," which also means that Freudian psychoanalysis must "insist in turn on seeing everything as being 'really' about something else."[30] This is no small point. The *aboutness* of Abraham and Torok differs radically from that of Freud. For while their theory is about things hidden and scarcely available to consciousness, those things nevertheless include actual psychic wounds, unmistakable effects, real secrets, and specific ancestral actors, however ghostly. They are hard to discover, sometimes impossible, but objectively, they existed, and so in principle, they might be discovered as part of a curative process. Torok delineates this difference in her 1975 essay "Story of Fear: The Symptoms of Phobia—the Return of the Repressed or the Return of the Phantom?" where she recalibrates dynamics surrounding phobias, fears, and anxieties that acquire pathological proportions in children and later in adults. Indeed, she does so to such a dramatic degree that anxious conflicts between repression and desire, most dangerously leading to a pervasive castration anxiety, might almost allow one to answer the question of who has done the castrating. And this because the dynamics surrounding fear and anxiety have been realigned to think about the agent of fear not just as a father figure, but as a troubling ancestor. Instead of being the displaced image of a castrating father or mother—all basically in a person's "head"—the agent might be something from the past that is secondary, yet deeply affecting to a given ego, with the result that, as Torok writes, "some people are completely detached from their own libidinal roots and only produce puppet emotions," emotions of others who haunt them.[31]

To think further on this point, we can return to Abraham's

preliminary thoughts in his late "Notes on the Phantom," where he draws attention to a central problem of the phantom concerning "detachment" from one's "libidinal roots":

> Let me offer, among others, one idea to explain the birth of a phantom. The phantom counteracts libidinal introjection; that is, it obstructs our perception of words as implicitly referring to their unconscious portion. In point of fact, the words which the phantom uses to carry out its return (and which the child sensed in the parent) do not refer to a source of speech in the parent. Instead, they point to a gap, that is, to the unspeakable. In the parent's topography, these words play the crucial role of having to some extent stripped speech of its libidinal grounding. Summoning the phantom occurs, therefore, as the recognition at the opportune moment of the gap transmitted to the subject with the result of barring it from specific introjections he seeks at present.[32]

On this view, the work of the phantom coincides with Freud's "death instinct" or "death drive," as Abraham spells it out, and in several ways: it has no energy of its own; "it pursues in silence its work of disarray," "sustained by secreted words, invisible gnomes whose aim is to wreak havoc, from within the unconscious, on the coherence of logical progression"; and its endless repetition "eludes rationalization."[33]

But this work of disarray, with its expression in endless repetitions, also eludes something Abraham doesn't really spell out, namely, the *agency* of the subject. Attached to the phantom is seemingly an abundance of intention, notwithstanding its status as a ghostly psychic gap (much as we see in the later personification by Torok's collaborator Rand). Hence, unsurprisingly, and as Abraham himself adds, the phantom also remains "beyond the reach of the tools of traditional analysis," only to be expelled from the victim "once we recognize its radically heterogeneous nature with respect to the subject—to whom it at no time bears any direct reference. In no way can the subject relate to it as his or her own repressed experience."[34]

Derrida's Specters

What is Derrida's place in all of this? In Chapter 3, I invoked Derrida as the master theorist-philosopher of the trace—a fundamentally linguistic trope, but one that understands language as stealthily pervading entire worlds, nook and cranny, from omicron to omega. Perhaps it should come as no surprise, then, that Derrida's more political and materialistic *Specters of Marx* should have caused a deluge of hauntology studies to flood academia once it appeared in 1993, especially after it came out in English translation in 1994. *Specters of Marx* brings Derrida's implicit investment in specters and ghosts out into the open, evolving, it would seem, not just from his Marxist preoccupations, but from 1980s-oriented psychoanalysis, all natural outgrowths of his attention to trace and voice. Indeed, the launchpad of the book is Marx and Engels's famous opening of *The Communist Manifesto* (1848)—"A specter is haunting Europe, the specter of communism"—while Marx's ghost-filled *Eighteenth Brumaire* ghosts *Specters of Marx* throughout.

And yet Derrida's curiosities about haunting date back to the 1950s, when he took a profound interest in the work of Abraham and Torok, especially the former, becoming something of an Isaac to Torok's Abraham over the next couple decades.[35] In 1976, the year after Abraham died, Torok published the couple's book on cryptonomy with a lengthy foreward by Derrida entitled "*Fors*: The Anglish Words of Nicolas Abraham and Maria Torok," initiating a process of memorializing and legacy building.[36] In 1979, Derrida's translator, Peggy Kamuf, offered some witty words about Derrida's role in Torok's continued work on Abraham's preliminary theories of phantoms, riffing on legacy, family, and plots—all motifs with which I've been preoccupied throughout this book:[37]

> Abraham's two other texts on this question [of phantoms] are published posthumously, annotated by Maria Torok and issued in his name as commemoration and legacy. What is described there, however, is another sort

> of legacy, a disruptive one which dissociates the beneficiaries from their potential investments by having them assume title to the family fortune, by giving them the role of accomplice and guardian in the family plot. Are these two ghosts distinguishable, or was Abraham's text dictated already from that "beyond-the-Self" and beyond a grave, the unspecified circumstance which is finally his own death? What has Nicolas Abraham left us in his will?
>
> Maria Torok, a survivor, would defer this question to her co-beneficiary, Derrida. In her prefatory remarks to *L'Ecorce et le noyau* [1978], she explains that she has not written a lengthier introduction because "the step crossing the threshold of the work has already been accomplished . . . I refer to the important introductory remarks of Jacques Derrida."[38]

In fact, a principal motivation behind Derrida's foreword was to locate the crack that might make it possible to unlock the legacy of the ancestors, to understand what's left behind in the crypt. Note that the English translation of the book as *The Wolf Man's Magic Word: A Cryptonomy* strays far from the original French, *Cryptonomie: Le verbier et L'Homme aux loups*, where "cryptonomie" is the main title. Here "verbier"—which might be rendered "verbarium" (as Kamuf translates it) or word play—and *l'Homme aux loups* are separate entities relegated to the subtitle.[39]

Understanding that difference means understanding what the crypt is intended to be. As form, object, concept, and place, the crypt is elusive because its very nature is not to present itself. Indeed, its topography produces a cleft in space by virtue of the partitions it erects in order to protect the self.

Besides which, the intellectual genealogies signaled in the title reveal much about the protections it's meant to afford. The crypt exists to spare selves and others from harm, to save them, however bad a job it does of it. Per Kamuf: in much the same way as Freud's famously depressive "wolf man," whose case is the subject of *Cryptonomie: Le verbier et L'Homme aux loups / The Wolf Man's Magic Word*, tried to save the inhabitants of his own crypt, Abraham and Torok looked to save a part of Freud, much as Derrida was working to save Abraham and Torok.[40] But what haunts this history are not just attempts at "saving" one's contemporaries and ancestors, but the fact that a day can come when these acts of saving simply stop. In the case of Derrida, they ended abruptly. Derrida abandoned the crypt after publishing his foreword to *Cryptonomie*. He said nothing more on the subject after 1976 until sixteen years later, when he published his highly influential *Spectres de Marx*, putting the proverbial last nail in the coffin by omitting all mention of Abraham and Torok (unless one counts a single footnoted bibliographical reference to his own foreword to *Cryptonomie*).

In sum, and as Davis and others highlight, substantial differences ultimately divided Derrida's hauntological spectrality from Abraham and Torok's transgenerational haunting. Nicholas Royle's wonderful book on the uncanny tallies the differences, noting, first, that Derrida's preoccupation with spirits, revenants, and phantoms is vested, differently from Abraham and Torok's, in the experience of unutterable language, akin to the ghostly Derridean trace of *différance*, and second, that Derrida's spectrality is consequently nonlinear and nonteleological, "time out of joint," constantly deferred, in contrast to the linear familial time at work in Abraham and Torok. Third, he notes that both Abraham (especially) and Torok see the possibility, indeed the necessity, of cures through a kind of psychoanalytic exorcism—what I've referred to above as utilitarian therapies—where Derrida sees only repetition and endless disavowal;[41] and fourth, that Derrida's specters lie forever in the future, if less damagingly than Abraham's (and again, let's add Torok's). Like the casualties Fabio and Rita wished they could have helped or wished could have helped them, Abraham and Torok's victims of secrets and crypts are continually haunted by the past.[42]

Crypts and Tombs

More than Derrida's theories, then, Abraham and Torok's—as popularized by Ancelin Schützenberger in the way that touched Fabio and Rita—have consequences for dealing with the dead.

"*The phantom which returns to haunt bears witness to the existence of the dead buried within the other*," writes Abraham toward the end of his "Notes on the Phantom."[43] Or as Rand puts it, "In the psychoanalytic realm, laying the dead to rest and cultivating our ancestors implies uncovering their shameful secrets, understanding their nameless and undisclosed suffering. We should engage in this unveiling and understanding of the former existence of the dead not because we may want to appease them or prevent them from perpetrating their nocturnal pranks, but because, unsuspected, the dead continue to lead a devastating psychic half-life in us."[44]

Giving this some credence, I am struck that in the Moreschi case, the phantom's haunting has prompted remembrances around the dead as ways of coping with them, memorializing them to honor them, but also to overcome their phantomatic forms. Even when detrimental, phantoms have helped provide psychic knowledge and finally relief. But honoring and overcoming them means remembering them not just psychically and mentally, but materially and performatively. Burials, with the various rites and rituals surrounding them, have served to externalize the inner psyche as they gather dead ancestors together in concrete tombs that transform the topography of psychic crypts, vaulted deeply beneath consciousness, into the above-ground architecture of the graveyard. Entombing the dead, as expressed by the literal, yet symbolically loaded phrase "burying the dead" and by the symbolic action of placing the dead underground, italicizes the fact of *encrypting the dead* in life. Even though psychic and physical burials are nowise the same thing, the rituals that burials entail work to decode and encode what is psychically encrypted.

By inaugurating a handsome tomb in 1900 to conjoin their families, Alessandro Moreschi and Pietro Rinaldi made a bequest to subsequent generations without meaning in that moment to encrypt lives that only a short time later would become severely wounded by Guendalina's falling out with her father, Pietro, by 1902, and with her abandonment of Alessandro and Giulio in 1907. Leapfrogging forward over the generations, we come to Rita and Fabio. When I first encountered them in May 2010, they had no knowledge of Pietro Rinaldi's identity, much less any purchase on why he shared a tomb with Rita's great-grandfather, as I learned at Taverna Antonina and then at the cemetery, where Fabio and I went the same day in 2010. And indeed, Rita's memoir remembers nothing of Pietro Rinaldi or any of the circumstances or persons from Guendalina's natal family, not even Guendalina's surname. Only from research carried out with my then research assistant, Martina Piperno, in early summer 2010 did Rinaldi's identity as Guendalina's father (along with her last name) come quickly to light. Innumerable questions persisted, ones Fabio was more eager than Rita to have answered. Rita hung back, not just because she was unwell by then, but because she was generally more sad than curious about family affairs and family history with a sadness that haunts her memoir and many family stories. Alessandra had been all of eighteen when Rita was born, after which her mother spent much of her time out on the town, while Rita's beloved grandparents mostly raised her. And as she writes with disarming frankness in chapter 2 of *In viaggio con lo zio*, mother and daughter had never been compatible:

> The idea for writing these notes came to me during the funeral for my mother, Alessandra, who was cut down suddenly by a heart attack in August of 1994.
>
> I never got along with my mother, and even as a young child, I understood that for no explicable reason, our relationship was based on mutual hostility. Basically, we never loved each other. In the final years of her life, we never saw each other or tried to reach each other by either phone or letter. Every now and then, we would hear about each other from some third party, but that was the end of it—we never did anything to try to fix our relationship. The hostility that had drawn us apart so many years before had gradually transformed into indifference. I never imagined that her death would hurt me, yet I felt a profound sadness.
>
> My father Riccardo had died three years before, and the year before [i.e., before Alessandra's death], Uncle Federico had passed away, followed a few

> months later by my beloved Aunt Giulietta. Even my two grandmothers, Ida (paternal) and Vittoria (maternal), had recently died. I was alone. My mother's death marked the end of an important chapter in my life, in fact more than half of it, seeing as I was almost fifty at the time. It's a time to balance things, I told myself, and so the idea of this book quickly formed.

Giulio's death had fallen hard on Rita, and still much harder Vittoria's, decades later. She worked continually to exorcise demons in the face of her bitter relationship with her mother, which finally lacerated all sense of kinship.[45]

Rita's feelings about family troubles shaped her last wish not to be entombed with family members at the Cimitero del Verano. By the time of her death, my periodic get-togethers with Fabio usually began at the Fellini store (which, owing to Rita's illness, he was generally manning with help only from his assistant, Paolo Corrado) and then progressed to the cemetery. I would typically arrive before noon and mingle among customers, many of them tourists who were dropping in and out of shops while ambling along the Corso. Often I picked up gifts while waiting until Fabio could make his getaway for a meal and conversation. On times when we visited the cemetery, we would groom the gravestone, weeding the surrounding earth and clearing away any debris, and then place flowers on it.

But my first return trip to Rome, in early summer 2011, well before Rita's death, surprised me. Shortly after our first meeting, Fabio had begun adorning the tomb's central column using genealogical data I had unearthed with Martina Piperno.[46] From the plain, pockmarked stone rising above what had originally been a sole picture of Rinaldi on the pedestal, the tomb had been transmuted by addition of seven porcelained photos to the middle of its column.[47] The additions, with birth and death data, effectively formed a three-tiered pictorial genosociogram. Arrayed along the lower tier were, left to right, the young castrato-uncle of Alessandro's, Domenico Salvatori, then Alessandro himself, and to the right Alessandro's nephew, Amerigo. Moving upward and gesturing toward a younger generation came (right to left) Vittoria Cevasco, Giulio Moreschi, and (slightly above them) Alessandra Moreschi. And sitting at the top was Julio Salvador Solinas Moreschi.[48]

By late spring 2012, Rita had been added—the only photo in color and the only one of a person so memorialized who is not actually buried in the tomb (figs. 5.1 and 5.2). She is thus a cenotaph, a stand-in and a crypt with no secret because it is empty. Fabio explained why. Rita was too sorrowful about the family to want to be laid to rest there. Although she had joined forces with her brother, Julio, to renovate the tomb in the mid-1990s, when parts of it were crumbling, she did not want to be part of the remembering (re-*membering*) through acts of reassembling that a family plot entails.[49] And yet in the iconography that now gathers the family together, she is nevertheless a member. Most especially, she is sister to Julio and granddaughter to Vittoria, with both of whom she shares, commemoratively, a border.

Coda: Phantom Riccardo in Fellini's Dream Books

Federico Fellini's explicit interest in ancestral phantoms circumvented his real family and hometown to zoom as far backward as the ghosts of Roman antiquity in *Fellini Satyricon* (1969) and a good way forward to the Rimini experienced by the two brothers in *Amarcord* (1973). *Satyricon*, based loosely on Petronius, together with bits of Ovid, Horace (*Satires*), and Suetonius, drew together what Fellini called "disconcerting analogies between [late] Roman society"—"cynical . . . impassive, corrupt and frenzied"—and the society of his day.[50] By evoking the past not through strict historical record or textual fidelity, but in the way "an archeologist does, when he assembles a few potsherds or pieces of masonry and reconstructs not an amphora or a temple, but an artifact in which the object is implied," Fellini could suggest the past as something fragmentary, evoking lost codes and operating to disinter distant forebears.[51] Alberto Moravia noted that although Fellini's dream of antiquity lost its meanings, his distant ancestors made their "presence felt at all

Figure 5.1. Close-up of porcelained pictures added to the Moreschi-Rinaldi tomb in 2011 and 2012. *Bottom row, left to right*: Domenico Salvatori, Alessandro Moreschi, Amerigo Moreschi. *Middle row, left to right*: Giulio Moreschi, Vittoria Cevasco. *Top row, left to right*: Alessandra Moreschi, Julio Salvador Solinas Moreschi, Rita Fellini. Photograph by the author.

Figure 5.2. Fabio Panconesi regarding the tomb with photographs recently added, June 2012. Photograph by the author.

times."[52] Fellini's dream lingered as a leave-taking, a spectral, inaccessible residue that nevertheless entwined with the present.

Only four years after making *Satyricon*, and despite an ambivalent nostalgia for his youth, Fellini tackled more recent forebears with *Amarcord*, striding straight into the Fascism that had beset the Rimini of Federico and Riccardo's youth before their exodus in 1939. As in *I vitelloni*, *Amarcord* made no real historical return to prewar and wartime Rimini, only to a fantastical, imaginary one. In an essay on Rimini explaining why, Federico wrote of escaping all the loyalties and debts of transgenerational history, not having to care about family justices and injustices in real life or revisit his hometown,[53] but just plunging into the world of Rome, the world of cinema, and the brave new world of his own cinematic creations.

"I have nephews and nieces whom I almost never see," he said elsewhere.[54] A charming thank-you note of Federico's in the Moreschi-Fellini Archive (fig. 5.3), addressed on Christmas Day 1972 to "Cara Rituccia," begs forgiveness from her "zio smemorato" (forgetful uncle), an uncle whom her memoir shows she adored.[55] And indeed, the note is a rare exception to the rule. Fellini's casual neglect of family was of a piece with his general disinterest in them. But that disinterest was less pointed in his younger years, even if he sought independence in Rome by drawing pictures and writing newspaper columns and radio plays, activities that extended his teenage work making caricatures for cinema in Rimini and then deepened with his cartoon work for Roman papers during the war, leading up to the Funny Face Shop started with his friend "O.G." (aka "Caporetto") in 1944.[56]

That same year, Fellini applied his graphic facility and narrative verve to his brother's engagement, producing a delightful wedding invitation, never before published, in the form of three cartoons voiced through the beaks of a waddling of ducks.[57] Look at the front (fig. 5.4a), and you see an anatine drum major, scroll in hand, quacking to three cloud-borne angel-ducklings, "Kids, book yourselves, because. . . . " Open the card (fig. 5.4b) and its width doubles to reveal why: "... Riccardo Fellini and Alessandra Moreschi have thought it a good idea to get married." The groom-duck chases the singing bride-duck up the church stairs as he warbles out the tenor solo that begins Bellini's duet "Prendi l'anel ti dono" (Take the ring I give you), a favorite of Riccardo's, watched by the three winged ducklings, who ask, "Where? How? When?"[58] Flip the card over, and you find two of the ducklings racing churchward (fig. 5.4c) as the scroll unfurls to read, "... on 12 June 1944 in the church of San Grisogono, 10am. Hurry up! Reservations at via Lungotevere Anguillara 11, no. 1." The whole sequence reads as a joyful little protocinematic storyboard.

Alas, relations with Riccardo became increasingly uneasy as the years went by. Although the list of those Fellini broke with or left in the dust grew over time, few in the sixties and seventies were so forcefully ejected from his lived life and waking consciousness as Riccardo, nor did any from his natal family preoccupy him as much. Only when Riccardo was bedridden at the end of his life did Federico search desperately for a nursing home and come to see him a few days before his death on March 26, 1991.[59]

Making sense of this requires a few passing stops through the vibrant landscape of Fellini's "dream books"—the heartland of his psyche and familial imaginary and what Tullio Kezich called "the realm where everything is possible."[60] Roaring with life, the dream books survive as two large physical albums (out of an original three; one has gone missing), plus a number of fragments and loose pages. They were undertaken by Fellini at the suggestion of his psychoanalyst, Ernst Bernhard, dealt with in Chapter 4, though Fellini's interest in dreams predates his association with Bernhard and may help explain what motivated it.[61]

The first, indeed foremost thing Fellini calls out in his fraternal relationship is a conflict over filmmaking, a conflict that deeply unnerved him in ways that are surprising and unsettling. He initially signaled them in a note of October 3, 1961, at an early stage in the dream books.[62] "What happened? Why did I dream that the little island . . . risked sinking into the sea? The day before I learned with certainty that my brother signed the film with the name Riccardo Fellini. This news was deeply disturbing to me, frightening, a sense of emptiness, of the end."[63]

Further dreams and drawings tell more. Later that month, on October 29, Fellini, though older and taller than Riccardo in real life, depicted himself as a small, perspiring child gazing up anxiously as his brother, who beams with glorious masculinity as he performs an iron cross on the rings. Their father, Urbano, looks on, applauding and exclaiming, "Bravo, bravo, Riccardo" (fig. 5.5).[64] Each dream reframes and refracts similar feelings, but also filters them, like an early phonographic recording. On December 11, Fellini's writes about another dream that expands on the business of Riccardo using the Fellini name:

> I decide to confront my brother about the issue of the "name." Our nocturnal meeting takes place on a large terrace surrounded by rooftops as far as the eye can see, under moonlight. We are not alone, there's a guy there who watches silently, and I can't talk to him with the aggressiveness and straightforwardness I'd intended to. Trying to keep calm, I list all the reasons why it seems to me opportune, useful, required that Riccardo sign his films with another name.
>
> My brother (who in my dream is an ill-mannered, unpleasant-looking girl) answers with a dry, insulting "No!" cynically adding that the Fellini name is useful to him, that he needs it in order to advance his career.
>
> I move on to begging, wheedling, I implore him, finally I am overcome with anger and I pummel him with slaps, punches, kicks.
>
> On the stairs I run into the old night watchman of a parking garage (Via Salaria?) and I tell him to go take a look at my brother, who I'd tossed beaten and bloody onto a bed, and in that very instant it seemed to me that he'd become incredibly small, a newborn. "Beaten and mistreated in that violent manner, he could die, suffocated under the sheets."
>
> I go out of that house and find myself in Rimini, before the big door to the building where I lived as a little boy.[65]

Federico, furious at the situation and frustrated at first by the stranger's presence, emasculates his brother by turning him first into a defenseless girl and then an infant. A week later, on December 18, a long, multipartite dream repeats the emasculation by reducing Riccardo's physical size while giving him a day job that "solves" the problem (fig. 5.6). The dream ends "with a vision of Riccardo (smaller than he really is), whistling with happiness because he finally has a safe, steady job. He even has his own little car"—the last echoing Riccardo's love of cars in real life and his sometime job as a used car salesman.[66] But the next year, on October 12, 1962, Fellini again records a dream that wrestles with the threat Riccardo poses. Federico is working at his Moviola, only to see his brother's shadow appear in a doorway, stiff, large, and menacing, its whole head obscured to view (fig. 5.7); in sum, a psychic specter. Like Fellini's text, which breaks off at the end ("Riccardo's shadow, taller and more massive. I am working at the Moviola when . . ."), the specter of Riccardo comes and goes unpredictably, menacing the arteries of Federico's lifeblood.[67]

In real life, Riccardo did in fact direct a film, *Storie sulla sabbia* (Stories in the sand), a pleasant, ninety-five-minute-long omnibus feature released in 1963 that tells three stories of people who spend time on the beach and the dunes until eventually their stories intersect. Nothing followed until a 1982 television documentary about Italians and their animals, *Quegli animali degli italiani*.[68] For a while over that earlier period, which begins with the release of Federico's *8½* (1963), followed by *Juliet of the Spirits* (1965), his acute, anxious resentment seems to have eased, at least to judge from the oneiric record. Then, a few years later, Riccardo's specter reappears, unwelcome or even downright ominous and sometimes preening over his films. In a dream of January 23, 1966 (fig. 5.8), Federico's nighttime visions culminate in a rendezvous with Livia (presumably his friend Livia Rezin), who zips him over to do his military service at the barracks where they encounter Riccardo "with the long hair of an artist. In the vast squalid silent courtyard, beautiful Livia is amused to witness my shock and anger at finding myself in this dark place with my brother."[69] And in July 1966, Federico pictures Riccardo in stocky miniaturized form, but with an outsized head, a full head of hair in a kind of pompadour, and what look at first glance like black sunglasses, though the caption describes his eyewear more darkly: "My brother Riccardo, much shorter, in fact incredibly small, with a black band over his left eye. I insult him violently" (fig. 5.9).[70] Then, on May 22, 1967: "My brother stops by Via Veneto with a satisfied air, saying that it's because he'd finally found (better yet, 'they gave me') the lead actor for his film."[71]

The years 1965 to 1967 saw Fellini caught up in the unspooling and aftermath of what turned out to be the failed project of a film many think would have been one of his chief masterpieces, *Il viaggio di G. Mastorna* (The journey of G. Mastorna), so perhaps it's unsurprising that his dark dreams of Riccardo returned then.[72] And indeed, after 1967, Riccardo practically disappears from the dream books, returning only on December 12, 1975, when he wreaks havoc with Fellini's notoriously active and clandestine love life in an account accompanied by a picture of Riccardo with chicken eyes (fig. 5.10, lower left):

> A. gets out of the bed she was sleeping in with me because she heard a noise, she says there's someone in the house. I follow her along down a vast corridor and see my brother coming up the stairs. I know it's him, Riccardo, but I have to admit it doesn't look like him at all. I'm struck by his strange eyes. They're like those of a chicken, a bird: small, round, devoid of any human expression. My brother, who also has the slovenly air of a vagabond, n'er do well, immediately starts talking to me and says:
>
> *"Federico, I want you to know that your mother and sister have come back and found you weren't home last night. Good evening, signora."*
>
> *"How do you know signora A.?"*
>
> *"A friend of mine, a tall, tall young friend of mine named Mario (?), was crazy about her and the signora was crazy for him, too."*

> "What a pain! These two nuisances are back," I say to the woman who is making up the bed where I was lying with A. The woman chortles, entertained and maybe a little scandalized. Then she shows me the shards of a lens from my eyeglasses between the sheets of the big bed.
>
> *The glass shards of my eyeglasses.*[73]

Federico's dreams contrast sharply with the Riccardo beloved by friends and family members, not least his daughter. Like the beautiful novice actress Anna Orso featured in Riccardo's *Storie sulla sabbia*, Rita remembers him as warm, openhearted, and witty. She radiates at his attention to her at her confirmation (see Appendix 1: Photo Essay no. 17) and writes affectionately about him in her *In viaggio con lo zio*. Others would add that Riccardo was not just a talented singer, but a fine actor, widely regarded as handsome and athletic, jovial and confident. In footage filmed shortly before Rita's death and subsequently woven into the film *L'altro Fellini* (2013) on Riccardo and Federico's vexed relationship, Rita sounds a protective note: "My father was in grief because he couldn't think that someone could ask his brother to change his last name. You wouldn't expect this, would you?"[74] Not long after the whole debacle over the signing of his film, Federico appeared with his two siblings, Riccardo and Maddalena, in a photograph taken with their daughters, Rita and Francesca, together with their grandmother Ida Barbiani—a sign of détente, perhaps, though more likely a rare rendezvous made to appease the siblings' mother.[75]

To be sure, Riccardo had a hapless side. Money was always a problem, and he was often down on his luck. Once he became an actor, there were few jobs, and when he tried to make films, he had virtually insuperable problems raising funds. Even those few projects that came to fruition incurred expenses, so humiliations ensued: embarrassing loans, pleas to borrow more money, odd jobs and petty patronage jobs, troubles paying up. Topping that off was the unmitigated failure of his sole cinematic feature (narrated in a whisper by Riccardo himself), the reception of which prompted him to defend himself in public:

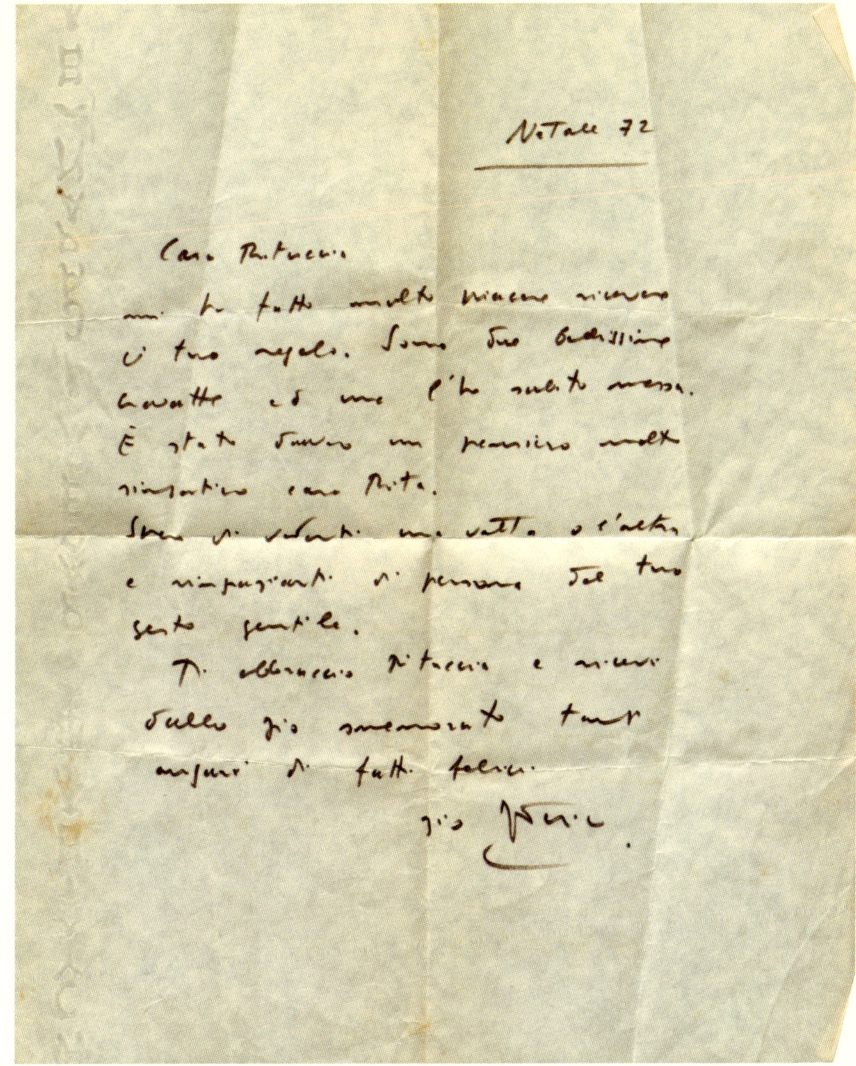

Natale 72

Cara Rituccia

mi ha fatto molto piacere ricevere il tuo regalo. Sono due bellissime cravatte ed una l'ho subito messa. È stato davvero un pensiero molto simpatico cara Rita. Spero di vederti una volta o l'altra e ringraziarti di persona del tuo gesto gentile.

Ti abbraccio Rituccia e ricevi dallo zio smemorato tanti auguri di fatti felici.

zio Federico

Figure 5.3. Thank-you note from Federico Fellini to Rita Fellini: "Christmas 1972. Dear Rituccia, it gave me great pleasure to receive your gift. They are two beautiful ties and one of them I put on immediately. Truly, it was a very dear thought, Rita. I hope to see you at one time or another and thank you in person for your kind gesture. I hug you, Rituccia, and please accept from your forgetful uncle many good wishes for happy occurrences [*fatti felici*]. Uncle Federico." Moreschi-Fellini Archive.

Figure 5.4a–c. Invitation drawn by Federico Fellini, cartoon style, for the wedding of Riccardo Fellini and Alessandra Moreschi. a) *Front*: "Bambini!! Prenotatevi perché . . ." (Kids, book yourselves, because . . .); b) *Inside* (shown below): ". . . Riccardo Fellini e Alessandra Moreschi hanno pensato bene di sposarsi!!! [in musical score: "Prendi l'anel che ti dono"] [*in balloon*: "Dove? Come? Quando?"] (Riccardo Fellini and Alessandra Moreschi have thought it a good idea to get married!!! . . . [*in musical score*: "Take the ring I give you"] [in balloon*: Where? How? When?]).*

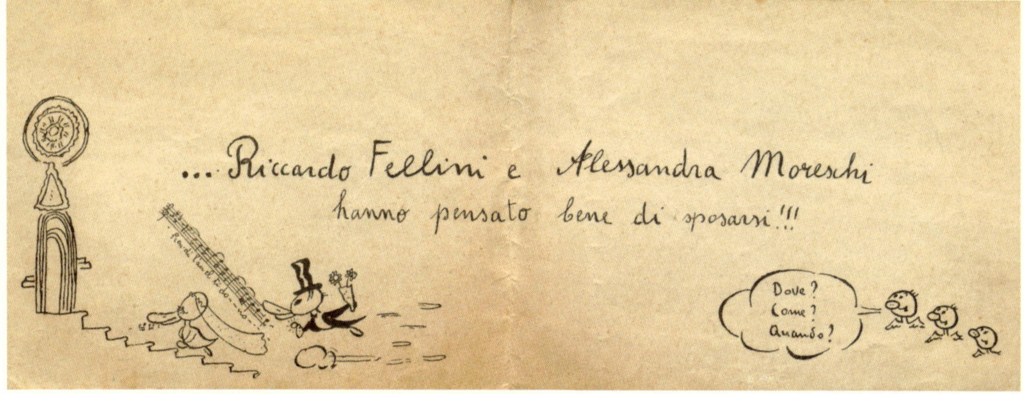

c) *Back*: " . . . [on scroll:] il 12 Giugno 1944 nella Chiesa di S. Grisogono . . . ore 10. Affrettatevi! Prenotazioni in via Lungotevere Anguillara 11-1" [*on scroll*: the twelfth of June 1944 in the church of San Crisognono at 10 a.m. Hurry up! Reservations at Lungotevere Anguillara no. 11, 1st floor].

gran corpo possente l'aria vibra come
attorno ad un colossale aereo che sta
per alzarsi... Un'oscuro terrore mi
raggela il corpo, e nel sonno mi
lamento, gemo faticosamente, balbetto
il nome di Giulietta invocandola che
mi scuota dal paralizzante torpore...
Mi sveglio ed ero in sala,
ansante per la paura.

x x x

Bernhard mi dice "Mi parli di suo
fratello Riccardo". Gli racconto allora
questo episodio (che illustro qui sotto),
della lontanissima infanzia...

Figure 5.5. Federico Fellini, *Libro dei sogni*, October 29, 1961, property of Fellini Museum Rimini, © Comune di Rimini and Francesca Fabbri Fellini. Reproduced by permission.

Figure 5.6. Federico Fellini, *Libro dei sogni*, December 18, 1961, property of Fellini Museum Rimini, © Comune di Rimini and Francesca Fabbri Fellini. Reproduced by permission.

Figure 5.7. Federico Fellini, *Libro dei sogni*, October 12, 1962, property of Fellini Museum Rimini, © Comune di Rimini and Francesca Fabbri Fellini. Reproduced by permission.

Figure 5.8. Federico Fellini, *Libro dei sogni*, January 23, 1966, property of Fellini Museum Rimini, © Comune di Rimini and Francesca Fabbri Fellini. Reproduced by permission.

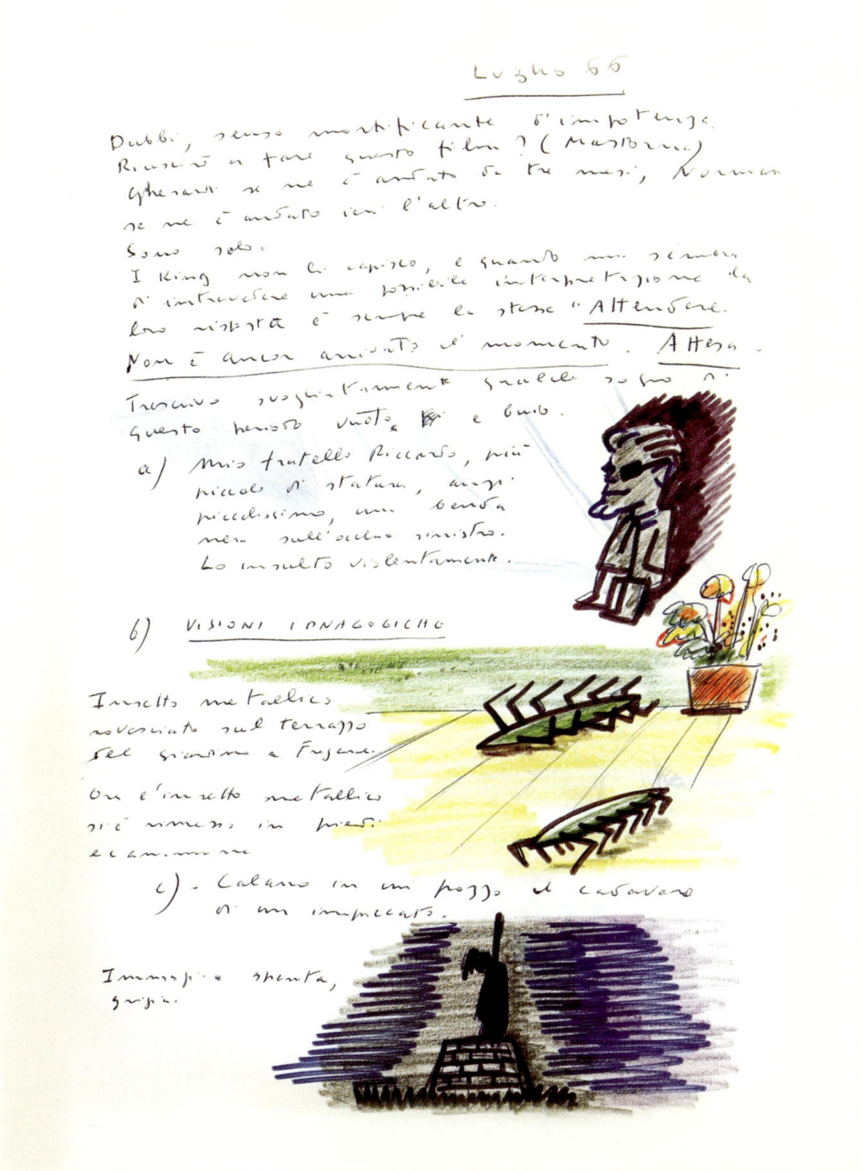

Luglio 66

Dubbi, senso mortificante d'impotenza.
Riuscirò a fare questo film? (Mastorna)
Gherardi se ne è andato da tre mesi, Norman
se ne è andato ieri l'altro.
Sono solo.
I King non li capisco, e quando mi sembra
di intravedere una possibile interpretazione la
loro risposta è sempre la stessa "Attendere.
Non è ancora arrivato il momento. Attesa.

Trascrivo suggestivamente qualche sogno di
questo penoso vuoto e buio.

a) Mio fratello Riccardo, più
piccolo di statura, anzi
piccolissimo, una benda
nera sull'occhio sinistro.
Lo insulto violentemente.

b) VISIONI IPNAGOGICHE

Insetto metallico
rovesciato sul terrazzo
del giardino a Fregene.

Ora l'insetto metallico
si è rimesso in piedi
e cammina

c) - Calano in un pozzo il cadavere
di un impiccato.

Immagine spenta,
grigia.

Figure 5.9. Federico Fellini, *Libro dei sogni*, July 1966, property of Fellini Museum Rimini, © Comune di Rimini and Francesca Fabbri Fellini. Reproduced by permission.

Figure 5.10. Federico Fellini, *Libro dei sogni*, December 12, 1975, property of Fellini Museum Rimini, © Comune di Rimini and Francesca Fabbri Fellini. Reproduced by permission.

> This year in Venice, my movie, like all the debut films presented, was not welcomed too kindly by the critics. I don't understand this fury towards debut films. A quite important critic from Milan defined my movie as "unreal, empty talk." I don't understand why. The originality of my first film lies in the stories themselves and in the choice to take performers from real life. . . . If I had to redo this movie, I would redo it in the same way, with the same people, with the same love and with the same passion. Maybe I'd like to be paid back in a different way.[76]

Different payback never came from Federico, who visited his brother only on his deathbed. The visits Riccardo made to Federico's dreams were of course a different matter. There, Riccardo takes the form of a superego who demands he be abused because the analysand's ego understands him as the one doling out abuse himself. In real life, of course, the demand, patently unfair, came from Federico himself. We can make sense of it, perhaps even understand it to a degree, however wrong and hurtful, as an objection to using a family name that could be erroneously ascribed to Federico and his creative work. Yet in Abraham and Torok's terms, it nonetheless reads as a gap in his psyche, a split in consciousness produced by a haunting whose uncanny, phantomic nature Federico objectified in Bernhard's office and through his dream books, endlessly revisiting the gap and at last desperately hoping to pacify it by suturing it in Riccardo's hospital room, where his illness might finally express itself in the form of a cure for Federico's "unfinished business." All that in a family sewn together by a variety of conflicts and more than one failed marriage that nevertheless produced the lively, bright, and sympathetic person of Rita, the Moreschi great-granddaughter and Fellini daughter/niece who was saddened by family life, but not defeated by it. Few others from the Moreschi line now survive, of whom the most direct, genealogically, if not biologically, is Alessandro's great-great-grandson, also Giulio's biological great-grandson, Alessandra's grandson, and Julio's son, Alessandro Solinas Moreschi (2006–) (Appendix 1, 33).

EPILOGUE

The Castrato Inheritance

> We lived through many moves, and with every move, letters and objects pertaining to the previous generation were lost, thrown away. . . . I saw that bit by bit, as time passed, less and less remained. Houses were sold, people moved. And so what one might be able to salvage is this: a book.
>
> —Fabio Panconesi, March 23, 2015

> How do we reckon with what modern history has rendered ghostly?
>
> —Avery Gordon, *Ghostly Matters*

The ambivalence that shadowed Moreschi's G & T recordings anticipated two transformations in the manufacture of art music. On one end was the castrato's final and complete disappearance, which from an art-music perspective hardly counted by then; on another end was the metamorphosis of opera from a living art form to something of a museum art.[1] Although moving pictures in Moreschi's time were still in their budding stages, they soon exploded into prominence, overtaking opera as a site of cultural production. Sound film did not arrive until 1929–1930. Once it did, the industry distinguished itself by its dogged practice of dubbing (*doppiaggio*), codified during Fascist times, when thousands of films had to be dubbed in keeping with the nationalist program carried out by a giant workforce of dubbing artists and technicians. Even after the Second World War, new soundtracks were routinely created after image editing. By staggering the emission of sound from the movement of bodies, Italian film underscored a looming absence: the absence not just of a tight relation of body and voice, but the absence, endemic to all sound recordings, of a visible source synching sound to a verifiable body and all its entailments.

Dislocations of the kind suggest we might think further about the singing bodies of castrati. What kinds of dislocations did castrato bodies conjure if not something like the time delays, bad syncing, and acousmatic effects of sound recordings, dubbed movies, and even radio? Not unlike those, they failed to confirm much sonically about the visible bodily source—above all, its gender. That had been the case for centuries, of course. Everyone in early modern times, from elite rulers to starstruck commercial ticketholders, had gazed upon castrated male bodies piping out high parts. What was new in these crepuscular years was that the price of such dislocations had steadily shot up to an unbearable degree. Tolerance for sound/body and sound/sight disjunctions, epitomized by Fellini's intentionally exaggerated misalignments of voice and body in the dubbing process, may have been present in the case of falsettists, but falsettists sang with a shaved-down male voice available to all men. Castrati, by contrast, sounded more like big-voiced females. Moreover, they sounded that way while masking a secret shared by church and state that finally rendered them ontologically and politically impossible.

Bonnie Gordon makes a compelling argument that from the time of their origins in the sixteenth century, castrati participated in what we might call (after Longinus) an artificial sublime. Gordon's castrati represent a technological triumph in the marriage of humans to machines, or perhaps better said, in the marriage of humans to machinic technologies. But in the Italy of this period, something else was at play. Well before Moreschi's death, Fascism was already on a steep rise, and Mussolini—chief promoter of what Barbara Spackman calls "fascist virilities" and born in the same year of 1883 that Moreschi was inducted into the Sistine Chapel—was to become prime minister three months after his death.[2] Masculinist tropes of Fascism, already powerful in the late nineteenth and early twentieth centuries, had also externalized themselves on the male body in the form of mustaches, iconic marks of masculinity that distinguished castrati from noncastrati—a fact on glaring display in a circa 1880s photograph of six Roman singers and another of two of Moreschi's friends (figs. E.1 and E.2). Yet in an ironic twist, with mustaches came attacks on modernity. As Sandro Bellassai has shown, the mustache fastened the knot between traditional Italian notions of virility and antimodernist discourse, including condemnation of the bourgeoisie and intelligentsia.[3] The mustache expressed a nineteenth-century repulsion toward feminine decadence and degeneration, manifested in fears of an "excess of 'civilization'" that were heaped onto Italian society after the establishment of the modern Italian state, with all its political and technological trappings.

Indeed, it's not unreasonable to think that maximally extended, those fears turned into Fascist fetishizations of heroic masculinity, which ended by rejecting anything that ruptured its ideal forms. They also led to castrati being heaved out of conscious memory. Moreschi, without whom in his heyday a colleague said no performance in Rome could succeed, was not even remembered in *L'osservatore romano*, the official mouthpiece of the Vatican, after he died on April 21, 1922.[4]

The erasure was all but total, but not permanent. Four years after Giulio Moreschi's death at age fifty-one and following decades of muteness about Italy's role in the making and use of castrated male singers, a book appeared, *Degli "evirati cantori": Contributo alla storia del teatro* (On emasculated singers: Contribution to the history of theater), published in 1959 by the prominent Roman theater director, cineaste, photographer, scholar, journalist, impresario, and art theorist Anton Giulio Bragaglia (1890–1960). The focus of *Degli "evirati cantori"* on the cross-dressing and sexual ambiguity of

Figure E.1. Six Roman musicians photographed in the 1880s. *Standing, left to right*: Filippo Mattoni (alto), Gaetano Capocci (composer, organist, and maestro di cappella), and Domenico Salvatori (castrato); *seated, left to right*: Alessandro Moreschi (castrato), Antonio "Toto" Cotogni (baritone), and Giovanni Cesari (castrato). Note the mustaches on all the unaltered men. Image from an unidentified late nineteenth-century newspaper. Wikimedia Commons.

Figure E.2. Two unaltered mustachioed friends of Moreschi's, Luigi Forini (signed 1911) and Roberto Fattorini (signed 1910), bearing the fashionable waxed mustaches of the day. Moreschi-Fellini Archive.

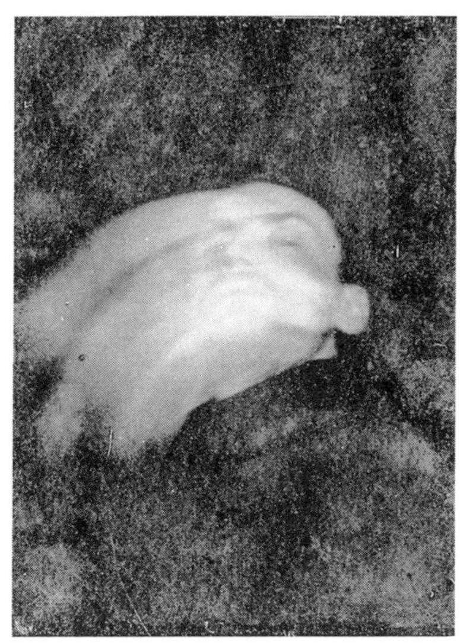

Figure E.3. Anton Giulio Bragaglia (1890–1960), "Un Gesto del Capo" (self-portrait), 1911. Gelatin silver print. 17.8 x 12.7 cm (7 x 5 in.). Metropolitan Museum of Art, Gilman Collection, gift of The Howard Gilman Foundation, 2005 (accession no. 2005.100.246). Rights and reproduction © 2022 Artists Rights Society (ARS), New York. Reproduced by permission.

early modern castrati aligned Bragaglia's scholarly ambitions with his avant-garde artistic visions. With his brother, he had invented photodynamism while still in his teens (as seen in an early self-portrait in figure E.3), a project inspired by the experimental work of Étienne-Jules Marey and the thought of Henri Bergson and delineated by Bragaglia in his *Fotodinamismo futurista* (1911), published when he was twenty-one.[5] By age twenty-six, he had written a manifesto on Italian futurist cinema and within another year made the quasi-futurist, protoexpressionistic film *Thaïs* (fig. E.4).[6]

The appearance of *Degli "evirati cantori"* cleared space for discourse about castrati, or at least indexed the possibility of it, effectively breaking codes of silence and intervening in the politics of erasure that marked Rome's antebellum and wartime years and their conformist aftermath. The book called attention to the euphemism through its quotation marks around "cantori evirati," taking up castrati in an idiosyncratic, yet sustained account, but eliding them with present times by hailing Moreschi as a living part of the author's own youthful experience, someone he knew in his Roman

Figure E.4. Film still from *Thaïs* (1917), directed by Anton Giulio Bragaglia, sets by Enrico Prampolini.

neighborhood around via de' Banchi Vecchi, where Moreschi lived for a time (fig. E.5) and whom he used to pass on the street. In this way, Bragaglia assimilated Moreschi to earlier "evirati cantori," instead of resurrecting them solely from the tombs of distant pasts.[7] All this set *Degli "evirati cantori"* apart from the shabby little book produced by Gino Monaldi four decades earlier, a book that failed to mention Moreschi or any other castrati remotely of Monaldi's time.[8] More than that, Bragaglia attended to the deeper implications of Italy's castrato past, mustering texts from obscure literary manuscripts that he interpreted with erudition and witty insight.[9] His was a first salvo in treating castrati as a serious object of study.

It's hard to say how great a role Bragaglia's book played in restoring castrati to Italian consciousness or Italians' intellectual horizons. Before the early music boom hit the still-nascent institution of Italian musicology in the 1980s, *Degli "evirati cantori"* remained largely islanded with respect to Italian scholarship. And in any case, when the 1980s did roll around, scholarship had turned its focus to the seventeenth-century and eighteenth-century repertories then

Figure E.5. Via dei Banchi Vecchi 58, one of Alessandro Moreschi's residences and the one where Bragaglia would have seen him circa 1910. Photograph by the author.

being revived by early music groups, using middle-voiced and high-voiced female sopranos and especially male countertenors, rather than to the embarrassments of recent history.

Yet something else began stirring right after Bragaglia's death that warrants a brief detour here. From 1961 onward, castrati occasionally popped up in Roman films, harnessing the power and meaning of their ghosts before books and public discourse could do so.

The castrato is dead, long live the castrato. In this most anachronous of moments, Pietro Germi's brilliantly funny *Divorzio all'italiana / Divorce Italian Style* (1961) inserted a castrato episode, giving a public airing to what must otherwise have been only murmured allusions. As with other cinematic references that appeared over the next two decades, Germi's materialized as a sendup in the register of the joke—unsurprisingly so, for what is the work of jokes if not to paper over repressions with nervous laughter or bring them to the surface, only to drive them away? The well-known plot of *Divorce Italian Style* follows the Sicilian baron Ferdinando Cefalù, called Fefè (Marcello Mastroianni), who wants to push his wife,

Rosalia (Daniela Rocca), into an affair so he can knock her off in an honor killing and marry his young cousin. In an early episode to which no one has seemingly paid much attention, Fefè tries to interest his wife in a beardless male soprano with the diminutive name Tonino, reminiscent of the infantilizing nicknames given many past castrati. On first encounter, Tonino is swooning over an onstage tenor as he reaches the climax of Donizetti's "Una furtiva lagrima." Fefè gazes at Tonino from an adjacent box (fig. E.6), latching onto him as the right sort to tempt his opera-loving wife before hearing a secret whispered in his ear that will sink his plan (fig. E.7).[10]

At the opera house, the tenor singing on stage:

Fefè [silently, to himself]: "Perhaps an encounter with an artistic type, a soul mate. Who knows, maybe Tonino Gambacorta would do?"[11]

At church, Tonino singing in a choir loft in church "Ave Maria, gratia plena, dominus tecum . . . ," surrounded by boys.

Fefè [whispering to his wife]:"What a lovely voice Tonino has!"

Rosalia: "What?" [Giggling] "Ah, Tonino. Yes, poverino!"

Fefè: "Why 'poverino'?"

The "Ave Maria" heard in the background . . .

Rosalia: "Why, don't you know?!" [whispers in his ear, then giggles more]

With the "Ave Maria" still sounding, Fefè looks up at the choir loft and clucks in disappointment.

Fefè [silently, to himself]: "Ah, Tonino won't do."

It hardly seems coincidental that once the couple finds themselves hearing Tonino in church, the "Ave Maria" he sings is the same Bach-Gounod setting famously recorded by Moreschi in 1904 (not, for example, Schubert's setting) or that the film surrounds Tonino with a boys' choir (fig. E.8), much as Moreschi would have been surrounded by 1905 after the Vatican's final ban on castrati and the deaths and retirements of castrato colleagues left him as the sole castrated soprano amidst a soprano section well-peppered with boys (fig. E.9).[12] The numerous cinema people who clustered around

Figure E.6. Film still from *Divorzio all'italiana* (1961), directed by Pietro Germi, showing Fefè at the opera, gazing at Tonino across their boxes, wondering if he would be suitable for an affair with Fefè's wife while a queer Tonino swoons over the tenor on stage.

Figure E.7. Film still from *Divorzio all'italiana* showing Fefè's wife whispering to Fefè that Tonino is a castrato.

Figure E.8. Film still from *Divorzio all'italiana* depicting Tonino in a choir loft singing the Bach-Gounod "Ave Maria" surrounded by boy choristers.

Figure E.9. Group of singers, including Sistine boy singers, August 16, 1905. Private collection, BDDS Photo Trouvée. Copy held at the Archivio moderno della Cappella Sistina at via Monte della Farina.

Moreschi's son in the wartime and postwar years had to have known the proud place Alessandro's recordings had in Giulio's studio—precisely what Giulio made much of in his will—and others would have known that setting of the "Ave Maria" as well. Germi himself developed as a filmmaker during and after the war years in Rome, when Giulio figured among the city's most prominent voice teachers, with such students as Teddy Getty, Riccardo Fellini, Alberto Sordi, Noëlle Norman, and others, most of whom acted, sang, and danced in the giant film business and all of whom would almost inevitably have studied this setting of the "Ave Maria" under Giulio's tutelage. The allusion is not generic, nor was it taken from Giovanni Arpino's 1957 novel *Un delitto d'onore* (An honor killing), on which the film is loosely based. Inserted into *Divorzio all'italiana* as an early comic stumble in Fefè's effort to ensnare his wife, it seems to have doubled as an inside joke.

Tonino, in sum, is an Alessandro Moreschi avatar, deferred, abjected, and repressed. But something more is happening here. Germi and his cowriters reimagine the cause of Tonino's sexual deficiency by eliding it with contemporaneous Italian notions of male sexuality. And those notions apprehend his sexuality through binary understandings that oppose putatively normal family relations, genealogies, and sexual impulses to abnormal ones. Through this rigid logic, Tonino becomes more than impotent. He becomes feminine, passive, and thereby implicitly homosexual, as suggested by our first glimpse of him mooning over the tenor. The effect reverberates with that of the father in Elsa Morante's novel *L'isola di Arturo* (1957) who falls in love with a male prisoner on the island's penitentiary, infuriating his son, who in turn feels betrayed and leaves their enchanted island off the bay of Naples.[13] Notwithstanding his apparently sweet, innocuous nature, Tonino is queer, aberrant, and therefore disturbing. And like the father's "aberration" in *L'isola d'Arturo*, Tonino's is pointed. It does not just reside in the material fact of his castration or constitute the trace of its means of production, but contains a difference that emerges under the sign of abnormal masculine passivity—specifically, that of a passive homosexual—a difference produced through a historically specific social projection tied to a repression. We might well think of Tonino as a literal (if fictive) embodiment of the return of the repressed.

If that return remains muted in *Divorce Italian Style*, the same can't be said of Pasquale Festa Campanile and Massimo Franciosa's comedy *Le voci bianche* (White voices) (the Italian term for any male treble, including boys and castrati). Released three years later, it makes castrati out explicitly as queers. In *Le voci bianche* a young Roman man of circa 1700 tries to escape a life of poverty by signing on to become a castrato (never mind that he is postpubescent, this is fiction), but then bribes the surgeon not to carry through with it. Already virile, he goes on to seduce several wealthy women, using his castrato pretext in a film that exploits an old trope that depicted castrati as attractive lovers because sterile. Eventually he gets caught and is forced to go through with the operation. Early on, to convince an effeminate castrato in the conservatory that he can sing, he croons out something like a Roman dialect *stornello*, a street song full of sexual innuendo about hanging lemon blossoms and chicory blossoms, using his already deepened, beautifully modulated low adult voice. Laughing, the young castrato, dressed in prissy eighteenth-century attire, reacts by encouraging him to get the surgery (fig. E.10). "Ah! Beh? Aside from the wobble in your voice from laughing, you sing well. *Mica male* (not bad). You have Fortune by the forelock! What are you waiting for, huh?"

The moral of the story is that if you're a promising young male singer, and therefore suitable to be castrated, you may become rich, but you'll also end up queer. The only two castrati Fellini ever depicted took the form of an absurd duo in *Casanova* (1976) that entertains guests at a surreal eighteenth-century dinner party hosted by a hunchback. Dressed in aristocratic garb, they're represented as "fairy" types, femme and campy. And not only by Fellini and his costume designer, Danilo Donati. Nino Rota's score

Figure E.10. Film still from *Le voci bianche* (White Voices) (1964), directed by Pasquale Festa Campanile and Massimo Franciosa. The protagonist, Meo (Paolo Ferrari), is about to sing for a young castrato to show him that he's fit to become a castrato.

has them crooning out goofy, nonsensical melodic semitones in a bouncy four-square unison in between a yawning refrain of pseudo-oriental chromatics (example E.1).

We have come full circle from castrati better known nowadays, specifically, those staged in the operas and oratorios of Handel, Jommelli, and early Mozart, from whom Roman and specifically Vatican castrati descended. Where earlier castrati were effectively sacralized as heroes onstage during festive seasons or in oratorios performed during penitential ones Germi, Festa Campanile/Franciosa, and Fellini all desacralize the castrato onscreen by rendering him as an alterity and turning him into the butt of humor. In fact, in all three of their films, not only is he a joke, but a new kind of sexual danger, or a newly resuscitated one, bearing the negative signs of a (largely passive) homosexual that only a joke can easily contain.[14]

Thinking about these paradoxes has required me to write something far from a sequential modernization narrative.[15] The very

Example E.1. Nino Rota's music for the two castrati who sing at a dinner party in Fellini's *Casanova*. Score reduction by Mark Yeary.

idea of recording a castrato, even photographing one, is something of an oxymoron. Notwithstanding Moreschi's professional genealogy as an early modern type of figure, he took part in the full spectrum of modern life—by marrying, wearing the fashionable attire of his time, attending the opera, claiming a son, and signing a contract to record for the vaunted Gramophone & Typewriter Company, whose name says it all. Modernity was meant to supersede the magical premodern, above all in its technological forms, which comprised what Jonathan Sterne calls "the promise of science, rationality, and industry and the power of the white man to co-opt and supersede domains of life that were previously considered magical."[16] On this reckoning, Moreschi was a modern white man, but not a proper white man since he lacked the physiology to qualify. More than that, he was an ana/chronism in a literal sense: a modern man trapped in an early modern body, a man out of time. Yet he had recourse to the latest technologies of the stenograph, the typewriter, the telegram, and the railroad, all of which participated in the same magic as those that engaged the senses artistically: the gramophone, the film camera, the movie projector.[17]

Indeed, it turns out that members of Moreschi's immediate family were directly involved in related shifts in institutional and media forms. From 1917 to 1925, thus including the last five years of Alessandro's life, Alessandro's nephew, Amerigo, ran a movie house next door to the old Antico Caffè Castellino at via Cesare Battisti 135 (in current numbering), off piazza Venezia near the south end of the Corso. It's hard to imagine that his uncle didn't frequent it. And when Amerigo died in 1925, the theater was taken over for five years by Vittoria and Giulio.[18]

Vittoria reportedly described it to her grandniece and grandnephew as an impressive place outfitted with three great shutters ("tre grandi serrate") streetside that were lowered at the end of each evening's show. Notices in the *Guida Monaci* bear her out, and other sources highlight the theater's elegance. Among surviving ones are preliminary architectural plans drawn up as early as 1911 to transform the old Roman pharmaceutical society that had originally occupied the site into a movie theater.[19] The upper cross-section in figure E.11a shows the inner front part of the theater with an ornamental pediment set in a cove reading "Anno 1911," plus an original skylight and windows, while the lower cross-section shows a cone of visibility from the projection room to the 12.5-foot screen, which was to cover the preexisting windows. Edwardian-styled spectators view it from in front of the projectionist's room. Plans for the ground floor (fig. E.11b) include numerous appurtenances and spaces in which patrons could circulate: a waiting room and corridor space spread over its two stories, an orchestra box, and (in the bottom drawing, giving an elevation seen from outside) a back exit onto vicolo del Mancino designed to facilitate foot traffic. The back exit should have prevented or ameliorated problems such as fires and crowds, but Vittoria recounted that the theater was closed down during "Fascist times" because of "skirmishes" alleged to have taken place outside it. According to the *Guida Monaci*, the closing

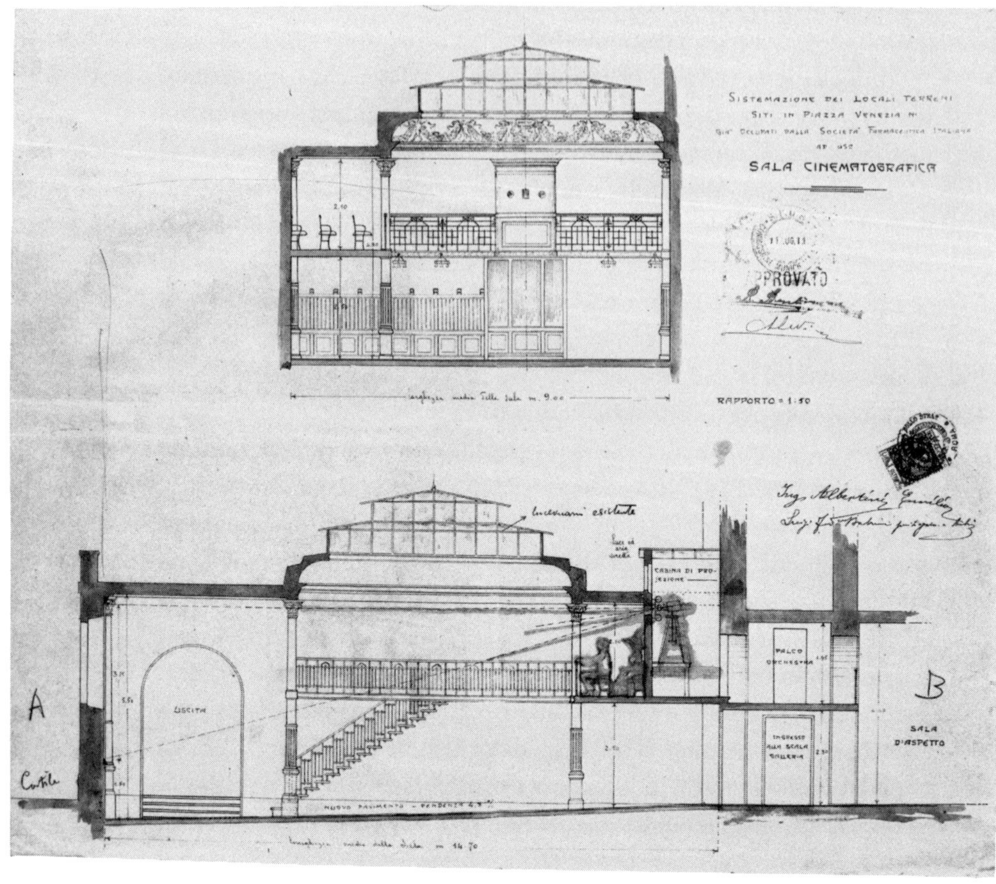

Figure E.11a. "Architectural refiguration into a cinema of local sites at piazza Venezia formerly occupied by the Società Farmaceutica Italiana, 1911." *Above*: Cross section showing inner front part of theater with added ornamental pediment set in a cove reading "Anno 1911." Original elements of the old Pharmaceutical Society are visible on the ground floor paneling and cabinets along the upper gallery. The building was well lit by an original skylight, built like a conservatory, and by many windows. *Below*: Crosssection showing the cone of visibility from the projection room to the screen, with spectators seated in front of the projectionist's room. The screen, 12.5 feet high, must have been placed over preexisting windows. Archivio Capitolino, Rome. Reproduced by permission.

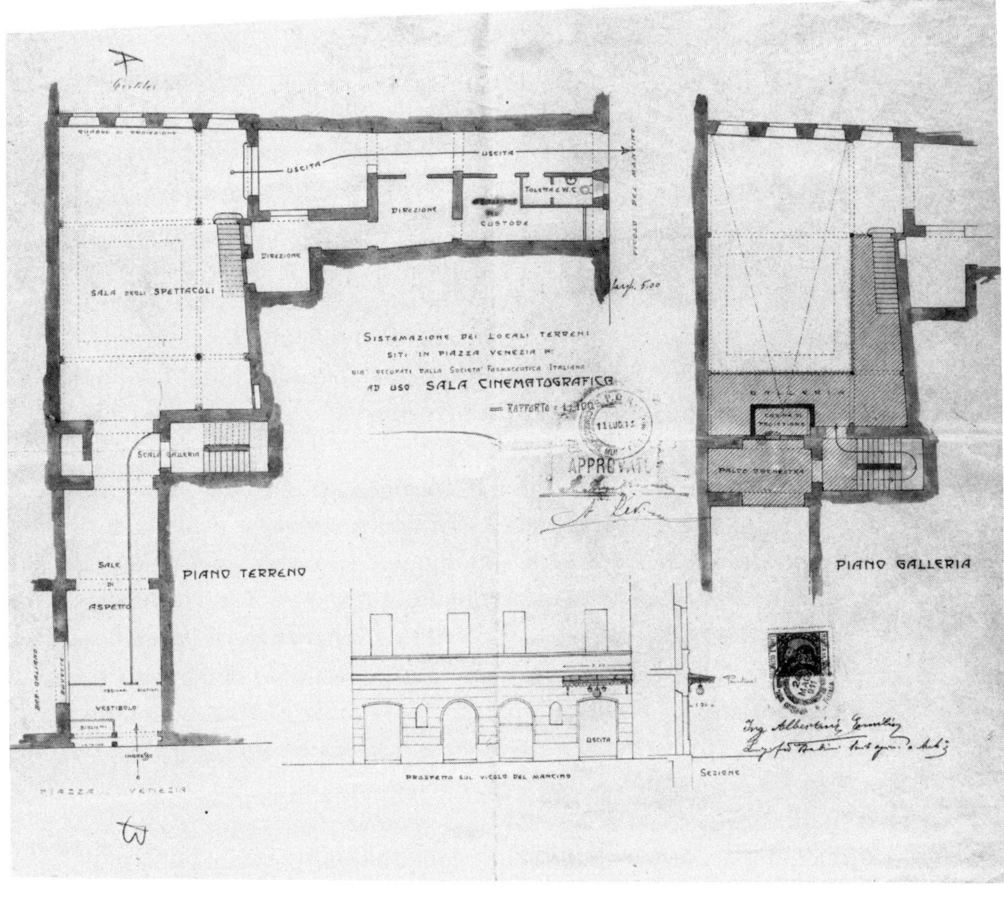

Figure E.11b. "Architectural refiguration into a cinema of local sites at piazza Venezia formerly occupied by the Società Farmaceutica Italiana, 1911." *Left*: Plan of ground floor showing the entrance from the Piazza Venezia side, ticket window, vestibule, drinking fountains, waiting room (*sala di aspetto*), viewing room (*sala degli spettacoli*), staircases to gallery, offices, closet, lavatory, and back exit onto vicolo del Mancino. *Right*: Plan of upper gallery showing the orchestra box, projection room (*cabina di proiezione*), gallery of the viewing room, and staircase with balustrade leading to gallery seating. *Bottom*: Partial elevation showing the façade of the back exit. Archivio Capitolino, Rome. Reproduced by permission.

would have happened in 1930. The date should come as no surprise if the reasons for closing the theater were trumped up, as was likely the case. After Mussolini opened his offices in Palazzo Venezia just one year earlier, the government was rapidly coopting and demolishing numerous buildings around the piazza to centralize political operations and build a central corridor from piazza Venezia into the Corso to be used for mass propaganda speeches.[20]

Given the temporal folds of these complex and mediated histories, it's unsurprising that Alessandro, while much loved and admired by his descendants, has haunted the Moreschi and Fellini families, much as Tonino haunts Fefè. In turn, Moreschi has also haunted us. Like many other castrati, but unique among them for having made recordings, he has invaded our cyber highways as an uncanny specter of a past that can never be fully incorporated into our modern and postmodern consciousnesses, but resides instead as a repressed remainder. Moreschi's voice conjures the ghost of modernity by its very failure to belong to it, by its provenance in the preindustrial technology of man-made production of voice. Indeed, this is true not just for Moreschi, but for those prior castrati who never recorded, but have made sonic returns as male countertenors and high-voiced females throughout much of the twentieth and twenty-first centuries.[21] All told, they have generated an impressive industry in repertory revivals, iconography, novels, digital media, movies, streaming sites, journalism, podcasts, blog posts, essays, and monographs, including the one I am writing now.

Still, Moreschi occupies a singular place in all of this, and not just because he made recordings. When his solos were digitally reissued in 1984, a "last" was finally established, a historiographic cadence stuck onto the whole centuries-long capitalistic enterprise of castrating for song.[22] At last we had the "last castrato." Branding Moreschi as such exposed the commerce for what it was while turning "last" into a loaded sign, at once a brand and a label. The label functions to justify Moreschi's *proprietary position* in old histories, but also signifies *surplus* in the sense Derrida intended when he spoke of what "presents itself as . . . an overabundance of value" that must "be subtracted, although it makes all commerce possible."[23] Precisely by circulating overabundantly while signifying what is no longer there—no more castrati to be born, castrated, and then die; no more men who produce ravishing song, but cannot procreate—precisely by this means, Moreschi got added as a kind of excess to the history and commerce of those who came before him. In purely Rankean terms—the terms of an essentially positivist history grounded in sources, empirical observation, and narrative—he also *completed* them, being not just the "last" to die, but as things turned out, the last to be born, castrated, and joined to the papal choir.[24] But beyond that, by virtue of the inscribing needle and the photographic lens, Moreschi has *lasted*, however vexedly, in that other common sense of *enduring*, if only as a bump in the temporal road, a hiccup in time that, like Derrida's *différance*, involves a time lapse in the circulation of meanings: differences deferred (*in* time). And so it is not only Moreschi who continues to ghost our present, but castrati all told. For as Avery Gordon has taught us, ghosts are collective, and furthermore what they haunt most poignantly are descendants of slavery, genocides, and colonial displacements—and we might add, castrations, which coincide with and tacitly participate in colonial projects. And this because haunting in all these spheres is not just the work of individuals, but of their "pater ex machina," as Peggy Kamuf calls them: the pope, the nobles, the dictator, the papal monarchy, the absolutist prince or king, and latterly the state-supported church.[25]

At the end of May 2015, the Fellini belt shop on the Corso closed down. Fellini was one of a clutch of small stores nestled on the ground floor of a larger edifice whose landlord took over all of them. The owners fought the takeover for a long time, but finally lost. Closing up shop was hard on Fabio. The shop was his occupation, his daily ritual, and his livelihood. More than that, it was a business started and run by Rita, who by then had been gone for over three years. The shop represented his marriage and his extended family, figuratively and literally.

As I sit finishing this book, I'm glad to put things to rest, for Fabio and others and for myself. For reasons I can't explain, I take a last look at the Archivio Luce of Cinecittà. More than once over the years, I visited it in person or used its digital archive without finding all I was hoping for. This time, when I type in "evirato"—still the term preferred by many educated and especially older Italians for a castrated man—a photograph comes up, dated January 15, 1929, showing the torso of a nude Black man, painfully thin, captioned "Il corpo di un indigeno evirato" (body of an indigenous [or "native"] emasculated man). The picture comes from the series "Franchetti Expedition in Dankalia [Base camp of the expedition, Dankalia, genres and customs, the protagonists of the traveling expedition]," located in present-day Eritrea reaching into Ethiopia. Other photos show the same man seated, or with arms outstretched, or with a doctor, always with genital areas fully visible.

The *evirato* is a man from Gaharre, a 165-meter hill situated near Bela'ita Shet' some 382 miles from the modern Eritrean capital of Asmara. Nowadays, to reach Gaharre from Asmara, you drive forty minutes northeast along the Asmara-Massawa Road toward the Red Sea, then cut sharply south onto P6, continuing along the coastline for nearly five hours before turning inland. In November 1928, the Franchetti Expedition had sailed from Italy to the coastal port of Assab, southeast of Gaharre, caravanning on camelback to set up camp in Dankalia under the leadership of the wealthy Italian Baron Raimondo Franchetti (1889–1935).[26]

Many things in this land attracted the intense curiosity of the white men, but few more than the *evirato*.[27] In one photo, a doctor stands beside him, scribbling in a notebook. The *evirato* reappears in a thirteen-minute-long *cortometraggio*, the work of a filmmaker sent along by the Instituto Nazionale Luce, then an arm of the Fascist government. One and a half minutes in, a scrolling intertitle proclaims the expedition has extended "the glorious tradition of those

Italian explorers who, from the beginnings of the last century, opened imperious and unknown regions to the path of civilization." It adds that 10 white men and 160 indigenous Black men made up the caravan, of which 11 indigenous men perished, "slaughtered by raiders" or "victims of thirst." Of 156 camels, only 23 survived "the harsh labors of the trek." None of the white men went thirsty and none of them died. Throughout the film, we see buffalo, elephants, tigers and lions, rhinoceroses, desert birds, many in large herds or flocks that nowadays would be scarce, victims of heedless hunters, species erosion, and ecodisasters. Rifles are exchanged, porters and sherpas wooed, colonizers charmed by naked children. And then comes a shock midway through: footage of the doctor handling the *evirato*, the camera zooming in on his torso, then his genital area only, then lingering there in extreme close-up.

The *evirato* of the Archivio Luce is unlike an Italian one. His testicles remain intact, but he is without penis. Still, the interest he meets with from the expeditionists feels somewhat familiar. How not to think of the imperial gazes trained on Italian castrati by eighteenth-century Habsburgs and Stuarts or by young nobles galivanting through Europe on Grand Tours paid for by West Indian slave plantations?[28] How not to think of those castrati endlessly displayed on stages, collected in scores and portraits, and latterly exhumed and scrutinized by scientific teams in the form of ghostly skeletal remains?[29] It strikes me that seven years after Moreschi's death, the Archivio Luce film frames the indigenous *evirato* for the eye of history and not just in a random way, but as an explicit object of colonial attention, a modern object to be photographed, filmed, annotated, studied, analyzed, catalogued, archived. And there in the archives he has sat for nearly a hundred years, like the castrato still awaiting rescue from the never-ending crucible of abjection, condescension, and dehumanization that haunts both their histories.

Chicago, Illinois, September 29, 2024

Acknowledgments

This book, like others I've written, has evolved from the residue of previous ones: A book on opera in Italian cities emerged from the theoretical residue of one on madrigals in Venetian city culture; a book on castrati from a bulbous early draft of the opera book. With the residues come a growing number of debts. The first are to the institutions and granting entities. The John Simon Guggenheim Memorial Foundation and the American Council of Learned Societies subsidized earlier work on castrati that bled into work for this book. Direct funding for it came from the Franke Institute for the Humanities at my home institution of the University of Chicago, followed by a Special Research Fund gifted by the University of Chicago's Humanities Advisory Council.

I owe much to the various deans of the Division of Arts and Humanities and chairs of the Department of Music at the University of Chicago for their generous support. My sincere thanks to deans Martha Roth, Anne Walters Robertson, and Deborah Nelson and department chairs Robert L. Kendrick, Anne Walters Robertson, Berthold Hoeckner, Larry Zbikowski, and Anna Schultz for backing this venture into terra incognita. I also thank Jim Chandler, head of the Franke Institute for the Humanities when I was in residence there in 2012–2013, for his collegiality, critical acumen, and warm friendship.

My greatest thanks go to Fabio Panconesi, without whose input this book would not exist. Thank you, Fabio, for all the help rendered to me from winter 2010 onward: endless questions answered, meals shared, graveside visits made, and outings spent visiting the dead, literally and figuratively. And thank you, Rita, for being distantly part of those conversations, even in your absence, and for your fascinating memoir.

My intellectual debts seem only to grow greater over time. The help given me for this project has never felt more crucial.

To Françoise Meltzer, thank you for your clear-eyed wisdom and steely gaze, for giving me the courage to persevere, and for your savvy comments on psychoanalysis in Chapter 5.

To Bonnie Gordon, my first full-draft reader: thank you for steering me off errant pathways and holding me to a crisper logic and diction.

To Judith Zeitlin, thank you for the companionship and for surprising insights from across the pond and around the globe.

To Ramona Naddaff: you are the editor I always longed for. Thank you devouring every word, for the canny feedback, and for sticking with the project from alpha to omega.

To Maria Anna Mariani, thank you for reading me with sympathy, intuition, and poetry, and for your rich understanding of modern Italy.

To the brilliant trio who traveled from as far away as Hong Kong to sit with me in our own private workshop:

Thank you, Giorgio Biancorosso for trusting in the tensile strength of dreams, for nuanced thoughts about aesthetics and screens, and for believing that I would have landed on Fellini's films regardless of the family connection.

Thank you, Suzanne Cusick, for the incisiveness and wit. Thank you for insisting that I pay careful attention to the needs of younger colleagues and less familiar readers and for always letting me know what I'm really saying, or mean to say, or need to say.

Thank you, Elisabeth Le Guin, for the decades of "enmeshment," for showing us all what true intellectual courage and commitment look like, and for your crystalline, unstinting critiques.

To others who gave indispensable feedback on parts of the manuscript, my dear aunts Johanna (Ann) Reiss and Annie Stanfield Hagert, my stepdaughters Emily Bauman and Rebecca Bauman, and my friend Jessica Peritz, brilliant all: thank you!

As I was bringing this book to a close, trudging through endnotes spade in hand, I realized once again how much I owe to scholars who came before me, including ones I don't know personally.

To Robert Buning, thank you is not enough. Without your pioneering, meticulous spadework on Moreschi's voice and recordings and the rich histories in which they were embedded—contained in what is really a doctoral thesis disguised as an MA thesis—and without all the insights that emerged from it, I don't know how this book could have been written.

For all the quarries dug on the Cappella Pontificia, thank you to Angela Pachovsky, thank you to the late Leopold Kantner, and thank you to Salvatore De Salvo Fattor.

Thank you, Will Crutchfield, for your unparalleled knowledge of voice, singing, and early recordings, your lively intelligence, your outstanding musicianship, your alacrity, and your bottomless generosity, without which writing parts of Chapter 3 would have been impossible.

Thank you also to Nicholas Clapton for the spirited and intriguing forays into Moreschiland that preceded mine.

Thank you, Shawn Keener and Keener Editorial, for such clever, capable, and stalwart assistance in the end stages.

To my pandemic writing partners: thank you Daniel Callahan for getting me to Zoom-write with you in 2020. Thank you, Judith Zeitlin and Rebecca Bauman for jumping in soon afterward. Thank you, all, for easing the isolation and power-charging the writing process.

Special thanks to Rebecca for sharing deep knowledge about Italian cinema, masculinity, and Fascism and for driving through the farmlands of Emilia Romagna to visit Tonino Guerra.

Thank you, Emily Bauman, for sharing your understanding of the angels you know intimately and for being one to me.

Thank you, Luciano Luciani, now among the angels, for opening your remarkable archive to me, which is how it all began.

Thank you, Emanuela Dessy Saddì, for careful help with parsing the Solinas Moreschi side of the family.

Thank you, Rebecca West, for your sharp reading of Rita's memoir.

Thank you to all who assisted with the research. Above all, a deafening shout-out to Martina Piperno, now an award-winning professor at La Sapienza, but back in 2010 a college student who to my great good fortune needed to earn some cash. Your input in 2010–2011 and again in 2016, on the verge of your meteoric rise, gives new meaning to the word indispensable.

Thank you, Courtney Quaintance, for unfailing friendship, for adventures through Roman statuary and domestic architecture, and for fine-tuning my transcriptions of notarial documents.

Thank you, Mark Yeary, Martha Sprigge, and Pete Smucker for skilled assistance in the earliest stages of this project.

Thank you, Giancarlo Rostirolla, for information and support on the ground and all your work with IBIMUS on behalf of Roman sacred music.

Thank you, Team Castrato—Bonnie Gordon, Freya Jarman, Hedy Law, Jessica Peritz, and Emily Wilbourne—for acting as brain trust, inspiration, moral support, and dining partners.

To the wonderful people at Zone Books: especially to Meighan Gale, managing editor par excellence; Bud Bynack, the most insightful, nuanced, and attentive copyeditor I've yet to encounter; and Julie Fry, for beautiful designs.

My thanks to the University of Chicago Press for permission to reprint parts of "Vocal Deliriums (Five Proposals)," *Critical Inquiry* 52 (Autumn 2025), in Chapters 3 and 4 of this volume and for permission to recast some of "The Castrato as Subject, Dead or

Alive," *Portable Gray* 8 (Fall 2025), small parts of which are scattered throughout the present volume.

Thank you to the many audiences who listened and gave important feedback: at the Harvard Music Department's Barwick Colloquium (2016); the Columbia Society of Fellows series on "Altered States," Columbia University (2016); the University of Pennsylvania, Music Department Colloquium series (2016); the University of California at San Diego Department of Music Distinguished Lecture Series (2017); the Institut für Musikwissenschaft, University of Vienna (2018); the conference on "Opera and the City: Technologies of Displacement and Dissemination," at the National Theater of São Carlos and Portuguese Cinemateca, CESEM/NOVA-FCSH, Lisbon (2019); the Center for Gender and Sexuality Studies, Iris Marion Young Lecture, University of Chicago (2020); the American Musicological Society Annual Meeting (online 2020); the "Concerted Realisms" conference, University of Chicago (2020); the "Character, Caricature, Characterization" conference, Department of Music, Case Western Reserve University; Humanities Day, the University of Chicago (2021); the roundtable "Folded Time, Shifting Borders: Toward New Castrato Histories" at the Quinquennial Meeting of the International Musicological Society, Athens, Greece (2022); the symposium "Sounding the Spectral," University of Chicago (2023); Cankarjev dom, Ljubljana (2023), organized by Mladen Dolar; and the Italian Studies graduate student conference "The Spell of the Voice: Perspectives on Italian Literature and Culture," organized by Alessandro Minnucci, Caterina Nicodemo, and Fara Taddei (2024).

Thank you in myriad ways Carolyn Abbate, Siel Agugliaro, Valentina Anzani, Marco Bertozzi, Alessandro Borgognone, Devon Borowski, Seth Brodsky, João Pedro Cachopo, Michele Callela, Alexandros Constansis, Victoria Cooper, James Davidson and Alberto Cedillo, Fabrizio Della Seta, Mladen Dolar, Giuseppe Fuà, Gigi Gaston, Bob Kendrick, Darren Kusar, David Levin, Armando Maggi, Ivana Maričič, Tom Mitchell, Ewa Gorniak Morgan, Robert Morgan, Anne Monique Pace, Roberto Parisi, Susan Pildes, Franco

Piperno, Martha Pollak, Hilary Poriss, Carmel Raz, Barbara Rogeli, Lovrenc Rogeli, Maria Ryan, Tommaso Sabbatini, Mindy Schwartz, Emanuele Senici, Mary Ann Smart, Gianmarco Tonelli, Kate van Orden, Claudio Vellutini, and Michael Wyatt, as well as to all my students.

Thank you to staff members at Rome's Cimitero del Verano, Archivio Storico Capitolino, Comune di Roma, Archivio Notarile Distrettuale di Roma (especially Drs. Maria Olinda Ceci and Maria Cristina Pacetti), the Archivio Storico Diocesano del Vicariato, the Archivio Segreto del Vaticano, the Fondazione per il il Centro Sperimentale di Cinematografia and Cineteca Nazionale, and especially Mario Musumeci, Joanna Hughes at the EMI Archive Trust, and Danielle Cordovez, NYPL Performing Arts.

Finally, to my beloved Patricia Barber, always my first and last reader: thank you for reading with the restraint of a poet and the wisdom of a sage, for the many scribbles, and for making sure I let the light in. You are the light.

APPENDIX ONE

Photo Essay

Unless otherwise noted, all images in this Appendix are from the Moreschi-Fellini Archive.

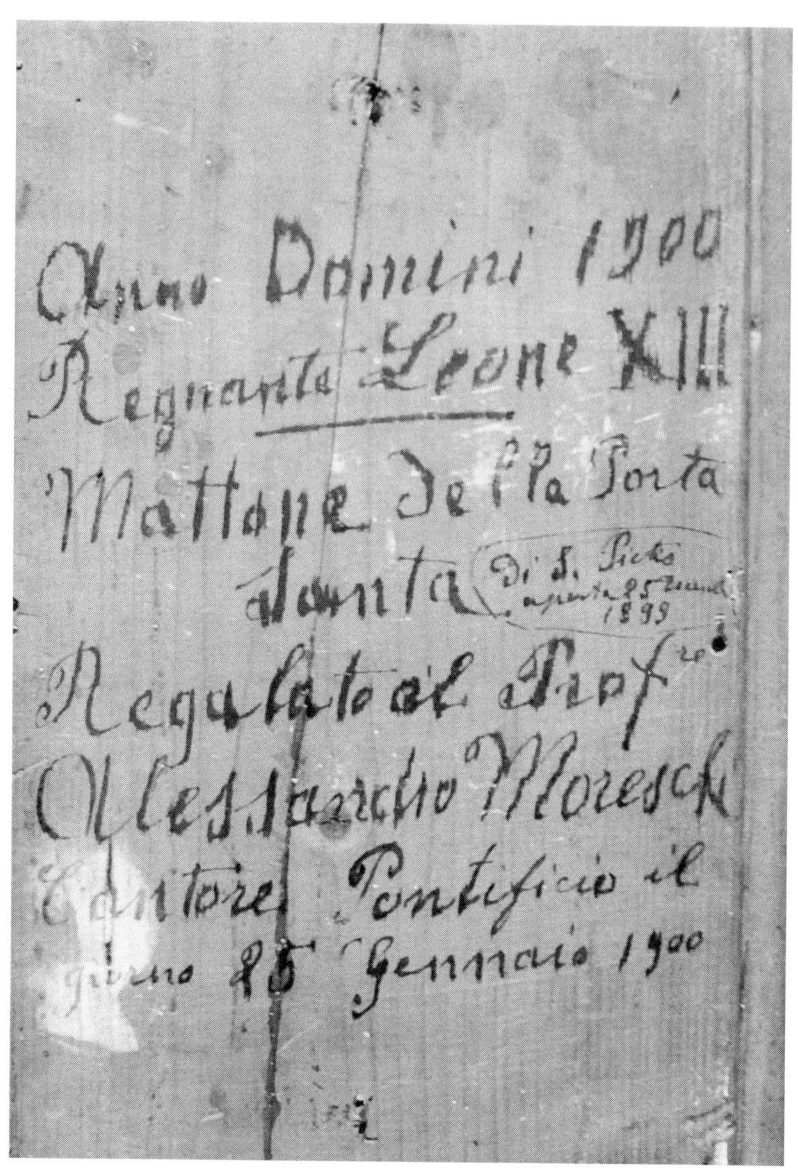

1. Mattone gifted to Alessandro Moreschi for the papal jubilee with the inscription “Anno Domini 1900/Regnante Leone XIII/Mattone della Porta/Santa [inserted: di S. Pietro aperta 25 dicembre (?) 1899]/Regalato al Prof[esso]re/Alessandro Moreschi / Cantore Pontificio il / giorno 25 Gennaio 1900.” (Year of our Lord 1900, reign of Leo XIII, mattone on the Porta Santa [of San Pietro, opened 25 December {?} 1899], gifted to Professor Alessandro Moreschi, papal singer, on 25 January 1900.” Holes are visible from where the original wooden object, now lost, was pounded into the wall. Reproduced from a photograph in the Moreschi-Fellini Archive.

2. Giulio Moreschi, about age ten, circa 1914, marked by Vittoria on the verso as "Giulietto."

3. Vittoria Cevasco at age twenty (per inscription on verso), circa 1919.

4. Vittoria marked the photo with the words "Vittoria e Giulio sposi" (Vittoria and Giulio married). Presumably it was taken in Genoa on their wedding day, April 25, 1925.

5. Vittoria, probably in 1924, posing as Madame Butterfly in Giulio's studio. Compare figures 1.2 and 6, which come from the same photo session.

6. Giulio Moreschi, photographed in his studio, probably 1924, since Vittoria added the annotation "Giulio Moreschi. 20 anni" (Giulio Moreschi, 20 years old). Note the photograph of Verdi just barely visible behind him. It was signed to Alessandro Moreschi by Verdi on April 15, 1893, and alluded to in Giulio's will of 1954 along with other photographs signed by illustrious musical figures mentioned there. Compare figures 1.2 and 5 from the same photo session.

7. A large dinner party in Rome attended by Giulio Moreschi and the famous tenor Giacomo Lauri-Volpi, probably early 1930s.

8. Giulio Moreschi and his daughter, Alessandra Moreschi, 1933.

9. Giulio Moreschi and Alessandra Moreschi, probably about 1941 or 1942.

10. Giulio Moreschi and colleagues singing a three-voice canzonetta by Claudio Monteverdi, captioned "Su su pastorelli vezzosi, correte, venite a mirar." Anonymous sketch dated April 2, 1943, and marked "canzonetta con cembalo."

11. Riccardo Fellini and Giulio Moreschi in Montecompatri, mid-1940s(?).

12. Riccardo Fellini and Giulio Moreschi on the beach, probably late 1940s.

13. Giulio Moreschi with Sistine Choir members and boy singers, circa 1950.

14 

14. Portrait of Maria Rita (Rita) Fellini as a small child, circa 1949 or 1950.

15. Arriving at Rita's confirmation, circa 1953. *Left to right*: Alessandra Moreschi, Rita Fellini, Giulietta Masina (holding Giulietta's hand).

16. (facing page, top) At Rita's confirmation, circa 1953. *Left to right*: Giulietta Masina, Rita Fellini, Riccardo Fellini, Vittoria Cevasco, and Alessandra Moreschi, who looks into the camera.

17. (facing page, bottom) Riccardo Fellini with his daughter, Rita, at her confirmation, circa 1953.

15 

16

17

18. Leaving Rita's confirmation, circa 1953. *Left to right*: Vittoria Cevasco, Alessandra Moreschi, Rita Fellini (reaching for Giulietta's Masina's hand), Giulietta Masina, and Riccardo Fellini, plus various strangers in the background.

GIULIO MORESCHI

N. 15 - 3 - 1904 M. 14 - 7 - 1955

✝

Requiem aeternam, nella pace del Signore,

a Te che l'inesorabilità della Morte ha folgorato, strappandoti alla tua laboriosa esistenza prematuramente e crudelmente, negandoti il raggiungimento delle tue sublimi mète.

Soave anima di artista, esempio fulgido di vità cristiane, di abnegazione al lavoro e alla famiglia.

Spirto buono e cordiale che diffondevi serenità e gaiezza e che suscitasti in quanti ti conobbero i più cari sentimenti di affetto.

Nel cordoglio e rimpianto nel quale Tu ci ai lasciati, ci sia sollievo è indelebile tuo pensiero e l'inimitabili doti.

Riposa in pace, nella gloria di Dio

Amen

19. Giulio Moreschi's requiem card, marked "born March 15, 1904, died July 14, 1955."

20. Vittoria Cevasco in 1957, aged fifty-eight, pictured before the console at via Lungotevere degli Anguillara 11, where Giulio's portrait stands between two large candelabra in front of a commanding eighteenth-century mirror.

21

22

23

21. Head shot of Alessandra Moreschi, presumably taken when she was still living in Mexico. An inscription on the verso signs the picture to her mother from S. Josè de Costarica on April 2, 1962, sending her "immense affection." Pearls and head scarves with large polka dots were fashionable at the time.

22. Giovanni Antonio ("Chico") Solinas, second husband of Alessandra Moreschi, who she evidently married in Mexico City circa 1960 or 1961. He was the father of Julio Salvador Solinas Moreschi, Rita's half brother, and grandfather of Alessandro Solinas Moreschi. Probably taken in Mexico City in the 1960s.

23. Julio Solinas Moreschi, Rita Fellini, Alessandra Moreschi, and Vittoria Cevasco at home in the kitchen at via Lungotevere degli Anguillara 11, circa 1968.

LIC. ANGEL CARDENAS CH.
AV. MORELOS 58-1204,
MEXICO, 1 D. F.
M E X I C O.

México, D. F., a 6 de Febrero de 1971.

SRA. ALESSANDRA MORESCHI C.,
LUNGOTEVERE ANGUILARA No. 11,
ROMA ITALIA - ITALIA.

Mi estimada y fina señora:

Es bastante penoso para mí, tener que dirigirme a usted para darle la fatal noticia que más adelante le narraré.

Desde el mes de Junio de 1969 GIOVANNI se fué a un poblado del estado de Queretaro, llamado Tequisquiapan a-dar unas clases de Italiano por cuatro meses, posteriormente se quedó a vivir en ese pueblo, y con frecuencia me visitaba; es el caso que el día 20 de Enero me llamarón por télefono indicandome que se encontraba bastante delicado de salud y recluído en un Hospital al tener conocimiento de tal noticia me traslade a dicho poblado y lo traje a un buen Sanatorio donde le brindarón la atención del caso, pero desde luego al no tener de que disponer es decir dinero con que curarse tuve la necesidad de recurrir a la embajada Italiana en esta ciudad, misma que se encargo de todo y desgraciadamente falleció el día 26 a las 7 de la mañana hora de México.

Al inicio de mi carta le indico que es lamentable; porque este hombre murió en la desgracia y procedí a recoger todas sus pertenencias consistentes en papeles de valor personal, fotógrafías de familia, y recuerdos de la guerra publicados en la prensa de la época donde hablan de sus hazañas todo esto lo tengo en casa y a disposición de usted.

Espero me conteste y me indique lo que deba hacer con lo que tengo en mi poder y deceo con todas el alma se conserve usted bien de salud en unión de GIULIO y RITA así también hago extensivos mis deceos a su señora madre.

Su atento y S. S.

LIC. ANGEL CARDENAS CHAVEZ.

24. Letter of February 6, 1971, from Ángel Cárdenas Chavez to Alessandra Moreschi informing her of Giovanni Antonio Solinas's death in the village of Tequisquiapan in the Mexican state of Querétaro, where he had gone in 1969 to teach Italian. Julio Solinas Moreschi had recently turned ten at the time of his father's death.

25. Rita and Fabio at their wedding reception at via Lungotevere degli Anguillara 11, September 14, 1973.

26. Rita at her wedding reception at via Lungotevere degli Anguillara 11, September 14, 1973. Fabio asked that the photo be included in this book because it shows Rita as "she would have liked to be remembered."

27. Wedding of Riccardo Fellini to his second wife, Lina Chelo, circa 1985(?). *Left to right*: Giulietta Masina, Fabio Panconesi, Lina Chelo, Riccardo Fellini, Rita Fellini, plus three unknown persons (including two women behind Lina and Riccardo and an unknown man behind Riccardo and Rita).

28. Julio Solinas Moreschi as a boy singer, circa 1972. Formerly posted on the web by Solinas Moreschi. Online screen grab.

29. Rita Fellini speaking at a memorial event for her uncle Federico Fellini, probably in Rimini in late 1993 or after.

30. Julio Solinas Moreschi, acting in travesty, probably in the 2000s. Online screen grab.

DNEWS
VENERDÌ 15_OTTOBRE_2010

Il lutto

Addio a Solinas attore e regista tra teatro e Tv

Cenni biografici
Julio Solinas era nato a Roma 49 anni fa. Mercoledì è stato colpito da un infarto che ne ha stroncato la carriera teatrale.

>> È morto mercoledì scorso a Roma stroncato da un infarto all'età di 49 anni l'attore e regista Julio Solinas. Dopo una formazione tra teatro, danza e canto, Solinas ha debuttato sul palcoscenico nel 1974 a soli 14 anni e da allora ha intepretato innumerevoli testi, dai classici a testi originali, per poi esordire nel 1997 alla regia: aveva diretto una trentina di opere, alcune delle quali lo vedevano anche autore. Parallelamente all'attività teatrale, durante la quale aveva dedicato molto tempo ed energie anche all'insegnamento agli attori emergenti, Solinas era apparso a partire dalla metà degli '80 in diverse fiction televisive, spot pubblicitari e film. <<

31. Obituary for Julio Solinas Moreschi, published on October 15, 2010, following his death from a heart attack two days earlier at age forty-nine. Saved by Rita along with a childhood photo.

32. Alessandro Solinas Moreschi, great-great-grandson of Alessandro Moreschi, born September 18, 2006, photographed here at age seventeen. Photograph courtesy of Emanuela Dessy Saddì.

APPENDIX TWO

Enrico Panzacchi, "Cantores!" (1885)

1 Io non penso, mia dolce amica, d'aver demeritata la vostra stima. E fosse pur vero tutto quello che voi siete andata fantasticando dopo la mia lettera di martedì, o credete voi proprio che anche in un desiderio a prima vista disumano, grottesco, bislacco e un pochino teratologico, non possa nascondersi un alto senso di poesia? E sopratutto un alto senso di verità?

2 Voglio che m'ascoltiate attentamente e pacatamente.... Ora io sento di potervi parlare con calma e voi non avete più a temere nè crudezza di linguaggio biblico, nè impeti di "liricismo forsennato" come dite voi. Sono calmo, v'ho detto, e sopratutto non ho mai cessato di essere uomo! Anzi ho in me il convincimento, — dopo tutto quello che è passato nell'animo mio nei giorni addietro — che un aspetto nuovo della umanità mi si è svelato e s'è in qualche modo aggiunto all'essere mio d'uomo. Perchè l'arte (abbiatelo per certo) non è sempre solo una imitazione della natura, ma qualche volta ne è la continuazione e il complemento.

3 Vedete dunque che io non ho niente da rimproverarmi e voi niente da sospettare sul conto mio....

4 Ed ecco come andò.

5 Io nemmeno sapevo che quella fosse la festa dell'Ascensione. Avevo pranzato solo e di buona ora all'Albergo *Milano*. Come passare meno male il tempo in quel lungo dopo pranzo? A Roma, in casi simili, io ho sempre la risposta pronta. Salgo in una botte[1] e mi faccio condurre a San Pietro. Ho

1 I do not think, my sweet friend, that I have been unworthy of your esteem. And that everything you have been fantasizing since my letter of Tuesday might be true — or do you really believe that even in a desire at first glance inhuman, grotesque, whimsical, and a bit teratological, a high sense of poetry cannot be hidden? And above all, a high sense of the truth?

2 I want you to listen to me carefully and serenely. . . . Now I feel able to speak to you with calm and you no longer have to fear either the severity of biblical language or the fervor of a "raving lyricism," as you put it. I am calm, I told you, and above all I have not ceased to be a man! Rather I have the conviction — after all that has passed through my soul in the last days — that a new aspect of humanity has revealed itself to me and that has in some way added to my being as a man. For art (you have it, to be sure) is not always a mere imitation of nature, but sometimes the continuation of and complement to it.

3 So you see that I have nothing with which to reproach myself, and you nothing of which to suspect me. . . .

4 And here is how things went.

5 I did not even know that this was the feast of Ascension. I had lunch alone and at an early hour at the Albergo Milano. How to pass the time well in that long postprandial time? In Rome, in similar situations, I always have a ready answer. I climb into a carriage and take myself to San Pietro. I have

per quella grande piazza elittica una specie di passione strana che alimenta in me una bramosia inesauribile di riverderla. Il getto superbo di quelle due fontane, illuminate dal sole, pare ogni volta che mi slarghi il petto e mi faccia ballare il cuore di gioia, mentre l'immane colonnato curvilineo, serrandomi a destra e a sinistra l'orizzonte, e tutte quelle statue poggianti ritte sopra l'attico e in atto di osservarmi severe, par che mi avvisino che io sono entrato in un vecchio mondo misterioso e magnifico. Anche per l'insieme della basilica vaticana io ho sempre avuta una forte ammirazione, e la sento dentro aumentare e ingigantire di mano in mano che mi si raffreddano i romantici entusiasmi per certe architetture gotiche.... So che anche voi, mia cara, mi condannate per questo; ed io chino il capo rassegnato, aspettando che il tempo mi renda giustizia. Lento ma ottimo giustiziere il tempo, non è vero?.... Voi lo sapete per prova.

6 Arrivai dunque in piazza San Pietro un'ora circa prima del tramonto del sole. Cominciavano le grandi ombre a stendersi dalle moli colossali. Delle due fontane, quella ch'io vedeva, arrivando, alla mia sinistra, pareva tutta raccolta e tranquilla nella calma dell'ombra vespertina; ma l'altra, dardeggiata obliquamente dal sole, era tutta una letizia di raggi e di zampilli e di nebbia luminosa e cangiante, diffusa all'intorno per largo tratto. Un gruppo di signori forestieri, uomini e donne, stava fermo ad ammirarla; e parevano tutti contenti d'essere inaffiati da quella rugiada.

7 Credevo, come al solito, di trovare la grande chiesa, a quell'ora, deserta; ma m'ingannai.

8 La festa dell'Ascensione aveva chiamata là molta gente: forestieri delle provincie, romani di Roma, inglesi, suore, trasteverini, minenti, frati, preti, pifferari; la turba mista e bizzarra che San Pietro accoglie in alcuni giorni dell'anno e che inutilmente cerchereste altrove. Le centinaia e le migliaia che si sparpagliano, povero formicaio umano, sotto le navate enormi e si perdono, come ombre, dietro i piloni smisurati, non facendo nemmeno sentire il fruscio dei loro piedi.

9 Mentre spingevo il pesante tendone della porta, m'arrivò subito una modulazione musicale. Era un istrumento? Era voce umana? Così alla prima non potei capire. Era un suono di timbro e d'acutezza insolita,[2] esilissimo, eppure vibrante per quella vastità in modo che pareva tutta riempirla. Fatti

a kind of strange passion for that great elliptical piazza, which nourishes in me an inexhaustible desire to see it once again. The magnificent jet of those two fountains, illuminated by the sun, seems to slow my breath and make my heart dance for joy every time, while the curvilinear colonnade, closing the horizon to the right and left, and all those statues placed upright along the attic in the act of observing me sternly—each time they seem to warn me that I've entered a mysterious and magnificent old world. I have always had a strong admiration for the whole of the Vatican basilica as well, and inside it I feel it augment and magnify my whole body bit by bit, chilling my romantic enthusiasms for certain Gothic architecture.... I know that you, my dear, condemn me for this too; and I bow my head in resignation, waiting until time does me justice. A slow, but excellent lawbringer time is, is it not?... You know it by proof.

6 So I arrived in piazza San Pietro about one hour before sunset. The great shadows had begun to spread out from the colossal pillars. Of the two fountains, the one I saw, arriving on my left, seemed all collected and tranquil in the shadow of Vespers; but the other, obliquely darting out from the sun, was a whole merriment of rays and jets and luminous, changing vapors, diffused all about for a large stretch. A group of foreigners, men and women, stood still admiring it, all seeming content to be sprayed by that dew.

7 I believed that as usual I would find the great church empty at that hour, but I was mistaken.

8 The feast of the Ascension had called forth many people: foreigners from the provinces, Romans from Rome, Englishmen, nuns, residents of Trastevere, minents,[3] clerics, priests, pipers; the mixed, bizarre crowd that San Pietro welcomes on certain days of the year and that you would look for in vain elsewhere. The hundreds and thousands who scatter themselves, a poor human anthill, under the enormous naves and get lost, like shadows, behind the immense pylons, not letting you hear so much as the rustle of their feet.

9 While I pushed open the heavy curtain of the door, a musical sound suddenly struck me. Was it an instrument? Was it is a human voice? At first I could not understand. It was the sound of an unusual timbre and highness, very fine, yet vibrant for this vast space in a way that seemed to fill it completely. After taking a few steps in the basilica, I heard distinctly notes

alcuni passi nella basilica sentii distintamente[4] la frase di un versetto biblico arrivarmi colle note all'orecchio. Era dunque canto umano senza dubbio.

10 E quale canto, signora! Immaginate una voce che fonda insieme la dolcezza del flauto e l'animata soavità della laringe umana; una voce che salga, salga leggera e spontanea come vola per l'aria un'allodola, quando s'inebria del sole; e allor che vi pare che questa voce siasi posata sugli altimissimi vertici della gamma sopracuta, ecco che spira ancora altri voli, e sale e sale sempre egualmente leggera, egualemente spontanea, senza la più piccola espressione di sforzo, senza il più tenue indizio d'artificio, di ricerca, di stento; una voce infine, che vi dà l'idea immediata "del sentimento fatto suono" e dell'ascensione d'un'anima verso l'infinito sull'ali di quel sentimento.

11 Che vi dirò di più? Ho sentito la Frezzolini e la Barbi in camera e la Patti in teatro; ho ammirato Masini, Vögel, Cotogni; ma in mezzo alla mia ammirazione rimaneva sempre qualcosa di inappagato in fondo al mio desiderio; rimaneva da togliere un certo dissidio fra l'intenzione dell'artista, non di rado elevata e fine, e la piena condiscendenza de' suoi mezzi vocali.... Qui invece tutto il mio essere era mirabilmente soddisfatto. Non la minima asprezza nel passaggio da un registro all'altro della voce, non penuria di estensione, non disuguaglianza di timbro[5] da nota a nota, ma un linguaggio musicale calmo, dolce, solenne, intonatissimo, che mi stupiva e mi rapiva a un punto solo con la potenza di una gratissima sensazione, non provata innanzi mai!

12 Mi spinsi avanti per la basilica con passi affrettati, verso quella voce e quel canto.... Nel giorno dell'Ascensione i cantori della Cappella Sistina scendono in San Pietro e prendono parte alla celebrazione della festa. Cantano sotto la cupola di Michelangelo, in una piccola cantoria eretta all'uopo, accompagnati da un piccolo organo, che anch'oggi, come al tempo di Ettore Berlioz, è messo sovra delle rotelle per il pavimento.

13 La folla si faceva di mano in mano più densa, ma io m'adoprai in modo che dopo una diecina minuti ero arrivato proprio sotto la cantoria e guardavo in faccia il mio solista.

14 Eseguivano un mottetto dell'Allegri quasi tutto affidato a lui. Il coro entrava di tanto in tanto con brevi risposte; e l'organo, con pochi accordi tenuti, aiutava a sostenere l'intonazione perfetta.

of a phrase from a Biblical verse reach my ears. So without doubt it was a human voice.

10 And what a voice, signora! Imagine a voice that combines the sweetness of the flute and the lively mellifluousness of the human larynx, a voice that rises, rises light and spontaneous, as a skylark flies through the air when it's inebriated by the sun; and then, when it seems that this voice must be poised on the highest vertices of the topmost range, takes further flight, and rises and rises, always with equal lightness, equally spontaneous, without the least expression of force, without the slightest hint of artifice, of searching about, of effort—a voice that, in sum, gives you the immediate sense "of feeling made sound" and of the ascendency of a soul toward the infinite on the wings of that feeling.

11 What more can I tell you? I have heard Frezzolini and Barbi in the salon and Patti in the theater; I admired Masini, Vögel, Cotogni;[6] but in the midst of my admiration there was always something unsatisfied at the root of my desire—what remained was to eliminate a certain discrepancy between the intention of the artist, often elevated and refined, and the full cooperation of his vocal means.... Here instead my entire being was wondrously satisfied. Not the least bitterness in the *passaggio* from one register of the voice to another, no lack of extension, no disparity of timbre from note to note, but rather a musical language that was calm, sweet, solemn, and perfectly in tune, that stupefied and ravished me both at once with the power of a most welcome sensation, never before felt!

12 I pushed myself further into the basilica with hurried steps, toward that voice and that singing... On Ascension Day the singers of the Sistine Chapel descend into St. Peter's and take part in the celebration of the feast. They sing under the dome of Michelangelo, in a small cantoria erected for this purpose, accompanied by a small organ, which, still today, as in the time of Hector Berlioz, is rolled around over the paving on wheels.

13 The crowd grew denser from one person to the next, but I did my best such that within ten minutes I had arrived just beneath the cantoria and was watching the face of the soloist.

14 They executed a motet by Allegri almost completely entrusted to him. The choir entered from time to time with brief responses, and the organ, with a few held chords, helped keep things perfectly in tune.

15 Finalmente ho intesa la voce vera del soprano. Vadano a riporsi le signore cantatrici che usurpano questo nome! Le chiameremo, se vogliono, soprane; ma è da augurare per il bene dell'arte del canto, declinante a grandi passi, ch'esse smettano una buona volta la sciagurata ambizione d'assorgere cogli sforzi della loro laringe a certe acutezze diatoniche solo leggittimamente consentite ai soprani veri, ai soprani sacri, ai soprani per diritto divino.

16 Oh, chi ridona all'arte i vecchi contralti, così giustamente rimpianti da Gioacchino Rossini! Una sciagurata ambizione, accesa dalla cupidità del guadagno, sciupa le nostre più belle voci femminili, mutando la nota vellutata e intonata in uno strillo squilibrato e sgradevole....

17 Ne vi paia strano, o signora, ch'io in quel giorno abbia anche compreso e partecipato il disgusto di Parini per i soprani in teatro:

Abborro sulla scena
Un canoro elefante[7]

18 Sì, quella voce eccezionale e quasi sorvolante agli orizzonti della vita è fatta per esprimere slanci di preghiera e puri rapimenti di estasi religiosa. Non è fatta per disposarsi alle torbide passioni del dramma umano nè per concorrere, profanandosi, al divertimento scenico. Nella scena essa doveva perdere il suo prestigio mistico senza acquistare il vigore, la pieghevolezza e la verità dolorosa del dramma; e questo forse spiega perchè il vero dramma musicale moderno comincia e coincide col bando dei veri soprani dalla nostre scene melodrammatiche. Però, se comprendo l'ammirazione dei nostri nonni elevata al più alto grado, trovo impossibile e ridicola la passione. L'amore di Sarazine per Zambinella e la sanguinosa avventura a cui riesce, per quanto magistralmente narrati da Balzac, mi lasciano freddo ed incredulo. Meglio comprendo gli epigrammi scritti dal popolo napoletano sulla casa costrutta da Caffariello.... [8]

19 Io guardavo attento il mio soprano. Era un giovane alto, pallido, non grasso, con una barbetta rada e gentile, ritto e composto nella sua cotta bianchissima davanti al leggio. Mentre la sua voce si elevava come un razzo canoro serpeggiando in trilli e scale, dispiegandosi in magnifiche declamazioni, raccogliendosi in cadenze elegantissime, io non riuscivo a notare in lui il più piccolo segno di fatica e di sforzo. La testa era lievamente inchinata sulla musica che teneva con le due mani immobili. Cantava a quel modo e

15 Finally I heard[9] the true voice of the soprano. Let the female sopranos who usurp this name hide themselves! We will call them "soprane," if they like; but it is to be hoped that for the sake of the art of singing, which is greatly declining, that they once again cease the wretched ambition of rising through the efforts of their larynx to certain diatonic vertices only legitimately permitted to true (male) sopranos, to sacred sopranos , to sopranos by divine right.

16 Oh who might restore to art the old altos, so justly lamented by Gioacchino Rossini! An unfortunate ambition, fired up by the cupidity of financial gain, spoils our most beautiful female voices, changing their silky, lyrical notes into a twisted and horrible screech. . . .

17 Nor should it appear strange to you, signora, that on that day I should also have understood and shared the disgust of Parini for male sopranos in the theater:

I abhor on the stage
A singing elephant.

18 Yes, this exceptional voice, practically soaring over the horizons of life, is made to express the urges of prayer and the pure convulsions of religious ecstasy. It is not made to be disposed to the murky passions of human drama or to contribute, profaning itself, to scenic diversions. On the stage it had to lose its mystical magic without acquiring the vigor, the pliability, and the sorrowful truth of the drama. Perhaps this explains why real modern musical drama begins and coincides with the banishment of true sopranos from our operatic stages. However, if I understand the admiration of our grandparents elevated to the highest level, I find the passion impossible and ridiculous. The love of Sarrasine for Zambinella and the bloody adventures to which he succeeds, however magisterially narrated by Balzac, leave me cold and incredulous. I understand better the epigrams written by the Neapolitan populace on the house built by Caffarelli. . . .

19 I watched my soprano attentively. He was young, tall, pale, not fat, with a light peach fuzz, erect and composed in his bright white surplice before the lectern. While his voice was raised like a singing ray, snaking its way around in trills and scales, unfurling itself in magnificent declamations, gathering itself in very elegant cadences, I did not manage to note in him the slightest sign of effort and labor. His head was slightly tilted over the music that he held immobile in his two hands. He sang like that, and it seemed

pareva che leggesse. Solo i suoi occhi si dilatavano, illuminandosi tratto tratto, allorchè una frase musicale toccava il suo momento d'espansione; solo le rughe della sua fronte di spianavano e si contraevano un poco assecondando le movenze del ritmo.

20 Ebbene, guardando quegli occhi illuminati e il tremito di quella fronte, io ho sentito che quel giovane cantore gustava in quell'ora una felicità alta ed intensa come io e voi, mia cara, non abbiamo probabilmente gustata mai.... Egli era felice; ma più che di tutta quella folla attenta e rivolta a lui, e del lieve mormorio di ammirazione contenuta che le sue mirabili note suscitavano sotto la più augusta cupola del mondo, egli era, io credo, felice della bellezza del suo canto, che si sentiva ripiovere sull'anima come una rugiada celeste.

21 Io l'ho compreso e l'ho invidiato. Nel calore del mio entusiasmo ho pronunciato dentro di me il pazzo augurio, che ho avuto la franchezza di significarvi e che mi ha tirato addosso le espressioni del vostro orrore.

22 Che volete ch'io vi dica? Durante quel mottetto dell'Allegri uno strano cambiamento è avvenuto in me; e mi pareva che nell'animo mio si facesse una gran luce improvvisa. In quella luce io vedevo, — bizzarra visione, — gli antichi Coribanti che menavano intorno, con gesti e grida di gente estatica, una danza vertiginosa; e in mezzo a quella ridda vedevo alzarsi la figura grave e serena di Origene che, tendendo una mano e gli occhi verso le stelle, esclamava: *beati!*... Al tempo stesso mi venivano in mente certe parole con cui il duca di Richelieu ringraziò la bontà divina quando si accorse d'esser giunto al termine della sua carriera d'uomo; non quella diplomatica, nè militare, s'intende.

23 E pensavo: — quando questo giovane sarà anch'esso innanzi cogli anni e un giorno s'accorgerà di non aver più la voce atta al mistico ufficio a cui ora la consacra, con che parole ringrazierà egli Dio della sua carriera compiuta?.... In sostanza la mia mente s'andava arrampicando su per delle guglie perigliose e splendide. Mi tininnavano negli orecchi e mi sentivo vibrare per tutto l'essere, accordi e dissonanze piene di voluttà ignota.... Alzavo gli occhi e mi pareva che anche gli Evangelisti, dai giganteschi pennacchi della volta, mi accennassero colla testa che avevo ragione. Sarò stato pazzo, se volete, ma ero superbo e felice.

24 Potete condannarmi; ma, sinceramente, a compiangermi avreste torto.

as if he was reading. Only his eyes widened, lighting up from time to time when a musical phrase reached its moment of expansion. Only the wrinkles of his brow expanded and contracted a little, following the movements of the rhythm.

20 Well, looking at those shining eyes and the trembling of that brow, I felt that the young singer enjoyed in that hour a great and intense happiness such as you and I, my dear, have probably never experienced.... He was happy; but more than that whole crowd, attentive and turned toward him, and the slight murmuring of contained admiration that his miraculous notes aroused under the most August cupola in the world, he was, I believe, happy with the beauty of his singing, which he felt rain down on his soul like a heavenly dew.

21 I understood it and I envied it. In the heat of my enthusiasm I pronounced to myself a mad wish, which I had the candor to express to you and which threw your expressions of horror onto me.

22 What do you want me to tell you? During that motet of Allegri's a strange change occurred in me, and it seemed that suddenly a great light shone in my soul. In that light I saw a bizarre vision—the ancient Corybantes who, with gestures and cries of ecstatic people, led around a vertiginous dance, and in the middle of that welter I saw rising up the weighty and serene figure of Origen who, extending a hand and his eyes straining toward the stars, was exclaiming: blessed!... At the same time, certain words came to mind with which the Duke of Richelieu thanked the divine goodness when he realized that he had reached the end of his career as a man—not meaning the diplomatic or the military one, of course.

23 And I thought: when this young man will likewise have moved on with the years and one day will realize that he no longer has a voice apt for the mystical office to which he now consecrates it, with what words will he thank God for his accomplished career?... In essence, my mind went clambering up through the perilous and splendid spire. I felt chords and dissonances ring in my ears and vibrate throughout my whole being, full of strange, voluptuous pleasures... I raised my eyes and it seemed to me that even the Evangelists, from the gigantic plumes of the vault, were nodded to me with their heads that I was right. I must have been mad, if you like, but I was proud and happy.

24 You can condemn me. But truly, you would be wrong to feel sorry for me.

Notes

During production of this book, the Moreschi-Fellini Archive has resided in New Buffalo, Michigan. Once the book is published, the archive will be placed in a public institution.

PROLOGUE

The epigraph is from Marianne Hirsch, *Family Frames: Photography, Narrative, and Postmemory* (Cambridge, MA: Harvard University Press, 1997), p. 3. In "Life and Death," Gregory Batchen echoes: "Photography has been haunted by . . . the specter of death." *Suspending Time: Life, Photography, Death*, with essays by Yoshaki Kai and Masashi Kohara (Tokyo: Nohara Publishing and IZU Photo Museum, 2010), p. 108.

1. A short biography of Luciani, who was born in Civitavecchia on January 14, 1954, appears in Salvatore De Salvo Fattor, *La cappella musicale pontificia nel Novecento* (Rome: Fondazione Giovanni Pierluigi de Palestrina, 2005), p. 217. Luciani joined the papal choir in 1988 and would have retired from a thirty-year term in 2018. He passed away at age sixty-seven on May 30, 2021, after which his book was published, *"Initia musices": Incipitario testuale per la consultazione dei fondi musicale Cappella Giulia e Cappella Sistina della Biblioteca Apostolica Vaticana*, ed. Giancarlo Rostirolla (Rome: IBIMUS, 2022), dedicated to the Sistine Chapel maestro di cappella Domenico Bartolucci (1917–2013), a musician and from 2010 a cardinal. Luciani's large collection is now part of the archive of the Cappella Musicale Pontificia "Sistina" at via del Monte della Farina 64, Rome.

2. Courtney Quaintance helped on that second trip. My sincerest gratitude to both her and Hilary Poriss.

3. Luciani subsequently published evidence of these events derived from documents in his collection, especially the diaries of Sistine alto Luigi Gentili; see "La professione

dei cantori romani di musica sacra," in *Il giardino armonioso: Studi e testimonianze in onore di Giancarlo Rostirolla da parte dei Soci dell'IBIMUS in occasione del suo 70° compleanno*, ed. Saverio Franchi and Orietta Sartori (Rome: IBIMUS, 2011), pp. 79–152.4. Cinema Treasures, "Band Box Theatre," http://cinematreasures.org/theaters/13298.

5. Martha Feldman, *The Castrato: Reflections on Natures and Kinds* (Oakland: University of California Press, 2015), including chapter 3 on castrato vocality with reference to Moreschi especially on pp. 80–90.

6. Fellini's biographer Tullio Kezich mentions Giulio Moreschi and his student Riccardo Fellini, but without connecting Giulio to his castrato father; see his *Federico Fellinii: His Life and Work* (New York: Faber & Faber, 2006), p. 23 (the only place where Giulio is mentioned by name) and p. 73.

7. The restaurant is located at via della Colonna Antonina 48.

8. My specific hope was to deepen arguments to include falsettist students of Alessandro Moreschi, the teaching of Giulio Moreschi, and Riccardo Fellini's singing. For the last, absent living memories, I had only Fellini's second feature *I vitelloni* (1953) to go on. (See Chapter 2 below.) See Feldman, *The Castrato*, chapter 3, "Red Hot Voice," and chapter 4, "Castrato De Luxe."

9. Rita and Fabio talked about Alessandra's move to Mexico City, on which Rita elaborates in her unpublished memoir, *In viaggio con lo zio*, chapters 8 and 10.

10. Federico said his brother never much practiced singing; see Chapter 2 below.

11. Sadly, because of her long illness and my fear of imposing, I never actually encountered Rita in the flesh. But her voice, her presence in the background of conversations with Fabio preceding her death, which continued between them in the background of mine with Fabio, and his reports to me of their conversations following her death have all stayed with me, however mediated, and informed my thinking.

12. An important source on the Spanish castrati in mid to late sixteenth-century Rome is Giuseppe Gerbino, "The Quest for the Soprano Voice: Castrati in Sixteenth-Century Italy," *Studi musicali* 32.2 (2004), pp. 303–57. Secondary sources on Italian singing castrati include Franz Haböck, *Die Kastraten und ihre Gesangskunst: Eine gesangsphysiologische, kultur- und musikhistorische Studie* (Stuttgart: Deutsche Verlags-Anstalt, 1927); Anton Giulio Bragaglia, *Degli "evirati cantori": Contributo alla storia del teatro* (Florence: Sansoni, 1959); John Rosselli, "The Castrati as a Professional Group and as a Social Phenomenon, 1550–1850," *Acta musicologica* 60 (1988), pp. 143–79; Isabelle Moindrot, *L'opéra seria, ou le règne des castrats* (Paris: Fayard, 1993); Sylvie Mamy, *Les grands castrats*

napolitains à Venise au XVIIIe siècle (Liège: Mardaga, 1994); Naomi André, *Voicing Gender: Castrati, Travesti, and the Second Woman in Early-Nineteenth-Century Italian Opera* (Bloomington: Indiana University Press, 2006); Corinna Herr, *Gesang gegen die "Ordnung der Natur": Kastraten und Falsettisten in der Musikgeschichte* (Kassel: Bärenreiter, 2013); and Bonnie Gordon, *Voice Machines: The Castrato, the Cat Piano, and Other Strange Sounds* (Chicago: University of Chicago Press, 2023). There exist various studies of individual castrati; important ones include Sandro Cappelletto, *La voce perduta: Vita di Farinelli, evirato cantore* (Turin: EDT, 1995); Lowell Lindgren, "An Intellectual Florentine Castrato at the End of the Medicean Era," in *'Lo stupor dell'invenzione': Firenze e la nascita dell'opera*, Quaderni della Rivista italiana di musicologia 36 (Florence: Leo Olschki, 2001), pp. 139–63; Roger Freitas, *Portrait of a Castrato: Politics, Patronage, and Music in the Life of Atto Melani* (Cambridge: Cambridge University Press, 2009); Anne Desler, "'Il novello Orfeo' Farinelli: Vocal Profile, Aesthetics, Rhetoric," PhD diss., University of Glasgow, 2014; Patricia Howard, *The Modern Castrato Gaetano Guadagni and the Coming of a New Operatic Age* (New York: Oxford University Press, 2014); Anne Desler, "'The little that I have done is already gone and forgotten': Farinelli and Burney Write Music History," *Cambridge Opera Journal* 27.3 (November 2015), pp. 215–38; Anne Desler, "From Castrato to Bass: The Late Roles of Nicolò Grimaldi," in Catherine Haworth and Lisa Colton, eds., *Gender, Age and Musical Creativity* (Farnham: Ashgate, 2015), pp. 61–80; and Valentina Anzani, *Il castrato Antonio Bernacchi: Virtuoso e maestro di canto bolognese* (Lucca: Libreria Musicale Italiana, 2022).

For the wider phenomenon of castrated males (who went by different terms), important sources include: Shaun Tougher, *The Eunuch in Byzantine History and Society* (London: Routledge, 2008); Piotr O. Scholz, *Eunuchs and Castrati: A Cultural History*, trans. John A. Broadwin and Shelly L. Frisch (Princeton: Markus Wiener, 2001); Laura Engelstein, *Castration and the Heavenly Kingdom: A Russian Folktale* (Ithaca: Cornell University Press, 2003); and Larissa Tracy, ed. *Castration and Culture in the Middle Ages* (Cambridge: D. S. Brewer, 2013).

13. See Claudio Annibaldi, *La cappella musicale pontificia nel Seicento* (Rome: Fondazione Giovanni Pierluigi da Palestrina, 2011), p. 85 and p. 150 n. 58. For important background, see Rosselli, "The Castrati as a Professional Group and as a Social Phenomenon, 1550–1850"; Freitas, *Portrait of a Castrato*; and especially Robert Anthony Buning, "Alessandro Moreschi and the Castrato Voice," MA thesis, Boston University, 1990, pp. 66–68, overall the best-researched work on Moreschi's voice including various related contexts and histories.

14. See André, *Voicing Gender*, chapter 2, "Haunting Legacies: The Castrato in the Nineteenth Century"; Marco Beghelli and Raffaele Talmelli, *Ermafrodite armoniche: Il contralto nell'Ottocento* (Varese: Zecchini Editore, 2011); John Potter, *Tenor: History of a Voice* (New Haven: Yale University Press, 2009), chapter 2, "Handel, Mozart, and the Tenor-Castrato Connection"; Heather Hadlock, "Women Playing Men in Italian Opera, 1810–1835," in Jane A. Bernstein, ed., *Women's Voices Across Musical Worlds* (Boston: Northeastern University Press, 2004), pp. 285–307; Feldman, *The Castrato*, chapter 6, "Shadow Voices, Castrato and Non"; and Jessica Gabriel Peritz, *The Lyric Myth of Voice: Civilizing Song in Enlightenment Italy* (Oakland: University of California Press, 2022).

15. J. Q. Davies, *Romantic Anatomies of Performance* (Berkeley: University of California Press, 2014), chapter. 1.

16. On, for example, the rapid diffusion of castrati into North Italian courts during the later sixteenth century, see Richard Sherr, "Guglielmo Gonzaga and the Castrati," *Renaissance Quarterly* 33.1 (spring 1980), pp. 33–56.

17. Rome has four papal basilicas, granted special privileges by the pope: the Arcibasilica di San Giovanni in Laterano (Archbasilica of St. John Lateran), the Basilica di San Pietro (St. Peter's Basilica) at piazza San Pietro, the Basilica di San Paolo Fuori le Mure (St. Paul "Outside the Walls") at Piazzale San Paolo, and the Basilica di Santa Maria Maggiore (St. Mary Major).

18. The number of castrati in the Sistine Chapel in 1900 was eight or nine, depending on how you count. (See Chapter 1 below.) By that time, there were some reinforcements through the use of boys, as well as ad hoc replacements of castrati.

19. Buning's is the best account of this: "Alessandro Moreschi and the Castrato Voice," chapter 1.

20. On the papacy as a monarchy up to about 1650, the classic work is Paolo Prodi's *The Papal Prince: One Body and Two Souls. The Papal Monarchy in Early Modern Europe*, trans. Susan Haskins (Cambridge: Cambridge University Press, 1987).

21. See Italo Insolera, *Roma moderna, da Napoleone I al XXI secolo*, new expanded ed. with the collaboration of Paolo Berdini (Turin: Einaudi, 2011).

22. On the possibility that castrati besides Moreschi can be heard in choral parts on the 1902 and 1904 recordings, see Christian Zwarg's short liner note accompanying *Alessandro Moreschi, Soprano-Castrato (1858–1922): Complete Gramophone Co. Recordings (Rome, 1902–1904)*, Truesound Transfers TT-3040 (2009). He believes they might be heard on a 1904 recording of Palestrina's madrigal "La cruda mia nemica," but as I note in Chapter 1

below, by then, other Sistine castrati had retired or died (Cesari on March 10, 1904). Cesari's voice may sound on choral numbers recorded in 1902, although since those sessions used a large number of singers almost certainly including boys, it would be virtually impossible to pick out his voice.

23. For evidence, see Rosselli, "The Castrati as a Professional Group 1550–1850," expanded in Feldman, *The Castrato*, chapter 1. Bruce Alan Brown has studied the phenomenon and given public talks on it, including "Castration as Microhistory: The Many Worlds of Bartolomeo Nucci of Pescia," at the conference "Castrato Singers in Opera: The Current State of Research," Villa Vigoni–Centro Italo-Tedesco per il Dialogo Europeo, Italy/online, October 2021), and "'Alla mia scuola hà cantato robbe anche difficilissime . . .': The Material Remains of the *scuola di canto* of Cavaliere Bartolomeo Nucci," at the Biennial International Conference on Baroque Music, Cremona, Italy, July 2018, and the Annual meeting of American Musicological Society, San Antonio, November 2018.

24. Michael Omi and Howard Winant, *Racial Formation in the United States*, 3rd ed. (New York: Routledge, 2014), p. 110.

25. Cesare Lombroso, *L'uomo delinquente studiato in rapporto alla antropologia, alla medicina legale, ed alle discipline carcerarie . . . con incisioni* (Milan: Hoepli, 1876).

26. Of the numerous studies on Lombroso, important to me have been Delia Frigessi, *Cesare Lombroso* (Turin: Einaudi, 2003), and David Horn, *The Criminal Body: Lombroso and the Anatomy of Deviance* (New York: Routledge, 2003).

27. For the date 1871, related to Haböck by Moreschi himself, see Haböck, *Die Kastraten und ihre Gesangskunst*, p. 206 (and see Chapter 1 below). Since Moreschi did not turn thirteen until November 11, he was probably twelve at the time. See John Pollard, *Catholicism in Modern Italy: Religion, Society, and Politics since 1861* (London: Routledge, 2008), chapter 3, "The Catholic Recovery (1870–1914)."

28. A good summary of the circumstances appears in Paul Corner, "State and Society, 1901–1922," in Adrian Lyttelton, ed., *Liberal and Fascist Italy* (Oxford: Oxford University Press, 2002), pp. 17–43, esp. pp. 30–36.

29. In reaction, Jesus and Mary feast days were added to the liturgical calendar. Pilgrimages and devotions increased around Marian cults, especially the cults of the Sacred Heart, which functioned to repair the damage done by rowdy Carnival celebrations. New religious orders cropped up, catechisms were strengthened, and feast days for local saints proliferated.

30. Manuel De Landa, *A Thousand Years of Nonlinear History* (New York: Zone Books, 1997), and Elizabeth Freeman, *Time Binds: Queer Temporalities, Queer Histories* (Durham: Duke University Press, 2010).

31. Freeman, in *Time Binds*, first explains "queer time" on p. x (quote on p. xi). See also Carolyn Dinshaw, *Getting Medieval: Sexualities and Communities, Pre- and Postmodern* (Durham: Duke University Press, 1999), and *How Soon Is Now? Medieval Texts, Amateur Readers, and the Queerness of Time* (Durham: Duke University Press, 2012); as well as Kara Keeling, *Queer Times, Black Futures* (New York: NYU Press, 2019), for other takes on queer temporalities. For an important gloss on the role that queer time plays in music history, see Jessica Gabriel Peritz, "Overhearing (Music) History with Vernon Lee," (in preparation), which the author kindly allowed me to read in draft.

32. Jacques Derrida, *Specters of Marx: The State of the Debt, the Work of Mourning, and the New International*, trans. Peggy Kamuf (New York: Routledge, 1994), p. xix.

33. The intergenerational approach is one I unfold in Chapter 5. Key to my thinking has been Avery F. Gordon's wonderful *Ghostly Matters: Haunting and the Sociological Imagination*, 2nd ed. (1997; Minneapolis: University of Minnesota Press, 2008).

34. Sara Danius, *The Senses of Modernism: Technology, Perception, and Aesthetics* (Ithaca: Cornell University Press, 2002), pp. 11–17.

35. See Vladmir Jankélévitch, *Music and the Ineffable*, trans. Carolyn Abbate (Princeton: Princeton University Press, 2003), and Carolyn Abbate and Michael Gallope, "The Ineffable (and Beyond)," in Tomás McAuley, Nanette Nielsen, Jerrold Levinson, and Ariana Phillips-Hutton, eds., *Oxford Handbook of Western Music and Philosophy*, December 2020, DOI: 10.1093/oxfordhb/9780199367313.013.36. Studies of ineffability align with work on spectrality and reenactment, most signally in the work of Rebecca Schneider, who explores the haunting play of past and present in reenactments in her *Performing Remains: Art and War in Times of Theatrical Reenactment* (New York: Routledge, 2011).

Some recent music studies have taken up reenactment and haunting, among them: Jessie Fillerup, "Lucia's Ghosts: Sonic, Gothic, and Postmodern," *Cambridge Opera Journal* 28.3 (November 2016), pp. 313–45; Gina Arnold, "There's a Spectre Haunting Hip-Hop: Tupac Shakur, Holograms in Concert and the Future of Live Performance," in Barbara Lebrun and Catherine Strong, eds., *Death and the Rock Star* (New York: Routledge, 2016), pp. 177–88; Elliott H. Powell, "The Ghosts Got You: Exploring the Queer (After) Lives of Sample-Based Hip Hop," in Justin D. Burton and Jason Lee Oakes, eds., *The Oxford Handbook of Hip Hop Music*, August 8, 2018, https://doi.org/10.1093

/oxfordhb/9780190281090.013.29; Naomi André, *Black Opera: History, Power, Engagement* (Urbana: University of Illinois Press, 2018), chapter 4, "Haunted Legacies: Interracial Secrets from *The Diary of Sally Hemings*"; Carlo Lanfossi, "Ghosting Agrippina: Genealogies of Performance in Italian Baroque Opera," *Journal of Musicology* 36.1 (2019), pp. 1–38; Tracy McMullen, *Haunthenticity: Musical Replay and the Fear of the Real* (Middleton: Wesleyan University Press, 2019); Timothy Hampton, "'Murder most foul' and the Haunting of America," *MIT Press Reader*, April 3, 2020, https://thereader.mitpress.mit.edu/murder-most-foul-and-the-haunting-of-america; Tamara Dee Turner, "Affective Temporalities of Presence and Absence: Musical Haunting and Embodied Political Histories in an Algerian Religious Community," *Culture, Theory and Critique* 61. 2–3 (2020), pp. 169–86; and Jessica Gabriel Peritz, "The Castrato Remains—or, Galvanizing the Corpse of Musical Style," *Journal of Musicology* 39.3 (2022), pp. 371–403. See also the special issue, "Sounding the Spectral," ed. Seth Brodsky and Martha Feldman, appeared in *Portable Gray* 8 (Fall 2025).

For theoretical underpinnings, see signally (among much else) Gordon, *Ghostly Matters*; Alexander G. Weheliye, *Phonographies: Grooves in Afro-Sonic Modernity* (Durham: Duke University Press, 2005); and María del Pilar Blanco and Esther Pereen, eds., *The Spectralities Reader: Ghosts and Haunting in Contemporary Cultural Theory* (London: Bloomsbury, 2013), including a hefty opening chapter by the editors, "Introduction: Conceptualizing Spectralities," pp. 1–27, and their interpolated commentary throughout.

36. Miriam Bratu Hansen, "The Mass Production of the Senses: Classical Cinema as Vernacular Modernism," *Modernism/Modernity* 6.2 (1999), p. 60.

37. The term is Pollard's, from *Catholicism in Modern Italy*, chapter 7, which covers the years 1945 to 1958.

38. Pollard, *Catholicism in Modern Italy*, chapter 8; Jonathan Dunnage, *Twentieth-Century Italy: A Social History* (London: Longman, 2002), pp. 170 and 183.

39. The seventeenth-century heyday in the production of castrati widely framed castration for singing as a sacred renunciation that compensated for an irremediable social loss, in sum a sacrifice marked by bloodshed, some degree of cloistering, and total dedication to singing for the church, for a divinely ordained sovereign, or for one of their proxies. Prior to the nineteenth century, the eternal church and the eternal sovereign were, formally speaking, one and the same. Hence, any verbal articulation of castration for singing in terms of sacrifice was also a tacit confession that such a castration had actually been done. See further in my *The Castrato*, esp. the preface and chapter 1.

40. Giulietta commented on Federico's dislike of social obligations, especially toward relatives, as quoted in Tullio Kezich, *Gulietta Masina* (Bologna: Nuova Casa Editrice Cappelli, 1991), p. 22. (Fuller context in Chapter 2 below.)

41. The picture survives in the Moreschi-Fellini Archive, as I explain further below.

42. From the outset, filling gaps in their "genosociogram" (a socially elaborated genealogy) and thus looking to generate better family histories were motivating forces, especially for Fabio. At our first meeting, I offered to try hunting down certain genealogical and historical facts, hoping that memories about the dead preserved by the living would produce new and varied histories compatible with my own interests, which they have.

43. Nicholas Clapton journeyed to the tomb before me and was understandably puzzled by the information in papers he obtained from the cemetery office; see his *Moreschi and the Voice of the Castrato* (London: Haus Books, 2008), pp. 190–94, including his photograph of the tomb as it stood in the mid-2000s on p. 191.

44. As of this writing, Martina Piperno holds the title of Ricercatore in the Dipartimento di Studi Europei Americani e Interculturali (SEAI) at Sapienza Università di Roma; an award-winning author, she has published prolifically. Franco Piperno is an emeritus Professore Ordinario di Musicologia e Storia della musica at La Sapienza, a former dean there, and past president of ADUIM (Associazione docenti universitari italiani di musica). Franco Piperno occasionally suggested research contacts to us, for which I am grateful.

45. Emanuela Dessy Saddì notes that Julio's father, Giovanni Antonio ("Chico") Solinas, was a career military man who "had had 'problems' at the end of the war (although he was later acquitted in 1945)" and that he was working in the 1950s "for something military in South America." She adds that he was "married in 1940 in Italy to Gradiska Curatola Romeo and later in Mexico to Alessandra Moreschi in the early 1960s"—this at a time when divorce in Italy was illegal—and that he was born in the Sardinian city of Cagliari on June 21, 1914, son of Salvatore Solinas and Vitalia Marongiu. (The paternal surname is also that of the Cagliari-born screenwriter Franco Solinas [1927–1982], who wrote *The Battle of Algiers*.) A letter to Alessandra Moreschi of February 6, 1971, from a man named Angel Cardenas Chavez, executor of Chico Solinas's estate and a close friend, announces Chico Solinas's death on December, 26, 1970, while alluding to the "problems" Dessy Saddì mentions—see Appendix 1: Photo Essay no. 24.

46. The only other Moreschi still living is the great-great-grandson of Alessandro

Moreschi, whose full name is Alessandro Carlo Leone Solinas Moreschi, born September 18, 2006, son of Emanuela Dessy Saddì and the late Julio (Giulio) Salvador Solinas Moreschi, who was the castrato's great-grandson and Rita's half brother. My sincere thanks to Dessy Saddì for providing me with information about that part of the family. (Email of August 25, 2020.)

47. When the marriage took place, in Genoa on April 25, 1925, Giulio was twenty-one and Vittoria was twenty-six. A copy of the marriage certificate survives in the Archivio di Stato di Roma, Atti di Matrimonio, parte II, series A, no. 909, transcribed from the Genoese document on May 28, 1925. It shows the couple were married at the Casa Comunale in a public civil ceremony and describes young Giulio as "prof. di musica." Vittoria is listed as daughter of Carlo Cevasco and Teresa Lauro, who entered a formal request that the couple be joined in matrimony. Present at the ceremony was also Antonio G. Lauro, aged forty-two, likely Vittoria's maternal uncle, who, according to Fabio, was Vittoria's benefactor. The groom's mother was not present, but gave her legal consent.

48. The unidentified man could be Umberto Giuli, named as Giulio's executor in his will. Archivio Notarile di Roma, Repertorio no. 15297, Raccolta no. 7583, notaio Alfredo de Martino; see Chapter 3 below.

49. During the war years, Theodora (Teddy) Getty, née Lynch (later Getty Gaston) often joined the Moreschi family and Giulio's other students at the ristorante, La Cisterna, in Travestere, near the Moreschi-Cevasco home on via Lungotevere degli Anguillara 11, where they would all sing during and after meals; see Theodora Getty Gaston with Digby Diehl, *Alone Together: My Life with J. Paul Getty* (New York: HarperCollins, 2013), p. 133, and further in Chapter 3 below. The osteria, still in operation today, traced its origins to 1630 on a former, now-defunct website, and has a new one seemingly in the process of being rebuilt: https://lacisternatrastevere.it. In an interview about her book, Getty Gaston talks about Moreschi: Daryn Hinton, Teddy Getty Gaston 'Alone Together' J. Paul Getty Inverview by Darcy Hinton video by Daryn Hinton," YouTube, 2014, https://www.youtube.com/watch?v=Hrn_6DXvmxo&t=180s, at 00:28 to 00:59 and elsewhere.

50. See Chapter 2 below for Federico's account. Rita writes of her mother in *In viaggio con lo zio*, chapter 2: "She loved to go out shopping, or to the movies or the theater, and she had a special passion for dancing. But it was with singing that she expressed herself best, and she was ecstatic whenever anyone asked her to perform at some party she had been invited to. She didn't need much encouragement: being at the center of

attention was like a drug for her, and there was a strong family tradition for music." Unpublished translation by Rebecca Bauman.

51. Susan Sontag, *On Photography* (New York: Farrar Strauss and Giroux, 1977), p. 154, emphasis mine.

52. Ibid., pp. 15–16.

53. Roland Barthes, *Camera Lucida: Reflections on Photography*, trans. Richard Howard (New York: Hill and Wang, 1981), p. 6, emphasis mine. Also fascinating on issues of temporal displacement and imagery is Georges Didi-Huberman, *Devant le temps: Histoire de l'art et anachronisme des images* (Paris: Éditions de Minuit, 2000).

54. Tingting Xu, an art historian specializing in early photography, tells me that "small portable cameras had been very popular" by this time, including for "globe trotters" such as missionaries in China. (Email exchange, June 21, 2023.)

CHAPTER ONE: PHANTOMS IN THE ARCHIVE

1. The shop was opened by Rita in 1976, three years after her marriage to Fabio, and closed by Fabio in May 2015 three years after Rita's death, when the landlord of the large building containing it as part of a contiguous set of shops on the ground floor decided to repurpose the spaces. (See the Epilogue.) On the history of the shop and its place in the wider context of Fellini-named businesses, see Rebecca Bauman, "The Fellini Brand: Marketing Appropriations of the Fellini Name," in Frank Burke, Marguerite Walker, and Marita Gubareva, eds., *A Companion to Federico Fellini* (Hoboken: Wiley Blackwell, 2020), p. 95.

2. Fabio's grandfather, Niccolò Panconesi received a medal for distinguished service in the African campaign of 1906. On his return to Italy, his ship encountered difficulties, and while awaiting the next ship, he fell ill and was sent to a Cairo hospital. He later married the woman who nursed him there, Giuseppina Bertola? (last name uncertain). Their son, Fabio's father, Edoardo Panconesi (1917–2013), was born in Cairo, but later moved the family to Rome.

Fabio's maternal grandmother Georgette Bernier (Paris 1890 – Rome 1973), orphaned as an adolescent, lived in the countryside with her grandparents until returning to Paris to work in a pastry shop, where she met the Bulgarian pastry chef Christo Martinoff(?) with whom she moved to Cairo to open their own pastry shop. Fabio's mother Marie Martinoff(?) (Cairo 1921 – Rome 2017) was born there, the youngest of their three daughters. Fabio recounts that when Marie was still young, her father went to school to pick up her two sisters, after which they all disappeared from the country along with Marie's documents. Thereafter Georgette was prevented from seeing her older daughters. She continued living in Egypt with young Marie, but in perpetual fear of losing her if Christo were to return. Eventually, Georgette formed a relationship with an expatriate Anatolian Greek, Louis Prelorenzo (Smyrna 1888 – Rome 1962; surname probably Italianized), who adopted Marie (her premarital documents read "Maria Martinoff Prelorenzo"), making it eventually possible for her to marry Fabio's father.

Edoardo was Giuseppina's second child; an older half-sister of his, Egizia Siliotti (Cairo 1899-Rome 1984), joined the family's move to Rome in January 1961 when Fabio was nine and a half. (Emails from Fabio Panconesi of March 24 and 25, 2025.)

3. Their marriage on April 25, 1925, discussed in the Prologue above, took place in Genoa when Giulio was twenty-one and Vittoria twenty-six. "L'anno millenovecentoventicinque addì 28 di maggio a ore nove e minuti dieci nella casa Comunale di Roma io Gr Uff. Avv. Carlo Scotti elettore delegato ad Ufficiale dello Stato Civile di Roma, avendo ricevuto dall'ufficiale dello Stato Civile del Comune di Genova copia d'atto di matrimonio l'ho per intero ed esattamente trascritta: L'anno millenovecentoventicinque, addì 25 di aprile a ore dievi e minuti venti, nella casa comunale di Genova aperta al pubblico. Avanti di me Giuseppe Guelfi elettore ufficiale dello Stato Civile, vestito in forma ufficiale, sono personalmente comparsi 1) Giulio Moreschi, celibe, di anni ventuno, nato in / residente in Roma, prof di musica, figlio di fu Alessandro, residente in / e di Guendalina Rinaldi, residente in Roma. 2) Vittoria Cevasco, nubile, di anni ventisei, nata in / residente in Genova, figlia di Carlo, residente in / e d Teresa Lauro residente in Genova, i quali mi hanno richiesto di unirli in matrimonio, a questo effetto mi hanno presentato i documenti sotto descritti, dall'esame di questi, nonché di quelli già prodotto all'atto delle pubblicazioni, i quali tutti , muniti del mio visto, inserisco nel volume degli allegati a questo registro, risultandomi nulla ostare alla celebrazione del loro matrimonio, ho letto agli sposi gli articoli centotrenta, centotrentuno e centotrentadue del codice civile, e quindi ho domandato allo sposo se intende di prendere in moglie la qui presente Vittoria Cevasco, e a questa se intende di prendere in marito il qui presente Giulio Moreschi; ed avendomi ciascuno risposto affermativamente a piena intelligenza anche dei testimoni sottoindicati, ho pronunciato in nome della legge che i medesimi sono uniti in matrimonio. A quest'atto sono stati presenti: Antonio G. Lauro di anni 42 industrial.[ista][?], Alessandro Patena di anni 52 commerc.[ialista] entrambi residenti in questo comune. I documenti presentati sono i certificati delle pubblicazioni eseguite qui a Roma li 12 e 14

corrente. Al matrimonio consentì a madre dello sposo. Letto e firmato ff. G. Moreschi, Vittoria Cevasco, A. Lauro, Alessandro Patena, G. Guelfi." Archivio di Stato, Documenti di Stato Civile: Matrimoni, 1925, vol. 2, part 2, series A, n. 209, p. 15.

4. Some of this information comes from Fabio and some from Rita's *In viaggio con lo zio*, especially chapters 2, 4, and 6. As of this writing, the book remains in unpublished typescript, although Rebecca Bauman and I have translated parts of it.

5. Comune di Roma, Richiesta di Operazioni Cimiteriali nel Cimitero di Verano, made on behalf of Vittoria Cevasco, deceased December 27, 1985; request by Alessandra Moreschi, December 30, 1985.

6. Maria Rita Fellini, *In viaggio con lo zio*, chapter. 10. In the Comune di Roma, Cimitero del Verano, Capitolini, Anagrafe, Giulio Moreschi's death is listed as July 14, 1955 (buried July 16), son of Alessandro Moreschi and Guendalina Rinaldi and "professore di musica." Document signed by Vittoria Cevasco's "son-in-law," Riccardo Fellini. Giulio's parents are listed the same way there, "Estratto per riassunto dal registro degli atti di morte dell'anno 1955," August 9, 1994 (the day after Alessandra's death). Giulio died of complications from diabetes, which runs in the family. (Rita Fellini and Fabio Panconesi, private communication, May 21, 2010.)

7. See Richard Sherr, "Guglielmo Gonzaga and the Castrati," *Renaissance Quarterly* 33.1 (Spring 1980), p. 56, on the sixteenth-century case. Most important on other castrato marriages are: Helen M. Berry, *The Castrato and His Wife* (Oxford: Oxford University Press, 2011), on Giovanni Ferdinando Tenducci's marriage in Dublin in 1766; Mary E. Frandsen, "Eunuchi conjugium: The Marriage of a Castrato in Early Modern Germany," *Early Music History: Studies in Medieval and Early Modern Music* 24 (2005), pp. 53–124, a meticulously documented study of castrato Bartolomeo Sorlisi's partial marriage near Leipzig in the early 1660s; and Johann Friedrich Schütze, *Hamburgische Theater-geschichte* (Hamburg: J. P. Treder, 1794), pp. 193–207, on Filippo Finazzi's 1761 marriage outside Hamburg. On castrato marriages within larger themes of biological and social reproduction, see Martha Feldman, *The Castrato: Reflections on Natures and Kinds* (Oakland: University of California Press, 2015), chapter 2, esp. pp. 49–55.

8. Biblioteca Apostolica Vaticana, Fondo Cappella Sistina 642, pp. 416–78. A transcription can be found in Leopold M. Kantner and Angela Pachovsky, *La cappella musicale pontificia nell'Ottocento* (Rome: Hortus Musicus, 1998), pp. 193–99, with lifting of the celibacy requirement on p. 198.

9. I owe thanks to Luciano Luciani for a copy of a score of Moreschi's on which

there is a stamp of his address, showing via Palombella 38. Although no date is associated with the address there, it provided a lead that made it possible to retrieve data from the parish records, *gli stati delle anime*. Residents of the Moreschi household are named in the *registri* at the Archivio Storico Diocesano del Vicariato di Roma, Stati delle anime, Parocchia di Sant' Eustachio, via Palombella 88, 1901–1906. (The number of the residence apparently toggled between 88, which appears on the parish record, and 38, which is given on the stamp on Moreschi's score and used on the present-day building. There is no via della Palombella 88 in present-day Rome.)

The *stati delle anime* are a kind of census of the parishioners conducted by churchmen and parish secretaries before the unified Italian state took over that function and substituted lay censuses for the previous religious ones. Up until the second half of the nineteenth century, parish registers therefore tend to be quite accurate, whereas after 1850–1860, they become both less reliable and fewer and fewer in number. As of 2010, the parish registers of Rome were stored in the narrow premises of the Archivio Diocesano del Vicariato, piazza di San Giovanni in Laterano 6, with no real indexing. As of 2024, a website exists at https://www.diocesidiroma.it/category/uffici/archivio-storico, but as of this writing it includes no digitizations of actual historical parish records.

The nephew was Amerigo [= Americo] Moreschi (1882–1925), whose birth record survives at the Comune di Monte Compatri, Dipartimento di Stato Civile, certificato di nascita, registri, part 1, series 78: Americo Moreschi, born July 27, 1882 to Agostino Moreschi and Celestina Felici (the latter also buried in the Moreschi-Rinaldi tomb). He was thus the son of one of Alessandro's brothers. Also boarding at the flat in 1902 and 1903 was a student, likely Alessandro's, whose name in 1902 looks like *Mario* Costa and in 1903 like *Maria*. A male singer is far more likely to have been a live-in student.

10. Information on the concession of the tomb survives at Cimiteri Capitolini, Archivio, Atto di Concessione, Alessandro Moreschi / Pietro Rinaldi, April 24, 1900. The tomb and records were previously accessed by Nicholas Clapton, *Moreschi and the Voice of the Castrato* (London: Haus Books, 2008), who tells his story on pp. 190–94.

11. The evidence that he passed away without heirs comes from a much later cemetery document stating that he died "senza lasciare eredi" (without leaving heirs); Comune di Roma, Decentramento Amministrativo, Verbale di ricevimento di dichiarazione, made by Alessandra Moreschi, January 17, 1986. The death certificate reads: "L'anno millenovecentoventiquattro addì ventisei [ventitré?] maggio a ore tredici e minuti quaranta nella casa comunale. Io cav. rag. Ciro Ciccolini Segretario delegato del sindaco il

22 ottobre 1909 con atto approvato ad Uffiziale dello stato Civile del Comune di Roma, avendo ricevuto dal Pretore del 6° Mandamento un avviso in data diciotto corr[ente] mese, relativo alla morte di cui in appresso [?] e che, munito del mio visto, inserisco nel volume degli allegato a questo registro, do [?] atto che a ore due e minuti / del giorno diciassette corrente mese in Roma è morto Rinaldi Pietro di anni ottanta scalpellino residente e nato in Roma dai furono Giacomo e Nicati Anna, coniugato Pirioli Irene. [signature]." Archivio di Stato di Roma, Stato Civile Italiano, Roma, Morti, 1924, vol. 4, part 2, series B, no. 1995, p. 72. The original can't be consulted, because the archive was destroyed by fire in 2015. (Email communication from Vincenzo De Meo, Archivio di Stato di Roma, March 3, 2024.) Courtney Quaintance kindly amended my transcription insofar as it was possible to do so. Guendalina's birth certificate survives in the Archivio di Stato di Roma, Documenti di Stato Civile, Nati, 1872, vol. 1, series D, no. 91, pp. 29–30.

12. Alessandro Gabrielli, "Appendice: Riassunto delle conversazioni sulla storia delle Cappelle musicali romane. III. La Cappella Sistina dall'Ottocento ad oggi," *Rassegna dorica: Cultura e cronaca musicale* 10.3 (January 1939), p. 256: "la sua vita intima, familiare, non fu tranquilla." Within a year after Mussolini's racial laws of 1938, the *Rassegna dorica* had become a virulently Fascist publication; see "Rassegna Dorica (1929–1942)," https://www.ripm.org/pdf/PeriodicaMusica/RADintroEnglish.pdf, pp. ix–x. On Gabrielli, see Giancarlo Rostirolla, "GABRIELLI, Alessandro (romano; n. il 22.XII.1882 - 4.V.1941†) Soprano falsettista": "Eccellente voce, fin dagli anni Venti fu attivo nella CS, dove entrò di ruolo il 1°.V.1935. Appassionato di storia musicale sacra ha offerto parecchi contributi alla storia delle cappelle musicali romane e dei loro protagonisti (cfr. la bibliogr. in fondo a questo Dizionario). Fece parte del Quartetto Vocale Romano, insieme con Luigi Gentili, Ezio Cecchini e Augusto Dos Santos," in Giancarlo Rostirolla, *Musica e musicisti nella Basilica di San Pietro: Cinque secoli di storia della Cappella Giulia*, APPENDICE VII: I cantori di San Pietro dal 1513 al 1979, http://dhi-roma.it/fileadmin/user_upload/pdf-dateien/Online-Publikationen/AM51-Rostirolla-Anhaenge/AM51_Rostirolla-Appendice-07.pdf, p. 171.

13. See Chapter 4 below, note 67, for the birth record at the Archivio di Stato di Roma. Giulio's birth was also reported in Luigi Gentili's diaries, preserved in Luciano Luciani's private archive, now at the Cappella Musicale Pontificia "Sistina" at via del Monte della Farina 64, Rome; see his presentation delivered at the Festival Moreschi 2011, Montecompatri, on June 11, https://www.youtube.com/watch?v=oaSlBJ7MlJs, beginning at 4:16, and his "La professione dei cantori romani di musica sacra," in Saverio Franchi

and Orietta Sartori, eds., *Il Giardino armonioso: Studi e testimonianze in onore di Giancarlo Rostirolla da parte dei Soci dell'Ibimus in occasione del suo 70° compleanno* (Rome: IBIMUS, 2011), p. 117. In 1904, a "Giulio" from Montecompatri was added to the parish record of the Moreschi household, with his age given as "21," his parentage and place of origin the same as Amerigo's ("fu Agostino," son of the late Agostino, and from Montecompatri), as if he were a nephew of Alessandro's; and in the 1903 parish record, the name "Giulio" is already penciled in, seemingly after the other data were recorded in ink (data from the Archivio Storico Diocesano del Vicariato di Roma, Parrocchia di S. Eustachio, Stato delle anime, for the 1901 decade). It's unclear whether this represents obfuscation of some kind.

14. Besides sharing a tendency to put on substantial weight, Giulio and Amerigo look uncannily alike, especially their eyes (which Julio's also resemble; see RB Casting, "Julio Salvador Solinas Moreschi," https://www.rbcasting.com/rb/web/juliosolinas).

15. The diarist is Luigi Gentili (see note 13 above), who dates Guendalina's flight without using her name. The relevant page is reproduced in Luciani, "La professione dei cantori romani di musica sacra," p. 128, with discussion on p. 118, also without identifying her by name.

16. The manuscript in its present form was compiled and edited by Fabio Panconesi. It's notable that it partly contradicts his oral account of Guendalina's flight and theft.

17. According to Vittoria, as remembered by Rita and Fabio, Guendalina's younger son, Saverio, came to see Giulio at the cinema the couple ran at piazza Venezia during what Vittoria called "Fascist times" (see the Epilogue below), presumably to bring them news of Guendalina. Vittoria also told Rita and Fabio stories of Guendalina herself going there regularly to ask Giulio for money. Efforts to trace Guendalina's whereabouts through documents dating from after 1907 have not yet proved successful, but her second son, Saverio Mancini, who was distinctly remembered for his club foot, reported her death to Alessandra through a letter (privately owned) sent in 1957 from Thiene in the Veneto. (See the end of this chapter.) When Giulio died, on July 14, 1955, his holograph will—published on behalf of the Comune di Roma, Stato Civile, by an Alberto Roselli and signed on July 18, 1955—listed him explicitly as son (rather than adoptive son) of the late Alessandro and late Guendalina Rinaldi ("nato in Roma da fu Alessandro e da fu Rinaldi Guendalina"). Document in Archivio Notarile di Roma, repertorio no. 15297, raccolta 7582 (richiesta 11465, p. 6). All other legal documents that I've seen do so as well.

18. According to Fabio, the genealogical research on the family being done by the late genealogist Jérôme Blanc, who died in 2015, led him to believe Guendalina was in Naples in 1932. Guendalina seems to have married the croupier, whose last name was apparently Mancini, the name borne by Guendalina's second son. (See Figure 0.1.) Future researchers will undoubtedly be able to uncover biographical details of the family beyond those I offer here.

19. The specifications of an imperial-style console and an eighteenth-century mirror come from the back of Figure 7.1a, which was inventoried, presumably for sale and probably in 1984 or 1985.

20. Moreschi's death certificate reads: "L'anno millenovecentoventidue addì ventidue di Aprile a ore diciannove e minuti trenta, nella Casa Comunale. Avanti di me Collera Cav. Domenico, segretario, delegato del Sindaco il 26 maggio 1921, Uffiziale dello Stato Civile del Comune di Roma, con atto debitamente approvato, sono comparsi Benedettini Giovanni, di anni cinquantadue, commesso, domiciliato in Roma, e Mochetti Pietro, di anni settantasei, commesso, domiciliato in Roma, i quali mi hanno dichiarato che a ore otto e minuti quaranta di ieri, nella casa posta in V. Plinio al numero 19 è morto Moreschi Alessandro, di anni sessantaquattro, musicista, residente in Roma e nato in Montecompatri da fu Luigi, domiciliato in |, e da fu Ippoliti Rosa, | domiciliata in |, Coniugato Rinaldi Luisa. A quest'atto sono stati presenti quali testimoni, Rolando Mario di anni trentanove, commesso, e Artusi Egidio, di anni sessantatre, commesso, ambi residenti in questo Comune. Letto il presente atto a tutti gl'intervenuti, meco lo firmano, tranne un teste perché imperito [firme]." Archivio di Stato di Roma, Stato Civile Italiano, Atti di Morte, 1922, vol. 5, part 1, series 1, p. 174, n. 1923. The author of the document mistakenly refers to a Luisa Rinaldi.

21. Lucy Hughes-Hallett, *Gabriele d'Annunzio: Poet, Seducer, and Preacher of War* (New York: Knopf, 2013), pp. 33–34, 150–54, 409–15. I also wonder whether he may have heard D'Annunzio's inflammatory speech at the Teatro Costanzi in May 1915, when D'Annunzio advocated for Italy's entry into the Great War on the side of the Entente Allies, denouncing "Giolittismo," named for Giovanni Giolitti, the five-time prime minister of Italy who opposed Italy's intervention. Ibid. pp. 51–52. See the illustration by Achille Beltrame at World War I Today, "Gabriele D'Annunzio," https://wwitoday.com/ww1ScPersonDetail.php?id=18.

22. This is recorded in a document titled "Commissione nominate nell'Assemblea Generale dei Cantori di Musica Sacra. 5 Feb. 1919, per concretare le tariffe delle esecuzioni

musicali sacre." Preserved in the archive of Luciano Luciani and in the Moreschi-Fellini Archive is a "Relazione delle adunanze della commissione nominata nell' Assemblea Generale dei Cantori di Musica Sacra il giorno 5 febbraio 1919 per concretare le tariffe delle esecuzioni musicali sacre" that lists Moreschi among five attendees.

23. See the document listed in note 22 above.

24. Fred Gaisberg, "Recordings of Actual Performances: Notes from My Diary," *Gramophone* (September 1944), p. 13. Moreschi probably looked older than he was as a result of prepubertal castration, which could lead to premature wrinkling (as some photographs confirm he had); see, for example, Kantner and Pachovsky, *La cappella musicale pontificia nell'Ottocento*, p. 279, upper image.

25. Harold Schonberg, "History's Last Castrato Is Heard Again," *New York Times*, September 16, 1984, a review of the Opal transfer of Moreschi's 78s. Franz Haböck, *Die Kastraten und ihre Gesangskunst: Eine gesangsphysiologische, kultur- und musikhistorische Studien* (Stuttgart: Deutsche Verlags-Anstalt, 1927), p. 208, gives a firsthand account of Moreschi's voice (as high and metallic) and his appearance (short and plump, "mittelgroß"). The latter account matches surviving images of him. He differs physically from a number of other castrati (including his colleagues Giovanni Cesari and Domenico Salvatori), who had unusually long limbs and great height as well as unusually large jaws and chests owing to prepubertal deprivation of testosterone, which caused the epiphyseal plates of the joints to fail to fuse at the proper time in the growing process.

26. My information about Pietro Moreschi (full name Pietro Luigi, born 1809) comes partly from a genealogy by an unknown author/creator in the Moreschi-Fellini Archive and partly from Luigi Devoti, who reports on Pietro Moreschi in "Alessandro Moreschi, detto 'L'angelo di Roma,' 1858–1922," in Renato Lefevre and Arnaldo Morelli, eds., *Musica e musicisti nel Lazio* (Rome: Gruppo Culturale di Roma e del Lazio with Fratelli Palombi, 1985), p. 463, with information repeated in Robert Anthony Buning, "Alessandro Moreschi and the Castrato Voice," MA thesis, Boston University, 1990, pp. 106–107, Clapton, *Moreschi and the Voice of the Castrato*, pp. 54–55, and elsewhere. Luigi Moreschi was the son of Francesco Moreschi and Antonia Carrari. Moreschi's mother, Rosa Pitolli, was the daughter of Giuseppe Pitolli and Antonia Salvatori. The godparents were Pietro Moreschi and Agnese Fortunati.

Some speculate that an already existing Roman connection to the Moreschi family may have determined Alessandro's future—a priest named Terenzio Moreschi, who was one of Baini's correspondents in the 1840s. See J. A. La Fage, *Essais de diphthérographie musicale* . . . (1864; Amsterdam: Knuf, 1964), p. 533. But nothing else seems to connect Terenzio to Alessandro.

27. A forty-five-page publication was made twenty-five years after the cholera epidemic by P. F. Francesco Saverio di S. Giuseppe carmelitano scalzo, *Brevi cenni storici della miracolosa immagine di Maria SS. detta del castagno che si venera nella sacra edicola sul colle Tuscolano a Monte-Compatri* (Rome: Tipografia Agostiniana, 1892), reported briefly by the Photo Club Controluce, https://www.controluce.it/edizioni/notizie-storiche-sulla-madonna-del-castagno.

28. See Haböck, *Die Kastraten und ihre Gesangskunst*, p. 206, and Kantner and Pachovsky, *La cappella musicale pontificia nell'Ottocento*, pp. 181–82. Further elaborations appear in Clapton, *Moreschi and the Voice of the Castrato*, especially chapters 3 and 4.

29. Haböck, *Die Kastraten und ihre Gesangskunst*, p. 206, which also states specifically: "As a child he had been singing in the Chapel of the Madonna dal Castagno in Montecompatri, where he was already allowed to sing solo. His first musical study began with Nazzareno Rosati, a famous tenor at the Sistine Chapel." I have smoothed the German for the sake of readability. See also Alessandro Gabrielli, "Appendice: Riassunto delle conversazioni sulla storia delle cappelle musicali romane tenuto da Prof. Alessandro Gabrielli, in Roma," *Rassegna dorica* 10.2 (December 1938). p. 239.

30. See Salvatore De Salvo, s.v. "Salvatore Meluzzi," *Dizionario biografico degli italiani*, vol. 73 (2009), https://www.treccani.it/enciclopedia/salvatore-meluzzi_%28Dizionario-Biografico%29; Alberto De Angelis, "La Schola cantorum di S. Salvatore in Lauro e l'Accademia di Santa Cecilia," *Santa Cecilia: Rivista dell'Accademia Nazionale di Santa Cecilia* 9.3 (June 1960), pp. 42–45, esp. p. 44; Kantner and Pachovsky, *La cappella musicale pontificia nell'Ottocento*, pp. 25, 52, 59, 168, 182, 199, 245, 269, 287; and Salvatore De Salvo Fattor, *La cappella musicale pontificia nel Novecento* (Rome: Fondazione Giovanni Pierluigi da Palestrina, 2005), pp. 4, 12, 19, 41–45, 60, 71. The school was officially called the Schola Cantorum A. Braschi and was contained within the church of San Salvatore in Lauro, located in a small piazza of the same name just off the via dei Coronari. Chosen boys were traditionally first placed in orphanages, so named — in nineteenth-century Rome, the Pia Casa degli Orfani di Santa Maria in Aquiro, or the Ospizio degli Orfani di Santa Maria in Acquiro (on which see Kantner and Pachovsky, *La cappella musicale pontificia nell'Ottocento*, pp. 24–25, 41, 50, 141, 144, 161, 176, 181, 186, 188, 266, 377) — but in 1871, Moreschi went straight to San Salvatore in Lauro, which had opened three years earlier. On the roles of Alessandro and Giulio Moreschi in the Cappella Giulia, see Giancarlo

Rostirolla, *Musica e musicisti nella Basilica di San Pietro: Cinque secoli di storia della Cappella Giulia*, vol. 2, *Dal 1804 ai giorni d'oggi* ([Vatican City]: Edizioni Capitolo Vaticano, 2014).

31. Leopold M. Kantner, "Capocci, Gaetano," *New Grove Dictionary of Music and Musicians*, https://www.oxfordmusiconline.com/grovemusic/display/10.1093/gmo/9781561592630.001.0001/omo-9781561592630-e-0000004847 (subscription required); *Enciclopedia dell'arte contemporanea*, s.v. "Capòcci, Gaetano," https://www.treccani.it/enciclopedia/gaetano-capocci.

32. Buning, in "Alessandro Moreschi and the Castrato Voice," rightly counts Capocci as a major cause of this aspect of Moreschi's singing style (pp. 116–17).

33. Ibid, p. 115. See Kantner and Pachovsky, *La cappella musicale pontificia nell'Ottocento*, pp. 266–69, for a list of the participants. The "Ospizio Orfanelli" indicated with the performance personnel of the motet may refer to the orphanage founded at the Church of S. Maria in Aquiro in piazza Capranica (see note 30 above). For the Tata Giovanni, see Carlo Luigi Morichini, *Degl'istituti di pubblica carità ed istruzione primaria e delle prigioni in Roma* (Rome: Marini e compagno), Morichini, *Estratto della memoria sacra sopra Tatagiovanni* (n.p. , n.d.); Morichini, *Rendiconto del denaro raccolto per l'Ospizio di Tata Giovanni*. Extract from the *Giornale Arcadico*, vol. 53, undated.

34. Alberto De Angelis, *Domenico Mustafà: La Cappella Sistina e la Società Musicale Romana* (Bologna: N. Zanichelli, 1926), p. 89.

35. In this period, those called contraltos or altos were falsettists or high tenors, depending on the work being performed and the kind of performance desired.

36. A reasonable summary, albeit with a Germanophilic bias, is given by Siegfried Gmeinwieser, "Cecilian Movement (Ger. Cäcilianismus)," *Grove Music Online* (January 20, 2001), https://www.oxfordmusiconline.com/grovemusic/display/10.1093/gmo/9781561592630.001.0001/omo-9781561592630-e-0000005245?rskey=Iqb1zD&result=1 (subscription required), which begins by describing Cecilianism as "a 19th-century movement, centered in Germany, for the reform of Catholic church music. Reacting to the liberalization of the Enlightenment, the Cecilians sought to restore traditional religious feeling and the authority of the church. They regarded 'true, genuine church music' as being subservient to the liturgy, and intelligibility of words and music as more important than artistic individuality." The name of the movement honors the patron saint of sacred music, St. Cecilia. Even if its roots in Germany were strong, early on, the movement spread far beyond Germany alone, especially to France.

37. Buning, "Alessandro Moreschi and the Castrato Voice," also points out that

leaders of the Cecilian movement were widely influenced by Franz Kandler's German version of Baini's study of Palestrina, edited by Raphael Georg Kiesewetter (p. 115 n. 5).

38. Ibid., p. 116, and Kantner and Pachovsky, *La cappella musicale pontificia nell'Ottocento*, pp. 51–55.

39. In 1883, Lent began on February 7, Easter Sunday on March 25, so Maundy Thursday was on March 22. I discuss the *Miserere* in question in Chapters 3 and 4 below, for which the go-to text is Graham O'Reilly, "*Allegri's* Miserere" *in the Sistine Chapel* (Woodbridge: The Boydell Press, 2020).

40. Biblioteca Apostolica Vaticana, Diarii Sistini, no. 290, "Diario della Cappella Pontificia compilato dal Signor Emilio Calzanera di Roma, Segretario Puntatore Del R. Collegio dei Capellani Cantori Pontifici nell'anno del Signore 1883 Regnante la Santità di Nostro Signore Papa Leone XIII," fols. 4', 8, 23, 46, 47, 51, 64, 67, 68'.

41. Art historian Tingting Xu has graciously informed me that the tone of this albumen print is typical of the 1870s–1880s and that it was probably done through a gelatin dry plate process because a wet plate collodion process would have produced more sharpness. (Private communication, August 25, 2021.) Her dating accords with my general impression based on Moreschi's appearance.

42. Lillie de Hegermann-Lindencrone, *The Sunny Side of Diplomatic Life* (New York: Harper & Bros., 1914), p. 119.

43. Gabrielli, "Appendice: Riassunto delle conversazioni sulla storia delle Cappelle musicali romane. III. La Cappella Sistina dall'Ottocento ad oggi," pp. 255–56. On the vocal demands of Abigaille's music see Will Crutchfield, "Unsafe at Any Speed: The Dangers of Singing Abigaille in *Nabucco*," *Opera News* 65.9 (March 2001), pp. 36–41.

44. Devoti, "Alessandro Moreschi, detto 'L'angelo di Roma,' 1858–1922,": "La celebre soprano Durand, che sarebbe dovuta intervenire nel concerto, non vuole cantare temendo il confronto" (p. 468). (And see Clapton, who speculates the year may have been 1889, in *Moreschi and the Voice of the Castrato*, p. 122.)

45. See Gabrielli, "Appendice: Riassunto delle conversazioni sulla storia delle Cappelle musicali romane. III. La Cappella Sistina dall'Ottocento ad oggi," p. 255.

46. Hegermann-Lindencrone, *The Sunny Side of Diplomatic Life*, pp. 118–19.

47. Clapton, *Moreschi and the Voice of the Castrato*, pp. 73–81, esp. p. 74. I put forward a critique of gender-bending tendencies in 1990s castrato scholarship in "Castrato Acts," in Helen M. Greenwald, ed., *The Oxford Handbook of Opera* (Oxford: Oxford University Press, 2014), pp. 404–10.

48. Susan Sontag, *Notes on Camp* (1961; New York: Penguin Books, 2018), p. 1. See also Devon J. Borowski, "Camping Empire: Melophilia and the Castrato Voice in Georgian Britain," *Journal of Musicology* 42.1 (Winter 2025), pp. 1–30, https://online.ucpress.edu/jm/article/42/1/1/205015/Camping-EmpireMelophilia-and-the-Castrato-Voice-in, for a consideration of camp with respect to eighteenth-century castrati and their patrons.

49. Violino, "Corrispondenza da Pisa," Supplement to *La nuova musica*, year 2, 1.10 (June 30, 1897), p. 7, col. 3, emphasis mine. Also singled out was the bass Capocci, together with the alto Mori (possibly Tommaso Mori, though he is listed as a soprano falsettist in De Salvo Fattor, *La cappella musicale pontificia nel Novecento*, p. 219, and tenor Zoli (?). Alessandro Gabrielli, "Appendice: Riassunta delle conversazioni sulla storia delle Cappelle musicali romane, III: La Cappella Sistina dall'Ottocento ad oggi (continuazione)," *Rassegna dorica* 10.3 (January 1939), mentions other Sistine tours in the 1890s with little comment (p. 256), and indeed they are not easy to trace. See also Haböck, *Die Kastraten und ihre Gesangskunst*, p. 204.

50. The first funeral was held on August 9, 1900, per the 1911 *Encyclopædia Britannica*, s.v. "Humbert, Ranieri Carlo Emanuele Giovanni Maria Ferdinando Eugenio, King of Italy," https://en.wikisource.org/wiki/1911_Encyclop%C3%A6dia_Britannica/Humbert,_Ranieri_Carlo_Emanuele_Giovanni_Maria_Ferdinando_Eugenio,_King_of_Italy; the second was held on September 13.

A painting of the occasion by Adriano Ferraresi is housed at the Museo di Roma (Palazzo Braschi); *The funeral of King Umberto I. in the Pantheon in Rome*, https://www.akg-images.com/archive/The-funeral-of-King-Umberto-I.-in-the-Pantheon-in-Rome-2UMDHURYYPPZ.html.

51. "La divina fra le arti ha pianto anch' essa con noi, a Roma, al Pantheon presso la salma venerata del Martire, il tristissimo avvenimento che colpì la nazione italiana. Vi furono due solenni funerali. Per il primo, il Ministero della Pubblica Istruzione chiamò il maestro Mascagni, che seppe in questa dolorosa circostanza mostrarsi all'altezza del nome suo, dandoci nuova prova del suo così vario ingegno. . . .

Mirabile la direzione mascagniana, e mirabile l'esecuzione della centosessanta voci, tra cui le migliori del nostro conservatorio musicale.

Il secondo funerale, nel *trigesimo*, fu altra degna commemorazione del nostro povero Re defunto. Vi presero parte le stesse messe corali, tra cui *i sopranisti* della Cappella Sistina, compreso il celebre Moreschi. Questa volta la direzione venne affidata al maestro Stanislao Falchi (il noto autore del *Trillo del Diavolo*), che diresse anch'egli in modo magnifico.

Il programma era fatto da cinque parti d'una *Messa* di autore ignoto del XVI secolo (scuola di Palestrina), del *Dies irae* del Pitoni, del *Peccavimus* di Palestrina e del Libera del Falchi stesso, scritta anche questa pei funerali di Vittorio Emanuele II.

Il maestro Alessandro Vessella, direttore della Banda Comunale, compose in quei giorni di dolore una elaborate *Marcia funebre*." A. Roberto Colombo, "Corrispondenze da Roma," *La nuova musica*, year 5, 2.57 (September 1900), pp. 164–65. Haböck, *Die Kastraten und ihre Gesangskunst*, pp. 206–207, states he sang for the funerals of both Vittore Emanuele II (died 1878) and Umberto I.

52. About the items, Giulio's will states: "La spilla e l'orologio del Re Umberto e Vittorio Emanuele III Re d'Italia con le relative lettere d'accompagno andranno sempre conservati con la maggior cura." Archivio Notarile di Roma, notaio Alfredo de Martino, Repertorio no. 15247, Raccolta no. 7582, holograph will of Giulio Moreschi, 23 August 1954, with official manuscript copy. See Gabrielli, "Appendice: Riassunto delle conversazioni sulla storia delle Cappelle musicali romane. III. La Cappella Sistina dall'Ottocento ad oggi," p. 256, who writes: "Nel 1900, con speciale permesso del Santo Sede cantò al Pantheon per i funerali di Re Umberto I. l'attuale Monarca lo rimeritò con un regale orologio e catena d'oro." Gabrielli states that the gift given was a gold watch and chain, whereas Giulio's will—correctly, no doubt—calls it a watch and pin.

53. Before rules about celibacy and prohibitions on marriage were lifted for Sistine lay singers by the new constitution of 1891, a number of Sistine singers made declarations (now in Sistine diaries) of not being married. After 1891, the change was still far from radical, for being able to generate continued to be a requirement for sex and marriage. Technically, the new rules therefore applied only to those capable of procreation, but the obligation of celibacy was revoked somewhat coyly, by noting that it was only "for those who are not otherwise constrained, whether by castration or membership in the priesthood." What was indeed radical in the 1891 constitution was secularizing the entire, previously clerical nature of the office of papal singer by allowing nonclerical dress when off duty, freeing singers from taking the *prima tonsura* (shaving of the top of the head as a sign of initiation), and allowing those who were not priests to engage in other professions with papal approval. It seems the change of rules gave Moreschi an opening to do what many before him had wanted to, but that he, as part of a general drift toward a more bourgeois, secular model of manhood, was able to do. Notably, notwithstanding the semiprivate ceremony, his marriage was widely recognized by others. A letter of January 1, 1897, to Moreschi from a G. Felice sends regards to Moreschi's wife (Moreschi-Fellini Archive), and Luigi Gentili uses the word "marita" in the diary entry cited in note 13 above.

Prior to the 1891 constitution, singers in the papal chapel were also not allowed to vote in political elections. A letter from 1890 addressed to the "Beatissimo Padre" by all the Sistine singers addresses the fact of a singer having voted in political elections and uniformly condemns it: "I sottoscritti Cappellani Cantori Pontifici prostrati ai Piedi della Santità Vostra umilmente espongono essere venuto a loro cognizione che un qualcuno di essi abbia recato grave dispiacere alla Santità Vostra trasgredendo il divieto di non prender parte alle elezioni politiche." Diario della Cappella Pontificia compilato da Sebastianelli Vincenzo, segretario puntatore del R. Collegio dei Capellani Cantori nell'anno del Signore 1890 del Pontificato di Leone XIII," no. 292, fol. 31.

54. See in Chapter 4 below the full text of the marriage certificate, preserved in the Archivio di Stato di Roma, Documenti di Stato Civile, Matrimoni, 1896, vol. 1, part 2, series B, no. 13, p. 10.

55. Maria Rita Fellini, *In viaggio con lo zio*, unpublished typescript.

56. "L'anno milleottocentottantadue questo dì 12 maggio alle ore una pomeridiana in Roma nell'Ufficio di Stato Civile della seconda Regione posto in Via dell'Archetto avanti a me Cavalier Augusto Castellani Consigliere di questo municipio delegato ad Ufficiale di Stato Civile con atto del cinque maggio corrente anno deliberatamente approvato è comparso il Signor Pietro Rinaldi di Giacomo di anni ventisei scalpellino nato e domiciliato in Roma il quale mi dichiara che alle ore un quarto antimeridiane del dì otto corrente mese nel suo domicilio in via Monterone numero ottantadue piano terzo Rione Sant'Eustachio la propria moglie signora Giulia Ferrucci fu Giovanni di anni ventuno seco convivente ha dato alla luce un neonato di sesso femminile cui vengono posti i nomi di Guendalina, Emma, Maria. La nascita e il sesso furono accertati dal Medico Municipale avendo dispensato dalla presentazione del neonato per ragioni igieniche. A questa dichiarazione sono testimoni i Signori Giuseppe Monico di anni quarantadue, cocchiere e Gaetano Frigieri di anni venticinque, domestico, qui residente. L'atto presente previa lettura accettato un testimone illetterato è stato dai suddetti e da me firmato. A quanto segue si annulli la parola incapellata e si legga Giugno. Postilla approvata [firme]. L'Ufficiale di Stato Civile Augusto Castellani." Archivio di Stato di Roma, Documenti di Stato civile, Nati, 1872, vol. 1, series D, no. 91, pp. 29–30.

57. For the contract see Chapter. 3, note 54 below.

58. See De Salvo Fattor, *La cappella musicale pontificia nel Novecento*, pp. 21–24. While castrati were not admitted to the Cantoria, the falsettists apparently continued to be present among the high voices with the job of acting as a "guide" to the boys.

59. See note 13 above.

60. The initial release was entitled *Alessandro Moreschi: The Complete Recordings* (Sparrows Green, East Sussex: Opal; distributed by Qualiton Imports, Long Island City, NY, 1984), with standard publisher no. 9823 for both CD and LP. Opal was a division of Pavilion Records. The title *Alessandro Moreschi, the Last Castrato: Complete Vatican Recordings* seems to date principally from the 1987 reissue and continue into later issues, although some WorldCat records list that title for 1984 issues. More recently, a German company used a similar title, *Alessandro Moreschi, der letzte Kastrat* (Hamburg: Membran Music, 2009), standard publisher no. 232596.

61. *Alessandro Moreschi: Soprano Castrato (1858–22): Complete Gramophone Co. Recordings, 1902–1904* (Berlin: Truesound Transfers, 2004).

62. See the *Oxford English Dictionary Online*, s.v. "endure": "Etymology: < Old French *endure-r* to make hard, to endure, = Provençal *endurar* , Italian *indurare* < Latin *indūrāre*, < *in-* (see in- prefix1) + *dūrāre* to harden, to endure, < *dūrus* hard." The meanings of "endure" are given there as "1. 1. To indurate, harden. Hence *figurative* to make callous or indifferent. Also in good sense: to make sturdy or robust, to strengthen." And "2. To last; to suffer continuously. . . . " a. *intransitive*. To last, continue in existence. Also, to persist, 'hold out' in any action, etc. †Formerly also, to continue in a certain state or condition, remain in a certain place (with complement expressing the state or place)."

63. The full contemporaneous title of the *cappella papale* was Collegio dei Cappellani Cantori della Cappella Pontificia, called in later times Cappella Pontificia. I mostly use Cappella Sistina or Sistine Chapel as the name widely known in the Anglophone musicological world from the work of Franz Xaver Haberl (1840–1910) and later Josephus [José] M. Llorens, most signally, Franz Xaver Haberl, et al., *Giovanni Pierluigi da Palestrina: Werke*, 33 vols. (Leipzig: Breitkopf & Härtel, 1863–1907); Franz Xaver Haberl, "Bibliographischer und thematischer Musikkatalog des päpstlichen Kapellarchivs im Vatikan zu Rom," supplements to *Monatshefte für Musikgeschichte* 19 (1887); and "Die römische Schola Cantorum und die päpstlichen Kapellsänger bis zur Mitte des 16. Jahrhunderts," *Vierteljahrschrift für Musikwissenschaft* 3 (1887), pp. 189–296, as well as Josephus M. Llorens, *Capellae Sixtinae codices, musicis notis instructi sive manu scripti sive praelo excussi* (Vatican City: Biblioteca Apostolica Vaticana, 1960), and Josephus M. Llorens, *Le opere musicali della Cappella Giulia*, vol. 1: *Manoscritti e edizioni fino al '700* (Vatican City: Biblioteca Apostolica Vaticana, 1971).

64. On the Chinese case during the first half of Qing rule, 1644–1800, see Norman

A. Kutcher, *Eunuch and Emperor in the Great Age of Qing Rule* (Oakland: University of California Press, 2018).

65. Buning, "Alessandro Moreschi and the Castrato Voice," p. 61.

66. Buning, in ibid., p. 61, cites the remark from John Rosselli, "The Castrati as a Professional Group and as a Social Phenomenon, 1550–1850," *Acta musicologica* 60 (1988), p. 150.

67. Emily Wilbourne, "The Queer History of the Castrato," in Fred Everett Maus and Sheila Whiteley, eds., *The Oxford Handbook of Music and Queerness*, pp. 441–54, September 10, 2018, https://doi.org/10.1093/oxfordhb/9780199793525.013.14.

68. I elaborate on this sacrificial aspect and the rhetorical and anthropological dimensions of evasive explanations in Feldman, *The Castrato*, preface and chapter 1, "Of Strange Births and Comic Kin."

69. Saidiya Hartman, "The Belly of the World: A Note on Black Women's Labors," *Souls: A Critical Journal of Black Politics, Culture, and Society* 18.1 (2016), pp. 166–73. I expand on the notion that castrations in this Italian and more widely European context were matters of male generation in *The Castrato*, chapter 2, "The Man Who Pretended to Be Who He Was: A Tale of Reproduction." A disability gloss informs Katherine Crawford's analysis of eunuchs and castrates in *Eunuchs and Castrati: Disability and Normativity in Early Modern Europe* (New York: Routledge, 2019).

70. See Peter Browe, *Zur Geschichte der Entmannung: Eine religions- und rechtsgeschichtliche Studie* (Breslau: Müller & Seiffert, 1936), pp. 88–89; and Buning, "Alessandro Moreschi and the Castrato Voice," pp. 69–70, and on vocal registers, in particular, chapter 3. Male singers who took alto parts in the nineteenth century used a combination of head and chest, whether designated "falsettists" or high tenors, also because the alto parts were on the low side.

71. Buning, "Alessandro Moreschi and the Castrato Voice," p. 67.

72. I adapt the translation in ibid., p. 66, whose translation principles are given on p. 66 n. 1. The bull, he notes, was never canonically revised. For further on the brief see Giuseppe Gerbino, "The Quest for the Soprano Voice: Castrati in Sixteenth-Century Italy," *Studi musicali* 32.2 (2004), pp. 334–39.

73. See Frandsen, "'Eunuchi conjugium,'" n. 29.

74. Of course women were not permitted to sing in church anywhere on Italian soil. Despite having read many Roman and papal documents concerning the nineteenth- and early twentieth-century papal chapel history, I remain much indebted to Kantner and

Pachovsky, *La cappella musicale pontificia nell'Ottocento*, and De Salvo Fattor, *La cappella musicale pontificia nel Novecento*, for that history as a whole.

75. The proscription was made explicit in a British version of the Napoleonic code: "Every person, guilty of the crime of castration, shall undergo the penalty of perpetual hard labor. If death has resulted therefrom, before the expiration of forty days, next after the crime, the criminal shall undergo the penalty of death." See *The Penal Code of France, translated into English, with a Preliminary Dissertation and Notes* (London: H. Butterworth, and Baldwin, Craddock, and Joy, 1819), book 3, section 2, article 316.

76. Kantner and Pachovsky, *La cappella musicale pontificia nell'Ottocento*, p. 24 and see n. 56, quoted from the Diarii Sistini, p. 221. Pachovsky notes that even during the sanctification of May 24, 1807, two tenors were chosen "by sovereign order," rather than two sopranos. On the banning in 1797 of "the infamous castrati" in occupied Brescia by the provisional democratic government, see Andrea Chegai, *L'esilio di Metastasio: Forme e riforme dello spettacolo d'opera fra Sette e Ottocento* (Florence: Le lettere, 1998), p. 108. I discuss the gradual process during which castrati came to be reviled in light of French Enlightenment discourse, especially in the latter half of the eighteenth century, in *The Castrato*, chapter. 5, "Cold Man, Money Man, Big Man Too."

77. The secretary of state was Ercole Consalvi, as quoted in Kantner and Pachovsky, *La cappella musicale pontificia nell'Ottocento*, p. 24.

78. Angela Pachovsky points out as much. Ibid., p. 24. Nonetheless, there were many analogues in opera; see my "Denaturing the Castrato," *Opera Quarterly* 24.3–4 (2008), pp. 178–99, and *The Castrato*, chapter 5.

79. Kantner and Pachovsky, *La cappella musicale pontificia nell'Ottocento*, p. 24, citing the Diarii Sistini 235 (1819), fol. 4r.

80. See Salvatore Di Giacomo, *Il conservatorio di Sant'Onofrio a Capuana e quello di S.M. della Pietà dei Turchini* (Milan: Remo Sandron, 1924).

81. In late 1828, Franz Kandler described the institution of the Pia Casa degli Orfani as a nursery for young castrati, in "État actuel de la musique à Rome," *Revue musicale* 3 (1828), p. 51, calling it "l'instituzione degl' Orfanelli."

82. Unless it's the case that surgeons accompanied agents on their scouting expeditions—we just don't know.

83. This is Buning's view, too, "Alessandro Moreschi and the Castrato Voice," pp. 96–97.

84. Gabrielli, "Appendice: Riassunto delle conversazioni sulla storia delle Cappelle

musicali romane. III. La Cappella Sistina dall'Ottocento ad oggi," p. 253: "L'ultima ammissione di sopranisti in blocco, fu quella di 1861. Inviata persona alla ricerca di questi residui di barbarie, ne furono trovati, dopo pazienti ricerche, tre, fra Alatri e Frosinone, zona che per il passato, ne aveva forniti parecchi. . . . Tutti e tre analfabeti, perchè figli di contadini, vennero condotti a Roma, e internati nell'Ospizio degli Orfani a S. Maria in Aquiro, a spese del Collegio. Si insegnò loro a leggere, a scrivere, e per la musica ed il canto fu dato loro a maestro, Gaetano Capocci."

85. A possible exception was the castration of Mustafà, whose parents, Francesco Mustafà and Petronilla Vitali, *contadini* from Sterpara, near Sellano (Perugia), seem to have taken him to Rome, where he was taught by Giovanni Matteo Tubilli, a former castrato soprano in the Cappella Giulia and Cappella Pontificia. See De Angelis, *Domenico Mustafà*, p. 8, translated in the epigraph to Chapter 4 below.

86. Haböck, *Die Kastraten und ihre Gesangskunst*, pp. 197 and 202–203. More accounts of why boys were castrated are given in Rosselli, "The Castrati as a Professional Group and as a Social Phenomenon, 1550–1850," pp. 152–56, and Feldman, *The Castrato*, chapter 1.

87. Haböck, *Die Kastraten und ihre Gesangskunst*, p. 203. "Ihm war sein Schicksal angeblich schon in der Wiege bereitet worden, indem er in einem unbewachten Augenblicke von einem Schwein angefallen wurde, welche Erzählung mir geschätzte Wiener Schriftsteller und Feuilletonist Hugo Wittmann mitteilte, der seinerzeit mit Mustafà in Rom und zur Sommerszeit in Albano persönlich viel verkehrt hatte."

88. I elaborate on this tendency in *Opera and Sovereignty: Transforming Myths in Eighteenth-Century Italy* (Chicago: University of Chicago Press, 2007), chapter 6, "Myths of Sovereignty."

89. See De Salvo Fattor, *La cappella musicale pontificia nel Novecento*, p. 210.

90. Haböck, *Die Kastraten und ihre Gesangskunst*, pp. 203–204. "Die älterer Sopranistin wurden pensioniert, nur drei—die letzten!—Salvatori, Sebastianelli und Moreschi blieben Mitglieder der Cappella Sistina und gleichzeitig der Cappella Giulia. Salvatori und Moreschi waren zu Ostern 1914, als ich drei Monate vor Ausbruch des Weltkriegs zum letztenmal in Rom war, in der Cappella Giulia noch tatig. Sebastianelli war schon damals hoch in den Sechzigern und machte nicht mehr regelmassig Chordienst. . . . Auch er war in seiner Jugend 'von einem wilden Schwein' gebissen worden." The last comment about the bite by a wild pig is repeated uncritically by De Angelis, *Domenico Mustafà*, p. 175 n 17.

91. De Angelis, *Domenico Mustafà*, pp. 7–8.

92. Haböck, *Die Kastraten und ihre Gesangskunst*, p. 197.

93. Cornell University, Legal Information Institute, UNITED STATES, Petitioner, v. Richard M. NIXON, President of the United States, et al. Richard M. NIXON, President of the United States, Petitioner, v. UNITED STATES, https://www.law.cornell.edu/supremecourt/text/418/683. Sex abuse numbers in my own state of Illinois alone are staggering; see Ruth Graham, "Sex Abuse in Catholic Church: Over 1,900 Minors Abused in Illinois, State Says," *New York Times*, May 23, 2023.

94. Kantner and Pachovsky, *La cappella musicale pontificia nell'Ottocento*, p. 25.

95. According to the Sistine Diaries, in April 1870 the Collegio chose to instruct at its expense a "young '*evirato*' *naturale* of naturally awakened talent," the sixteen-year-old Costantino Maddalena, but once the papal state was dissolved, that idea seems to have dissolved as well. Ibid., p. 25. Since the Sistine Diaries do not exist for 1899–1933 (or as late as 1935), the organization of the Collegio having fallen down considerably during that time, information is missing about some particulars. See De Salvo Fattor, *La cappella musicale pontificia nel Novecento*, p. xvii, and my thanks to the late Luciano Luciani for clarifications. (Private communication, February 7, 2016.) On Vissani, see Kantner and Pachovsky, *La cappella musicale pontificia nell'Ottocento*, p. 188, and De Salvo Fattor, *La cappella musicale pontificia nel Novecento*, p. 225.

Moreschi's activity in the Sistine Chapel is documented in the *Annuario Pontificio per l'anno 1914* (Rome: Poliglotta Vaticana, 1914), p. 413. I accessed only the volumes for 1915 and 1917. I can say that the 1916 volume lists him as a singer in the "Cappella Pontificia," whereas the 1918–1922 volumes list him as "emerito." Kantner and Pachovsky imply that Moreschi sang only at the Cappella Giulia after 1913. *La cappella musicale pontificia nell'Ottocento*, p. 168.

96. Kantner and Pachovsky, *La cappella musicale pontificia nell'Ottocento*, p. 25, suggest that by around 1902, only Salvatori, Sebastianelli, and Moreschi were active, although Cesari was singing in the Sistine Chapel until his death on March 10, 1904, and neither Pesci nor Vissani nor Meniconi had formally retired.

97. Kantner and Pachovsky give a transcription of the new constitution in ibid., pp. 198–99.

98. Ibid., article 1h, p. 199. The diary of January 1, 1898, shows nine sopranos (including the director), six contraltos, nine tenors, and eight basses, subdivided into "cappellani cantori" (religious) and "cantori pontefici" (lay).

99. Letter of January 23, 1891, quoted in De Angelis, *Domenico Mustafà*, p. 48.

100. De Angelis, *Domenico Mustafà*, p. 51.

101. Ibid.

102. These are listed in the Diario Sistina 298, fols. 35–36r. For a transcription, see Kantner and Pachovsky, *La cappella musicale pontificia nell'Ottocento*, pp. 251–52.

103. I provide the original Italian for articles 7 through 9 here—important not only because the language is sometimes ambiguous and obfuscating in a way that makes it hard to render in English, but also because it is revealing precisely in its ambiguity:

"VIIo. Delle mensili L. 100 delle quali all' art[icol]o 4o e delle altre di L. 140 delle quali all'art[icol]o 5o disporrà il maggiordomo di sua santità per il mantenimento ed educazione religiosa, letteraria e musicale di due fanciulli evirati, che dovranno poi servire nella classe dei soprani della Cappella Sistina.

VIIIo. Della educazione religiosa, letteraria e musicale dei due fanciulli sopranotati sarà responsabile il Collegio dei Cappellani Cantori e Cantori Pontificii e per esso il maestro *pro tempore*.

Resta in facoltà del Collegio affidare i detti due fanciulli o ad uno dei componenti il Collegio o ad un istituto ecclesiastico ed anche civile di Roma.

IXo. Vacato un posto di soprano nella Cappella Sistina, se uno dei due giovanetti, a giudizio del Collegio, è abile per fare parte del Collegio stesso, sarà senz'altro sostituito nel posto vacante di soprano e percipirà le L. 90 (novanta) mensili come all'art[icol]o 4o.

Se nessuno dei due giovanetti fosse giudicato abile, si provvederà al posto vacante come di consueto.

Se poi non verificassero vacanze nella classe dei soprani e intanto ambedue i giovanetti fossero abili a cantare, dovranno prestare l'opera loro a cantare in Cappella come *cantori aggiunti* percipiendo le sole L. 50 (cinquanta) che già si spendevano per ciascuno di loro e per conseguenza non si sceglieranno altri giovanetti per essere educati, fino a tanto, che i due cantori aggiunti non entrano di numero nel Collegio.

Il disposto di questa seconda parte dell'art[icol]o 9 vale ancora se uno soltanto dei giovanetti fosse riconosciuto abile ad essere *cantore aggiunto*."

Kantner and Pachovsky, *La cappella musicale pontificia nell'Ottocento*, pp. 251–52.

104. See ibid., from acts of the secretary, protocollo n. 628, November 16, 1897.

105. Mustafà's fury is recounted by De Angelis from contemporary oral reports; see the epigraph to Chapter 4 below.

106. De Angelis, *Domenico Mustafà*, p. 139.

107. Ibid., p. 62, quoting Professor Hermann Wichmann from the *Allgemeine Musik*

Zeitung, October 14, 1898, on the occasion of Mustafà's jubilee in the Sistine Chapel, which was richly celebrated. See also Kantner and Pachovsky, *La cappella musicale pontificia nell'Ottocento*, pp 49–55 for the period of Mustafà up to 1898.

108. See Feldman, *The Castrato*, pp. 122–25.

109. Haböck, *Die Kastraten und ihre Gesangskunst*, p. 203. Gabrielli had good reason to compare his compositions to his vocality and to Bernini's sculptural style: "I suoi lavori che mai volle pubblicare, assomigliano alle arti plastiche del Bernini, sono barocche, sono l'espressione più avanzata delle fioriture, delle sovrapposizioni, degli abbellimenti, sia pure tradizionali, ma portati alla forma sfacciata e teatrale." "Appendice: Riassunto delle conversazioni sulla storia delle Cappelle musicali romane. III. La Cappella Sistina dall'Ottocento ad oggi," *Rassegna dorica* 10.2 (December 1938), p. 239.

110. I share the opinion Buning expresses in "Alessandro Moreschi and the Castrato Voice," p. 98.

111. This included a rival who openly filed a *giunta* against him; Kantner and Pachovsky, *La cappella musicale pontificia nell'Ottocento* , p. 50.

112. De Angelis, *Domenico Mustafà*, p. 8.

113. For this history, see Kantner and Pachovsky, *La cappella musicale pontificia nell'Ottocento*, pp. 49–57, De Angelis, *Domenico Mustafà*, pp. 79–80 and appendix, document 6, pp. 181–85.

114. In 1881, for example, a bass named Giuseppe Brucchietti was expelled for having been married two years earlier, though he was readmitted in 1891 under the terms of the new constitution. Kantner and Pachovsky, *La cappella musicale pontificia nell'Ottocento*, p. 49 and p. 146 n. 299, DS 289 fol. 48r. Other singers submit certificates to prove that they are not married, as recorded in the papal diaries. The diary of 1891, kept by Moreschi, shows a "certificato negativo di matrimonio" dated 1881 for a singer named Carlo Girelli (?) affirming that he has not contracted a marriage in the Comune di Roma and another likewise for a tenor Giuseppe Bernardini from the same year (dated 1 June). A third, Emilio Calzanera, attested that he got married after the constitution of 1891 passed. Document of December 31, 1891.

115. See Kantner and Pachovsky, *La cappella musicale pontificia nell'Ottocento*, p. 97.

116. Some sopranos, meaning castrati, did take up positions in the period. Domenico Salvatori was moved from the alto section of the Cappella Giulia to the soprano section of the Cappella Sistina in 1877; Vincenzo Sebastianelli took up a spot in the soprano

section of the Cappella Sistina in 1879. Kantner and Pachovsky, *La cappella musicale pontificia nell'Ottocento*, p. 183.

117. Kantner and Pachovsky list all the repertories performed throughout the nineteenth century. Ibid., pp. 88–116.

118. See the account of Mario Rinaldi, *Lorenzo Perosi* (Rome: Edizioni De Santis, 1967), pp. 187–88, and for the quote, De Angelis, *Domenico Mustafà*, p. 80 n. 1. See also the interview with Mancini discussed in Chapter 3 below.

119. Pope Pius X, *Tra le sollecitudini:* Instruction on Sacred Music. *Motu proprio* promulgated by Pope Pius X on November 22, 1903, Adoremus, https://adoremus.org/1903/11/tra-le-sollecitudini.

120. The new Medicean edition began publication in 1871. Friedrich Pustet of Ratisbon had an exclusive papal privilege to publish it, but it never appeared free from an atmosphere of resistance by monastic paleographers and liturgical reformists. See Robert F. Hayburn, *Papal Legislation on Sacred Music, 95 A.D. to 1977 A.D.* (Collegeville: Liturgical Press, 1979), pp. 115–247. See also Katherine Bergeron, *Decadent Enchantments: The Revival of Gregorian Chant at Solesmes* (Berkeley: University of California Press, 1998), p. 130, for the introduction of the Solesmes usage in the midst of the 1904 Gregorian Congress in Rome; and see Chapter 3 below.

121. Pope Pius X, *Tra le sollecitudini.*

122. See Kantner and Pachovsky, *La cappella musicale pontificia nell'Ottocento*, chapters 3 and 4, on repertory and musical works.

123. Emphasis mine, with translations modified from Pope Pius X, *Tra le sollecitudini.* (See note 119 above.) The *motu proprio* went on to forbid piano, bells, cymbals, drums, and bands (only a few winds were allowed in special cases, with special consent) and to stipulate that liturgical musical numbers not take longer than the length of time required to perform liturgical actions. See Chapter 3 below.

124. The rescript was called "Urbis et Orbis": De Angelis, *Domenico Mustafà*, p. 80 n. 1; De Salvo Fattor, *La cappella musicale pontificia nel Novecento*, pp. 14–21; and see Clapton, *Moreschi and the Voice of the Castrato*, pp. 165–66 and 175–77.

125. See Zsuzsanna Domokos, "Wagner's Edition of Palestrina's *Stabat mater*," *Studia musicologica academiae scientiarum hungaricae* 47.2 (June 2006), pp. 221–32, and more broadly, Martin Geck, "Richard Wagners Beschäftigung mit geistlicher Musik während seiner Dresdner Zeit," in Matthias Herrmann, ed., *Die Dresdner Kirchenmusik im 19. und 20. Jahrhundert* (Laaber: Laaber-Verlag, 1998), pp. 121–32.

126. Daniel Albright, ed., *Modernism and Music: An Anthology of Sources* (Chicago: University of Chicago Press, 2004), p. 11.

127. See notes 95 and 96 above. In the *Annuario Pontificio per l'anno 1914* (Rome: Poliglotta Vaticana, 1914), p. 413, Moreschi is listed as a regular singer, despite having reached his jubilee in 1913. *The Annuario Pontificio* lists him only as emeritus in 1918 (p. 475) and subsequent years, through and including the year of his death.

128. The funeral register survives in the Moreschi-Fellini Archive. Passages from the *Giornale d'Italia* are quoted in translation in Clapton, *Moreschi and the Voice of the Castrato*, p. 189. The same funeral home was used for Giulio Moreschi's funeral, as shown on the funeral card for his death. Moreschi-Fellini Archive.

129. On the status of Rita with respect to the tomb, see Chapter 5 below. On Celestina Felici as buried there, see note 9 above.

CHAPTER TWO: THE SACRED VERNACULAR

The epigraph is from Federico Fellini, *Making a Film*, trans. Christopher Burton (New York: Contra Mundum Press, 2015), p. 101.

1. The spaces that make up the scene are heavily laden with the baggage of histories old and recent. As Giorgio Biancorosso notes, in mapping the opening minutes of *La dolce vita*, Fellini bypasses entirely the "monumental, self-aggrandizing interventions" of Mussolini, namely, the via della Conciliazione and the via dei Fori Imperiali. (Private communication, June 12, 2024.) On the reworking of Mussolini's "'oceanic' meetings of the Fascist faithful in Piazza Venezia" in the piazza of St. Peter's and the grandiose via della Conciliazione that extends from it, see John Pollard, *Catholicism in Modern Italy: Religion, Society, and Politics Since 1861* (London: Routledge, 2008), p. 125.

2. Alessandro Carrera, *Fellini's Eternal Rome: Paganism and Christianity in the Films of Federico Fellini* (London: Bloomsbury Academic, 2019), chapter 3 and p. 39.

3. M. Thomas Van Order, *Listening to Fellini: Music and Meaning in Black and White* (Madison: Fairleigh Dickinson University Press, 2009), p. 213.

4. The term "paparazzi" was birthed from the film.

5. See, too, the fierce blimp of a bedridden mother in *Roma* (1972), the *tabacchaia* in *Amarcord* (1973), the impish clown in *La voce della luna* (1990), and other such figures too numerous to count.

6. Carrera calls her a female pope (*Fellini's Eternal Rome*, p. 40). The dress was actually an invention of the time, a "pretino" as worn by Ava Gardner, as well; see The

Editors, "Fellini and Fashion, a Two-Way Street: An Interview with Gianluca Lo Vetro," in Franke Burke, Marguerite Waller, and Marita Gubareva, eds., *A Companion to Federico Fellini* (Chichester: Wiley Blackwell, 2020), pp. 154–55.

7. Carrera, *Fellini's Eternal Rome*, pp. 40–41.

8. Carrera, ibid., p. 143, compares this to the capture of the moon in Fellini's *Voce della luna*. Not unimportantly, the miracle scene, too, had an antecedent in real life. See Tullio Kezich, *Federico Fellini: His Life and Work* (New York: Faber & Faber, 2006), p. 201.

9. See also *La strada* (1954) and the Divino Amore scene in *Le Notte di Cabiria / Nights of Cabiria* (1957). Giorgio Biancorosso notes "more than a hint of mise-en-abyme in these sequences, culminating in *8 ½*" and points to Carmelo Bene's critique in "Carmelo Bene contro il cinema, Fellini, Pasolini regista e il '68," *Birdmen Magazine*," https://www.youtube.com/watch?v=UY1bFZnK2pM. (Private communication, June 12, 2024.)

10. Carrera, *Fellini's Eternal Rome*, p. 43. For the boundary (or "border") figures in the film as viewed from a feminist and decolonial perspective, see the marvelous article by Marguerite Waller, "'*Il Maestro*' Dismantles the Master's House: Fellini's Undoing of Gender and Sexuality," in *A Companion to Federico Fellini*, pp. 311–23, esp. on Rita Hayworth, pp. 318–20.

11. I quote from Italo Calvino," "A Spectator's Autobiography," in Fellini, *Making a Film*, p. xliv, but my main text uses the more mellifluous and familiar English title "Autobiography of a Spectator" instead of White's "A Spectator's Autobiography."

12. Ibid., p. xli.

13. See Gianfranco Angelucci's preface, "Felliniesque: A Glimpse behind the Curtain," in *A Companion to Federico Fellini*, p. xxxiii.

14. See Jacqueline Risset's now-classic *L'incantatore: Scritti su Fellini* (Milan: Scheiwiller, 1994).

15. The idea that castrati functioned as angels and were assimilated to them has been taken up often, together with the idea that high voices can register the angelic. See, for instance, Felicia Miller-Frank, *The Mechanical Song: Women, Voice, and the Artificial in Nineteenth-Century French Narrative* (Stanford: Stanford University Press, 1995), which argues that the artificial voice of the female singer represents at once the sublime and the modern; Hubert Ortkemper, *Engel wider Willen: Die Welt der Kastraten — Eine andere Operngeschichte*, reprint edition (Munich: Deutscher Taschenbuch, 1995); Richard Somerset-Ward, *Angels and Monsters: Male and Female Sopranos in the Story of Opera, 1600–1900* (New Haven: Yale University Press, 2014); Saskia Maria Woyke,

"Die Metapher der Engelsstimmen: Beschreibungen von Frauen- und Kastratenstimmen in Venedig und Rom vor dem kulturellen Hintergrund des späten Seicento," in Saskia Maria Woyke, Anno Mungen, Stephan Mösch, and Katrin Losleben, eds., *Singstimmen: Ästhetik — Geschlecht — Vokalprofil* (Würzburg: Königshausen & Neumann, 2014), pp. 61–74; and Virginia [Ginger] Dellenbaugh, "From Earth Angel to Electric Lucifer: Castrati, Doo Wop, and the Vocoder," in Julia Merrill, ed., *Popular Music Studies Today: Proceedings of the International Association for the Study of Popular Music* (Wiesbaden: Springer, 2017), pp. 75–84. Recently, Freya Jarman has been working on cognate issues in her research on high voices. I engaged some of these ideas in *The Castrato: Reflections on Natures and Kinds* (Oakland: University of California Press, 2015), chapter 1.

16. The statue was designed by Bernini and carved in marble by Cosimo Fancelli. Bernini provided sketches for all the statues on the Ponte Sant'Angelo, but worked with a team of sculptors to execute them, at least some of those sculptors forming part of his circle. Since the statue with garment is the one that best matches the image in Fellini's film, but stands in middle of the Ponte Sant'Angelo, it seems as though Fellini had it filmed illusionistically such that viewers would imagine it standing along the bank where the heroine attempts her "suicide." The Fellini literature refers to the statue as the one holding the lance, but that description doesn't actually match the statue seen in the film. See "File:Angel Ponte Sant Angelo garment dice.jpg," Wikimedia Commons, https://commons.wikimedia.org/wiki/File:Angel_Ponte_Sant_Angelo_garment_dice.jpg, and "Roma. Ponte Sant'Angelo," https://en.wikipedia.org/wiki/Ponte_Sant%27Angelo#/media/File:%C3%81ngel._Puente_Sant'Angelo_01.JPG. My sincere thanks to Courtney Quaintance for making a site visit with me and helping me think this through.

17. As Stefania Parigi puts it in a summary of Fellinian angels, "When the white sheik descends to earth, he appears as merely one of many elements in the great ramshackle carnival that lies behind the false romanticism of the fotoromanzi." "Neorealism Masked: Fellini's Films of the 1950s," in *A Companion to Federico Fellini*, p. 49 (and see pp. 49–50).

18. Compare Sandra Milo, dressed in white on a swing in *Giulietta degli spiriti / Juliet of the Spirits* (1965), albeit with no such happy ending, cited in Jacqueline Risset, *Fellini: Le cheik blanc* (Paris: Éditions Adam Bito, 1990), p. 56 and figure 39, and the essay derived from it, Jacqueline Risset, "The White Sheik: The Annunciation Made to Federico," in Peter Bondanella and Cristina Degli Espositi, eds., *Perspectives on Federico Fellini* (New York: Macmillan, 1993), pp. 63–69.

19. I am indebted for what follows to Massimo Cacciari, *The Necessary Angel*, trans. Miguel E. Vatter (Albany: State University of New York Press, 1994); David Albert Jones, *Angels: A Very Short Introduction* (New York: Oxford University Press, 2011); and Emily Bauman, "Dreaming in Crisis: Angels and the Allegorical Imagination in Postwar America," PhD diss., University of Pittsburgh, 2003, who has shared her special insights about angels with me over the years.

20. See *The Castrato*, chapter 1.

21. Cacciari, *The Necessary Angel*, chapter 1.

22. Vera Lukomsky and Sofia Gubaidulina, "'The Eucharist in My Fantasy': Interview with Sofia Gubaidulina," *Tempo*, n.s., 206 (September 1998), p. 33.

23. Robert Anthony Buning, "Alessandro Moreschi and the Castrato Voice," MA thesis, Boston University, 1990, pp. 78–79 and 91.

24. On Mustafà's relationship to Moreschi, see Chapter 1 above.

25. Feldman, *The Castrato*, pp. 3–5. On García Márquez's story and for a reading of the racial dimension, see Vera M. Kutzinski, "The Logic of Wings: Gabriel Garcia Marquez and Afro-American Literature," *Latin American Literary Review* 13.5 (January–June 1985), pp. 133–46. My thanks to Emily Bauman for the reference. For Meluzzi, see Chapter 4 below.

26. Cacciari, *The Necessary Angel*, pp. 9–10.

27. See note 17 above.

28. Kezich, *Federico Fellini*, pp. 120–21.

29. See Risset's beautiful analysis in "The White Sheik."

30. Rivoli, married to a nightmarish mother figure he cannot do without, is a type Fellini would revisit often, including with Sordi. It bears comparison with Ernst Bernhard's analysis of the Italian male discussed in Chapter 4, here articulated by Fellini and his colleagues through careful montage.

31. See Peter Bondanella, *The Cinema of Federico Fellini* (Princeton: Princeton University Press, 1992), p. 86, on the parallels in editing and their pronounced distance from the neorealism that Fellini learned from Rossellini.

32. Jones stresses the point about angels in *Angels*, p. 28. See also p. 62 on the "ministering spirits" of angels.

33. Jones, *Angels*, p. 24.

34. Or, to step from the screen to the world, Fellini said often, and in many different ways, that his wife, Giulietta, was the essence of Christian goodness and like a

fairy to him. See below and Charlotte Chandler, *I, Fellini* (New York: Random House, 1995), pp. 43–44, 104, 159, including: "Something I have always loved about Giulietta is her unending hopefulness. She never loses it. Sometimes she lives in Fairy Tale Land, but she will fight like a knight, not like a damsel in distress, to defend the walls of Fairy Tale Land against the assaults of the marauders" (p. 43).

35. The end of *The White Sheik* invited a critical misfire on the matter by Peter Bondanella, who takes pains to point out that the published screenplay wrongly directs Wanda to gaze up at the statue of an angel and wonders why the scriptwriters, Fellini, Tullio Pinelli, and Ennio Flaiano, would designate as an angel what appears in the film as one of the 140 saints that grace the colonnade at St. Peter's. His solution is to call the textual designation a mistake and to correct the discrepancy by renaming the statue in the last frame a "saint giving his benediction." Bondanella, *The Cinema of Federico Fellini*, p. 88 n. 27.

36. A common trope of sentimental comedy and comic melodrama, the remarriage was explored by Stanley Cavell in *Pursuits of Happiness: The Hollywood Comedy of Remarriage* (Cambridge, MA: Harvard University Press, 1981).

37. As Courtney Quaintance suggested to me, the statue could well be St. Olympia, hence not a male saint, but rather a female one parallel in gender to Cabiria. See "The 140 Saints of the Colonnade" 11. St. Olympias," StPetersBasilica.Info, http://stpetersbasilica.info/Exterior/Colonnades/Saints/St%20Olympia-11/StOlympia.htm. It's hard to be certain because in the film, the image appears only fleetingly and only from the side.

38. I wonder whether Fellini would have been less amenable to immortalizing Giulio as the reappearing desk clerk in later years, since by about 1960, he had backed away from his brother. See Chapter 5 below.

39. Aldo Tassone, "From Romagna to Rome: The Voyage of a Visionary Chronicler (*Roma* and *Amarcord*)," in Peter Bondanella, ed., *Federico Fellini: Essays in Criticism* (Oxford: Oxford University Press, 1978), p. 275, and see esp. p. 270 and pp. 275–76. Extending a suggestion there by an assistant of Fellini's, Tassone says Fellini wrote the sequel to *I vitelloni* as "the trilogy of Moraldo in the city" (without that film itself): "In the ideal order, with *Roma*, *La Dolce Vita*, and *8½*, Fellini has written the continuation of *I Vitelloni*, the trilogy of Moraldo in the city" (p. 276).

40. Fausto Tozzi was slated to play Fausto, but was replaced with Franco Fabrizi. Fellini explained how he fit roles to actors (and specifically in *I vitelloni*) in "My Experiences as a Director, in *Federico Fellini: Essays in Criticism*, pp. 5–7.

41. Italo Calvino, "The Autobiography of a Spectator," in *Perspectives on Federico Fellini*, p. 26. Fellini surely agreed with this; see *Federico Fellini: Essays in Criticism*, p. 63 (also pp. 8 and 24). Kezich is explicit that the movie should not be seen as autobiographical, but he protests a bit too much. *Federico Fellini*, p. 132. Fellini himself explained its relationship to his own life with more nuance as conveyed in Chandler, *I, Fellini*, pp. 100–101.

42. The quote is prefaced with "In my early teens, I would stand with my young friends and we would study the women and speculate on who wore a brassiere and who didn't. We would position ourselves at the bicycle stand in the late afternoon, when the women came for their bicycles, so we could watch from behind with the best view as they sat on their bicycles." Ibid., p. 100.

43. Federico Fellini, *Ciò che abbiamo inventato è tutto autentico: Lettere a Tullio Pinelli*, ed. Augusto Sainati (Venice: Marsilio, 2008). Related comments are countless, e.g. in the title of the chapter "Miscellany III—'I see no dividing line between imagination and reality,'" in *Fellini on Fellini*, trans. Isabel Quigley (New York: Delacorte Press, 1974), pp. 150–58.

44. Fellini critics have debated the etymology of the Italian title at length; see Kezich, *Federico Fellini*, pp. 131–32, as well as Bondanella, *The Cinema of Federico Fellini*, pp. 89–90 (though importantly, Fellini seems to have coined the term himself). As Fellini notes, the title means something like "big veals," but with an etymological origin that may connote big eaters from a small-town bourgeois family. The American-release title *The Young and the Passionate* is totally misleading since the *vitelloni* may be too passionate about some things, but too languid and feckless about others.

As for their Catholicism and fantasy world, Germaine Greer had choice things to say in a now-classic interview with Fellini where she elides the Latin man's tenuous relationship to reality with the Italian experience of the church, again in the way of Ernst Bernhard (see Chapter 4 below): "The Latin man stays on the threshold of reality. He postpones realization to an indefinite tomorrow because he prefers the dream, the fantasy. That is the great wrong done to us by the Catholic Church and at the same time the great protection that our religion gives us. It locks us into this phase of appetency, of excitement and desire." Germain Greer, "Fellinissimo," in *Perspectives on Federico Fellini*, p. 227.

45. Innocent of where he is going, the viewer learns more, years later, from Fellini himself: "I thought of a film for this character, called *Moraldo in città*, and it should be a continuation of *I vitelloni*. It should tell of Moraldo's adventures in Rome." Quoted in *Fellini: Essays in Criticism*, p. 10 (translation lightly modified). The film was never made,

but the arc was repeated often, not just in the newlyweds' arrival in *The White Sheik* (1952), but in *La dolce vita* (the journalist who's come to Rome from the provinces), *8½* (ditto for Marcello), and *Roma* (1972, the adolescent Fellini who lands in the Roman railway station).

46. About his own marriage into the Moreschi family, word had it that Riccardo used to joke that he'd gotten hitched after singing Bellini's "Prendi l'anel ti dono" one too many times ("Take this ring I give you, which the dear beloved spirit who smiled upon our love once bore to the altar"), at least according to Kezich (*Federico Fellini*, p. 23). The aria is a delicate, high-pitched barcarolle-styled *aria di grazia* from *La sonambula*, delivered by the leading man, Elvino, as he offers his orphaned fiancée his late mother's wedding ring. See Chapter 5 below and note 58 there for Fellini's incorporation of the aria into the invitation he made for Riccardo and Alessandra's wedding.

47. See. Bondanella, *The Cinema of Federico Fellini*, p. 92. The "Ave Maria" of Schubert that Riccardo sings in *I vitelloni* is the same one he sang at the wedding of the brothers' friend, painter Rinaldo Geleng, in June 1943, and played on a small portable reed organ (a "harmonium") at Federico and Giulietta's wedding—quietly, to keep the event out of earshot of draft recruiters. See Kezich, *Federico Fellini*, pp. 50 and 73.

48. Federico Fellini, I vitelloni *e* La strada*: Soggetto e sceneggiatura de Federico Fellini, Tullio Pinelli e Ennio Flaiano* (Milan: Longanesi, 1997), p. 53.

49. Lillie de Hegermann-Lindencrone, *The Sunny Side of Diplomatic Life* (New York: Harper & Bros., 1914), pp. 118–19.

50. Chandler, *I, Fellini*, p. 23. See Kezich, *Federico Fellini*, p. 50.

51. The voice is already familiar from the film's opening, where Riccardo croons into a mic at a summertime restaurant hosting the Miss Siren beauty contest, judged by some minor starlets from the big city.

52. Edward Branigan, "The Spectator and the Film Space: Two Theories," *Screen* 22.1 (1981), pp. 72–77.

53. Chandler, *I, Fellini*, p. 101.

54. Ibid. Indeed, Moraldo became the basis for several future iterations—in addition to the sequel to *I vitelloni*, never made, the additions of two alter egos, Marcello in *La dolce vita* and Guido in *8 ½*. As Fellini said, "Marcello and Guido . . . are actually extensions of Moraldo in *I Vitelloni"* (ibid., p. 125); and later, further extending the autobiographical: "Moraldo was looking for the meaning of life as I, myself, was doing. Moraldo became Guido about the time that I understood that perhaps I wasn't going to find life's

meaning after all. It was then that the Moraldo in me disappeared, or at least hid himself, embarrassed by his naïveté" (ibid., p. 141).

Film scholars have disputed the status of Moraldo. See Brunello Rondi, *Il cinema di Fellini* (Rome: Edizioni di Bianco e nero, 1965), pp. 100–27; Zygmunt G. Baranski, "Antithesis in Fellini's *I vitelloni*," *The Italianist* 1 (1981), pp. 24–42; and Bondanella, *The Cinema of Federico Fellini*, pp. 93–98, who puzzlingly sees Moraldo as a failed figure who just escapes, with no sense of future direction or purpose.

55. Calvino, "A Spectator's Autobiography," p. xlvi (translation much modified).

56. My thanks to Tom (W. J. T.) Mitchell for awakening me to the Christlike nature of Guido's escape upward.

57. *Fellini on Fellini*, p. 57.

58. See Alberto Moravia's comment, quoted below in Chapter 4, at note 108.

59. Various English translations of the essay are available. I refer here to the version published as Pier Paolo Pasolini, "The Catholic Irrationalism of Fellini," trans. Frank Demers and Pina Demers, *Film Criticism* 9.1 (Fall 1984), pp. 63–72. The essay was originally published as "L'rrazionalismo cattolico di Fellini," *Filmcritica* 40.94 (February 1960), pp. 80–84, and is also available in translation in *Perspectives on Federico Fellini*, pp. 101–109. John David Rhodes, in "Scandalous Desecration": *Accattone* against the Neorealist City," *Framework: The Journal of Cinema and Media* 45.1 (Spring 2004), pp. 7–33, explains some of the conflict and the aesthetic divide that led to Fellini failing to provide funding for Pasolini's first film and leading to a lasting bitterness. The essay is reprinted as chapter 3 in Rhodes's *Stupendous Miserable City: Pasolini's Rome* (Minneapolis: University of Minnesota Press, 2007).

60. Pasolini, "The Catholic Irrationalism of Fellini," p. 67.

61. Ibid.

62. Demers and Demers wrongly translate "paratattici" as "parataxic," a word the *Oxford English Dictionary* defines as "Of, relating to, or designating a mode of interpersonal relationship in which projection of memories, feelings, etc., creates distorted perception or expectation of others." Pasolini's word "paratattici" instead refers to the formal properties of Fellini's camera work as "one would say speaking of literature," so the translation should be "paratactic": "Relating to or involving parataxis; coordinative" (*OED*). "Paratactic," from the noun "parataxis," means "The placing of propositions or clauses one after another, without indicating by connecting words the relation (of coordination or subordination) between them, as in *Tell me, how are you?*" (*OED*). See Pasolini's original: "Quasi sempre, all'attacco di un episodio, la macchina da presa è

in movimento, e i suoi movimenti non sono mai semplici: paratattici, come si direbbe parlando di letteratura." *Filmcritica* 40.94 (February 1960), p. 81. See also note 65 below.

63. Pasolini, "The Catholic Irrationalism of Fellini," p. 67 (emphasis mine).

64. Ibid., p. 68.

65. Pasolini has the wonderful characterization of the syntax as "subordinating and halting, with rapid, willful shudders of interjections and of simple, spoken, orderly statements." Ibid.

66. Ibid., p. 70.

67. Ibid.

68. The responses by Fellini noted here come from: "Éntretiens avec Federico Fellini," interview with Dominique Delouche, in *Les cahiers RTB, Série Télécinéma* (Brussels: Radiodiffusion Télévision Belge, 1962), in translation in *Fellini on Fellini*, pp. 56–57; the statement about Pope John XXIII comes from an interview with Lillian Ross, *New Yorker*, October 30, 1962, excerpt reproduced in *Fellini on Fellini*, p. 56.

69. Federico Fellini, *Comments on Film*, ed. Giovanni Grazzini (Fresno: California State University, 1988), pp. 88–89, and interview with Valerio Riva in *Il film* Amarcord *di Federico Fellini*, ed. Gianfranco Angelucci and Liliana Betti (Bologna: Cappelli, 1974); in English as "*Amarcord*, the Fascism Within Us: An Interview with Valerio Riva," in Fellini, *Essays in Criticism*, pp. 20–26, which contains Fellini's most famous critique of the Catholic church.

70. Pasolini, "The Catholic Irrationalism of Fellini," p. 67.

71. It's possible that Rita kept no pictures of her parents' presence at the reception that took place at the apartment, though Fabio's memory is that Riccardo took off after the wedding, whereas Alessandra came to the reception (August 30, 2022). A number of eight-by-ten-inch photos of the reception survive in the Moreschi-Fellini Archive, but none of Alessandra or Riccardo.

72. Conversation of May 23, 2015; see the longer quote given in the epigraph in Chapter 5 below.

73. Kezich, *Federico Fellini*, p. 73.

74. In English as "Letter to a Jesuit Priest," written to Dr. Charles Reinert, Swiss Jesuit and film publicist, in *Fellini on Fellini*, p. 66.

75. *Fellini on Fellini*, "Whom Do You Most Admire?" p. 142. Fellini explains there that Franzscheina is the Romagna dialect version of Franceschina.

76. Carrera, *Fellini's Eternal Rome*, p. 139.

77. Ibid., p. 45.

78. *Fellini on Fellini*, p. 54.

79. Liliana Betti, *Fellini*, trans. Joachim Neugroschel (Boston: Little, Brown, 1979), p. 71.

80. Ibid., p. 63 (translation lightly modified).

81. *In viaggio con lo zio*, chapter 12.

82. Masina became a muse for many Italians who got solutions to daily problems from the eight-year run of her column in *La Stampa* (Turin) "Risponde Giulietta Masina." Others wrote her on the weekly radio program *Lettere aperte a Giulietta Masina*, which ran for three years, addressing topics ranging from the burdens of life to love, woman problems, father/son relationships, and marital relations. See Giulietta Masina, *Il diario degli altri* (Turin: Società Editrice Internazionale, 1975).

83. "Delle voci concitate mi arrivavano dal fondo del locale, dove si trovava l'officina. Continuavo ad avanzare in quella direzione, chinandomi a guardare sotto ogni macchina, col pensiero di fare una sorpresa a Claudio, quando ebbi un tonfo al cuore! Le voci dal fondo si erano fatte più concitate, si erano alzate di tono, e in mezzo ad esse avevo riconosciuto distintamente, l'inconfondibile voce di zia Giulietta. Mi accovacciai nel tentativo di non farmi vedere. Udivo di nuovo la sua voce, quella maschile di uno sconosciuto, dei rumori metallici coprirono la conversazione, poi tutto tacque, infine le voci ripresero la conversazione in tono ancora più animato. Carponi cercai di avvicinarmi il più possibile senza farmi vedere, le voci si udivano nitide, le persone che discutevano si stavano muovendo nella mia direzione, entrando nel garage. Se la zia mi avesse visto, non avrei saputo giustificare la mia presenza in quel luogo, perciò, incurante del vestito nuovo, m'infilai sotto una vettura e restai immobile. A due macchine di distanza da me vidi avanzare i piedi di mia zia, quelli di un uomo che indossava una tuta blu, e quelli di una ragazza che calzava delle scarpe basse. Non riuscivo a distinguere altri particolari. Strisciando cercai di avvicinarmi il più possibile. Adesso riuscivo a captare interi brani della conversazione. Il tono di voce della zia Giulietta era duro, asciutto, strano per lei. Anche l'uomo davanti a lei non era da meno, anzi mi spaventai per quanto la sua voce fosse arrogante. Non era questo il modo di parlare a mia zia. La ragazza taceva. Mi avvicinai ancora un poco. Ora potevo comprendere il senso completo della discussione. La ragazza, non riuscivo a capire chi fosse, doveva in qualche modo essere una protetta della zia, che in questo momento ne stava difendendo con foga le virtù e i meriti, presentandola come una vera fortuna per l'uomo che l'avesse sposata. Provai un inaspettato

senso d'invidia per quella sconosciuta, ma dovetti ricredermi subito. L'uomo rispose con una risata sguaiata. Non riuscivo proprio a capire chi fosse quella ragazza, perché la zia non la nominava mai, ma ne parlava usando termini come "la ragazza", "questa giovane", "questa creatura", ma non pronunciava mai il suo nome. Morivo dalla curiosità, ma non potevo avvicinarmi ulteriormente. Ero certa che la ragazza fosse una protetta della zia Giulietta, molto impegnata in opere di beneficenza di vario genere, per cui in fondo non c'era molto da stupirsi, se non fosse stato per la stranezza della scena cui stavo assistendo. L'uomo continuava a usare un tono molto sprezzante ogni volta che si rivolgeva alla zia. Poi all'improvviso, una frase mi svelò di colpo tutto l'intreccio di quella discussione. La ragazza, per quanto protetta, era riuscita a farsi mettersi incinta dall'uomo con la tuta blu, sicuramente dopo avergliela tolta, pensai in uno scatto sarcastico di ostilità nei confronti della sconosciuta. L'uomo, lungi dall'assumersi le sue responsabilità, buttava la situazione sull'osceno e sul grottesco. Anzi, di più. Minacciava e chiedeva del denaro per normalizzare la situazione e sposare la ragazza. Oppure un bell'aborto. Il tono si era fatto ancora più minaccioso, la zia Giulietta ancora più dura e risoluta, la ragazza sfinita dalla tensione si perse la pipì che finì sul pavimento del garage a due metri dalla mia faccia, poi scoppiò a piangere istericamente. Doveva essere stremata dalla paura e dalla vergogna. Sinceramente non avrei voluto essere al suo posto, anche se all'inizio avevo provato invidia per lei, che in qualche modo mi rubava l'affetto della zia Giulietta. Desideravo follemente uscire dal mio nascondiglio per difendere la zia e vedere che faccia avesse quella ragazza. La litigata terminò lì e i tre uscirono dal garage. Strisciando fuori da sotto la macchina voltai lo sguardo e vidi Claudio dall'altro lato del garage, anche lui sotto un'automobile. Aveva ascoltato tutto anche lui, e con un dito sulle labbra mi stava facendo segno di tacere. L'uomo in tuta era il proprietario del garage, e Claudio era informato di tutta la vicenda. Mi sentivo piena di rabbia e di tristezza, triste per la zia Giulietta e per com'era stata trattata. Compresi allora certi suoi silenzi, la riservatezza che circondava lei e lo zio Federico, il timore di essere di continuo avvicinati da sconosciuti. Quest'ansia di riservatezza però li aveva fatto un poco allontanare anche dal resto della loro famiglia." From Maria Rita Fellini, *In viaggio con lo zio*, chapter 16.

84. "Ho continuato ad adorare senza riserva la mia famiglia, forse ho perfino idealizzato papà e mamma perche non sono vissuta con loro a tempo pieno. In questo sono diversissima da Federico, che detesta ogni tipo di obbligo a cominciare da quelli verso i parenti. Papà e mamma non mi hanno mai scaricata, sia ben chiaro. Hanno voluto semplicemente offrirmi un'apertura che i miei fratelli non hanno avuto. Per l'educazione

che mi hanno impartito, li ho sempre considerati perfetti. Le prediche in casa non le ho sentite mai. Anzi, forse mi hanno viziata, e cosi i miei fratelli. Continuavano a dirsi l'un l'altro: Giulietta sta con noi cosi poco, lasciamola fare quello che vuole. E io, stando a Roma ed essendo la sorella maggiore, sono diventata presto molto matura." From Tullio Kezich, *Gulietta Masina* (Bologna: Nuova Casa Editrice Cappelli, 1991), pp. 22–23.

85. Masina, *Il diario degli altri.*

86. On the funeral, see Salvatore De Salvo Fattor, s.v. "Moreschi, Alessandro Nilo Angelo," *Dizionario biografico degli Italiani*, vol. 76 (2012), https://www.treccani.it/enciclopedia/alessandro-nilo-angelo-moreschi_(Dizionario-Biografico)/?search=MORESCHI%2C%20Alessandro%20Nilo%20Angelo%2F.

87. Susan Handelman, "Walter Benjamin and the Angel of History," *Cross Currents* 41.3 (Fall 1991), p. 346.

88. Lesley Stern, *Diary of a Detour* (Durham: Duke University Press, 2020), p. 14.

89. Freya Jarman, "The Voice of an Angel? The Unfillable Vocal Gap Between the Divine and the Mundane," presented at the conference "Vicarious Vocalities, Simulated Songs," hosted online by University of Portsmouth, September 2020.

90. See Feldman, *The Castrato*, preface.

91. Jarman, "The Voice of an Angel?," traces the negative valence of high male voices, manifested in the operas of Richard Wagner in the characters of Klingsor (*Parsifal*), for which Mustafà was approached, Beckmesser (*Die Meistersinger von Nürnberg*), and Albrecht (*Das Ring des Nibelungen*), figures who were often elided with that of the Jew, who "creaks, squeaks, and buzzes, and breaks." See also David J. Levin, "The Gesamtkunstwerk and Its Discontents: The Wounded Voice In (and Around) Alexander von Zemlinsky's *The Dwarf*," on the dwarf in Alexander von Zemlinsky's *Der Zwerg* (Cologne, 1922), with libretto by Georg C. Klaren, in Martha Feldman and Judith T. Zeitlin, eds., *The Voice as Something More: Essays Toward Materiality* (Chicago: University of Chicago Press, 2019), pp 209–26.

92. The word in the original is *lenocinio*, meaning cheap tricks or procurement (as in prostitution).

93. Quoted in Luigi Devoti, "Alessandro Moreschi detto 'l'angelo di Roma,'" in Renato Lefevbre and Arnaldo Morelli, eds., *Musica e musicisti nel Lazio* (Rome: Gruppo Culturale di Roma e del Lazio F.ll Polombi Editori, 1985), p. 466.

94. The gloss grounds the anecdotal book by Somerset-Ward, *Angels and Monsters.*

95. Devoti, "Alessandro Moreschi detto 'l'angelo di Roma,'" pp. 472–73.

96. Feldman, *The Castrato*, pp. 3–5.

97. Franz Haböck, *Die Kastraten und ihre Gesangskunst: Eine gesangsphysiologische, kultur- und musikhistorische Studie*, ed. Martina Haböck (Berlin: Deutsche Verlags-Anstalt Stuttgart), pp. 197 and 203.

98. Nicholas Clapton, *Moreschi and the Voice of the Castrato* (London: Haus Books, 2008), pp. 58 and 61.

99. Ibid., p. 59.

100. My presumptions here differ from those voiced by Clapton in *Moreschi and the Voice of the Castrato*, pp. 60–62 and 75, and Devoti in "Alessandro Moreschi detto "l'angelo di Roma," pp. 467–68, who thought Don Pietro Moreschi must have performed the operation. Generally speaking, I tend toward the view of Buning, "Alessandro Moreschi and the Castrato Voice," p. 110, who suspected surgeries were often performed at the Pia Casa degli Orfani a S. Maria in Aquiro (the Ospizio di S. Maria in Aquiro), although evidence is highly mixed and obscure for either argument. The French-style legal code imposed after the fall of Rome in 1870 made castration formally illegal, but since the aspiration to "find" more castrated boys was still blatantly discussed within the Collegio in 1896–1897, discussions that were officially recorded, one has to think backward in time and infer that castrations could still have been masterminded and even carried out in Rome during the first two-thirds of the nineteenth century (see Chapter 1). Giovanni Cesari was placed there by country parents from Frosinone at age nine (Diario Sistino 276, fol. 48v and Diario Sistino 267, fol. 23r); Giuseppe Ritarossi (1841–1902) was placed there by country parents from Alatri at age eleven (Diario Sistino 276, fol. 47r); and Giosafat Anselmo Vissani (born 1841) was placed by his country parents from Castelfranco in a different orphanage, the Oszpizio di Termini, and at age twelve was transferred to S. Maria in Aquiro. (See Clapton, *Alessandro Moreschi and the Voice of the Castrato*, p. 70, who thinks boys were transferred to Rome at an older age.) All these are also documented in Leopold M. Kantner and Angela Pachovsky, *La cappella musicale pontificia nell'Ottocento* (Rome: Hortus Musicus, 1998), pp. 150, 181, 188. What seems quite possible, then, is that "celibate" priest-musicians ensured the "sacrifices" of boys, participating in this way in male-on-male sacrificial practices, and did so either without the knowledge of the natal parents or with some turn-the-other-cheek, barely tacit form of their consent.

101. The scrapbook remains in the Moreschi-Fellini collection.

102. Burial with other papal singers at Chiesa di Santa Maria in Valicella was probably

impossible because it was more than full by the mid-nineteenth century, but it seems highly likely Moreschi would have chosen a family tomb in any case, given the other strategic pieces of family making he pursued prior to 1900.

103. Agamben, *Homo Sacer: Sovereign Power and Bare Life*, trans. Daniel Heller-Roazen (Stanford: Stanford University Press, 1998), pp. 71–72.

104. Martha Feldman, *Opera and Sovereignty: Transforming Myths in Eighteenth-Century Italy* (Chicago: University of Chicago Press, 2007), esp. chapters. 6 and 8.

105. Giorgio Agamben, *The Open: Man and Animal*, trans. Kevin Attell (Stanford: Stanford University Press, 2004), p. 36.

106. Ibid., p. 37.

107. A keen analysis along these lines, preceding Agamben's, but with rich reflections on relations between the body, eating, capital consumption, money, antisemitism, pigs, and other animals, is Jud Newborn's "Work Makes Free: The Hidden Cultural Meanings of the Holocaust," 4 vols., PhD diss., Department of Anthropology, University of Chicago, 1994.

108. On the continuities, see Uri Erman, "The Castrato, the Jew, and the Prima Donna: British Singers in the Public Discourse, 1760–1830," PhD diss., Hebrew University of Jerusalem, 2019, and Devon J. Borowski, "Navigating Voices: Song, History, and Humanity in the British Imperial Project, 1770–1836," PhD diss., University of Chicago, 2023, chapter 4, available at https://knowledge.uchicago.edu/record/14504?v=pdf.

109. Agamben, *The Open*, p. 38. For further on the Jew/castrato adjacency, see Uri Erman, "The Operatic Voice of Leoni the Jew: Between the Synagogue and the Theater in Late Georgian Britain," *Journal of British Studies* 56.2 (2017), pp. 295–321, esp. pp. 309–10. Erman's *Made to Sing: Opera, Gender, and National Identity in Britain, 1760–1830* (Oxford University Press, forthcoming) will make an important intervention here.

110. Accounts are numerous. A succinct one appears in Christopher Duggan, "Politics in the Era of Depretis and Crispi, 1870–96," in John A. Davis, ed., *Italy in the Nineteenth Century, 1796–1900* (Oxford: Oxford University Press, 2000), pp. 154–58.

111. See Adrian Lyttelton, ed., *Liberal and Fascist Italy* (Oxford: Oxford University Press, 2002), and Pollard, *Catholicism in Modern Italy.*

112. Martha Feldman, "Castrato/Trans," forthcoming in Martha Feldman, Bonnie Gordon, and Kara Keeling, eds., *Errant Voices: Performances beyond Measure* (in preparation).

113. But see also the canny reading by Stefan Jonsson, *A Brief History of the Masses: Three Revolutions* (New York: Columbia University Press, 2008), chapter 30, "Saints,"

which situates Agamben's theories in relation to challenges to democracy also taken up by Jacques Derrida.

114. Bonnie Gordon, *Voice Machines: The Castrato, the Cat Piano, and Other Strange Sounds* (Chicago: University of Chicago Press, 2023), chapter 7, and Serena Guarracino, "Voci da sud: La voce castrata e la dislocazione dello sguardo," in Luigi Cazzato, ed., *Orizzonte Sud: Sguardi, prospettive, studi multidisciplinari su mezzogiorno, mediterraneo e sud globale* (Nardò: Salento Books, 2010), pp. 293–304; in English as "Voices from the South: Music, Castration, and the Displacement of the Eye," in Luigi Cazzato, ed., *Anglo-Southern Relations: From Deculturation to Transculturation* (Nardò: Salento Books, 2012), pp. 40–51.

CHAPTER THREE: HAUNTING VOICES

The epigraphs are from Alessandro Gabrielli, "Appendice: Riassunto delle conversazioni sulla storia delle cappelle musicali romane. III. La Cappella Sistina dall'Ottocento ad oggi," *Rassegna dorica* (January 1939), p. 255 ("White voices" (*voci bianche*) is the Italian way of speaking of male trebles, used for boys and high-voiced men), and Walter Benjamin, "The Work of Art in the Age of Its Technological Reproducibility: Second Version," trans. Edmund Jephcott and Harry Zohn, in *The Work of Art in the Age of Its Technological Reproducibility, and Other Writings on Media*, ed. Michael W. Jennings, Brigid Doherty, and Thomas Y. Levin (Cambridge, MA: Belknap Press of Harvard University Press, 2008), p. 3, https://monoskop.org/images/6/6d/Benjamin_Walter_1936_2008_The_Work_of_Art_in_the_Age_of_Its_Technological_Reproducibility_Second_Version.pdf.

1. J. Q. Davies, *Romantic Anatomies of Performance* (Berkeley: University of California Press, 2014), chapter 1, and Naomi André, *Voicing Gender: Castrati, Travesti, and the Second Woman in Early-Nineteenth-Century Italian Opera* (Bloomington: Indiana University Press, 2006), chapter 2.

2. See Edmond Michotte, *Richard Wagner's Visit to Rossini (Paris, 1860) and An Evening at Rossini's in Beau-Sejour (Passy), 1858*, trans. Herbert Weinstock (Chicago: University of Chicago Press, 1968), pp. 73–74 (paraphrasing Rossini's remarks to Wagner on a visit Wagner made to Rossini in 1860), and pp. 109–10. Both were originally published by Michotte in 1906. For Michotte's detailed notes on these visits, see Weinstock's preface to *Richard Wagner's Visit to Rossini*, pp. v–x.

3. Jessica Peritz, who has read deeply in Lee's extensive oeuvre, assures me that Lee never called them "castrati." (Private communication, July 11, 2021.) Lee's avoidance is

unsurprising inasmuch as it follows Italian practice that extends through the twentieth century and beyond. See Martha Feldman, "*L'evirato castrato* and Other Castrato Conundra," in Andrea Chegai and Simone Caputo, eds.,"*Tu Duca, Tu Segnore e Tu Maestro*": *Studi in onore di Franco Piperno* (Rome: Neoclassica, 2023), pp. 423–32.

4. On Lee's feelings about Pacchierotti, see Jessica Gabriel Peritz, "The Castrato Remains—or, Galvanizing the Corpse of Musical Style," *Journal of Musicology* 39.3 (2022), pp. 371–403, and Bonnie Gordon, *Voice Machines: The Castrato, the Cat Piano, and Other Strange Sounds* (Chicago: University of Chicago Press, 2023), pp. 290–94, both of which attend to the old tousled gardens that so stimulated Lee's imagination. See also Anthony Teets's attention to haunting in "Singing Things: The Castrato in Vernon Lee's Biography of a 'Culture-Ghost,'" *The Sibyl, A Journal of Vernon Lee Studies*, May 5, 2018, https://thesibylblog.com/singing-things-the-castrato-in-vernon-lees-biography-of-a-culture-ghost-by-anthony-teets.

5. See Peter Gunn's *Vernon Lee: Violet Paget, 1856–1935* (London: Oxford University Press, 1964), pp. 37–38, itself quoting Lee's *Juvenilia: Being a Second Series of Essays on Sundry Aesthetical Questions* (Boston: Roberts Brothers, 1887), pp. 414–16. I learned of the quote from Peritz, who quoted part of it in "Empathy for the Castrato," paper given at the quinquennial meeting of the International Musicological Society, Athens, Greece, August 26, 2022. That work is now developing as part of her book *Opera and the Limits of History* (in preparation), chapter 1, "Affective History: The Queer Musical Temporality of Vernon Lee," and part of it is quoted in Peritz's "Overhearing (Music) History with Vernon Lee."

6. Peritz, "Overhearing (Music) History with Vernon Lee." Peritz shrewdly points out that in recounting this anecdote, Lee puts her own theory of affective memory on display.

7. Gordon, *Voice Machines*, "Epilogue."

8. He was also a member of the Royal Austrian Music-Pedagogical Association (Österreichischen musikpädagogischen Reichsverbands).

9. Franz Haböck, *Die Gesangskunst der Kastraten*, vol. 1, *A, Die Kunst des Cavaliere Carlo Broschi Farinelli. B, Farinellis berümte Arien* (Vienna: Universal, 1923), and *Die Kastraten und ihre Gesangskunst, eine gesangsphysiologische, kultur- und musik- historische Studie* (Stuttgart: Deutsche Verlsags-Anstalt, 1927).

10. Haböck, *Die Kastraten und ihre Gesangskunst*, p. 207. This was reported in the Roman *La tribuna* on December 28, 1902; see Alberto De Angelis, *Domenico Mustafà: La*

Cappella Sistina e la Società Musicale Romana (Bologna: N. Zanichelli, 1926), p. 80 n. 1. Haböck wrote on singing physiology in *Die physiologischen Grundlagen der altitalienischen Gesangschule* (Berlin: Schuster & Löffler, 1909).

11. On the castrato's *messa di voce*, see Martha Feldman, *The Castrato: Reflections on Natures and Kinds* (Oakland: University of California Press, 2015), pp. 112–16.

12. Peritz, "The Castrato Remains."

13. The full passage reads as follows: "Seit Jahren erstreckt sich aber der Umfang seiner Stimme nur mehr von a bis g. Die Tone im Zentrum der Stimme zwischen f und d waren 1914 noch von einer Schönheit und Wucht, die man sich kaum vorstellen kann, wenn man sie nicht gehört hat. Die Höhe vom e' an war etwas unsicher und weniger klangschön, si ging (meist schon bei d') mit einem leisen Bruch in die reine Kopfstimme über, welch letztere schwächer und flachernd schien. Alle meine Gewährsmänner versicherten, Moreschis Stimme sei in seiner Glanzzeit von einer Schönheit und Stärke gewesen, die sie niemals bei einer Frauen- oder Männerstimme gehört hätten. Die richtige Beweglichkeit des Koloraturgesanges habe er aber nie besessen, auch mangelte ihm der Triller, Hingegen war sein Schwellton von jeher unvergleichlich." (For years, however, the range of his voice has only extended from a to g''. In 1914, the notes in the center of the voice between f' and d' were still of a beauty and power that one can hardly imagine if one has not heard them. The high notes from e'' onward were somewhat uncertain and less beautiful; they moved (usually at d), with a slight break, into pure head voice, which seemed weaker and flatter. All my informants assured me that in its heyday, Moreschi's voice was of a beauty and strength that they had never heard in a female or male voice. However, he never had the right flexibility for coloratura singing, nor did he have a trill. On the other hand, his swell was always incomparable.) Haböck, *Die Kastraten und ihre Gesangskunst*, p. 208.

14. Tom Gunning, "Terror and the Mythology of the Technological Voice," in Martha Feldman and Judith T. Zeitlin, eds., *The Voice as Something More: Essays Toward Materiality* (Chicago: University of Chicago Press, 2019), pp. 325–35.

15. Michel Chion, *The Voice in Cinema*, trans. Claudia Gorbman (New York: Columbia University Press, 1999); Steven Connor, *Dumbstruck: A Cultural History of Ventriloquism* (New York: Oxford University Press, 2000); Mladen Dolar, *A Voice and Nothing More* (Cambridge, MA: MIT Press, 2006); and Brian Kane, *Sound Unseen: Acousmatic Sound in Theory and Practice* (New York: Oxford University Press, 2014). See also Alexander G. Weheliye, *Phonographies: Grooves in Sonic Afro-Modernity* (Durham: Duke University Press, 2005), and Giorgio Biancorosso, *Situated Listening: The Sound of Absorption in*

Classical Cinema (New York: Oxford University Press, 2016), for fascinating insights on the relationships between sound, source, voicer, and listener.

16. Much has been written about early sound recording as a means to preserve the voices of dying speakers, which in turn promotes the idea of sound as an archive. Very early recordings were themselves ephemeral, as well, but by 1901–1902 had become far less so because of the advent of flat shellac records, pioneered as early as 1898. See "The History of 78 RPM Recordings," Irving S. Gilmore Library, Yale University, https://web.library.yale.edu/cataloging/music/historyof78rpms.

17. Jonathan Sterne, *The Audible Past: Cultural Origins of Sound Reproduction* (Durham: Duke University Press, 2003), p. 26, and see p. 295. As early as about 1836, an Italian pamphlet was given the title *Imbalsamazione* (Embalming)—an extract from the *Esculapio napolitano* 30.111 (March 1836). See also Dario Campani, *Nuovo processo di imbalsamazione* (Pisa: Tip. Del Folchetto, 1889).

18. Sterne, *The Audible Past*, p. 290, and see Friedrich Kittler's classic *Gramophone, Film, Typewriter*, trans. Geoffrey Winthrop-Young and Michael Wutz (Stanford: Stanford University Press, 1999).

19. Quoted in Sterne, *The Audible Past*, p. 308, from "Voices of the Dead," *Phonoscope* 1.1 (November 15, 1896), p. 1. On these issues, see also John M. Picker, *Victorian Soundscapes* (New York: Oxford University Press, 2003).

20. It did do so in advertisements, however, for example, for the 1904 chants and other sacred music: "By a happy thought the Gramophone Company has determined that the triumphs of voice-reproduction achieved for the Concert Room and the Council Chamber should be accomplished for the Church. Faithful 'Records' of the Music performed during the International Gregorian Congress held in Rome on the occasion of the Thirteenth Centenary of St. Gregory the Great, 1904, have been taken with the full approval and assistance of the Holy Gather and of the highest musical authorities." Quoted in Katherine Bergeron, *Decadent Enchantments: The Revival of Gregorian Chant at Solesmes* (Berkeley: University of California Press, 1998), p. 133.

21. Nor is the difference simply that between preelectrical and microphonic phonography, a difference that may also in some respects be exaggerated.

22. "Tutte le fotografie degli artisti esposte nel mio studio, gli autografi del Maestro Perosi che sono in una cartella della libreria dovranno essere sempre esposti a eterna gloria di mio padre Alessandro Moreschi così pure dovranno essere conservati nella miglior maniera i suoi dischi fonografici affinche i figli e tutti i discendenti di Rita conoscano la

gloria artistica di mio padre di cui c'è anche un libro con tutti gli articoli dei giornali e appunti della sua vita." Quoted from the holograph will of Giulio Moreschi, August 23, 1954, Archivio Notarile di Roma, Repertorio n. 15297, Raccolta n. 7583. The will was copied and notarized by the notary Alfredo de Martino on July 21, 1955, a week after Giulio's death. See Figures. 3.1a and 3.1b.

The contents of the apartment were itemized in detail in an inventory made on October 12, 1955 (hence after Giulio's death), and were registered at Rome on the following November 29 (contained in the Moreschi-Fellini Archive).

23. Perosi's signed portrait remains in the Moreschi-Fellini Archive. Three others, of Enrico Caruso, Pietro Mascagni, and Beniamino Gigli, are now in the Hanna Holborn Gray Special Collections Research Center of the University of Chicago. While the Caruso and Mascagni portraits are signed to Alessandro, the Gigli portrait is signed to Giulio. See also note 92 below.

24. Notably, other copies of those 78s are exceedingly rare.

25. Robert Anthony Buning, "Alessandro Moreschi and the Castrato Voice," MA thesis, Boston University, 1990. Crucial, too, are the discographies of William Shaman, "The Vatican G & T's," *The Record Collector* 28.7–8 (December 1983), pp. 147–91, and "The Vatican G & T's: An Addendum," *The Record Collector* 30.12–13 (December 1985), pp. 287–93, based on the EMI company registers (now the EMI Archive Trust), as well as a goodly number of original 78s. The "Addendum" has crucial corrections to the initial article.

See Bergeron, *Decadent Enchantments*, pp. 129–42, for reflections on the 1904 sessions from the Solesmes perspective. Joe K. Law, "Alessandro Moreschi Reconsidered: A Castrato on Records," *Opera Quarterly* 2.2 (summer 1984), pp. 1–12, had little to say that still holds up, but he does pick up on the appoggiatura, or acciaccatura, that I unpack here, as well as Mendelssohn's attention to it (pp. 9–11).

26. Jerrold Northrop Moore, *A Voice in Time: The Gramophone of Fred Gaisberg, 1873–1951* (London: Hamish Hamilton, 1976).

27. Ibid., p. 35.

28. Ibid., pictured after p. 40, top of page.

29. Moore, *A Voice in Time*, pp. 51 and 66, with the full story on pp. 66–70. The pope was not "nearly ninety," as Moore says (p. 68), but ninety-two by the time the recordists reached the Vatican.

30. The fuller passage is snide: "These singers [castrato singers of the Sistine Chapel choir] are seldom good musicians, but their strange voices allow them to take the place

of women. Occasionally some of them are excellent musicians. . . . Moreschi's voice is of an agreeable quality and he may be called the prima donna of the choir." *Musical World* 2.9 (October 1902), p. 121.

31. "The Fred Gaisberg Diaries, Part 7," *Talking Machine Review* 63–64 (Autumn 1981), p. 1765: The passage continues: "During the last session an accident happened that might have proven serious. A fire started where we were working, and in a moment there was a big blaze. All the singers rushed out panic-stricken. Will & I and the Michaelises worked like Trojans and soon gained the upper hand, and saved the Company from big damages, as we were working in a salon of the Palace of the Bishop of Rome. Reports of this occurrence reached London & America and appeared in the Italian papers. Will and I under private guidance went through some inaccessible parts of the Vatican and St. Peter's." Hugo Strötbaum has made available an online edition of the diaries, *The Fred Gaisberg Diaries, Part. 1: USA & Europe (1898–1902)*, http://www.recordingpioneers.com/docs/GAISBERG_DIARIES_1.pdf, quote on pp. 103–104. See also Moore, *A Voice in Time*, pp. 69–70.

32. Buning, "Alessandro Moreschi and the Castrato Voice," p. 13.

33. Fred Gaisberg, "Notes from My Diary: Recording of Actual Performances," *Gramophone* 22.256 (September 1944), p. 43.

34. Ibid.

35. The terms "power source," "sound source," and "sound modifiers" come from David M. Howard, "Acoustics of the Castrato Voice," in Nicholas Clapton, *Moreschi and the Voice of the Castrato* (London: Haus Books, 2008), p. 230.

36. John Franklin Botume, "Success of the Cosmopolitan Singer," *Musical World*, Pictorial Supplement 2.9 (October 1902), p. 116.

37. For a helpful discography of Moreschi's solos, as well as those of opera singers recorded during the Vatican sessions, the remarkable site http://78opera.com/content/discographies, previously created and maintained by Robert Johannesson, of Kristianstad, Sweden, proved invaluable, and I am much indebted to it. Johannesson has apparently not been seen on this site since 2017, and when last checked, the URL yielded "Site off-line. The site is currently not available due to technical problems." As of this writing, his discographies now live in the Internet Archive at: https://archive.org/search.php?query=creator%3A%22Robert+Johannesson%22. He originally built this goldmine of unpublished internet discographies on his now-defunct website.

I am immensely grateful to Robert Johannesson for correspondence in 2016 and for answering my queries and above all for sharing his discographies with me, including an unpublished discography of the 1904 sessions by the late Alan Kelly that I discuss here, which is the best discography of the sessions to date.

38. Buning understandably thought no tenor named Primo Vitti ever existed and that the name was probably a transcription error that made its way onto the published disks. "Alessandro Moreschi and the Castrato Voice," p. 14 n. 3. In fact, Vitti was not on the rolls of the Sistine Chapel, but as Will Crutchfield notes, he was a tenor in a basilican chapel, the Cappella Liberiana. (*Miscellanea francescana di storia, di lettere, di arti* [Foligno: La Direzione, 1906], vol. 15, p. 163), who also sang in Monteverdi's *L'incoronazione di Poppea* and did other "early music" programs (*Rivista musicale italiana*, 1912). (Private communication, March 22, 2021.) See also Luciano Luciani, "La professione dei cantori romani di musica sacra," in Saverio Franchi and Orietta Sartori, eds., *Il giardino armonioso: Studi e testimonianze in onore di Giancarlo Rostirolla da parte dei Soci dell'Ibimus in occasione del suo 70° compleanno* (Rome: Ibimus, 2011), pp. 94, 98, and 151 (where there are two pictures of Vitti), and Giancarlo Rostirolla, *Musica e musicisti nella basilica di San Pietro: Cinque secoli di storia della Cappella Giulia*, vol. 2, *Dal 1804 ai giorni d'oggi* (Rome: Edizioni Capitolo Vaticano, 2014), p. 979 n. 196 (and see pp. 919, 940, 1307).

39. See Shaman, "The Vatican G & T's," pp. 170–72.

40. Documentation on the point is slim because the Sistine Chapel diaries are basically nonexistent for the relevant years after 1897.

41. Gabrielli, "Appendice: Riassunta delle conversazioni sulla storia delle Cappelle musicali romane," p. 256.

42. The Joyce Project, "Whiteeyed kaffir," http://www.joyceproject.com/notes/120013whiteeyedkaffir.htm.

43. Moore, *A Voice in Time*, pp. 79–80.

44. See Regula Burckhardt Qureshi, "Female Agency and Patrilineal Constraints: Situating Courtesans in Twentieth-century India," in Martha Feldman and Bonnie Gordon, eds., *The Courtesan's Arts: Cross-Cultural Perspectives* (New York: Oxford University Press, 2006), pp. 311–31, esp. p. 318.

45. Figure. 3.3a in Moore, *A Voice in Time*, after p. 104.

46. Vikram Sampath, *My Name Is Gauhar Jaan! The Life and Times of a Musician* (New Delhi: Rupa Publications, 2010).

47. The first records with Gaisberg were made in a makeshift studio created in two rooms of a Calcutta hotel.

48. Film buffs know Begum Akhtar as the courtesan singer in the great Bengali director Satyajit Ray's film *Jalsaghar / The Music Room* (1958).

49. Moore, *A Voice in Time*, chapter 8. For the Egypt trip, see the photograph on a camel by the pyramids, plate 7a. See also Gavin Williams, *Format Frictions: Perspectives on the Shellac Disc* (Chicago: University of Chicago Press, 2024), pp. 51–54, on Gaisberg and the technological ambitions he entertained with colleagues, and pp. 65–73, on recollections of 78s in Singapore.

50. This is how Peter Martland characterizes it, s.v. "Gaisberg, Frederick William (1873–1951)," *Oxford Dictionary of National Biography* (2004), https://www.oxforddnb.com.

51. Lorraine Daston and Peter Galison, "The Image of Objectivity," *Representations* 40 (Autumn 1992), pp. 81–128, and *Objectivity* (New York: Zone Books, 2007). Some of the same spirit pervades Haböck, *Die Kastraten und ihre Gesangskunst*.

52. The Gramophone Monarch label apparently started in the same year of 1903. It was one of many sublabels of the London-based Gramophone Co. Ltd., of which the Gramophone and Typewriter Co. was another. See Discogs. "Gramophone Monarch Record," https://www.discogs.com/label/162080-Gramophone-Monarch-Record.

53. Reckoned using inflationhistory.com.

54. The signed contract and a draft of it is kept at the EMI Archive Trust, Hayes, Middlesex, England (see Figure 3.4). My thanks to curator Joanna Hughes for help with locating the document. This signed version reads:

"Con la presente scrittura privata da valere quale pubblici atto tra il Sig. Alfredo Michaelis quale direttore della The Gramophon Company (Italy) Ld. ed il Prof. Moreschi Alessandro si è stabilito quanto segue:

1. Prof. Moreschi Alessandro si obbliga di eseguire con alcuni cantori della Cappella Sistina coadiuvati da altri professori delle Patriarcale Basiliche di Roma Venti dischi ripetendo alcuni già fatti da fissarsi nel Grammofono Monarch.

2. Sig. Michaelis quale rappresentante e direttore della The Gramophon Company (Italy) Ld. si obbliga corrispondere Lire tremila (lire 3000) come esecuzione ed ingaggiamento.

3. Prof. Moreschi Alessandro si obbliga per la durata di un anno da incominciare dal 10 Marzo 1903 a tutto il Marzo 1904 di non fare eseguire sotto la sua direzione e di non cantare lui stesso in altre macchine parlanti in genere e per tale impegno riceve la somma di Lire Millecinquecento (Lire 1500) già comprese nelle Tremila Lire come nell'articolo 20:

4. All'atto della firma il Sig. Alfredo Michaelis verserà al Prof. Moreschi Alessandro Lire cinquecento (Lire 500) in accanto delle Lire Mille cinquecento (Lire 1500) per l'ingaggiamento versandogli la rimanenza cioè Lire Mille (Lire 1000) entro il mese di Aprile del corrente anno, tenendosi sciolto qualora non avenisse detto pagamento.

5. I pezzi saranno eseguiti dentro il Mese di Marzo corrente

6. In caso di impedimento da una parte o dall'altra i dischi si eseguiranno in epoca da stabilirsi entro l'anno.

7. Il pagamento delle Lire Millecinquecento (Lire 1500) per l'esecuzione dei dischi sarà fatto all'atto della suddetta.

Roma 1 Marzo 1903

[signed:] Alessandro Prof. Moreschi"

55. *Times* of London, quoted from Shaman, "The Vatican G & T's," p. 152. Reuter's Agency contradicted this, writing that the pope "entered the chapel walking and took his place in the Sedia Gestatoria at the Cappella della Pietà."

56. Both the *Times* of London and Reuters are quoted in Shaman, "The Vatican G & T's," pp. 152–53. Reuters gave the number of performers at about fifteen hundred and the *Times* of London gave about one thousand. For the figure 1,210 see Salvatore De Salvo Fattor, *La cappella musicale pontificià nel Novecento* (Rome: Fondazione Giovanni Pierluigi de Palestrina, 2005), p. 20, who also notes that a new precedent was established on April 11, 1904, for using these other choirs alongside the Cappella Pontificia, one that has lasted until present times. It involves executing psalmody, hymns, propers of the mass, and other chants with Gregorian melodies. See "Melodie gregoriane e canto di popolo nelle solenne funzioni papali," *Bollettino ceciliano* 37 (1942), quoted in De Salvo Fattor, *La cappella musicale pontificia nel Novecento*, p. 103 n. 15.

57. Reuters, quoted in Shaman, "The Vatican G & T's," p. 152.

58. Ibid., p. 153.

59. A point made by Bergeron, *Decadent Enchantments*, p. 130.

60. See ibid., p. 134 and her figure 3.0.

61. Shaman corrects the annotation in his discography that gives accompaniment by piano and bassoon obbligato, changing the latter to organ or more likely harmonium; see Shaman, "The Vatican G & T's," p. 173, and "Addendum," p. 289.

62. See Arman Schwartz, *Puccini's Soundscapes: Realism and Modernity in Italian Opera* (Florence: Leo S. Olschki, 2019), chapter 2, "Verismo Bells," on the precise situatedness of Puccini's *Tosca* in Rome.

63. On Giraud at the Teatro Costanzi, see Matteo Incagliati, *Il Teatro Costanzi, 1880–1907: Note e appunti della vita teatrale a Roma* (Rome: Tipografia Editrice "Roma," 1907), pp. 187–88, and Vittorio Frajese with Jole Tognelli, *Dal Costanzi all'Opera: Cronache, recensioni e documenti*, 4 vols. (Rome: Edizioni Capitolium, 1977), vol. 1, pp. 214–15.

64. Alessandro and Guendalina would likely have heard Giraud, Darclée, and Magini-Coletti at the Costanzi, too. See further below.

Perosi was no stranger to the Costanzi then, either, though his relation to it was as a composer of sacred music, not as a performer of profane opera. (Whether he was also an attendee at operas I don't know.) His oratorio *Resurrezione del Lazzaro* was given there in 1898, his *Mosé* under his own baton in 1900, and his *Stabat mater* and *Giudizio universale* both in 1904. All these used singers who were performing major roles in operas staged during festive parts of the season (as opposed to penitential ones). We therefore have to surmise that for Perosi and quite likely other reformers, the end of theatrical church music pertained specifically to the *liturgical*, rather the operatic or even the religious—and perhaps not to the realm of technological mediation, either. The aesthetic stance of the reformers probably contradicts the narrative of increasing ideological rigidity in Cecilianism. It surely also suggests that ideological rigidity pertained specifically to sacred music's function within the church and especially within church liturgy, without extending much outside of it.

Perosi's first cuts in the studio were made after Giraud's. Even if Perosi accepted the sacred/profane disjunction for his own repertory, he conducted the Cappella Sistina in classic Renaissance polyphony by Viadana and Palestrina, albeit having two of the three disks destroyed, presumably because they were not up to snuff. Afterward, he made way for the Vatican brass band (the Trombe d'Argento del Vaticano), which recorded a surprisingly up-tempo oompah number.

65. The "discorsi" were in a suffix i series recordings, while others were interpolated into a suffix I series. Helpful on the G & T, HMV, and EMI prefix/suffix systems are Hugo Ströthaum's charts, "Prefix/Suffix System of Matrix Series of The Gramophone (& Typewriter) Company / HMV / EMI," at www.recordingpioneers.com, http://www.recordingpioneers.com/docs/grurks/SUFFIX-PREFIX.pdf.

66. Recording 290i, "Prolusione al corso pratico per l'insegnamento del Canto Gregoriano."

67. Recording 303i.

68. Recordings 301i and 311i. See Shaman, "The Vatican G & T's," pp. 156–59 on the "discorsi."

69. J. Q. Davies, "'Veluti in speculum': The Twilight of the Castrato," *Cambridge Opera Journal* 17.3 (November 2005), pp. 271–301.

70. For the term "castrato revenant," see Grace Kehler, "Occult Charm and Social Ills: Vernon Lee's 'A Wicked Voice' and George Du Maurier's Castrated Texts," *Érudit*, November 11, 2004, https://www.erudit.org/en/journals/ron/1998-n10-ron824/009438ar.

71. See Peritz, "The Castrato Remains"; Gordon, *Voice Machines*, pp. 290–94; Carlo Caballero, "A Wicked Voice": On Vernon Lee, Wagner, and the Effects of Music," *Victorian Studies* 35.4 (Summer 1992), pp. 385–408; and Teets, "Singing Things."

72. Emma Calvé, *My Life: An Autobiography*, trans. Rosamond Gilder (New York: Arno, 1977), pp. 63–64. I attend to the vocal implications of Calvé's lessons in Feldman, *The Castrato*, pp. 122–24.

73. Mladen Dolar gives a concise account of Lacan's limp in causality in *A Voice and Nothing More* (Cambridge, MA: MIT Press, 2006), pp. 10–11.

74. Lillie de Hegermann-Lindencrone, *The Sunny Side of Diplomatic Life, 1875–1912* (New York: Harper and Brothers, 1945), p. 117.

75. See Lucia Marchi, "Rossini's *Stabat Mater* and the Aesthetics of 19th-Century Sacred Music," *Rivista internazionale di musica sacra* 32.1–2 (2011), pp. 341–62. I use Helmholtz pitch notation to indicate both pitch and octave, hence c' is middle C, c'' is one octave above middle C, and c''' is two octaves above middle C, etc.

76. See Feldman, *The Castrato*, pp. 95–96, 100, and 106 and literature cited there on these extensions of the castrato register.

77. Heather Hadlock, "Women Playing Men in Italian Opera, 1810–1835," in Jane A. Bernstein, ed., *Women's Voices Across Musical Worlds* (Boston: Northeastern University Press, 2004); John Potter, *Tenor: History of a Voice* (New Haven: Yale University Press, 2009); Marco Beghelli and Raffaele Talmelli, *Ermafrodite armoniche: Il contralto nell'Ottocento* (Varese: Zecchini, 2011); André, *Voicing Gender*; and Davies, *Romantic Anatomies of Performance*. In Pacchierotti's case, the lower extension veered toward approximating the newly prominent tenor voices that threatened to overtake male sopranos. It seems that the nineteenth-century Sistine castrato Giovanni Cesari also had a voice that developed a strong lower extension as he aged.

78. Buning, "Alessandro Moreschi and the Castrato Voice," has explained this well, understanding it in terms of vocal behaviors and traditions. In the "Inflammatus," he notes, "the greatest emphasis is on the c2 and g2 delineating the central fifth [that is, an octave and a fifth above middle c] which is considered technically foundational for the

highest notes. The item furthermore requires a strong lower mid-range, marked with use of g1, a1, and b1 flat," also requiring "a degree of ease at the extremes of a full two-octave compass, here c1 and c3" (p. 180). On using multiple registers and pushing the chest up high by select sopranos who studied with castrati, including Maria Malibran, sister of Manuel Garcia, Jr., see Buning, "Alessandro Moreschi and the Castrato Voice," pp. 345, 345 n. 2, and 390.

79. It is also the first one documented.

80. Hegermann-Lindencrone, *The Sunny Side of Diplomatic Life*, pp. 118–19. See Chapter 1 above.

81. Haböck, *Die Kastraten und ihre Gesangskunst*, p. 208.

82. Hegermann-Lindencrone, *The Sunny Side of Diplomatic Life*, p. 119.

83. Gabrielli, "Appendice: Riassunto delle conversazioni sulla storia delle cappelle musicali romane," pp. 255–56.

84. The fuller quote, by Mary Ann Smart, states that Stoltz had "excellent low notes and a strong but harsh upper register. She lacked agility and technical control, but her vocal colour and broad palette of timbres were universally praised." *Oxford Music Online*, May 15, 2009, s.v. "Stoltz, Rosine [Noël, Victoire]," https://www.oxfordmusiconline.com; and see Mary Ann Smart, "The Lost Voice of Rosine Stoltz," *Cambridge Opera Journal* 6.1 (March 1994), pp. 31–50. The opera was performed on December 2, 1840, at the Académie Royale de Musique (Salle Le Peletier). On Abigaille, see Will Crutchfield, "Unsafe at Any Speed: The Dangers of Singing Abigaille in *Nabucco*," *Opera News* 65.9 (March 2001), pp. 36–41. The role is still considered one of the most hazardous in the repertory. (Presumably Moreschi sang the part 2 scena "Anch'io dischiuso un giorno.")

85. I am deeply grateful to Will Crutchfield for the knowledge and materials he shared with me toward the writing of this section, as well as to Robert Buning's careful, penetrating work in "Alessandro Moreschi and the Castrato Voice," esp. pp. 381–90.

86. William Ashbrook, liner notes (copyright 1999) to *Eugenia Burzio: Verismo Soprano. Complete Operatic Repertoire* (Marston Records 52020-2.), https://www.marstonrecords.com/products/burzio. In *The Castrato*, pp. 82–89, I listened to contemporaneous recordings of sopranos singing the Bach / Gounod "Ave Maria" in the years from about 1904 to 1916, including Nellie Melba (1904), Adelina Patti (1905), Emma Eames (1906), and Eugenia Burzio (ca. 1912–1916), among all whom Burzio stands out as a kind of distant vocal cousin to Moreschi, with a far grittier and gutsier delivery, to say the least.

87. I don't engage here the whole problem of what exactly verismo is and what kind

of term it is. For a pithy take on the ironies of a term emphasizing the real in as unreal a genre as opera, see Ginger Dellenbaugh, *Maria Callas: Lyric and Coloratura Arias* (New York: Bloomsbury Academic, 2022), p. 38. As she says, opera will virtually always yield to the singing voice.

88. See Incagliati, *Il Teatro Costanzi, 1880–1907*, and Frajese and Tognelli, *Dal Costanzi all'opera*.

89. Some archives for the theater survive, but seemingly only accounts of ticket sales, not subscriber lists.

90. Incagliati, *Il teatro Costanzi, 1880–1907*, p. 187.

91. Gabrielli, "Appendice: Riassunto delle conversazioni sulla storia delle cappelle musicali romane," pp. 255–56.

92. The photos in question were auctioned by the Casa D'Aste Babuino in Rome in late 2010. Three additional photographs also went up for auction, including those signed to Alessandro Moreschi, by Giuseppe Verdi in 1897 and Lorenzo Perosi in 1904, and "the one" signed to Giulio Moreschi by the famously sob-filled Beniamino Gigli in 1937. All but Perosi were towering figures of Italian opera in their time. The photos of Verdi and Puccini were apparently purchased by anonymous private Italian collectors. The photo of Perosi remains in the Moreschi-Fellini collection, along with a fragment of Perosi's music that seems to have been owned by Alessandro Moreschi.

93. Adrien de la Fage, *Essais de diphthérographie musicale ou notice, descriptions, analyses, extraits et reproductions de manuscrits relatifs à la pratique, à la théorie et à l'histoire de la musique* (1864; Amsterdam: Frits A. M. Knuf, 1964), pp. 447–69, and Felix Mendelssohn Bartholdy, *Reisebriefe aus den Jahren 1830 bis 1832*, ed. Paul Mendelssohn-Bartholdy (Leipzig: Hermann Mendelssohn, 1869), available from the Hathi Trust at https://babel.hathitrust.org/cgi/pt?id=nnc1.cu01713370&seq=9.

94. For the following discussion of the upward appoggiatura, I'm again indebted to Will Crutchfield, who shared his spadework and insights on the subject.

95. La Fage, *Essais de diphthérographie musicale*, pp. 447–69.

96. Ibid., p. 454.

97. Ibid., p. 455.

98. Ibid., pp. 455, 463, etc.

99. Ibid., pp. 455–56, 459, 460, 461.

100. Ibid., p. 456. Here, as always, the cantus firmus ("canto fermo") comes first, then to the right of it the manner in which singers execute it in practice (labeled "si

canta"), with square notes used for the essential notes of the chant and diamond-shaped notes for the ornamental ones (small diamond-shaped notes for the trillo).

101. Ibid., p. 463. Buning, "Alessandro Moreschi and the Castrato Voice," p. 387, translates Baini's phrase "aspirazione fatta con impeto" as "glottal attack," which is obviously not literal, but rather captures the physiological referent intended and conveys its sonic effect.

102. Felix Mendelssohn-Bartholdy, *Letters of Felix Mendelssohn Bartholdy from Italy and Switzerland* (Philadelphia: F. Leypoldt, 1863), pp. 182–83.

103. "L'appoggiatura può andare ancora da una nota distante all'altra, purchè il salto non sia d'inganno." Pierfrancesco Tosi, *Opinioni de' cantori antichi, e moderni o sieno osservazioni sopra il canto figurato . . .* (Bologna: Lelio dalla Volpe, 1723), p. 22; in English in *Observations on the Florid Song*, trans. John Ernest Galliard (London: J. Wilcox, 1742 or 1743), p. 38 (in article 14).

104. Domenico Corri, *A Select Collection of the Most Admired Songs, Duetts, &c.: from Operas in the Highest Esteem, and from Other Works in Italian, English, French, Scotch, Irish, &c., &c. in Three Books. The First Consisting of Italian Songs, Duets, Terzetts, &c. The Second of English Songs, Duetts, Terzetts, &c. The Third of Airs, Rondos, Canzonette, Duettini, Terzetti, Catches, Glees, &c., All in Their Respective Languages* (Edinburgh: John Corri: [n.d.]), middle of p. 8. For the dating, I rely on the facsimile edition: *Domenico Corri's A Select Collection of the Most Admired Songs, Duetts, etc., Volumes 1–3*, ed. Richard Maunder (New York: Garland Publishing, 1993); see Maunder's introduction, pp. vii–viii, which explains why a date of issue earlier than late 1781 is very unlikely and why an issue date of 1782 or 1783 is much more likely.

105. Buyers may well have known the London production of the opera from a decade earlier, with Guadagni performing his most famous role. See Patricia Howard, *The Modern Castrato: Gaetano Guadagni and the Coming of a New Operatic Age* (Oxford: Oxford University Press, 2014), pp. 126 28.

106. Shane Butler, *The Ancient Phonograph* (New York: Zone Books, 2015).

107. Manuel Patricio Rodriguez Garcia, *Traité complet de l'art du chant: Première partie, deuxième edition; seconde partie, première edition*, 2 vols. (Paris: chez l'auteur, 1847). For an extended consideration of Garcia's elaborate annotations of Velluti's expression and ornamentations and their implications for the status of the castrato body and voice, see Davies, *Romantic Anatomies of Performance*, pp. 31–38.

108. See Will Crutchfield, "G. B. Velluti e lo sviluppo della melodia romantic,"

Bolletino del Centro Rossiniano di Studi 53 (2013), pp. 9–85, rich with musical examples that show the workings of Velluti's vocal ornamentational art and support Crutchfield's hypothesis that it influenced the ornamentational innovations in Frédéric Chopin's piano music. Crutchfield's book-in-preparation on nineteenth-century and early twentieth-century ornamentation practices, parts of which he has generously shared with me in advance of publication, will include many further examples of these practices, including via his variorum of Mercante's "Soave immagine d'amor di pace," comparing a number of early iterations in which upward appoggiaturas proliferate at the interval of the third.

109. Crutchfield tells me this is highly unusual for Rossini (email of September 20, 2023), and indeed, it seems like an early instance of trying to "record" and then print, in script, the singer's partly orally transmitted practice. A pass through Robert Crowe's edition of selected ornamented songs and arias of Velluti's shows some upward appoggiaturas at intervals ranging from a third to a ninth and including at the fourth, fifth, sixth, and octave, generally as a way of giving emphasis to an accented downbeat or other strong beat through an upward leaping grace note. See Robert Crowe, ed., *Songs and Arias Ornamented by Giovanni Battista Velluti, the Last Operatic Castrato* (Middleton: A-R Editions, 2020): no. 3, Giovanni Battista Velluti, "Quel tuo girar del ciglio," m. 27; no. 4, John Fane, Lord Burleigh, "L'amor timido," mm. 64 and 100; no. 5, John Fane, Lord Burleigh, "Placido zeffiretto," m. 22; no. 6, John Fane, Lord Burleigh, "Compagni, amici, addio—Deh non soffrir," m. 103; no. 10, Johann Simon Mayr, "Ah! Che per me non v'è," mm. 15 and 22; no. 11 Saverio Mercadante, "Soave imagine," mm. 7, 26, and 29; no. 14, Giuseppe Nicolini, "Nere funeste immagini," m. 8; no. 15, Giuseppe Nicolini, "Dite al mio bene," m. 25; no. 16, Giuseppe Nicolini, "Or che la luna," m. 19; and no. 24, Nicola Vaccaj, "Api erranti," m. 9. Many of the Velluti sources survive in scattered prints, others came to light early in the present century when the Fondo Velluti at the Biblioteca Civica in Belluno, Italy, was given to the library and endowed by a descendant (through a sibling) of Velluti's, Federico Velluti. Included in the Belluno archive are prints believed to have been Velluti's own; see ibid., p. 199.

110. Davies, *Romantic Anatomies of Performance*, chapter. 1.

111. This extremely rare print, *Treatise on Singing, Forming a Complete School of the Art in Three Parts* (London: Robert W. Ollivier, n.d.), survives at the Bibliothèque Nationale de France, the British Library, and the Biblioteca dell'Accademia Filarmonica di Bologna. It is usually dated "[184?]." The British Library gives no publisher for it and dates it to 1850.

112. Graham O'Reilly, *"Allegri's Miserere" in the Sistine Chapel* (Woodbridge: Boydell Press, 2020), and recording with Ensemble Byrd on Astrée (2002) with female soloist Catherine Greuillet singing the first soprano part. Mustafà explained why he wrote down all the expressive details; see Clapton, *Moreschi and the Voice of the Castrato*, pp. 131–32. The extant manuscript score is in Vatican City, Biblioteca Apostolica Vaticana, Fondo Cappella Sistina MS 375. It bears the title "Miserere di Bai ed Allegri," though all but verse 3 use Bai's version.

113. O'Reilly, *"Allegri's Miserere" in the Sistine Chapel*, pp. 45–51.

114. Transcription by O'Reilly in ibid., pp. 306–27, including appendices and published by Shorter House (London, 2018). The words "un fil di voce" appear repeatedly (mm. 63, 87, and 113). On "portando" and portamento, see ibid., pp. 234–38. The usage goes back to the seventeenth century at least. (See Feldman, *The Castrato*, p. 119.)

115. "N.B. Se al 1º soprano convenisse meglio di appoggiare il sol acuto potra prendere me prima il sol medio." The word "sol," which normally means G, here translates as C because an annotation at the beginning of Mustafà's *Miserere* instructs singers to perform the work at "il tono una quarta sopra," that is, at the pitch a fourth above.

116. O'Reilly, *"Allegri's Miserere" in the Sistine Chapel*, p. 172 n. 8, quoting Paul Renouard, *Rome pendant le semaine sainte* (Paris: Boussod, Valadon & Cie, 1891).

117. O'Reilly *"Allegri's Miserere*," p. 180.

118. See n. 61 above.

119. My thanks again to Will Crutchfield here.

120. Crutchfield describes the all-out sob as "an interruptive, uncontrolled phonation in head voice in the context of a passage otherwise executed in chest voice," continuing: "The interruptive sound can have a pitch near or identical to the adjacent musical notes sung in chest voice, or can be a random distant pitch (sometimes falling into the spectrum of 'un-pitched' sounds like some percussion and some speech." (Email communication, January 17, 2020.)

121. Excellent on the valence of such matters is Mary Ann Smart's *Mimomania: Music and Gesture in Nineteenth-Century Opera* (Berkeley: University of California Press, 2004).

122. Certainly, after Pope Benedict XIV's humongous treatise *De diocesana synodo* of 1748—which forbade clerics from attending the theater, even though clearly many continued to do so—the whole castrato phenomenon was variously tolerated, looked down on, or regarded by the church with a certain shame, always being complexly positioned between church and theater. The fact overlaps with Moreschi's storied second life as

a salon singer of female opera arias, singing Verdi and Donizetti alongside the likes of Francesco Marconi and Antonio Cotogni, and his function as a singer at the Laterano (from 1873) and then Sistine Chapel (from 1883), hence as a singer of the pope's.

123. Enza Venturini, s.v. "Capocci, Gaetano," *Dizionario biografico degli Italiani* vol. 18 (1975), https://www.treccani.it/enciclopedia/gaetano-capocci_(Dizionario-Biografico)/.

124. Alberto De Angelis, *La musica a Roma nel secolo XIX* (Rome: G. Bardi, 1944), p. 93. See also Clapton, *Moreschi and the Voice of the Castrato*, pp. 69–70 and 73–75. The reference prompted Clapton to speculate as much (p. 74), and I agree that it's fair to surmise that one of the two chapel singers was Mustafà.

125. This explains why information about them is scarce, though Georg Sievers and Karl Proske heard the performances at S. Filippo Neri's oratories in 1824 and 1835, respectively; see Georg Ludwig Peter Sievers "Über den heutige Zustand der Musik in Italien, besonders zu Rom," *Caecilia* 1.3 (1824), pp. 201–60, and Franz Xaver Haberl, "Zum hundertsten Geburtstag von Dr. Karl Proske," *Kirchenmusikalisches Jahrbuch* 9 (1894), pp. 22–47. Leopold M. Kantner and Angela Pachovsky, in *La cappella musicale pontificia nell'Ottocento* (Rome: Hortus Musicus, 1998), pp. 32–34, note that participating in performances outside the Cappella Sistina required a *licenza* granting permission, but only occasionally did it specify precisely the purpose for which permission was given. Excessive activity outside the Cappella Sistina was generally seen as impinging on the prestige of the pope's private chapel. In 1895, Antonio Comandini was punished for having taken part in a concert at the Accademia di Santa Cecilia, even though the concert was of Palestrina. Nineteenth-century Sistine singers were generally prohibited from singing on theatrical stages and could be expelled for having done so. Some singers did the reverse, joining the Sistine Chapel after having had a theater career.

126. On March 31, 1857, Mustafà was sentenced for having participated in an *accademia* in the house of a Protestant, as was Rosati, though the sentence was later commuted, and they were warned not to sing in Protestant *accademie* or *conversazioni* in the future. Ibid., p. 59 n. 119. By contrast, there are frequent testimonials about eighteenth-century Sistine chapel singers taking part in what were called *riunioni musicali* or *accademie* in the homes of Roman aristocrats or foreign diplomats in Rome (De Angelis, *La musica a Roma nel secolo XIX*, pp. 20–22; Kantner and Pachovsky, *La cappella musicale pontificia nel Ottocento*, p. 59 n. 121), even though from 1762 onward, singers were forbidden from participating in

accademie venali according to the orders given by Pope Clement XIII in an act known as *Cum retinendi* (August 31, 1762). Around 1820, some still took part at the baron Christian Karl Josias von Bunsen's Roman residence; Mendelssohn wrote that those *accademie* were held every Monday and were attended by Otto Nicolai and also took place at the house of the collector Fortunato Santini. Kantner and Pachovsky, *La cappella musicale pontificia nel Ottocento*, p. 33 n. 126.

127. Nino Angelucci, *Ricordi di una artista, Antonio Cotogni* (Rome: Roma, 1907), p. 21. De Angelis is the one who adds that Cotogni made his debut alongside Mustafà and Nazareno Rosati. *La musica a Roma nel secolo XIX*, pp. 89 and 93.

128. Biblioteca Apostolica Vaticana, Diarii Sistini 297, fol. 7r.

129. Incagliati, *Il Teatro Costanzi, 1880–1907*, p. 67.

130. Ibid. Remastered in The Harold Wayne Collection, vol. 4, audible at https://www.youtube.com/watch?v=CDnSdgxbd-c, at 3:11. They were recorded on Pathé-AICC cylinders and discs, Milan, 1903(?), matrix 84001, and on Zonophone, Milan, 1903?, matrix X-1546 or X-1547, catalogue X-1546. See Johannesson discographies in the Internet Archive, Artist Ba–Bi, p. 82.

131. Incagliati, *Il Teatro Costanzi, 1880–1907*, pp. 122–23.

132. The recording is not available online as of this writing. I heard it in a file supplied to me by Will Crutchfield. The Johannessen discographies, Artist F, p. 33, gives it as G & T Milan, December 1902, matrix 2925b, catalogue no. 53284.

133. The information comes from YouTube user "lido2008ve," "Soprano GEMMA BELLINCIONI — Cavalleria rusticana 'Voi lo sapete o mamma' (1903)," https://www.youtube.com/watch?v=gQggLVRZXcE, who gives the discographic inforamation as Milano, Matrix Con 574R, Catalogue no. G&T 053038, recorded on October 11, 1903. Listen at 3:10. Johannessen, Artist Ba-Bi, p. 81, lists Catalogue no. 053018, and also lists a Pathé recording of Bellincioni's of "Voi lo sapete" from 1904–1905, matrix 4393, catalogue10205 rr. Herr.

134. See Feldman, *The Castrato*, pp. 122–24.

135. Johannesson discographies, Artist C, p. 6, lists the following recordings of "Voi lo sapete": G & T, London July 1902, matrix no. 2063b, catalogue nos. 3286, Vic 5003, 91003; Zonophone, Paris, October to December 1902, matrix no. X-2033, catalogue no. X-2033; Victor, Camden NJ, April 22, 1907, matrix no. C4426-1, catalogue nos. 88086, 6053, 053183, 033030, DB160, AGSB6. A collector with the YouTube handle, "@Bassett HoundTrio," shows a photograph of the April 22, 1907 recording, matrix DB160, issued

by His Master's Voice, and lists it as "likely recorded in Philadelphia" with label (EMG Mark IX Gramophone). The last can be heard https://www.youtube.com/watch?v=wATZuQ5JLDc&t=14s. Listen from 2:52.

Burzio's singing of the end of "Voi lo sapete," on a recording made for Fonotopia in Milan on March 17, 1908 (matrix XPh3091, catalogue no. 92160), gives a point of comparison: https://www.youtube.com/watch?v=k7Ldpcgc-9U, from 3;20; catalogue information from Johannesson, Artist Bj-By, p. 163.

136. His Master's Voice DB 160, April 22, 1907, Philadelphia (?).

137. Seth Kim-Cohen, *In the Blink of an Ear: Toward a Non-Cochlear Sonic Art* (New York: Continuum, 2009), pp. 111–12, which quotes Mary Douglas's classic *Purity and Danger* (London: Routledge, 1966).

Numerous other examples of sobs exist on early recordings. I single out ones that are most proximate to Moreschi. Will Crutchfield has sent me some nineteen further examples. Among them are several interpretations of "Voi lo sapete," which all but demanded a sob at the end, including Isabella Paoli's (Zonophone X-1839, recorded in 1903) and Emma Longhi's (Gramophone). They also include Mattia Battistini's "Pura siccome un angelo" from Verdi's *Traviata*, act 2 (Gramophone Monarch Record: 054395, recorded 1903–1906); Elisa Bruno's renderings of Donizetti's "O mio Fernando" (Pathé 86150, recorded 1905) and "Connais tu le pays" from Thomas's *Mignon* (Pathé); Fernando De Lucia's "Una furtiva lagrima" from Donizetti's *L'elisir d'amore* (Phonotype M1754, recorded 1917); and Eugenia Burzio's "Deh! non volerli vittime" from Bellini's *Norma* (Pathé 86382, recorded in 1913).

138. See examples at Music Web International, "The Recording Angel Trademark," http://www.musicweb-international.com/friedman/page11.htm.

139. Jonathan Sterne is quite brilliant on the implications of gramophone writing for ontology, otology, and scripture; see *The Audible Past: Cultural Origins of Sound Reproduction* (Durham: Duke University Press, 2003), especially chapter 1.

140. Originally published as "Typewriter Ribbon: Limited Ink (2) ('within Such Limits')," trans. Peggy Kamuf, as the last piece in the last section, "Materiality Without Matter," of *Material Events: Paul de Man and the Afterlife of Theory* (Minneapolis: University of Minnesota Press, 2001), pp. 277–360; also in Jacques Derrida, *Without Alibi*, ed. and trans. Peggy Kamuf (Stanford: Stanford University Press, 2002), pp. 72–160.

141. Derrida elaborated on time in *Given Time. 1: Counterfeit Money*, trans. Peggy Kamuf (Chicago: University of Chicago Press, 1994).

142. The event, Derrida notes, is proper to the organic, living being; automatic repetition is proper to the inorganic machine. But as Leonard Lawlor writes, "this paradox . . . announces . . . another kind of thinking, an impossible thinking: the *impossible event* [on the one hand, resembling the past, which thereby cancels its singularity, of course] . . . and the *only possible event* [i.e. a singular, nonresembling, nonrepeating one]." The question then is how in the future or ever to retain both since "the elements [of each] are internal to one another and yet remain heterogeneous." See Leonard Lawlor, s.v. "Jacques Derrida," *Stanford Encyclopedia of Philosophy Archive, Summer 2023 Edition*, ed. Edward N. Zalta and Uri Nodelman, https://plato.stanford.edu/archives/sum2023/entries/derrida. It strikes me that Derrida's imaginings in "Typewriter Ribbon" anticipate developments in sampling, AI, and much else.

143. Allen S. Weiss, *Breathless: Sound Recording, Disembodiment, and the Transformation of Lyrical Nostalgia* (Wesleyan: Wesleyan University Press, 2002), p. xii, a book dedicated to "those without voice."

144. Michel de Certeau, "Vocal Utopias: Glossolalias," trans. Daniel Rosenberg, *Representations*, no. 56 (Fall 1996), p. 29.

145. Black radical studies have taken up related phenomena, as I show in "Fugitive Voice," *Representations* 154.1 (Spring 2021), pp. 10–22.

146. Certeau, "Vocal Utopias," p. 30. Judith T. Zeitlin and I designated some of this along with some pertinent genres in our introduction "The Clamor of Voices," in *The Voice as Something More: Essays toward Materiality* (Chicago: University of Chicago Press, 2019), pp. 1–33 (discussion of Certeau on pp. 9–12, esp. on p. 10).

147. Carolyn Dinshaw, *Getting Medieval: Sexualities and Communities, Pre- and Postmodern* (Durham: Duke University Press, 1999).

148. Benjamin, "The Work of Art in the Age of Its Mechanical Reproducibility: Second Version," p. 31, with fuller context on pp. 30–32.

149. As Giorgio Biancorosso notes, theoretically speaking, this not unlike the differences in the profilmic elements of the film set — what the *camera* sees versus what the *viewer* sees — differences that arrive to us in the form of finished film strips. I'm grateful to him for the insight (shared on June 6, 2024) and for pointing me to Luigi Pirandello's brilliant exposition of the problematics in his 1915 novella *Shoot! The Notebooks of Serafino Gubbio, Cinematograph Operator*, trans. C. K. Scott Moncrieff (1915; Chicago: University of Chicago Press, 2005), with "Introduction: The Diva, the Tiger, and the Three-Legged Spider" by Tom Gunning.

150. See Garcia, *Traité complet de l'art du chant*, part 2, where ascending appoggiaturas and the closely related acciaccatura are explained on pp. 41–43. I borrow use of the term "petite note inférieure" from Will Crutchfield, who notes that Garcia "doesn't use 'petite note inférieure' as a consistent category-name for this particular kind of acciaccatura (which is what he more usually calls it). But since he uses that descriptor for a famous example of the device, and shows the device itself all over the place, it seems a good idea to press the phrase into service," also because it's "easily remembered and clear as to musical meaning." (Email of March 20, 2025.) The example in question comes from Donizetti's *Lucia di Lammermoor* and part 2, p. 13 (first column, third example down), where Garcia writes: "La syllabe posée sur la petite note inférieure permet à l'organe de gagner, au moyen d'un port de voix léger et rapide, la note élevée." (The syllable placed on the small lower note allows the organ to reach, by means of a light and rapid portamento, the high note.)

151. Recorded for Victor on December 30, 1906 (Victrola Red Seal Cat. 88049), available at https://www.youtube.com/watch?v=GyodNzbjVkw .

152. I'm most grateful to Domen Marenčič for his insightful and detailed work on "ovations" on early recordings—mostly, he argues, "orchestrated"—as well as for lively correspondence about these issues in fall 2023. Among the most pertinent of those he shared is baritone Mattia Battistini's 1902 recording of "Finch'è dal vino" from Mozart's *Don Giovanni*, available on *Great Opera Singers / The Complete Recordings / 1902–1911*, vol. 1, and at https://www.youtube.com/watch?v=w8haAwmwdIg, where to my ear, the ovation at the end sounds much more canned than the one Moreschi's colleagues deliver. Marenčič also kindly shared with me his paper "Towards a Better Understanding of Simulated Ovation on Early Recordings," given on May 19, 2021, at the conference "Early Recordings: Diversity in Practice," https://earlyrecordingsconference.wordpress.com/2021-conference.

153. See Feldman, *The Castrato*, p. 153. Callas's relationship with Rome was notorious because she later became a casualty of her "Rome walk-out" of January 2, 1958, when the producers at Rome's Teatro dell'Opera were either too parsimonious or too unthinking to have provided her with an understudy in case of illness.

154. Throughout this book, rather than delving into the various usages of "falsettist," I simply take the word to encompass any of various situations in which a man is singing in a register distinctly above his natural (or modal) chest. All unaltered adult sopranos were designated falsettists in the chapels of Rome during and after the period I deal with here.

155. Alessandro Gabrielli was the soprano in the Quartetto Vocale Romano Gabrielli-Gentili, which recorded under the name of the Sistine Chapel Quartet. (See Feldman, *The Castrato*, chapter 3.) I first heard the quartet when Luciano Luciani played the recordings for me in 2006. As for Mancini, the rumor that he was a castrato seemingly became hard to erase until he reached adulthood, when the truth that he was not became completely obvious. No one has yet to substantiate the claim that other castrati were also trying to get into the chapel during Perosi's time (see below). The notion was probably born from the distorted imaginings of Perosi, whose mental health was always precarious and became increasingly fragile.

156. This rarity is available on YouTube: https://www.youtube.com/watch?v=IBbCaBcyppg and https://www.youtube.com/watch?v=Pj5E2vVx2ZI, though the latter, while it provides English subtitles, contains an interpolated section not voiced by Mancini (at 1:23–2:23). The only copy of the original vinyl LP recording that I have found (listed on SBN) resides at the Biblioteca della Fondazione Giovanni Pierluigi da Palestrina, in Palestrina RM. SBN gives the album as *Le voci di Roma: Primo volume*, edited by Maurizio Tiberi, TIMA37 (Edizioni del Tima Club, 1981), track A4 (apparently side 1, track 4). It includes recordings by Antonio Cotogni, Domenico Mancini, Alessandro Moreschi, Bice Mililotti (listed there as Bice Mililotti de Reyna), Francesco Marconi, and Francesco Signorini, according to the track listings on Discogs.com: https://www.discogs.com/artist/1126217.

157. This of course resembles the master teacher / apprentice pupil relationship in numerous traditions worldwide—Indian and Chinese ones, for instance—as well as widespread systems of learning in early modern Europe. See, among many examples, Regula Burckhardt Qureshi, *Master Musicians of India: Hereditary Sarangi Players Speak* (New York: Routledge, 2007).

158. Davies, *Romantic Anatomies of Performance*; James Q. Davies, "Voice Belongs," in the colloquy "Why Voice Now?" convened by Martha Feldman, *Journal of the American Musicological Society* 68.3 (Fall 2015), pp. 677–81; and James Q. Davies, "'I am an essentialist': Against the Voice Itself," in Martha Feldman and Judith T. Zeitlin, eds., *The Voice as Something More: Essays Toward Materiality* (Chicago: University of Chicago Press, 2019), chapter 7.

159. The grammar is conversational in the original, and some of the syntax jumbled in incomplete sentences or sentences that don't "add up."

160. See Feldman, *The Castrato*, pp. 10–12.

161. For details of the argument, see Feldman, *The Castrato*, pp. 90–96, part of the evidence being textual, mainly from the eighteenth century, and part of it auditory, comparing Moreschi's "Ave Maria" with his contemporaries (ibid., pp. 83–86) and drawing on some scores.

162. On Perosi's mental state see Chapter 4, note 60 below.

163. The 1936 recordings were produced on the Paris Édition de musique sacrée (SEMS) label. They are strictly choral. Later recordings date from 1958, 1969, and 1970, etc. and are exceedingly rare. A number of recordings have surfaced at the Instituto Centrale per i Beni Sonori ed Audiovisuali in Rome, which I have yet to hear.

164. See Feldman, *The Castrato*, pp. 130–32.

165. Giorgio Biancorosso writes me apropos: "it is certainly striking that Giulio trained one of the most successful *doppiatori* (Sordi), one who defined the role for generations to come. . . . Of course, *doppiare la voce* is not the same as singing. Still they share an obsessive care for vocality and a preoccupation with substituting/inhabiting one body (person) for another. *Doppiare* and loose synchronisation are, at least as far as the voice is concerned, two sides of the same coin." (Email of June 13, 2024.)

166. By 1940, Norman had returned to Paris, where she first played the nurse in *Péchés de jeunesse* (released in Paris on November 16, 1941), directed by Maurice Tourneur. She went on playing in comedies (some musical), dramas, romances, and crime thrillers in France through 1959.

167. SecondHandSongs, "Assia de Busny," https://secondhandsongs.com/artist/128296, and https://music.metason.net/artistinfo?name=Assia+De+Busny&born=. Some were later anthologized on LPs. De Busny was born in Kyiv, then part of the Russian Empire, and died in Paris, according to the latter site.

168. My identification of the place in Figure 3.10 is based on its having clearly been taken at the same time and place as one included in Theodora Getty Gaston with Digby Diehl, *Alone Together: My Life with J. Paul Getty* (New York: HarperCollins, 2013). Unnumbered there and situated on unnumbered pages, it appears approximately midway through the group of tipped-in photographs and documents placed between pp. 144 and 145. The date given for the latter image is "during the war, in 1940," whereas the photograph in Figure 3.10 is marked in Vittoria Cevasco's hand "1939." I'm inclined to favor Vittoria's dating because she routinely marked family photographs with dates, people, and places and appears to have done so close to the time they were taken.

169. Getty Gaston, *Alone Together*, pp. 116–17. In 2015, I tried to obtain an interview

with her, but by the time I succeeded in making contact with her daughter Gigi Gaston, on July 18, 2021, her mother had passed away some four years prior, on April 8, 2017. I remain grateful to Gigi Gaston for our exchange.

170. Getty Gaston, *Alone Together*, notes that Giulio made some of these announcements in French (p. 117). Teddy later struggled with J. Paul Getty over remaining in Rome for the agreed-upon length of time she needed for study (ibid., p. 126). See also Darcy Hinton's interview with Getty Gaston following the book's release, videoed by Daryn Hinton, when Getty Gaston was one hundred (and still extremely sharp), where she mentions Moreschi and the lead-up to her arrest by the *questura*: https://www.youtube.com/watch?v=Hrn_6DXvmxo, at .00:27–1:50 .

171. Getty Gaston, *Alone Together*, p. 117.

172. Getty Gaston reports that Giulio "had sung as a member of the Cappella Sistina, and was a man devoted to pasta, the art of singing, and his love of people. Short in stature, with a sweet face and a huge smile, he greeted me at his doorway, dark-rimmed glasses hiding behind the gleam within his eyes" [sic]. Ibid.

173. "Ethi Junger, a beautiful coloratura soprano from Salzburg, was among Moreschi's most promising students." Ibid., p. 133.

174. Ibid., p. 137.

175. Ibid., pp. 137–38. Much of part 1 of the book recounts the travails of war in Italy when, having become a journalist, Getty Gaston spent part of her wartime years in jail and under house arrest. Ibid., chapters 18–23.

176. Ibid., p. 149. Giulio remained central to Getty Gaston's Roman life. See ibid., pp. 158–59 and 162–63 on his teaching and accompanying her and playing for her performances on the radio, and p. 173 on the family they formed and her enormous affection for him, including when it came time to part.

177. For the declaration of herself as an Aryan, see ibid., the unnumbered figure between pages 144 and 145. She is uncredited in *The Lost Weekend* itself, but listed as Theodora Lynch (her maiden name) in IMBD, https://www.imdb.com/title/tt0037884/fullcredits/?ref_=tt_cl_sm.

178. Possibly he was named Luigi [Loudovikos?] Coruno, but I'm uncertain of the name and have not yet tracked him down.

179. Getty Gaston also mentions a student named Delphi Valiani, "a beautiful Italian woman whose husband owned the restaurant in the Roma Termini," the central train station. *Alone Together*, p. 149. I've not yet found further trace of her.

CHAPTER FOUR: MASCULINITIES AND HERMAPHRODITES

The epigraph comes from Alberto De Angelis, *Domenico Mustafà: La Cappella Sistina e la Società Musicale Romana* (Bologna: Nicola Zanichelli, 1926), p. 8.

1. See the next note.

2. See De Angelis, *Domenico Mustafà*, pp. 7–9.

3. Marco Levi Bianchini, ed., *Sulla psicoanalisi: Cinque conferenze tenute nel settembre 1909 alla Clark University di Worcester Mass. in occasione del 20. anniversario di fondazione S. Freud*, 1st Italian translation of the 2nd German ed. of 1912 (Naples: R. Stab. Tip. F. Giannini & Figli, 1915); and Sigmund Freud, *Tre contributi alla teoria sessuale: Prima traduzione italiana autorizzata sulla quarta edizione tedesca del 1920 del prof. M. Levi Bianchini* (Zurich: Libreria psicoanalitica internazionale, 1921). According to the OPAC SBN (the Online Public Access Catalogue of the Servizio Bibliotecario Nazionale), three copies of the latter survive in Rome. On Levi Bianchini, see Alberto Zanobio, s.v. "Levi-Bianchini, Marco," *Dizionario biografico degli italiani*, vol. 64 (2005), https://www.treccani.it/enciclopedia/marco-levi-bianchini_(Dizionario-Biografico)/?search=LEVI%20BIANCHINI%2C%20Marco%2F. Also published in that period (and in Rome), but undated, is Sigmund Freud, *Enciclopedia sessuale*, trans. Francesco Adami (Rome: Elios, n.d. [1920?]). The speculative date is taken from OPAC SBN.

For further on Levi Bianchini, see Zanobio and his comment: "L. was trained in the Italian psychiatric school following the positivist and organicist orientation given by C. Lombroso. However, already open to the study of psychology, when toward the end of the first decade of the century he began to take an interest in psychoanalysis, he enthusiastically adhered to the doctrines of S. Freud, with whom he had an epistolary relationship, and promoted valid initiatives to promote their knowledge and diffusion in Italy, made difficult by philosophical-religious, scientific and political obstacles: in 1915 he founded the International Psychiatric Library, which from 1921 he called the Italian Psychoanalytic Library, and in 1920, he transformed the periodical *Il Asylum* into the *General Archive of Neurology and Psychiatry*, from the following year on, the *General Archive of Neurology, Psychiatry and Psychoanalysis*, which would become the official organ of the Italian Psychoanalytic Society; in 1925, he gave birth to the Italian Society of Psychoanalysis in Teramo, whose the generic character was that of an association of doctors interested in psychoanalysis, of which he was secretary until 1931. L. was not (and could not be, due to his training) a pure analyst, however, sensing the validity and depth of the Freudian conception, he brought valid contributions to psychoanalysis, of which he became one of the first and most significant Italian exponents, albeit within the limits of an extremely personal approach."

4. See Sigmund Freud, *Introduzione allo studio della psicoanalisi; prima traduzione italiana autorizzata sulla terza edizione tedesca del 1920 del dott. E. Weiss con prefazione di M. Levi Bianchini* (Zurich: Libreria Psicoanalitica Internazionale; Naples: Casa Editrice V. Idelson, 1922), including Freud's writings on lapsus (the famous Freudian slip), dreams, and his general theory of neurosis, a volume that was also published in other editions that year and is well preserved in Roman libraries, including two copies at Università degli Studi di Roma La Sapienza. Weiss published his own writings in the next few years: Edoardo Weiss, *Su alcuni concetti psicologici fondmentali della psicoanalisi* (Naples: Francesco Giannini & figli, 1924); *Su alcune critiche di autori italiani in tema di psicoanalisi* (Naples: Francesco Giannini & figli, 1924); and "Il simbolismo psicoanalitico," *Archivio generale di neurologia, psichiatria e psicoanalisi* 7 (1926), pp. 121–53. Later additions include Edoardo Weiss, *Elementi di psicoanalisi* (Milan: U. Hoepli, 1931), with an introduction by Freud, which appeared the same year Weiss moved to Rome. In 1939, a year after Fascist racial laws were put in place, the Jewish Weiss migrated to the United States, joining the staff of the Chicago Institute for Psychoanalysis in 1941, as well as practicing privately. See Paul Roazen, "Psychoanalytic Ethics: Edoardo Weiss, Freud, and Mussolini," *Journal of the History of the Behavioral Sciences* 27 (October 1991), pp. 366–74, on the Italian reception of Freud through Weiss, and Marco Conci, "Italian Themes in Psychoanalysis—International Dialogue and Psychoanalytic Identity," *International Forum of Psychoanalysis* 17 (2008), pp. 65–70.

5. An excellent account of these developments with attention to film and historical memory is Rebecca Bauman, "Visions of Virility: Masculinity and Memory in the Italian War Film," in Thomas Cragin and Laura A. Salsini, eds., *Resistance, Heroism, Loss: World War II in Italian Literature and Film* (Vancouver: Fairleigh Dickinson University Press, 2018), chapter 8.

6. Raffaella Sarti shows that shaving the beard became a hotly contested matter, notably in the Turin of 1907, when servants launched a fierce protest against proscriptions for servants growing mustaches, calling shaving a form of "facial mutilation." Hence while Moreschi was bourgeois and married, he was what the Fascist Pavese called "spiritually castrated," besides being physically so. See Sarti's "Fighting for Masculinity: Male Domestic Workers, Gender, and Migration in Italy from the Late Nineteenth Century to the Present," *Men and Masculinities* 13.1 (October 2010), pp. 16–43, esp. pp. 16–21,

and see Domenico Rizzi, "Liberal Decorum and Men in Conflict: Rome, 1871–90," *Journal of Modern Italian Studies* 10 (2005), pp. 281–96, and Sandro Bellassai, "The Masculine Mystique: Antimodernism and Virility in Fascist Italy," *Journal of Modern Italian Studies* 10 (2005), pp. 314–35. Also important are David G. Horn, *Social Bodies: Science, Reproduction, and Italian Modernity* (Princeton: Princeton University Press, 1994); Cecilia Dau Novelli, *Famiglia e modernizzazione in Italia tra le due guerre* (Rome: Edizioni Studium, 1994); and Daniel Pick, *Faces of Degeneration: A European Disorder, ca. 1848–1918* (Cambridge: Cambridge University Press, 1989).

7. See the Epilogue below and Joseph Albert North, "Martyrs on the Silver Screen: Early Church Martyrdom in Italian Silent Cinema (1898–1930)," PhD diss., Durham University, 2015, esp. the section "Rodolfo Kanzler: Between Archaeology, the Magic Lantern, and Cinema," pp. 78–103, as well as pp. 12 and 21–22.

8. Tullio Kezich, *Federico Fellini: His Life and Work* (New York: Faber & Faber, 2006), p. 220, and on Fellini's relationship with Bernhard, pp. 220–27, an encounter that prompted him to begin his dream books. Kezich gives the date 1961 there, but in his "*Somni explanation*, or In the Realm Where Everything Is Possible," trans. David Stanton, included in Federico Fellini, *The Book of Dreams*, ed. Sergio Toffetti in collaboration with Gian Luca Farinelli and Felice Laudadio, trans. Aaron Maine (New York: Rizzoli, 2020), he gives 1960 (p. 571).

9. To the extent that they survive, the so-called dream books were first published in relatively complete form as Federico Fellini, *Il libro dei sogni*, ed. Tullio Kezich and Vittorio Boarini, with a contribution from Vincenzo Mollica (Milan: Rizzoli, 2007), and later in English as Federico Fellini, *The Book of Dreams*, ed. Tullio Kezich and Vittorio Boarini, with a contribution from Vincenzo Mollica (New York: Rizzoli International, 2008). The 2020 edition cited in the preceding note includes added essays.

10. Ernst Bernhard, "Il complesso della Grande Madre: Problemi e possibilità della psicologia analitica in Italia," collected in Ernst Bernhard, *Mitobiografia*, ed. Hélène Erba-Tissot, trans. Gabriella Bemford, 3rd ed. (1969; Milan: Adelphi Edizioni, 1985), pp. 168–79.

11. Ibid., p. 169.

12. Suzanne Stewart-Steinberg, *The Pinocchio Effect: On Making Italians, 1860–1920* (Chicago: University of Chicago Press, 2007), pp. 4–5.

13. The crucial passage reads as follows: "La chiave che permette di schiudere l'enigma dell'anima italiana è la constatazione che in Italia regna la Grande Madre mediterranea, la quale, nonostante le molte civiltà sovrappostesi, non ha perduto nei milenni

né di potenza né di influenza. Essa è la premessa archetipa che si ravviva in ogni singola donna italiana se si fa appello alle sue qualità materne. Come un simbolo vivo cela sempre in sé un intero mito, così la Grande Madre rappresenta un'ampia rete di relazioni di cui la madre è protagonista." Bernhard, "Il complesso della Grande Madre," p. 169. (The key to unlocking the enigma of the Italian soul is the observation that Italy is ruled by the Great Mediterranean Mother, which in notwithstanding the many overlapping civilizations, has lost neither power nor influence over the millennia. It is the archetypal premise that is revived in every single Italian woman once one appeals to her maternal qualities. Just as a living symbol always conceals within itself a whole myth, so the Great Mediterranean Mother represents a wide network of relationships in which the mother is the protagonist." Bernhard, "Il complesso della Grande Madre," p. 169, and see again on p. 172.

14. Ibid., p. 170.

15. Ibid., pp. 171 and 172.

16. Ibid., p. 173.

17. Ibid., p. 174.

18. See Chapter 2 above. Bernhard ties these tendencies to manifest or latent homosexuality — not surprisingly for his generation — including in women. He also acknowledges that in his time, attachments to the church were in a state of ongoing decline, albeit without following through on the implications of that (p. 174).

19. David I. Kertzer, *The Pope and Mussolini: The Secret History of Pius XI and the Rise of Fascism in Europe* (New York: Penguin Random House, 2014), and *The Pope at War: The Secret History of Pius XII, Mussolini, and Hitler* (New York: Random House, 2023); Karlheinz Deschner, *God and the Fascists: The Vatican Alliance with Mussolini, Franco, Hitler, and Pavelic* (1965; Amherst: Prometheus Books, 2013).

20. Bernhard, "Il complesso della Grande Madre," pp. 175–76.

21. Ibid., p. 178.

22. And the way to get there is through transference and countertransference. Italian patients will require much patience on the part of the analyst, because owing to this national character, transference will take even longer than usual and be even more intense. Ibid., p. 179.

23. John Pollard, *Catholicism in Modern Italy: Religion, Society, and Politics Since 1861* (London: Routledge, 2014).

24. Stewart-Steinberg, *The Pinocchio Effect*, p. 3.

25. See Erica Moretti, *The Best Weapon for Peace: Maria Montessori, Education, and Children's Rights* (Madison: University of Wisconsin Press, 2021).

26. Stewart-Steinberg, *The Pinocchio Effect*, p. 4.

27. Martha Feldman, *The Castrato: Reflections on Natures and Kinds* (Oakland: University of California Press, 2015), chapter 1. I profited greatly there from Domenico Scafoglio and Luigi M. Lombardi Satriani, *Pulcinella: Il mito e la storia* (Milan: Leonardo, 1990). Since then, Karen T. Raizen's *Pulcinella's Brood: Popular Culture in the Enlightenment* (Toronto: University of Toronto Press, 2024) has appeared, a wonderful exploration of the cultures and biopolitics of Pulcinella.

28. On Pulcinella as simultaneously bird and castrato, see Feldman, *The Castrato*, pp. 22–26; on his relationship to money, pp. 26–27; and on amphibious issues of gender and reproduction, pp. 18–19.

29. Filippo Balatri, *Frutti del mondo, autobiografia di Filippo Balatri da Pisa (1676–1756)*, ed. Karl Vossler ([Palermo]: R. Sandron, 1924), is heavily edited and very heavily abridged. I've consulted the manuscript version from Munich, Bayerische Staatsbibliothek, cod. It. 39, 2 vols.

30. The caricaturist was Anton Maria Zanetti, and the castrato depicted was Antonio Bernacchi; see Feldman, *The Castrato*, p. 26 and figure 21.

31. Guided by the vantage points of Louis Althusser's "Ideological State Apparatus" (less by Walter Benjamin's thesis eliding the puppet with Marxist history, though see p. 23), Stewart-Steinberg understands state ideology as form of puppetry. Of the two, Benjamin strikes me as more relevant to the castrato condition. More than a metaphor, Benjamin's puppet in his "Theses on the Philosophy of History" figures historical materialism directly. In order to function, the puppet relies on theology—doctrine, religion, or whatever is axiomatic—to win every chess match imaginable. Walter Benjamin, *Illuminations* (New York: Schocken Books, 1969): "It can easily be a match for anyone if it enlists the services of theology" (p. 253). That said, the elision Stewart-Steinberg makes between the ideology and Italian maleness in the period is a particularly controversial part of her book. See Silvana Patriarca's review, which finds the take on Italian maleness totalizing, *Journal of Modern History* 82.2 (June 2010), pp. 479–81, or David G. Horn, *American Historical Review* 114.3 (June 2009), p. 859.

32. Beyond Stewart-Steinberg, *The Pinocchio Effect*, see Albert Russell Ascoli and Krystyna von Henneberg, eds., *Making and Remaking Italy: The Cultivation of National Identity Around the Risorgimento* (Oxford: Berg, 2001).

33. Fire-Eater, Mangiafuoco, a gruff sort who is actually kind and forgiving, was director and puppet master of the Great Marionette Theater.

34. Stewart-Steinberg and I each point this out, albeit in quite different terms: Stewart-Steinberg, *The Pinocchio Effect*, p. 25; Feldman, *The Castrato*, p. 75, and Martha Feldman, "Strange Births and Surprising Kin: The Castrato's Tale," in Paula Findlen, Wendy Wassyng Ryworth, and Catherine M. Sama, eds., *Italy's Eighteenth Century: Gender and Culture in the Age of the Grand Tour* (Stanford: Stanford University Press, 2009), pp. 129–31. On Balatri's account of his castration, see Feldman, *The Castrato*, pp. 55–56, and for a richly annotated recent edition of the text, see Filippo Balatri, *Vita e viaggi*, ed. Maria Di Salvo (Alessandria: Edizioni dell'Orso, 2020).

35. Achille Mbembe, *Necropolitics* (Durham: Duke University Press, 2011).

36. See Donna Haraway, *Simians, Cyborgs, and Women: The Reinvention of Nature* (New York: Routledge, 1991), and Paul B. [Beatriz] Preciado, *Testo Junkie: Sex, Drugs, and Biopolitics in the Pharmacopornographic Era*, trans. Bruce Benderson (New York: Feminist Press Books, 2013). This emerges more fully in my "Castrato/Trans," forthcoming in Martha Feldman, Bonnie Gordon, and Kara Keeling, eds., *Errant Voices: Performances Beyond Measure.*

37. Stewart-Steinberg, *The Pinocchio Effect*, p. 23.

38. Stewart-Steinberg glosses Francesco De Sanctis's *Storia della letteratura italiana* (1870–71; Turin: Einaudi, 1996), p. 615, in *The Pinocchio Effect*, p. 15.

39. See my *City Culture and the Madrigal at Venice* (Berkeley: University of California Press, 1995), chapter 5.

40. See Gianna Pomata, "Family and Gender," in John A. Marino, ed., *Early Modern Italy* (Oxford: Oxford University Press, 2002), pp. 69–86, and Dante E. Zanetti, *La demografia del patriziato milanesi nel secoli XVII, XVIII, XIX*, with appendix by Franco Arese Lucini (Pavia: Università, 1972). On the coincidence of patriliny and the castrato phenomenon, see Feldman, *The Castrato*, pp. xvi–xviii and 45–46, and Bonnie Gordon, *Voice Machines. The Castrato, the Cat Piano, and Other Strange Sounds* (Chicago: University of Chicago Press, 2023), chapter 7.

41. Gordon, *Voice Machines*, and Serena Guaraccino, "Voices from the South: Music, Castration, and the Displacement of the Eye," in Luigi Cazzato, ed., *Anglo-Southern Relations: From Deculturation to Transculturation* (Lecce: Negroamaro, 2012), pp. 40–51 originally published as "Voci da Sud: La voce castrata e la dislocazione dello sguardo," in Luigi Cazzato, ed., *Orizzonte Sud: Sguardi, prospettive, studi multidisciplinare su Mezzogiorno, Mediterraneo e Sud globale* (Nardò: Salento Books, 2010), pp. 293–304.

42. Mladen Dolar, *A Voice and Nothing More* (Cambridge, MA: MIT Press, 2006), p. 3.

43. Enrico Panzacchi, *Racconti incredibili ed credibili* (Rome: E. Perino, 1885). The work was reissued in further editions by printers in other Italian cities. The 1900 edition *I miei racconti*, 6th ed. expanded (Milan: Treves, 1900), forms the basis for the modern edition, Enrico Panzacchi, *Racconti*, ed. Valeria Giannantonio (Chieti Scalo: Vecchio Faggio, 1993), pp. 113–17. Already in 1880, Panzacchi's first stories appeared as *Racconti*, but without "Cantores!" For a short history of the textual issues, see Panzacchi, *Racconti*, ed. Giannantonio, p. 29, though her transcription omits the last five paragraphs of the 1885 edition.

44. For that reason, I call the character "Panzacchi" throughout my analysis.

45. The word I translate as "very fine" is *esilissimo*. It could be rendered as "slender," but in this context, it suggests acoustical focus.

46. Panzacchi, "Cantores!," in *Racconti*, ed. Giannantonio, pp. 114–15.

47. The tall soprano coloratura Giovanni Cesari (1843–1904), who took over as soprano soloist of the Allegri Miserere from castrato chapelmaster Domenico Mustafà, may have served as Panzacchi's prototype for "Cantores!," although the character in Panzacchi's story could well be purely fictionalized, its presentation within a pseudoautobiographical story imply a literary ruse. For Cesari's biography *in nuce*, see Leopold M. Kantner and Angela Pachovsky, *La cappella musicale pontificia nell' Ottocento* (Rome: Hortus Musicus, 1998), pp. 150–51, with his image on p. 151, bottom right. Robert Anthony Buning, "Alessandro Moreschi and the Castrato Voice" (MA thesis, Boston University, 1990), thinks Cesari's soloistic abilities started to drop by 1877 (pp. 97–98), at about age thirty-five, a crucial decade in the vocal life of many castrati, and that his voice seems then to have gone into lower range. Though Alessandro Moreschi was the most famous singer in the chapel, he was not tall and was never thin, so not a good candidate if what we're dealing with is some kind of direct prototype for the story.

48. Giannantonio situates Panzacchi between literary trends of "scapigliatura," verismo, and an intimate psychological mode. Panzacchi, *Racconti*, ed. Giannantonio, pp. 5–20, esp. p. 13.

49. The issue surfaces throughout Martha Feldman and Judith T. Zeitlin, eds., *The Voice as Something More: Essays Toward Materiality* (Chicago: University of Chicago Press, 2019), especially in Martha Feldman, "Voice Gap Crack Break," pp. 188–208; David J. Levin, "The *Gesamtkunstwerk* and Its Discontents: The Wounded Voice in (and Around)

Alexander von Zemlinsky's *The Dwarf*," pp. 209–26; and Seth Brodsky, "There Is No Such Thing as the Composer's Voice," pp. 227–46.

50. See especially Mladen Dolar, "The Object Voice," in Renata Sałecł and Slavoj Žižek, eds., *Gaze and Voice as Love Objects* (Durham: Duke University Press, 1996), pp. 7–31, and *A Voice and Nothing More*, p. 40; see also "Beyond Interpellation," *Qui parle* 6.2 (Spring–Summer 1993), pp. 75–96; and most recently, "Voices That Matter," in *The Voice as Something More*, pp. 339–55. For Shane Butler, it is Echo who figures as the real singer, envoicing the "continuous song" of Ovid's *Metamorphoses*; see "Is the Voice a Myth? A Rereading of Ovid," in *The Voice as Something More*, pp. 171–87.

51. Dolar, "The Object Voice," p. 15.

52. Butler, "Is the Voice a Myth?" and see Dolar, "Voices that Matter," p. 349.

53. The self-castration of Origen (185/6–254 AD) is recounted by Eusebius of Caesarea (ca. 263–339), following Matthew 19:12: "For there are some eunuchs, which were so born from [their] mother's womb: and there are some eunuchs, which were made eunuchs of men: and there be eunuchs, which have made themselves eunuchs for the kingdom of heaven's sake." Presumably, the reference to Richelieu that follows is to the Duke Armand de Vignerot du Plessis (1696–1788; grandnephew of Cardinal Richelieu), who was allegedly cured of conjugal impotence by Hermann Boerhaave (1668–1738). See *Institutions de Médicine de Monsieur Herman Boerhaave traduite de Latin en francois par Monsieur de la Maettrie, docteur de médecine*, vol. 2 (Paris: Huart, 1740), pp. 76–77, and Angus McLaren, *Impotence: A Cultural History* (Chicago: University of Chicago Press, 2007), p. 93.

54. Panzacchi, "Cantores!," in *Racconti*, ed. Giannantonio, p. 116.

55. In an act of extreme poetic license, Panzacchi alludes to "a motet by Allegri almost completely entrusted to him"—that is, to the castrato soloist—adding that "the choir entered from time to time with brief responses, and the organ, with a few held chords, helped keep things perfectly in tune." This makes it sound like he means to allude to Allegri's *Miserere*, certainly the most famous piece of Allegri's and the most famous in the choir's repertory, but besides the fact that it was not a motet, that work was never performed at Ascension and was not with organ. My thanks to Robert Kendrick for helping me parse this and for confirming that there was no "motet" of Allegri's done at Ascension by the Cappella Sistina in these years.

56. The Ensemble William Byrd, conducted by Graham O'Reilly (Astrée, 2002), has recorded the work from Mustafà's romanticized manuscript score. My thanks to O'Reilly for sharing a copy of the recording. Mustafà explained why he wrote down

all the expressive details. See Graham O'Reilly, *"Allegri's Miserere" in the Sistine Chapel* (Woodbridge: Boydell Press, 2020), chapter 7, as well as Nicholas Clapton, *Moreschi and the Voice of the Castrato* (London: Haus Books, 2008), pp. 131–32.

57. Castrati in the chapel were quietly aware that no new recruits were being made; see Kantner and Pachovsky, *La cappella musicale pontificia nell'Ottocento*, chapter 1, and Clapton, *Moreschi and the Voice of the Castrato*, pp. 127–32. In 1897, Mustafà made a pitch for training of two new castrated boys to become adult male sopranos in the chapel that did not come to pass. See Kantner and Pachovsky, *La cappella musicale pontificia nell'Ottocento*, pp. 54–55 and Chapter 1 above.

58. Dolar, "The Object Voice," p. 15.

59. See Mario Rinaldi, *Lorenzo Perosi* (Rome: Edizioni De Santis, 1967), chapter 26, and Salvatore De Salvo Fattor, *La cappella musicale pontificia nel Novecento* (Rome: Fondazione Giovanni Pierluigi da Palestrina, 2005), pp. 23–27.

60. Quoted in De Salvo Fattor, *La cappella musicale pontificia nel Novecento*, p. 14.

61. "Volendo dare un pubblico attestato di riconoscenza alla mia dilettissima moglie Guendalina Rinaldi in Moreschi la nomino mia erede universale raccomandando alla sua pietà e religione di suffragare l'anima mia. Roma 14 Dicembre 1896, Alessandro Moreschi." Archivio notarile distrettuale di Roma, atto notaio Balsi Matteo, 30 dic. 1896, Rep. n. 18.

62. Witnesses to Guendalina's birth certificate included a cook and a domestic worker. See n. 65 below.

63. The information is recorded in Guendalina's birth certificate, preserved in the Archivio di Stato di Roma, Documenti di Stato civile, Nati, 1872, vol. 1, series D. n. 91, pp. 29–30: "L'anno milleottocentottantadue questo dì 12 maggio alle ore una pomeridiana in Roma nell'Ufficio di Stato Civile della seconda Regione posto in Via dell'Archetto avanti a me Cavalier Augusto Castellani Consigliere di questo municipio, delegato ad Ufficiale di Stato Civile con atto del cinque maggio corrente anno debitamente approvato è comparso il Signor Pietro Rinaldi di Giacomo di anni ventisei scalpellino nato e domiciliato in Roma il quale mi dichiara che alle ore un quarto antimeridiane del dì otto corrente mese nel suo domicilio in via Monterone numero ottantadue piano terzo Rione Sant'Eustachio la propria moglie signora Giulia Ferrucci fu Giovanni di anni ventuno seco convivente ha dato alla luce un neonato di sesso femminile cui vengono posti i nomi di Guendalina, Emma, Maria. La nascita e il sesso furono accertati dal Medico Municipale avendo dispensato dalla presentazione del neonato per ragioni igieniche. A questa dichiarazione sono testimoni i Signori Giuseppe Monico di anni quarantadue, cocchiere

e Gaetano Frigieri di anni venticinque, domestico, qui residenti. L'atto presente previa lettura eccettuato un testimone illetterato è stato dai suddetti e da me firmato. A quanto segue si annulli la parola incapellata e si legga Giugno. Postilla approvata (firme) L'Ufficiale di Stato Civile Augusto Castellani."

64. Since Guendalina's mother was deceased by 1900, Guendalina and her father were almost certainly estranged by 1901–1902, and Guendalina was estranged from her husband and his family by June 1907, it's unsurprising that the only member of the Rinaldi family to have been buried in the tomb was Pietro.

65. "L'anno milleottocentonovantasei lì 30 Aprile a ore sedici nella casa posta in Via Corso V. Emanuele 187. Avendo Rinaldi Guendalina dimostrato con certificato medico l'impossibilità di recarsi nella casa comunale per celebrar il matrimonio io Avvocato Salvatore Bugarini, consigliere comunale delegato ad Ufficiale di Stato civile col mio Segretario comunale Anastasio Cocchi mi sono recato in questa casa ove ho trovato 1. Moreschi Alessandro di anni trentasette Maestro di Musica nato in Montecompatri, residente in Roma, figlio di Luigi e di Pitolli Rosa 2. Rinaldi Guendalina, di anni ventitré nata e residente in Roma figlia di Pietro e di Ferrucci Giulia, i quali mi hanno richiesto di unirli in matrimonio: a quest'effetto mi hanno presentato i documenti sotto descritti e dall'esame di questi e di quelli prodotti alle pubblicazioni, risultandomi nulla ostare al matrimonio, ho letto agli Sposi gli articoli 130, 131, 132 del codice civile quando ho domandato allo Sposo se intende di prendere in moglie Rinaldi Guendalina e a questa se intende di prender in marito Moreschi Alessandro, ed avendomi ciascuno risposto di sì, in presenza dei Testimoni sotto descritti ho pronunciato in nome della legge che i medesimi sono uniti in matrimonio. A quest'atto sono stati presenti Agostini Ottaviano di anni cinquanta, impiegato, Giancinquanta D. Giovanni, di anni cinquantanove, Salvatori Domenico di a. 41 cantante e Langeli D. Salvatore di a. 41. I documenti presentati sono il certificato delle pubblicazioni eseguite in Roma il diciannove e il ventisei Aprile corrente anno e il certificato del dottore Glori. Letto e firmato: Alessandro Moreschi, Guendalina Rinaldi, Ottaviano Agostini, Giovanni [L.?] Giancinquanta, Salvatore Langeli, Domenico Salvatori." Archivio di Stato, Documenti di Stato Civile, Matrimoni, 1896, vol. 1, part 2, series B, no. 13, p. 10. Marriages were also published, this one in Archivio di Stato, Documenti di Stato Civile: Matrimoni, pubblicazioni, vol. 1, part 1, series B, no. 38, p. 20. Alessandro was actually thirty-seven at the time, not thirty-six. In the same year, he also obtained official permission to become a full-fledged member of both the Lateran choir and the Cappella Giulia.

66. His actual age was forty-five at the time.

67. "L'anno millenovecentoquattro, addì diciannove di Marzo, ore diciannove, minuti dieci, nella Casa comunale. Avanti di me, Stefanelli cavalier Vincenzo Capo Sernone[?] delegato del Sindaco 10 marzo 1897 Ufficiale dello Stato Civile del Comune di Roma con atto approvato è comparso Moreschi Alessandro, di anni 38, artista di canto, domiciliato in Roma, il quale mi ha dichiarato che alle ore due e minuti trenta, del dì quindici del corrente mese, nella casa posta in Via Palombella al numero 38, da Rinaldi Guendalina sua moglie seco lui convivente è nato un bambino di sesso maschile, che non mi presenta, e a cui da il nome di Giulio Maria Pietro Luigi. A quanto sopra e a quest'atto sono stati presenti quali testimoni Davanti Antonio, di anni 52, impiegato, e Moreschi Amerigo, di anni 22, studente, entrambi residenti in questo Comune. La nascita ed il sesso furono accertati dalla levatrice Moreschi Maria, omessa la presentazione del neonato per igiene. Letto il presente atto agli interessati meco si firmano. Firmato; Moreschi Alessandro, Antonio Davanti, Moreschi Amerigo. L'Ufficiale Stefanelli[?]." A note on the left reads: "Il suddetto è morto a Roma il 14/07/1955, parte I, serie IV, vol. III, atto 947, anno 55, 26 ottobre 1955, il cancelliere [firma]." Archivio di Stato di Roma: Stato Civile Italiano, Atti di Nascita, 1904, vol. 3, part 1, series A, pp. 146–47 n. 1631.

68. Archivio di Stato di Roma, Stato civile italiano, Roma, 1899. Morti, n. 796-1591, vol. 2, part 1, series C, no. 827. She died on October 10, 1899, at age forty-eight.

69. Note, too, that the midwife, Maria Moreschi, apparently a member of the Moreschi family, was also registered in the parish archives as living with Alessandro and Guendalina beginning in 1903.

70. Luigi Devoti, "Alessandro Moreschi, detto 'L'angelo di Roma,' 1858–1922," in Renato Lefevbre and Arnaldo Morelli, eds., *Musica e musicisti nel Lazio* (Rome: Gruppo Culturale di Roma e del Lazio F.ll Polombi Editori, 1985), p. 467. Salvatore Meluzzi, Maestro di Musica della Cappella Giulia, letter of January 19, 1883, translation in Buning, "Alessandro Moreschi and the Castrato Voice," p. 122, lightly modified here. Clapton, *Moreschi and the Voice of the Castrato*, pp. 80–81, notes the rivalry Meluzzi felt toward Gaetano Capocci as part of the provocation for this nastiness, as well as Meluzzi's commitment to Cecilianism, which would lead two decades later to the expulsion of the castrati.

71. Peter Stallybrass and Allon White, *The Politics and Poetics of Transgression* (Ithaca: Cornell University Press, 1986).

72. Less likely would have been their attending to the elision with Il Panormita's

obscene fifteenth-century Latin text *Hermaphroditus* (1425), which takes the hermaphrodite to be a person of gender-mixed sexual proclivities, rather than gender-mixed anatomy. See Ugo Piscopo, *Alberto Savinio* (Milan: Mursia, 1973), pp. 78–79.

73. For Savinio's text I use Alberto Savinio, *Hermaphrodito*, with a note by Gian Carlo Roscioni (Turin: Einaudi, 1974).

74. The most relevant English-language writing on the brothers is Keala Jewell's *The Art of Enigma: The De Chirico Brothers and the Politics of Modernism* (University Park: Pennsylvania State University Press. 2004). On Savinio's hermaphrodite, see chapter 7, "Savinio's Jewish Hermaphrodite." Further biography appears in Nicol Maria Mocchi, "The Enigma of the Double: Sources and Symbols in Alberto Savinio's Poetics," *Italian Modern Art* 2 (July 2019), pp. 1–27. See also the complete issue.

75. On the early printings of parts of *Hermaphrodito*, see Roscioni's "Nota di testa," in Savinio, *Hermaphrodito*, p. 253.

76. Jewell, *The Art of Enigma*, p. 166.

77. Massimo Cacciari, "Saverio 'europeo,'" in *Mistero dello sguardo: Studi per un profilo di Alberto Savinio*, ed. Rosita Tordi (Rome: Bulzoni, 1992), p. 15, quoted in Franco Baldasso, "Impossible Homecoming: Alberto Savinio and His 'Hermaphrodito,'" *Italian Modern Art* 2 (July 2019), p. 21 n. 22.

78. Baldasso, "Impossible Homecoming," and "Alberto Savinio and the Myth of Babel: Homecoming, Genealogies, and Translation in *Hermaphrodito*," *Italianist* 49.1 (2020), pp. 44–65, and see the special issue "Alberto Savinio," *Italian Modern Art* 2 (July 2019). The questioning to which Baldasso draws attention does not simply reach back in time to build a new story of language but attempts something more far-reaching, expressed in the ontological challenges posed by the hermaphrodite: by discrediting the idea that Babel was the starting point of linguistic plurality, Baldasso claims, Savinio is able to use Babel to demonstrate "the absurdity of the founding myth of Western civilization, the original unity that supports all metaphysical systems from Plato onwards." "Impossible Homecoming," p. 3.

79. The principal theorist of errancy in more recent times is Édouard Glissant, whose *Poetics of Relation*, trans. Betsy Wing (Ann Arbor: University of Michigan Press, 1997), delineated the stakes in the notion that all relations are rhizomatic, made in relation to others, but also should be mobile, open, and ever evolving.

80. See Jacques Derrida, *Monolingualism of the Other; or, The Prosthesis of Origin*, trans. Patrick Mensah (Stanford: Stanford University Press, 1998), and on Derrida's critique

of ordinary language, Raoul Moati, *Derrida/Searle: Deconstruction and Ordinary Language*, trans. Timothy Attanucci and Maureen Chun (New York: Columbia University Press, 2014).

81. On this passage, see Baldasso, "Impossible Homecoming," p. 9, and for an English translation of just this part of *Hermaphrodito*, see *The Departure of the Argonaut*, trans. George Scrivani (London: Petersburg Press, 1986). Jewell, *The Art of Enigma*, illuminates the Jewish context, particularly of the Jews of Thessaloniki (Salonica) (pp. 173–75).

82. Roscioni stresses Savinio's antipathy toward the circle and his inclination toward jagged destinations, of which this is a principal one; Roscioni, "Nota di testa," in Savinio, *Hermaphrodito*, p. 237, for instance, Roscioni's emphasis on *equivoci*, oxymorons, and ambiguities, which he associates with the titling of the book (p. 246, and see Savinio, *Hermaphrodito*, p. 232).

83. That is, a box-shaped dwelling.

84. Jewell, *The Art of Enigma*, translates this as "pained guts" (p. 177), with an explanation on pp. 178–79. The term is refractory to translation.

85. "In una mia incursione di pocanzi, m'ero spinto fino alle porte della città ove si vedon nascere le case.

Ivi m'intoppai in un ebreo che aveva terminato di costruirsi un cuboide di mattoni, con tre aperture e un tetto a cuneo da cui si levava un palo che stava là con l'apatica imbecillità che può avere un parafulmine di legno.

Il tetto era ancora scoperto e rivelava la nuda piramide delle architravi su cui sventolavano due rami d'albero.

L'ebreo s'arrampicò in sul cocuzzolo e aprì le braccia come un re burlone. La sua voce secca e penetrante gridò poscia nel crepuscolo l'orazione grata per l'opera compiuta.

Proclamate all'aria libera, quelle dette da lui non erano parole sparse al vento: egli le pronunciava con cura e vigoria che davano loro il peso di gocce metalliche cascanti in un crogiolo solidificatore.

Quantunque fossi solo a musare davanti alla sua casascheletro e che, d'altronde, la mia presenza non l'avesse colpito, egli parlava con energia lungiportante e sembrava arringere larghe messi di popolo raccolte sotto di lui.

Sono uso di processare ogni mio plexus cerebrale, assolvendolo con plauso oppure condannandolo irrefutabilmente; per cui rischiai di compromettarmi di fronte alla mia coscienza che, sul principio, guidicai le fatiche oratorie sperperate dall'omuncolo, quali un indizio flagrante della sua imbecillità vanesia. Ma in tempo ravvisai l'errore e lo corressi: riterrò l'esempio per l'alterne vicende dei fatti a venire, e comporrò la mente mia in tal maniera si da esser pronto a un getto d'eroismi fuori dal fenomeno apparentemente più trito e più cretino.

Da quanto m'avvidì, il construttore semita, con ogni sua voce, stringeva un nodo attorno a un lungo anello mistico in cui s'andava inviluppando come entro un rosario di salsicce traendo a raccolta intorno a se una colonna di uomini, passati, presenti e futuri, che attraversava i secoli dall'una all'altra oscurità.

Nell'incomprensibile sanscrito di quell'uomo, intesi ch'egli riportava a se e in quella casa sua, tutti i fossili da cui aveva tratti il suo ingresso in questa vita storta; nonché suscitava intorno a se in quella casa sua tuttti gli zoidi che sarebbero germogliati da suo seme.

Egli era un uomo strano, vera macchina di mondo e degno d'illustrare la propria discendenza meglio che il Colleone di Venezia e il Tricouillard di Francia.

Come l'ebbi esaminato attenamente, scoprì la terribile fecondità rachiusa nel suo corpo bacato.

Prognosticai in lui un misto dei due sessi, con palese androginia e calcolo di patromaternità. Lo indovinai malato di un doppio motore genitale e sofferente così degli ovari che dei testicoli.

Benché la membratura mostrasse il travaglio di una cachessia progressiva, in essa era inciso il marchio dell'infallibile generazione—in osservanza della legge che moltiplica il fermento del germe su dalla vermina raggrumata.

Costui era votato alla procreazione e al conseguente problema del parto che lui, magari, avrebbe risolto da secolo.

Il sunto della diagnosi mi procurò la rivelazione affermata in appresso:

incinto tutti i nove giorni e mammelluto come un Teresias, l'uomo sul tetto butta dal meato puzzolente grappoli di carne che per terra si ritorcono, poi si levano e camminano, indi crescon con vigore—insufflati da un calore dilatante—e finalmente si fan uomini seriosi e dottrinari di morale." Savinio, *Hermaphrodito*, pp 228–30.

For a marvelous analysis of a shorter excerpt of this passage focusing on reproduction, see Jewell, *The Art of Enigma*, pp. 175–80.

86. In using male pronouns for the hermaphrodite here, I am following Savinio's text.

87. Perhaps better translated as "worm-devoured waste"—imagine the rot that worms help turn into compost.

88. Feldman, *The Castrato*, pp. 22–23.

89. Barbara Spackman, "Inter musam et ursam moritur: Folengo and the Gaping 'Other' Mouth," in Marilyn Migiel and Juliana Schiesari, eds., *Refiguring Woman: Perspectives on Gender in the Italian Renaissance* (Ithaca: Cornell University Press, 1991), pp. 19–34; Jewell, *The Art of Enigma*, p. 177.

90. See Katherine Meizel, *Multivocality: Singing on the Borders of Identity* (New York: Oxford University Press, 2020), who associates the boundary-busting of multivocal voices with the "movement and plasticity" of twenty-first-century searches for identity in response to neoliberal oppression (p. 2). Her analysis brings to mind such multivoiced twentieth-century singers as Maria Callas, Yma Sumac, and Nina Simone.

91. "Proclamate all'aria libera, quelle dette da lui non erano parole sparse al vento: egli le pronunciava con cura e vigoria che davano loro il peso di gocce metalliche cascanti in un crogiolo solidificatore." Savinio, *Hermaphrodito*, p. 228.

92. Baldasso illuminates the point with reference to an entry on Nietzsche in Savinio's much later *Nuova encyclopedia* (1977) that contains the following: "Nietzsche is a lyrical man. He is the most typical example of a lyrical man. He is the most lyrically complete man that I know of. Besides his work, his life itself is a lyrical fact. His philological excess, his philosophical excess, his philosophizing with a hammer, his will to power, his political excess, his ideas on states, on war are all forms of lyricism [and] they should be considered *more lyrici*, untied to any purpose—they should be taken as a game." Quoted in Baldasso, "Impossible Homecoming," p. 14; Alberto Savinio, *Nuova encyclopedia*, 7th ed. (Milan: Adelphi Edizoni, 2011), p. 270. On the hermaphrodite as proxy for Europe and antimasculinity, see ibid., p. 150. Feldman, *The Castrato*, chapter 3, "Red Hot Voice," talks about the castrato's control over multiple registers and timbres. On Callas's multiple registers as index of a kind of monstrosity in connection with divadom, see Wayne Koestenbaum, *The Queen's Throat: Opera, Homosexuality, and the Mystery of Desire* (New York: Poseidon Press, 1993). On multivocality as a contemporary tool of personal agency, see Meizel, *Multivocality*.

93. "Per quanto camminassi, non riuscì a slacciarmi dalla voce dello strano ermafrodito, che tagliava l'epoche da parte a parte. E pure invano volli cancellar la casa di mattoni: io la rividi sempre, e la rivedo ancora.

La casa, amici, la casa!
Chi fra di noi sapra mai sciogliere
l'enimmatico nodo di pietra?" Savinio, *Hermaphrodito*, p. 231.

94. Baldasso, "Impossible Homecoming," p. 10. And see Massimo Cacciari, "Savinio

'europeo,'" pp. 15–20, and Nicol M. Mocchi, *La cultura dei fratelli de Chirico agli albori dell'arte metafisica: Milano e Firenze, 1909–1911* (Milan: Scalpendi, 2017).

95. Savinio, *Hermaphrodito*, pp. 33–34, 39, 67, 110, 108, 117, 123, 56.

96. See Michael Denning and Gary Tomlinson, "Cantologies," in "Music and Sound at the Edges of History," ed. Martha Feldman and Nicholas Mathew, special issue, *Representations* 154.1 (Spring 2021), pp. 113–28. On the utopia of the hermaphrodite's realm, see Baldasso, "Impossible Homecoming," p.12.

97. "Poco fa, come fui rientrato nella camera venduta, mi tolsi un guanto e l'inchiodai alla parete. Il guanto penzoloni conserva la forma della mano vuota: io guardo in quel cadavere di mano il mio destino, che non è più di una cotenna sgonfia.

Nella tristezza dura che mi sta compagna, abbraccio la mia ultima amicizia.

Negligo la bestialità d'esser forte e salgo sul trapezio per l'esercizio finale: che si chiuderà in dramma—sì!—e, fra le berciate de' tromboni e gli strilli delle donne in platea, il giocoliere-equilibrista, stretto nel rosa-carne della maglia aderente, staccherà dal firmamento fulgido del circo, e, con un prillo tragico, piomberà nella segatura della pista, come una stella estiva.

Sul mondo mutante e medesimo, la mia casa non rimarrà, fra le case degli uomini."

(A short while ago, as I returned to the sold room, I removed a glove and nailed it to the wall. The dangling glove retains the shape of an empty hand: I look at my fate in that corpse of a hand, which is no more than a deflated rind.

In the harsh sadness that is my companion, I embrace my latest friendship.

I deny the bestiality of being strong, and I get on the trapeze for the final exercise: which will end in drama—yes!—and, among the barking of the trombones and the squeals of the women in the audience, the juggler-tightrope walker, clinging in the flesh-pink skin-tight shirt, the drama will detach from the shining firmament of the circus and, with a tragic twirl, will fall into the sawdust on the track, like a summer star.

On the changing and selfsame world, my house will not remain among the houses of men.) Savinio, *Hermaphrodito*, pp. 233–34.

98. For the relationship of Petronius's text to Fellini's film, see Dario Zanelli, ed., *Satyricon di Federico Fellini*, 2nd ed. (Rocca San Casciano: Cappelli, 1969), including Fellini's scenario treatment ("trattamento," pp. 105–45) and screenplay ("sceneggiatura, pp. 147–273), and Federico Fellini et al., *Making a Film* (1980; Contra Mundum Press, 2015), pp. 159–69, where Fellini talks about his attraction to Petronius's fragmentary and enigmatic text (on which further below). Peter Bonadanella, *The Cinema of Federico*

Fellini, with foreword by Federico Fellini (Princeton: Princeton University Press, 1992), pp. 253–61, supplies a trio of appendices summarizing the main elements of Petronius's text, Fellini's treatment, and the loose schematic divisions of the film print itself. The first two have colossal differences of narrative content that far outweigh their similarities, and there are also notable differences between the second and third sections.

99. The actor who plays the hermaphrodite goes uncredited in the film, as is true for many characters in *Satyricon*, but perhaps none as notable as this one. The credit is given in IMDB, https://www.imdb.com/title/tt0064940/fullcredits/?ref_=tt_cl_sm.

100. In the screenplay, it is not a woman.

101. See Martha Feldman, "*L'evirato castrato* and Other Castrato Conundra," in Andrea Chegai and Simone Caputo, eds., *"Tu Duca, Tu Segnore e Tu Maestro": Studi in onore di Franco Piperno* (Rome: Neoclassica, 2023), pp. 423–33, and see Àngel Medina, *Los atributos del capon: Imagen histórica de los cantores castrados en España* (Instituto Complutense de Ciencias Musicales, 2011), as well as Feldman, *The Castrato*, chapters 1–2.

102. Alessandro Carrera, *Fellini's Eternal Rome: Paganism and Christianity in the Films of Federico Fellini* (London: Bloomsbury Academic, 2019), p. 73.

103. Though boyish-looking in some respects, they were often taken to be older than they were; see the comments by Gaisberg and Hegermann-Lindencrone in Chapter 3 above.

104. Stephen Snyder, "Color, Growth, and Evolution in *Fellini Satyricon*," in Peter Bondanella, ed., *Federico Fellini: Essays in Criticism* (Oxford: Oxford University Press, 1978), p. 173 (see also p. 171).

105. "The presence of air is emphasized at the Villa of the Suicides by the toy of the young child, a glider 'airplane' . . . and by the solemn, unearthly, 'airy' behavior of the patricians in their act of suicide. There is intermittent wind present as the three thieves flee with the hermaphrodite, and 'its' loss of breath marks the end of this air/white section of the narrative." Snyder, "Color, Growth, and Evolution in *Fellini Satyricon*," p. 173.

106. Fellini, *Making a Film*, p. 167 (translation lightly modified).

107. See Mocchi, "The Enigma of the Double," p. 3.

108. Alberto Moravia, "Dreaming Up Petronius," trans. Raymond Rosenthal, *New York Review of Books* 14 (March 26, 1970); reprinted in *Federico Fellini: Essays in Criticism*, p. 166.

109. Ibid.

110. See Chapter 1 above. Even this, unsurprisingly, is a kind of fantasy of the past.

See Craig A. Monson's now-classic "The Council of Trent Revisited," *Journal of the American Musicological Society* 55.1 (Spring 2002), pp. 1–37. Fantasies of the past persist, along with dreams of resurrecting it. On December 20, 2023, AMS-Announce circulated the following message: "In 2025, Sacred Heart Parish in Grand Rapids, MI will be hosting Palestrina500, a yearlong festival honoring the life and legacy of composer Giovanni Pierluigi da Palestrina (1525–94) for the 500th anniversary of his birth. However, Palestrina500 is more than just a commemorative season of concerts: the festival aims to restore this Renaissance polyphony to its proper ritual context: the Latin Mass." Sacred Heart of Jesus Parish. "In the Year of Our Lord 2025, Palestrina 500," http://www.sacredheartgr.org/palestrina500.

111. Devoti, "Alessandro Moreschi, detto 'L'angelo di Roma,' 1858–1922," p. 467 (and see Clapton, *Moreschi and the Voice of the Castrato*, p. 79).

112. Franz Haböck, *Die Kastraten und ihre Gesangskunst, eine gesangsphysiologische, kultur- und musik- historische Studie* (Stuttgart, Deutsche Verlags-Anstalt, 1927), p. 208.

CHAPTER FIVE: SECRETS, PHANTOMS, AND CRYPTS

The second epigraph is from Nicolas Abraham, "The Phantom of *Hamlet* or The Sixth Act, *preceded by* The Intermission of Truth," in Nicolas Abraham and Maria Torok, *The Shell and the Kernel: Renewals of Psychoanalysis, Volume 1*, ed. and trans. Nicholas T. Rand (Chicago: University of Chicago Press, 1994), p. 190. (Translation lightly modified.)

1. In any case, Rita inherited very little, as confirmed by Fabio.

2. This is because, as Valerio Valeri writes, "survivors perpetuate around . . . [the remains of the dead] the exchanges and relations that made them exist socially when they were alive." "Mourning," in *Classic Concepts in Anthropology*, ed. Rupert Stasch and Giovanni da Col (Chicago: Hau Books, 2018), p. 167. Françoise Meltzer reminds me that in French "revenant" means literally "that which returns" (email, February 10, 2025).

3. Rebecca Schneider, *Performing Remains: Art and War in Times of Theatrical Reenactment* (New York: Routledge, 2011).

4. The book, published in English as Anne Ancelin Schützenberger, *The Ancestor Syndrome: Transgenerational Psychotherapy and the Hidden Links in the Family Tree*, trans. Anne Trager (East Sussex: Routledge, 1998), was originally issued as *Aïe, mes aïeux!: Liens transgénérationnels, secrets de famille, syndrome d'anniversaire et pratique du génosociogramme* (Paris: Epi-D De Brouwer: La Méridienne, 1993). It appeared in Italian twelve years after its initial publication, as *La sindrome degli antenati: Psicoterapia transgenerazionale e i*

legami nascosti nell'albero genealogico, trans. Francesca Garofoli (Rome: Di Renzo, 2005), achieving popularity with reissues in 2010, 2011, and 2019.

5. Ancelin Schützenberger extends J. L. [Jacob Levy] Moreno's work on "social atoms," which are instances of such networks and their statuses as they pertain to a given person. *The Ancestor Syndrome*, pp. 8–10. She also follows Henri Collomb's elaborations of Moreno (pp. 10–11) in arriving at the "genosociogram" as an "annotated family tree."

6. Typical would have been to name the child after Guendalina's father, Pietro, but Guendalina had clearly broken off relations with him by then, as evidenced in her calling herself "Guendalina Rinaldi fu Pietro" (Guendalina Rinaldi daughter of the late Pietro Rinaldi) in the parish records of 1902, when he was still very much alive (as noted in Chapter 1 above; see Figure 1.4b).

7. See Sigmund Freud, *The Uncanny*, trans. David McClintock (1919; New York: Penguin Books, 2003), pp. 123–66, esp. pp. 124–25 and 148, and relatedly, Jacques Derrida, *Specters of Marx: The State of the Debt, the Work of Mourning, and the New International*, trans. Peggy Kamuf (New York: Routledge, 1994), and *Archive Fever: A Freudian Impression*, trans. Eric Prenowitz (Chicago: University of Chicago Press, 1996). See also Mark Fisher, "What Is Hauntology?" *Film Quarterly* 66.1 (2012), pp. 16–24.

8. Nicholas Royle, *The Uncanny* (New York: Routledge, 2003), p. 8.

9. On the somewhat differing accounts by Rita and Fabio, see Chapter 1 above.

10. Ancelin Schützenberger, *The Ancestor Syndrome*, pp. 18 and 44–47. For an account of their theories of haunting, secrets, phantoms, and crypts situating them within contemporaneous Parisian psychoanalytic circles, see Syrine Slim, *L'Affaire Abraham et Torok: Légende, vie et secrets* (Paris: Presses universitaires de France, 2021).

11. See Ancelin Schützenberger's discussions of Abraham and Torok in ibid., pp. 44–48, 144–45 and 147–49, as well as pp. 12, 64, 141, and 164. Their work is collected for readers of English in Nicolas Abraham and Maria Torok, *The Shell and the Kernel: Renewals of Psychoanalysis, Volume 1*, ed. Nicholas T. Rand (Chicago: University of Chicago Press, 1994).

12. Abraham, born in Kecskemét, migrated to Paris in 1938, and Torok, born in Budapest, relocated to Paris in 1947. Most of *The Shell and the Kernel* appeared originally as *L'ecorce et le noyau* (Paris: Flammarion, 1987), twelve years after Abraham's death. A book on their work by Syrine Slim, *L'Affaire Abraham et Torok: Légende, vie et secrets* (Paris: Presses universitaires de France, 2021), takes up their theories of haunting, secrets, phantoms, and crypts and situates them in the thinking of contemporaneous Parisian psychoanalytic circles.

13. Nicolas Abraham, "Notes on the Phantom: A Complement to Freud's Metapsychology," trans. Nicholas T. Rand, in Françoise Meltzer, ed., *The Trial(s) of Psychoanalysis* (Chicago: University of Chicago Press, 1987), p. 75; the essay also appears in *The Shell and the Kernel*, pp. 171–76.

14. Jean Laplanche and Jean-Bertrand Pontalis, *The Language of Psycho-Analysis*, trans. Donald Nicholson-Smith (New York: Norton, 1973). Originally published as Jean Laplanche and J.-B. Pontalis, *Vocabulaire de la psychanalyse* (Paris: Presses universitaires de France, 1967). Abraham's review essay, "L'ecorce et le noyau," *Critique* 249 (1968), pp. 162–81, is published in English as Nicolas Abraham, "The Shell and the Kernel: The Scope and Originality of Freudian Psychoanalysis," trans. Nicholas T. Rand, in Abraham and Torok, *The Shell and the Kernel*, pp. 79–98, with Rand's editorial commentary on pp. 75–78. Abraham's proposals there almost oppose those that Jacques Lacan was making during almost the same time period. Abraham's preoccupation was the realm of the asemantic or antisemantic—the realm of what he called "anasemia," which is to say the antisymbolic—whereas Lacan's theories (very roughly put) look at how the subject is embedded in language but exceeds it. A useful review of the former is Maria Yassa's "Nicolas Abraham and Maria Torok: The Inner Crypt," *Scandinavian Psychoanalytic Review* 25.2 (2002), pp. 1–14, with an explanation of the shell and the kernel at pp. 3–5. See also Esther Rashkin, *Family Secrets and the Psychoanalysis of Narrative* (Princeton: Princeton University Press, 1992), which relies deeply on Abraham and Torok.

15. Jacques Derrida, "*Fors:* The Anglish Words of Nicolas Abraham and Maria Torok," trans. Barbara Johnson, in Nicolas Abraham and Maria Torok, *The Wolf Man's Magic Word: A Cryptonomy*, trans. Nicholas Rand (Minneapolis: University of Minnesota Press, 1986), pp. xi–xlviii. Rand's introduction to *The Shell and the Kernel* explains the basic problem of introjection as fundamental to psychic life, offering the following on its core principle and operation. "A preliminary definition might be that it is a constant process of acquisition and assimilation, the active expansion of our potential to accommodate our own emerging desires and feelings as well as the events and influences of the external world." Rand, "Introduction: Renewals of Psychoanalysis," in *The Shell and the Kernel*, pp. 9–10. Slim, *L'Affaire Abraham et Torok*, who interviewed various living associates and witnesses, devotes some attention to biography, including to Abraham's nephew Nicholas Rand, who married Torok some time after Abraham's death (according to Wikipedia in 1990) and became literary executor of the Abraham / Torok estate after the death of Torok in

1998. Slim points out fault lines in biographical sources used by Rand and others (Kindle edition, location 216–45 of 6068 etc.).

On Abraham and Torok's notions of introjection and incorporation, see also Nicolas Abraham and Maria Torok, "Mourning *or* Melancholia: Introjection *versus* Incorporation" (1972), in *The Shell and the Kernel*, pp. 125–38; Tom Goodwin, "The Haunted Delimitation of Subjectivity in the Work of Nicolas Abraham: Translator's Preface," *Diacritics*, 44.4 (2016), pp. 6–7; and Yassa, "Nicolas Abraham and Maria Torok," pp. 6–9.

16. Christopher Lane, "The Testament of the Other: Abraham and Torok's Failed Expiation of Ghosts," *Diacritics* 27.4 (Winter 1997), pp. 9–12. More appreciatively, Goodwin, in the course of explaining their term "anasemia," notes: "The neologism *anasemia* (translating the French *anasémie*) is the term by which Abraham defines all authentic psychoanalytic concepts. Combining *ana* from the Greek for 'up, back, again, anew' with a derivative of the Greek *sēma* pertaining to the production of meaning, it designates a discourse that has no reality or usage other than in its function of mediation between a *shell of phenomenal sense (or conscious reality)* and a *kernel of non-sense* whose continual displacement and disruption of the shell's meanings stands as their ever-deferred and traumatic origin. Between these realms, the distinctions between fiction and reality become more fluid, especially where clinical effectiveness is the purpose of interpretative construction." "The Haunted Delimitation of Subjectivity in the Work of Nicolas Abraham," n. 9 (emphasis mine).

17. Lane, "The Testament of the Other," p. 10 n. 9.

18. See Rand's introduction to part 4 of *The Shell and the Kernel*, "New Perspectives in Metapsychology: Cryptic Mourning and Secret Love," pp. 99–100.

19. I unpack this euphemism and some of the history and logics behind it in "*L'evirato castrato* and Other Castrato Conundra," in Andrea Chegai and Simone Caputo, eds., *"Tu Duca, Tu Segnore e Tu Maestro": Studi in onore di Franco Piperno* (Rome: Neoclassica, 2023), pp. 423–32.

20. Ibid.

21. Given that Vittoria married Giulio three years after Alessandro's death, she likely did not hear that from the castrato himself. If the speculation is correct, then Giulio lay biologically close to Alessandro. It's worth noting that Giulio and Amerigo seem to have been close. The death notice for Alessandro was signed by both together, and Giulio and Vittoria also took over the running of Cinema Venezia after Amerigo's death in 1925. Rita and Fabio wondered whether the father could instead have been the croupier with the last name of

Mancini, Guendalina's paramour with whom she ran away three years after Giulio's birth. If true, it would have made Giulio a cruel memento for Alessandro, having been publicly cuckolded, left, and bankrupted in a chain of events that led to his raising the abandoned son of the wife who abandoned them both and who shamed the family in acts that were ugly and disreputable, producing a distinct history of "we don't talk about it." But that may well have been the case even if the biological father was Amerigo and even if the child had been planned in advance. See Ancelin Schützenberger, *The Ancestor Syndrome*, p. 44.

22. Nicholas Rand, "Psychoanalysis with Literature: An Abstract of Nicolas Abraham and Maria Torok's *The Shell and the* Kernel," *Oxford Literary Review* 12.1–2 (1990), p. 59. See further on Abraham and Torok's crypts in Yassa, "Nicholas Abraham and Maria Torok," pp. 8–9; Goodwin, "The Haunted Delimitation of Subjectivity in the Work of Nicolas Abraham," p. 12 nn. 17–18; "Freud, the Wolf Man, and the Encrypted Dynamism of Revolutionary History," *European Journal of Psychoanalysis* (2012), https://www.journal-psychoanalysis.eu/articles/freud-the-wolf-man-and-the-encrypted-dynamism-of-revolutionary-history; Rashkin, *Family Secrets and the Psychoanalysis of Narrative*, pp. 175–76 and p. 175 n. 39; Dominique La Capra, "History and Psychoanalysis," in Meltzer, *The Trial(s) of Psychoanalysis*, pp. 9–38; and Gabriele Schwab, *Haunting Legacies: Violent Histories and Transgenerational Trauma* (New York: Columbia University Press, 2010).

23. See, for example, Judith T. Zeitlin, *The Phantom Heroine: Ghosts and Gender in Seventeenth-century Chinese Literature* (Honolulu: University of Hawai'i Press, 2007), and Ernesto De Martino, *Morte e pianto rituale nel mondo antico: Dal lamento funebre antico al pianto di Maria* (Turin: Edizioni scientifiche Einaudi, 1958). Especially pertinent on the literary dimension is Rashkin, *Family Secrets and the Psychoanalysis of Narrative*, particularly chapter 1, which deals with Abraham and Torok.

24. Colin Davis, "État present: Hauntology, Spectres, and Phantoms," *French Studies* 59.3 (2005), p. 374, and see p. 378 on the phantom as liar. Zeitlin, *The Phantom Heroine*, deals with Ming dynasty female ghosts. Extensive art and literature exists on the Chinese ghost Zhong Kui, the demon king of ghosts but also ghost vanquisher, dramatized in Huang Shuqin's riveting 1987 film *Woman Human Demon*, discussed in Haiyan Lee, "*Woman, Demon, Human*: Spectral Journey Home," in Chris Berry, ed., *Chinese Films in Focus II* (New York: Palgrave Macmillan, 2008), pp. 243–49.

25. The point is suggested indirectly in the summary of Abraham and Torok's contributions by Yassa, "Nicolas Abraham and Maria Torok," p. 8.

26. Davis, "État present," p. 377. See also Derrida, "*Fors*."

27. See Maria Torok, "Story of Fear: The Symptoms of Phobia—the Return of the Repressed or the Return of the Phantom?," in Abraham and Torok, *The Shell and the Kernel*, pp. 177–86.

28. Illegitimacy has figured elsewhere in analyses of transgenerational haunting, notably in Serge Tisseron's *Tintin chez le psychanalyste: Essai sur le création graphique e la mise en scène de ses enjeux dans l'oeuvre d'Hergé* (Paris: Aubier Montaigne, 1985), and *Tintin et le secret d'Hergé* (Paris: Hors Collection—Presses de la Cité, 1993), which analyze a sequence of adventures in which the protagonist is haunted by ancestors, the source of which Tisseron attributes to an illegitimate birth of the author, Belgian cartoonist Hergé, a pseudonym for Georges Remi (1907–1983). See Davis, "État present," p. 375.

29. See Chapter 1, n. 15 above.

30. Françoise Meltzer, "Introduction: Partitive Plays, Pipe Dreams," in *The Trial(s) of Psychoanalysis*, p. 1.

31. Torok, "Story of Fear," p. 179. Notably, as Françoise Meltzer reminds me (email of February 10, 2025), a prominent example of transgenerational haunting given by Abraham concerns a man who badly wants to be an aristocrat and keeps trying to understand why he does. It turns out that his father had the same wish, which his son inherited without knowing why. See Abraham, "Notes on the Phantom," pp. 76–77.

32. Abraham, "Notes on the Phantom," p. 78.

33. Ibid., p. 79.

34. Ibid. See Maria Torok, "The Illness of Mourning and the Fantasy of the Exquisite Corpse," in *The Shell and the Kernel*, pp. 107–24, and Derrida *"Fors,"* pp. xvi–xviii. See also Yassa, "Nicholas Abraham and Maria Torok," pp. 2, 5–8, and 12, and Rand in Abraham and Torok, *The Shell and the Kernel*, p. 100. On "secrets" as a matter of differentiation, see Davis, "État present," pp. 378–79.

35. See also Davis, "État present," p. 376.

36. Derrida, "*Fors.*"

37. On these relationships, coinvestments, and entanglements, see her brilliant review essay of several works of Abraham and Torok's: Peggy Kamuf, "Abraham's Wake," *Diacritics* 9.1 (1979), pp. 31–43.

38. Ibid., p. 38.

39. Nicolas Abraham and Maria Torok, *Cryptonomie: Le verbier et L'Homme aux loups* (Paris: Aubier-Flammarion, 1976).

40. See Kamuf, "Abraham's Wake," especially p. 39.

41. Of course, they were clinicians, unlike Derrida.

42. Nicholas Royle, *The Uncanny*, pp. 281–83. See also Davis, "État present," for a succinct delineation of differences between transgenerational haunting and deconstructive spectral haunting.

43. Abraham, "Notes on the Phantom," p. 79. Emphasis in the original.

44. Nicholas Rand, in Abraham and Torok, *The Shell and the Kernel*, "Part IV. Secrets and Posterity: The Theory of the Transgenerational Phantom," editor's note, p. 167.

45. One might almost think of the wounded kinship written of in Black American studies, for example David Marriott, *Haunted Life: Visual Culture and Black Modernity* (Brunswick: Rutgers University Press, 2007); Saidiya Hartman, *Lose Your Mother* (New York: Farrar Straus and Giroux, 2008); and Fred Moten, *In the Break: The Aesthetics of the Black Radical Tradition* (Minnesota: University of Minnesota Press, 2003).

46. At about that time, a freelance French historian-genealogist, Jérome Blanc, began working for an admirer of the castrato's who had befriended Fabio and Rita not long after my initial visit in May 2010. He and I had some limited correspondence before his death in 2015.

47. There is no evidence that might reveal who placed the picture of Pietro Rinaldi on the tomb, and Rita and Fabio did not know.

48. On March 23, 2015, when I recorded conversations with Fabio shortly before the closing of the Fellini shop, he told me: "I dreamt of Julio, and Rita was not yet dead, she was still living, he showed me . . . the street, because he was dead and had died falling on the street in front of a bus stop; and then he said to me, showing me the slope of the street, he said 'Fabio, dig here, I am dead, I fell here,' probably because when dying he had fallen, and the last thing he saw was the black of the sloping pavement; and . . . I said 'But no, Julio, you are not buried here, you are properly buried, I took you to the cemetery, I made a funeral for you, I know where you are, you aren't here."

49. The work on the tomb addressed the vandalism, which apparently involved architectural ornaments. It's hard to say what was actually stolen or ruined because the tomb was evidently damaged during Allied bombings, which also destroyed a number of documents in the cemetery archives.

50. Federico Fellini, preface to *Fellini's Satyricon*, ed. Dario Zanelli, trans. Eugene Waller and John Matthews (New York: Ballantine Books, 1970), p. 43; reprinted as "Preface to *Satyricon*," in *Federico Fellini: Essays in Criticism*, ed. Peter Bondanella (Oxford: Oxford University Press, 1978), pp. 16–19.

51. The quote, from Dario Zanelli, "From the Planet Rome," in *Fellini's Satyricon*, p. 4, is based on conversations with Fellini.

52. Alberto Moravia, "Dreaming Up Petronius," trans. Raymond Rosenthal, in *Federico Fellini: Essays in Criticism*, p. 163.

53. See Federico Fellini, "My Rimini," *Aperture* 172 (Fall 2003), pp. 24–37, with photographs by Marco Pesaresi (unattributed translation of an essay from 1967).

54. In *Federico Fellini: Comments on Film*, ed. Giovanni Grazzini, trans. Joseph Henry (Fresno: Press at California State University, Fresno, 1988), p. 28.

55. The note has never been published. It arrived as an addendum to the archive in a mailing from Fabio in April 2024, along with a cache of additional photographs and other documents.

56. See, among much else, Tullio Kezich, *Federico Fellini: His Life and Work* (New York: Faber & Faber, 2006), chapters 2, 3, 4, and 5, and Marco Bellano, "Fellini's Graphic Heritage: Drawings, Comics, Animation, and Beyond," in Franke Burke, Margherite Waller, and Marita Gubareva, eds., *A Companion to Federico Fellini* (Hoboken: John Wiley & Sons, 2020), pp. 59–77.

57. I received the card in a package from Fabio only on September 16, 2024, as this book was about to go into production. Although the invitation is apparently completely unknown, it was fairly obvious that it was Fellini's work. On the evening of the day it arrived, I nonetheless spent time looking through Fellini's comic-book drawings in an effort to confirm for myself that Fellini had to have made the invitation. The next day, on September 17, I got an email from Fabio asking if I'd received "Uncle Federico's" wedding invitation. Kezich describes invitations Fellini made the year before, for Rinaldo Geleng's wedding and again for his own wedding to Giulietta, in *Federico Fellini*, pp. 50 and 73–74.

The package that arrived also included two books. One was by the well-known psychologist and psychedelic drug advocate Timothy Leary with Joanna Leary and Lynn Wayne Benner, *Terra II: The Starseed Transmission* (San Francisco: Imprinting Press, 1974), which contains a hand-written dedication to Fellini. Fabio's impression was that the Learys' book was kept by Fellini all his life, but a fascinating volume on Fellini's library, Oriana Maroni and Giuseppe Ricci, ed., *I libri di casa mia: La biblioteca di Federico Fellini* (Rimini: Fondazione Federico Fellini with La Pieve Poligrafica Editore, 2008) — the other book in Fabio's package — does not include it among the 1,915 volumes catalogued there. Two other books of Timothy Leary's do figure among those catalogued, together with various other books on magic, psychology, the occult, psychedelics, and the supernatural. It may be that Rita borrowed *Terra II* as she worked on her manuscript *In viaggio con lo zio*, which deals with her adventures with Federico in exploring the occult and could explain why Fabio had the book in his possession in 2024.

58. Kezich, *Federico Fellini*, p. 23, remarks that Riccardo joked that he married the seventeen-year-old Alessandra when he himself was only twenty-two because "he'd sung *Prendi l'anel ti dono* from Bellini's *La sonambula* one too many times." Federico himself seems to have penned the score. The notation approximates the tenor's vocal line, though with some mistakes.

59. For a thoughtful exploration of Riccardo's life and his relationship with Federico, with interviews of Rita (albeit omitting the Moreschi connection), see the documentary film *L'altro Fellini* (2013), 1:9, directed by Stefano Bisulli and Roberto Naccari, produced by Paolo Pallavidino and Giusi Santoro, EiE film, Cinematica, and POPCult and distributed by Windrose, a film that was in the making during the time I was beginning to research this book. It is available with English subtitles, albeit with a paywall, at https://video.alexanderstreet.com/watch/l-altro-fellini and a trailer is available at https://www.youtube.com/watch?v=Dv5MHxvdoOE.

60. See Tullio Kezich, "*Somnii explanatio*, or In the Realm Where Everything Is Possible," in Federico Fellini, *The Book of Dreams*, ed. Sergio Toffetti with Gian Luca Farinelli and Felice Laudadio (New York: Rizzoli, 2020), pp. 571–79, originally published in the edition of 2007.

61. Kezich, "*Somnii explanatio*," who notes that Fellini's interest in dreams was longstanding, that after Bernhard's death on June 25, 1965, Fellini continued his therapy for "a certain period" with Bernhard's widow, Dora Friedlaender, and that prior to those sessions, in 1954, he had abandoned earlier Freudian sessions with Emilio Servadio (pp. 573–74). In *L'altro Fellini*, Vittorio De Seta takes credit for getting Fellini to the office of Bernhard (beginning at 25:00), although it was Bernhard who got Fellini started on recording his dreams.

62. I am not the first to remark on this. Note similarly the tagline for *L'altro Fellini*: "Two brothers united by the same dream: the Cinema, and separated by the same surname." The film spends some time on the matter.

63. Fellini, *The Book of Dreams*, i/75 and translation on p. 496 (my underlining, added to reflect the original). Presumably Riccardo had just signed his *Storie sulla sabbia* (1963) by then, an unprepossessing effort that did not meet with success (see below).

64. The caption reads "Bernhard says to me: 'Talk to me about your brother Riccardo.' So I tell him this episode . . . from my most distant childhood." Ibid., iii/16 and translation on p. 558.

65. Ibid., i/79, translation on p. 497.

66. Ibid., i/86, translation on p. 498.

67. Ibid., i/81, translation on p. 497. The term "Moviola" generally refers to a machine that makes it possible to view a film while it's being edited. Fellini's drawing suggests he had that in mind here.

68. Almost twenty years after *Storie sulla sabbia*, that documentary, about Italians and their pets, had a better reception. See *L'altro Fellini*, 41:30–48:50.

69. Fellini, *The Book of Dreams*, i/152, translation on p. 508.

70. Ibid., i/160, translation on p. 510.

71. Ibid., p. 515.

72. See Kezich, *Federico Fellini*, pp. 265–80, with a brief reference to the dreams on p. 274, and Federico Fellini, with Dino Buzzati, Brunello Rondi, and Bernardino Zapponi, *The Journey of G. Mastorna*, trans. Marcus Perryman (New York: Berghahn, 2013), with preface by Peter Bondanella (pp. ix–xi) briefly summarizing the circumstances that led to the catastrophic failure of the film to be made.

73. Fellini, *The Book of Dreams*, ii/49, translation on p. 533.

74. Starting at around 29:00, the film dilates on the brothers' break over Riccardo's use of their surname. Rita also offers an explanation there for the breakup of Riccardo and her mother Alessandra. *L'altro Fellini*, beginning at 20:55.

75. Francesca Fabbri Fellini, Fellini's niece via Maddalena Fellini Fabbri and her husband, Giorgio Fabbri, has shared the picture at https://www.federicofellini.info/giorgio-fabbri-racconta-il-suo-fellini, third photo down. See also a posting of a photograph showing (left to right) Giorgio Fabbri, Maddalena Fellini Fabbri, Giulietta Masina, Federico Fellini, Rita Fellini, Ida Barbiani Fellini, Urbano Fellini, Alessandra Moreschi, and Riccardo Fellini, presumably at the Fellini home about 1950, at https://www.facebook.com/photo/?fbid=2980830238645459&set=a.207813005947210&locale=bs_BA.

76. See *L'altro Fellini*.

EPILOGUE: THE CASTRATO INHERITANCE

The second epigraph is from Avery Gordon, *Ghostly Matters: Haunting and the Sociological Imagination*, 2nd ed. (Minneapolis: University of Minnesota Press, 2008), p. 18.

1. Lydia Goehr, *The Imaginary Museum of Musical Works: An Essay in the Philosophy of Music* (Oxford: Clarendon Press of Oxford University Press, 1992).

2. See Barbara Spackman, *Fascist Virilities: Rhetoric, Ideology, and Social Fantasy in Italy* (Minneapolis: University of Minnesota Press, 1996). April 3, 1926, saw the institutionalization of Fascist spectacle via the Federazione Nazionale Fascista Industriale dello Spettacolo. By that time, 225 movie theaters already existed in Italy. Mussolini's famed statement about populist cinema as a universalist phenomenon and coordinator of international education and order was issued in 1928. See Gian Piero Brunetta, *Storia del cinema italiano, 1895–1945* (Rome: Riunti, 1979), pp. 238 and 244–47; a condensed English version is available as *The History of Italian Cinema: A Guide to Italian Film From Its Origins to the Twenty-first Century*, trans. Jeremy Parzen (Princeton: Princeton University Press, 2009).

3. Sandro Bellassai, "The Masculine Mystique: Antimodernism and Virility in Fascist Italy," *Journal of Modern Italian Studies* 10 (2005), pp. 314–35, and especially *L'invenzione della virilità: Politica e immaginario maschile nell'Italia contemporanea* (Rome: Carrocci, 2011), which ties Italian virility to tradition, imperialism, colonialism, and Fascism and traces its decline after World War Two.

4. Giovanni Gavazzi, quoted in Alessandro Gabrielli, "Appendice: Riassunto delle conversazioni sulla storia delle Cappelle musicali romane. III. La Cappella Sistina dall'Ottocento ad oggi," *Rassegna dorica: Cultura e cronaca musicale* 10.3 (January 1939), p. 255.

5. Anton Giulio Bragaglia, *Fotodinamismo futurista* (Rome: Nalato, 1911). About this intriguing and enterprising figure, Sisto Sallusti notes: "From his father, capricious and biting, and his mother, tenaciously tied to the cult of her ancestor Ennio Quirino Visconti, he inherited a double nature: as a restless man of the theater inclined to extremisms and as a diligent and meticulous researcher." Sisto Sallusti, s.v. "Bragaglia, Anton Giulio," *Dizionario Biografico degli Italiani* 13 (1971): https://www.treccani.it/enciclopedia/anton-giulio-bragaglia_%28Dizionario-Biografico%29.

6. Anton Giulio Bragaglia, *Degli "evirati cantori": Contributo alla storia del teatro* (Florence: Sansoni, 1959). The futurist manifesto is titled "Il manifesto del cinema futurista," dated Milan, September 11, 1916. Many museums hold prints of Bragaglia's photographs. I consulted the rich collection of Bragaglia materials at the Biblioteca e Raccolta di Teatro Burcardo, now Biblioteca Museo Teatrale SIAE. There's much writing on Bragaglia and his brothers. See Alberto Cesare Alberti, *Poetica teatrale e bibliografia di Anton Giulio*

Bragaglia (Rome: Bulzoni, 1978) for a wide-ranging one, and Mario Verdone, *Anton Giulio Bragaglia* (Rome: Centro Sperimentale di Cinematografia and Edizioni di Bianco e Nero, 1965). On *Thaïs*, see Millicent Marcus, "Anton Giulio Bragaglia's 'Thaïs'; or, The Death of the Diva + The Rise of the Scenoplastica = The Birth of Futurist Cinema," *South Central Review* 13.2–3 (Summer–Autumn, 1996), pp. 63–81, which is highly critical of the film. Two other futurist films of 1917 and 1918, now lost, were also filmed by Bragaglia. For a general biographical overview, see the *Dizionario biografico degli italiani* entry cited in note 5 above.

7. Bragaglia, *Degli "evirati cantori,"* p. 35.

8. Gino Monaldi, *Cantanti evirati celebri del teatro italiano* (Rome: Ausonia, 1920). Bragaglia lambasts Monaldi's text (p. 7), citing glaring errors of fact. On Monaldi, who managed Rome's Costanzi and Argentina theaters from 1891 to 1893, see Biancamaria Brumana, s,v, "Monaldi, Gino," *Dizionario biografico degli italiani* 75 (2011), https://www.treccani.it/enciclopedia/gino-monaldi_(Dizionario-Biografico).

9. One of these inspired my reading of the castrato's linkage to the comic character of Pulcinella, in Feldman, *The Castrato: Reflections on Natures and Kinds* (Oakland: University of California Press, 2015), pp. 22–27.

10. I'm indebted to Rebecca Bauman for first drawing my attention to the episode.

11. Tonino's last name, Gambacorta, meaning "short leg," extends the joke metonymically, inasmuch as Tonino is short on something, if not his leg.

12. The actor who played the role of Tonino Gambacorta is uncredited.

13. My thanks to Armando Maggi, who encouraged me to read the novel and also think about the figure of the passive male homosexual that dominates Italian thinking of this period.

14. A fuller treatment of these films would include *Il marchese di Grillo* (The Marquis of Grillo, 1981), directed by Mario Monicelli, with Alberto Sordi again in the title role, where castrati play a minor part in one theater scene.

15. One could cite many models and precedents for writing nonsequential history. Two that explicitly argue for its value are Heather Love's *Feeling Backward: Loss and the Politics of Queer History* (Cambridge, MA: Harvard University Press, 2009) and Elizabeth Freeman's *Time Binds: Queer Temporalities, Queer Histories* (Durham: Duke University Press, 2010).

16. Jonathan Sterne, *The Audible Past: Cultural Origins of Sound Reproduction* (Durham: Duke University Press, 2003), p. 9.

17. Sara Danius, *The Senses of Modernism: Technology, Perception, and Aesthetics* (Ithaca: Cornell University Press, 2002), pp. 11–20.

18. The theater originally opened in 1906 as the Sala Vittorio Emmanuele to accommodate what *Il messaggero* called "the good taste of the owners," who succeeded in opening "a true jewel of elegance and comfort," which was to be "the preferred gathering spot [*ritrovo*] of the elite of Roman society and those who love to watch select spectacles with a refined understanding of art." On September 16, 1911, under the new proprietorship of Francesco Castellino, it was rebuilt, its name changed to Cinema Venezia, and the next year screened a filmic version of Puccini's *La bohème*. Vittoria is listed as owner in 1928–1929 and Giulio in 1930. The information about ownership comes from the *Guida Monaci* (Rome) for 1917, p. 1042 for 19281929, p. 825, and for 1930, p. 826. The gap in ownership in the years 1926 and 1927 could have resulted from the workings of a slow bureaucracy. Roberto Parisi suspected that Giulio carried on after Amerigo died, even though neither Giulio nor Vittoria was registered as owners until 1928. (Private communication, 2011.) I thank him for helping to track and parse matters of movie theater ownership in Rome.

A tie between the Castellino and Moreschi families must have extended to theater connections, and they apparently endured. Maria Sciandra (1830–1927), described as "in Castellino" (i.e. married into the Castellino family), was evidently related to Francesco Castellino—probably, given her age, as his mother. Upon her death, she was buried in the Moreschi-Rinaldi tomb, but only for one year before being moved to the newly opened Castellino tomb in 1928.

19. Archivio Capitolino, Verbale delle Deliberazioni Giunta Municipale di Roma, August 16, 1911, Prot. 79661, Copia all'Ufficio V. (I.E.), document issued based on a decision of July 11, 1911. The principal text reads: "13°= Al sig. Castellino Francesco per ridurre ad uso di Cinematografo e locali terreni con ingresso a via Nazionale 129 [now Cesare Battisti] e uscito sul vicolo Mancino a condizione che il lucernario della sala abbia sportelli apribili; che nei lavori di adattamento sia eliminato l'uso di materiali combustibili e salve le ulteriori condizioni imposte dalla Commissione Prefettizia per la sorveglianza dei teatri ecc."

20. See Spiro Kostof, *The Third Rome, 1870–1950: Traffic and Glory* (Berkeley: University Art Museum, 1973), pp. 56–59, and D. Medina Lasansky, *The Renaissance Perfected: Architecture, Spectacle, and Tourism in Fascist Italy* (University Park: Pennsylvania State University Press, 2004). My thanks to architectural historian Martha Pollak for the references and for help with reading the architectural plans.

21. As Freya Jarman discussed in her "Vexatious Voices: Madness and Other Metaphysical Journeys of Pitch," paper given at the conference "Errant Voices: Performances

Beyond Measure," University of Chicago, April 29–30, 2002, related to her book in preparation.

22. See Feldman, *The Castrato*, preface and chapter 1.

23. From Jacques Derrida, *The Archeology of the Frivolous: Reading Condillac*, trans. John P. Leavey, Jr. (Pittsburgh: Duquesne University Press, 1980), quoted in Robert Bernasconi, "Supplement," in Claire Colebrook, ed., *Jacques Derrida: Key Concepts* (New York: Routledge, 2015), p. 22.

24. See the literature cited in the Prologue, note 12.

25. Peggy Kamuf, "Abraham's Wake," *Diacritics* 9.1 (1979), p. 42.

26. Franchetti was a wealthy Mantuan Jewish man who published his account of the expedition: Raimondo Franchetti, *Nella Dancàlia etiopica: Spedizione italiana, 1928–29* (Milan: Mondadori, 1930).

27. The caption on the Archivio Luce reads "The doctor, perhaps Dr. Gregorini of the expedition, rests his hand on the arm of the emasculated indigenous man (= native), standing in the resting camp. Tents of the camp probably of Gaharre." Photo A00007235 in the archive. https://patrimonio.archivioluce.com/luce-web/detail/IL0000018944/12/un-medico-della-spedizione-visita-l-indigeno-evirato.

28. See Devon J. Borowski, "Navigating Voices: Song, History, and Humanity in the British Imperial Project, 1770–1836," PhD diss., University of Chicago, 2023, esp. chapter 1, and Devon J. Borowski, "Camping Empire: Melophilia and the Castrato Voice in Georgian Britain," *Journal of Musicology* 42.1 (Winter 2025), pp. 1–30.

29. See, for example, Maria Giovanna Belcastro et al., "Hyperostosis Frontalis Interna (HFI) and Castration: The Case of the Famous Singer Farinelli (1705–1782)," *Journal of Anatomy* 219 (2011), pp. 632–37, and Alberto Zanatta et al., "Occupational Markers and Pathology of the Castrato Singer Gasparo Pacchierotti (1740–1821)," *Scientific Reports* 6, 28463 (2016), https://doi.org/10.1038/srep28463.

APPENDIX TWO: ENRICO PANZACCHI, "CANTORES!"

1. A "botte" is a public horse-drawn carriage, used especially in Rome. See Enrico Panzacchi, *Racconti*, ed. Valeria Giannantonio (Chieti Scalo: Vecchio Faggio, 1993), p. 113 n. 3.

2. Elsewhere, the text reads: "Era un suono di timbro metallo di acutezza insolita." See Feldman, *The Castrato*, pp. 107–12 on the valence of the term *metallo* when used to describe the voices of castrati.

3. "Minenti" were Roman commoners, especially from Travestere, known from the early nineteenth century through to Panzacchi's time for shamelessly flaunting their new-found wealth, often achieved in artisanal trades. See https://www.museodiromaintrastevere.it/it/percorso/labito-popolare-romano-i-minenti# and https://gioachinobelli150.blogspot.com/2019/09/ggbelli-e-i-minenti-e-le-minenti.html. See also the review of *History of the Italian Language and Dialects*: *Saggi di prose e poesie de' più celebri scrittori d'ogni secolo*... selected by L. Nardini and S. Buonaiuti," *North American Review* 35.77 (October 1832), p. 313 and notes.

4. Elsewhere this reads "discretamente."

5. Elsewhere this reads "di metallo."

6. Erminia Frezzolini (1818–1884), Alice Laura Barbi (1858–1948), Adelina Patti (1843–1919), Angelo Masini (1844–1926), Heinrich Vogl [= Vögel] (1845–1900), and Antonio Cotogni (1831–1918).

7. The lines come from the beginning of Giuseppe Parini's ode "La Musica," composed circa 1769; https://it.wikisource.org/wiki/Odi_(Parini)/La_musica.

8. Don Fastidio, "La casa di Caffarello," *Napoli nobilissima* 8 (1898), pp. 119–21.

9. Heard or understood (*inteso*).

Index

Images are indicated by italic page number

Zone Books series design by Bruce Mau
Image placement and production by Julie Fry
Typesetting by Meighan Gale
Printed and bound by Maple Press